Hockey For Dummies ™

Quick Reference Card

The rink

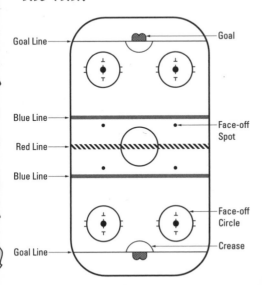

- Goal Line
- Goal
- Blue Line
- Face-off Spot
- Red Line
- Blue Line
- Face-off Circle
- Goal Line
- Crease

Tips on shooting and passing the puck

- ✔ The younger the player, the shorter the pass.

- ✔ Cradle the puck with your stick when you receive it.

- ✔ Don't pass to the player; pass to where he is going. And try to put the puck on the blade of his stick.

- ✔ Don't pass over two lines; that's against the rules, and the official will blow the whistle. Then he'll call a face-off, most likely in your defensive zone.

- ✔ Whenever possible, keep your passes on the ice. But if you must elevate the puck to get it to your teammate, try to make it land flat on the ice so it is easier to receive.

Penalties

Tripping: When a stick or any portion of a player's body is used to cause an opposing player to fall.

Hooking: When a player impedes the progress of an opponent by "hooking" him with his stick.

Interference: When a player interferes with or impedes the progress of an opponent who does not have the puck. Also assessed to a player who deliberately knocks the stick out of an opponent's hand, or who prevents a player who has dropped his stick (or any other piece of equipment) from picking it back up.

Elbowing: When a player uses his elbow to foul an opponent.

Slashing: When a player hits an opponent with his stick, or "slashes" him, either to impede his progress or cause injury.

Cross-checking: When a player makes a check with both hands on the stick.

Butt-ending: When a player jabs an opponent with the top end of his stick.

Spearing: When a player stabs at an opponent with the blade of his stick, whether he makes contact or not.

Fighting: Called "Fisticuffs" in the NHL rule book, it is assessed when players drop their gloves and throw punches at each other.

Checking from behind: Whistled when a player hits an opponent who is not aware of the impending contact and therefore cannot defend himself from behind.

Kneeing: When a player fouls an opponent by kneeing (of course!).

Roughing: Called when a player strikes another opponent in a minor altercation that the referee determines is not worthy of a major penalty.

...For Dummies: Bestselling Book Series for Beginners

Positions

Goalie: Perhaps the toughest position in all sports (remember this book is being written by a former net minder), the goalie is the one player who can control a team's confidence. His job is to keep the puck out of the net, and if he's good, he can take his team a long way. Good goalies win championships.

Defensemen: A team at full-strength has two, one on the left side and another on the right. Nowadays, there are three primary kinds of defensemen. One is creative and offensive-minded. He likes to handle the puck and lead the team up ice, but is not too physical. Another is defensive-minded, a stay-at-home bruiser who plays a physical game and doesn't often venture out of his zone with the puck. And there are those rare athletes who are a combination of the two.

Right wing: He works the right side of the ice for the most part. Needs to be a physical player who is good along the boards and in the corner. He is responsible for the opposition's left defenseman in the defensive zone.

Left wing: Traditionally a left-handed shot, but the NHL is seeing more right-handers playing this position now, a practice picked up from the Europeans. A right-hander has a better angle to shoot from when he's coming in on his wing. Again, he needs to be able to dig out the puck from the corners and battle in front of the net.

Center: He quarterbacks his club at both ends of the ice. Must be good at face-offs and passing, doesn't hurt if he possesses a good shot as well. Coaches want a lot of creativity in this position — and a lot of hockey smarts.

Hockey do's and don'ts

✔ Learn to skate properly, even if you're playing goalie. You can't do anything in hockey if you can't skate.

✔ Make sure your equipment, whether it's your skates, your stick, or your sweater (that's what the pros call a hockey jersey), fits well.

✔ On the bench, be alert. Watch what the opposing team is doing, and be prepared to play both ways, offensively and defensively.

✔ Don't be a puck hog; pass to your teammates.

✔ Don't stay out on your shift for too long. If you're working hard, an average shift on the ice should last no longer than a minute. Come off when it's your turn.

✔ Be ready when it's your turn to go onto the ice.

✔ Wear a helmet. But remember: Just because you have head protection, don't think you are invincible.

✔ Be careful with your stick; just because everybody wears headgear, don't think they're invincible either.

✔ Don't check people from behind.

✔ Keep your head up when you're going into the boards. If it's tucked in, the chances of a serious head injury rise if someone hits you from behind.

✔ Don't yap at the ref or other team. It's okay to be emotional and pull for the people on your team. But don't give the ref a hard time, or the opposing players.

✔ Get yourself in good physical shape.

✔ Work on your shooting and passing.

...For Dummies: Bestselling Book Series for Beginners

Praise For Hockey For Dummies

"My dog, Blue, and I loved it. We give it two paws up!"

— Don Cherry, Former NHL Coach and Coaches' Corner Commentator for Hockey Night in Canada

"Hockey is a way of life for me, and I've seen lots of books on the game, but nothing like *Hockey For Dummies*. JD's insight and sense of humor give die-hard fans and newcomers to the sport the inside edge!"

— Scotty Bowman, NHL's Winningest Coach and Coach of the Detroit Red Wings, 1997 Stanley Cup Champions

"Listen to the Beezer, *Hockey For Dummies* is a must read for all hockey fans!"

— John Vanbiesbrouck, Goaltender, Florida Panthers

"John Davidson is a better writer than he was a goalie (and he was a pretty good goalie). If you're a fan, you'll want this book. If you're not a fan yet, *Hockey For Dummies* will turn you into one."

— Mark Messier, NHL All-Star

"*Hockey For Dummies* makes understanding the game of hockey a cinch — with John Davidson's inside tips and techniques, you're sure to be an expert in no time."

— John Shannon, Executive Producer of Hockey Night in Canada

BUSINESS AND GENERAL REFERENCE BOOK SERIES FROM IDG

References for the Rest of Us!™

Do you find that traditional reference books are overloaded with technical details and advice you'll never use? Do you postpone important life decisions because you just don't want to deal with them? Then our *...For Dummies*™ business and general reference book series is for you.

...For Dummies business and general reference books are written for those frustrated and hard-working souls who know they aren't dumb, but find that the myriad of personal and business issues and the accompanying horror stories make them feel helpless. *...For Dummies* books use a lighthearted approach, a down-to-earth style, and even cartoons and humorous icons to diffuse fears and build confidence. Lighthearted but not lightweight, these books are perfect survival guides to solve your everyday personal and business problems.

> *"More than a publishing phenomenon, 'Dummies' is a sign of the times."*
> — The New York Times

> *"A world of detailed and authoritative information is packed into them..."*
> — U.S. News and World Report

> *"...you won't go wrong buying them."*
> — Walter Mossberg, Wall Street Journal, on IDG's ...For Dummies™ books

Already, millions of satisfied readers agree. They have made *...For Dummies* the #1 introductory level computer book series and a best-selling business book series. They have written asking for more. So, if you're looking for the best and easiest way to learn about business and other general reference topics, look to *...For Dummies* to give you a helping hand.

IDG BOOKS WORLDWIDE

5/97

HOCKEY
FOR
DUMMIES™

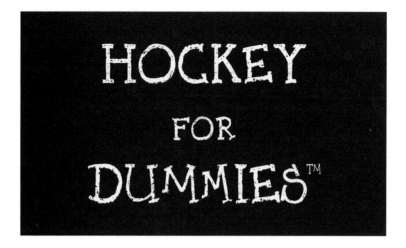

by John Davidson
with John Steinbreder

Preface by Mike Myers
Foreword by Wayne Gretzky

IDG Books Worldwide, Inc.
An International Data Group Company

Foster City, CA ♦ Chicago, IL ♦ Indianapolis, IN ♦ Southlake, TX

Hockey For Dummies ™

Published by
IDG Books Worldwide, Inc.
An International Data Group Company
919 E. Hillsdale Blvd.
Suite 400
Foster City, CA 94404
www.idgbooks.com (IDG Books Worldwide Web site)
www.dummies.com (Dummies Press Web site)

Library of Congress Catalog Card No.: 97-80182

ISBN: 0-7645-5045-4

Printed in the United States of America

10 9 8 7 6 5 4 3 2 1

1O/SS/QZ/ZX/IN

Distributed in the United States by IDG Books Worldwide, Inc.

Distributed by Macmillan Canada for Canada; by Transworld Publishers Limited in the United Kingdom; by IDG Norge Books for Norway; by IDG Sweden Books for Sweden; by Woodslane Pty. Ltd. for Australia; by Woodslane Enterprises Ltd. for New Zealand; by Longman Singapore Publishers Ltd. for Singapore, Malaysia, Thailand, and Indonesia; by Simron Pty. Ltd. for South Africa; by Toppan Company Ltd. for Japan; by Distribuidora Cuspide for Argentina; by Livraria Cultura for Brazil; by Ediciencia S.A. for Ecuador; by Addison-Wesley Publishing Company for Korea; by Ediciones ZETA S.C.R. Ltda. for Peru; by WS Computer Publishing Corporation, Inc., for the Philippines; by Unalis Corporation for Taiwan; by Contemporanea de Ediciones for Venezuela; by Computer Book & Magazine Store for Puerto Rico; by Express Computer Distributors for the Caribbean and West Indies. Authorized Sales Agent: Anthony Rudkin Associates for the Middle East and North Africa.

For general information on IDG Books Worldwide's books in the U.S., please call our Consumer Customer Service department at 800-762-2974. For reseller information, including discounts and premium sales, please call our Reseller Customer Service department at 800-434-3422.

For information on where to purchase IDG Books Worldwide's books outside the U.S., please contact our International Sales department at 415-655-3200 or fax 415-655-3295.

For information on foreign language translations, please contact our Foreign & Subsidiary Rights department at 415-655-3021 or fax 415-655-3281.

For sales inquiries and special prices for bulk quantities, please contact our Sales department at 415-655-3200 or write to the address above.

For information on using IDG Books Worldwide's books in the classroom or for ordering examination copies, please contact our Educational Sales department at 800-434-2086 or fax 817-251-8174.

For press review copies, author interviews, or other publicity information, please contact our Public Relations department at 415-655-3000 or fax 415-655-3299.

For authorization to photocopy items for corporate, personal, or educational use, please contact Copyright Clearance Center, 222 Rosewood Drive, Danvers, MA 01923, or fax 508-750-4470.

 is a trademark under exclusive license to IDG Books Worldwide, Inc., from International Data Group, Inc.

About the Authors

John Davidson has been a hockey analyst for the Madison Square Garden Network since 1976 and also serves as the top analyst for Fox Broadcasting. A longtime goaltender who broke in with the St. Louis Blues in 1973 and retired as a New York Ranger ten years later, JD is also a regular panelist for Hockey Night in Canada, appears frequently on ESPN Radio, and has his own Internet show on the NHL's Web site (nhl.com). He has won three New York Sports Emmys and one Ace Award and has covered two (with a third to come in February 1998) Winter Olympics. He lives in Bedford, New York, with his wife Diana, their daughters Lindsay and Ashley, three dogs, and a host of construction workers.

John Steinbreder is a former staff reporter for *Fortune* magazine and a writer/reporter for *Sports Illustrated*. The author of five books, John has contributed articles to several major newspapers and magazines, including *Golf Digest, Forbes FYI, The New York Times Magazine, Sky, Golf World, The Wall Street Journal, Time, Golf & Travel,* and *Outdoor Life*. He also works as a special contributor to ESPN and plays the occasional game of pond hockey. He lives in Easton, Connecticut with his daughter Exa.

(Photo by Alison M. Dunn)

Dedication

To our parents, Eunice and Jack Davidson, and Sandy and Cynthia Steinbreder, for giving us the chance to pursue our dreams.

ABOUT IDG BOOKS WORLDWIDE

Welcome to the world of IDG Books Worldwide.

IDG Books Worldwide, Inc., is a subsidiary of International Data Group, the world's largest publisher of computer-related information and the leading global provider of information services on information technology. IDG was founded more than 25 years ago and now employs more than 8,500 people worldwide. IDG publishes more than 275 computer publications in over 75 countries (see listing below). More than 60 million people read one or more IDG publications each month.

Launched in 1990, IDG Books Worldwide is today the #1 publisher of best-selling computer books in the United States. We are proud to have received eight awards from the Computer Press Association in recognition of editorial excellence and three from *Computer Currents'* First Annual Readers' Choice Awards. Our best-selling *...For Dummies®* series has more than 30 million copies in print with translations in 30 languages. IDG Books Worldwide, through a joint venture with IDG's Hi-Tech Beijing, became the first U.S. publisher to publish a computer book in the People's Republic of China. In record time, IDG Books Worldwide has become the first choice for millions of readers around the world who want to learn how to better manage their businesses.

Our mission is simple: Every one of our books is designed to bring extra value and skill-building instructions to the reader. Our books are written by experts who understand and care about our readers. The knowledge base of our editorial staff comes from years of experience in publishing, education, and journalism — experience we use to produce books for the '90s. In short, we care about books, so we attract the best people. We devote special attention to details such as audience, interior design, use of icons, and illustrations. And because we use an efficient process of authoring, editing, and desktop publishing our books electronically, we can spend more time ensuring superior content and spend less time on the technicalities of making books.

You can count on our commitment to deliver high-quality books at competitive prices on topics you want to read about. At IDG Books Worldwide, we continue in the IDG tradition of delivering quality for more than 25 years. You'll find no better book on a subject than one from IDG Books Worldwide.

IDG BOOKS WORLDWIDE

John Kilcullen
John Kilcullen
CEO
IDG Books Worldwide, Inc.

Steven Berkowitz
Steven Berkowitz
President and Publisher
IDG Books Worldwide, Inc.

Eighth Annual
Computer Press
Awards ≥1992

Ninth Annual
Computer Press
Awards ≥1993

Tenth Annual
Computer Press
Awards ≥1994

Eleventh Annual
Computer Press
Awards ≥1995

IDG Books Worldwide, Inc., is a subsidiary of International Data Group, the world's largest publisher of computer-related information and the leading global provider of information services on information technology. International Data Group publishes over 275 computer publications in over 75 countries. Sixty million people read one or more International Data Group publications each month. International Data Group's publications include: **ARGENTINA:** Buyer's Guide, Computerworld Argentina, PC World Argentina; **AUSTRALIA:** Australian Macworld, Australian PC World, Australian Reseller News, Computerworld, IT Casebook, Network World, Publish, Webmaster; **AUSTRIA:** Computerwelt Österreich, Networks Austria, PC Tip Austria; **BANGLADESH:** PC World Bangladesh; **BELARUS:** PC World Belarus; **BELGIUM:** Data News; **BRAZIL:** Annuário de Informática, Computerworld, Connections, Macworld, PC Player, PC World, Publish, Reseller News, Supergamepower; **BULGARIA:** Computerworld Bulgaria, Network World Bulgaria, PC & MacWorld Bulgaria; **CANADA:** CIO Canada, Client/Server World, ComputerWorld Canada, InfoWorld Canada, NetworkWorld Canada, WebWorld; **CHILE:** Computerworld Chile, PC World Chile; **COLOMBIA:** Computerworld Colombia, PC World Colombia; **COSTA RICA:** PC World Centro America; **THE CZECH AND SLOVAK REPUBLICS:** Computerworld Czechoslovakia, Macworld Czech Republic, PC World Czechoslovakia; **DENMARK:** Communications World Danmark, Computerworld Danmark, Macworld Danmark, PC World Danmark, Techworld Denmark; **DOMINICAN REPUBLIC:** PC World Republica Dominicana; **ECUADOR:** PC World Ecuador; **EGYPT:** Computerworld Middle East, PC World Middle East; **EL SALVADOR:** PC World Centro America; **FINLAND:** MikroPC, Tietoverkko, Tietoviikko; **FRANCE:** Distributique, Hebdo, Info PC, Le Monde Informatique, Macworld, Reseaux & Telecoms, WebMaster France; **GERMANY:** Computer Partner, Computerwoche, Computerwoche Extra, Computerwoche FOCUS, Global Online, Macwelt, PC Welt; **GREECE:** Amiga Computing, GamePro Greece, Multimedia World; **GUATEMALA:** PC World Centro America; **HONDURAS:** PC World Centro America; **HONG KONG:** Computerworld Hong Kong, PC World Hong Kong, Publish in Asia; **HUNGARY:** ABCD CD-ROM, Computerworld Szamitastechnika, Internetto online Magazine, PC World Hungary, PC-X Magazin Hungary; **ICELAND:** Tolvuheimur PC World Island; **INDIA:** Information Communications World, Information Systems Computerworld, PC World India, Publish in Asia; **INDONESIA:** InfoKomputer PC World, Komputek Computerworld, Publish in Asia; **IRELAND:** ComputerScope, PC Live!; **ISRAEL:** Macworld Israel, People & Computers/Computerworld; **ITALY:** Computerworld Italia, Macworld Italia, Networking Italia, PC World Italia; **JAPAN:** DTP World, Macworld Japan, Nikkei Personal Computing, OS/2 World Japan, SunWorld Japan, Windows NT World, Windows World Japan; **KENYA:** PC World East African; **KOREA:** Hi-Tech Information, Macworld Korea, PC World Korea; **MACEDONIA:** PC World Macedonia; **MALAYSIA:** Computerworld Malaysia, PC World Malaysia, Publish in Asia; **MALTA:** PC World Malta; **MEXICO:** Computerworld Mexico, PC World Mexico; **MYANMAR:** PC World Myanmar; **NETHERLANDS:** Computer! Totaal, LAN Internetworking Magazine, LAN World Buyers Guide, Macworld Netherlands, Net, WebWereld; **NEW ZEALAND:** Absolute Beginners Guide and Plain & Simple Series, Computer Buyer, Computer Industry Directory, Computerworld New Zealand, MTB, Network World, PC World New Zealand; **NICARAGUA:** PC World Centro America; **NORWAY:** Computerworld Norge, CW Rapport, Datamagasinet, Financial Rapport, Kursguide Norge, Macworld Norge, Multimediaworld Norge, PC World Ekspress Norge, PC World Nettverk, PC World Norge, PC World ProduktGuide Norge; **PAKISTAN:** Computerworld Pakistan; **PANAMA:** PC World Panama; **PEOPLE'S REPUBLIC OF CHINA:** China Computer Users, China Computerworld, China InfoWorld, China Telecom World Weekly, Computerworld, Electronic Design China, Electronics Today, Electronics Weekly, Game Software, PC World China, Popular Computer Week, Software Weekly, Software World, Telecom World; **PERU:** Computerworld Peru, PC World Profesional Peru, PC World SoHo Peru; **PHILIPPINES:** Click!, Computerworld Philippines, PC World Philippines, Publish in Asia; **POLAND:** Computerworld Poland, Computerworld Special Report Poland, Cyber, Macworld Poland, Networld Poland, PC World Komputer; **PORTUGAL:** Cerebro/PC World, Computerworld/Correio Informático, Dealer World Portugal, Mac*In/PC*In Portugal, Multimedia World; **PUERTO RICO:** PC World Puerto Rico; **ROMANIA:** Computerworld Romania, PC World Romania, Telecom Romania; **RUSSIA:** Computerworld Russia, Mir PK, Publish, Seti; **SINGAPORE:** Computerworld Singapore, PC World Singapore, Publish in Asia; **SLOVENIA:** Monitor; **SOUTH AFRICA:** Computing SA, Network World SA, Software World SA; **SPAIN:** Communicaciones World España, Computerworld España, Dealer World España, Macworld España, PC World España; **SRI LANKA:** Infolink PC World; **SWEDEN:** CAP&Design, Computer Sweden, Corporate Computing Sweden, Internetworld Sweden, it.branschen, Macworld Sweden, MaxiData Sweden, MikroDatorn, Nätverk & Kommunikation, PC World Sweden, PCaktiv, Windows World Sweden; **SWITZERLAND:** Computerworld Schweiz, Macworld Schweiz, PCtip; **TAIWAN:** Computerworld Taiwan, Macworld Taiwan, NEW ViSiON/Publish, PC World Taiwan, Windows World Taiwan; **THAILAND:** Publish in Asia, Thai Computerworld; **TURKEY:** Computerworld Turkiye, Macworld Turkiye, Network World Turkiye, PC World Turkiye; **UKRAINE:** Computerworld Kiev, Multimedia World Ukraine, PC World Ukraine; **UNITED KINGDOM:** Acorn User UK, Amiga Action UK, Amiga Computing UK, Apple Talk UK, Computing, Macworld, Parents and Computers UK, PC Advisor, PC Home, PSX Pro, The WEB; **UNITED STATES:** Cable in the Classroom, CIO Magazine, Computerworld, DOS World, Federal Computer Week, GamePro Magazine, InfoWorld, I-Way, Macworld, Network World, PC Games, PC World, Publish, Video Event, THE WEB Magazine, and WebMaster; online webzines: JavaWorld, NetscapeWorld, and SunWorld Online; **URUGUAY:** InfoWorld Uruguay; **VENEZUELA:** Computerworld Venezuela, PC World Venezuela; and **VIETNAM:** PC World Vietnam.   3/24/97

Authors' Acknowledgments

Writing, like hockey, is a team effort, and we could not have done this book without an enormous amount of help from our friends and colleagues. First off, thanks to Mark McCormack, Sandy Montag and Mark Reiter of the International Management Group for bringing us into this project and doing their best to keep us both solvent. We are also appreciative of the good work Sarah Kennedy of IDG did in getting this book off the ground, and of the fine editing skills of Bill Helling and Michael Simsic. Another key player was John Halligan, who served not only as our technical editor but also as a great source of ideas and information during the reporting process.

The folks at the National Hockey League lent invaluable assistance, and we would like to thank everyone who is a part of that organization, especially Gary Bettman, Bernadette Mansur, and David McConnachie. Darryl Seibel of USA Hockey also contributed a great deal to our efforts, and so did his counterparts at the Canadian Hockey Association, the International Ice Hockey Federation, the American Hockey League, and the International Hockey League.

We turned to a number of other sources as we put together this opus and are grateful for their time and support. Scotty Bowman and Colin Campbell graciously shared their insights on the game and so did Emile Francis, Don Cherry, Dick Irvin, Mark Messier, Brian Leetch, Wayne Gretzky, Mike Gartner, Gary Roberts, Mike Vernon, Sergei Nemchinov, Al MacInnis, Ron Hextall, Eric Lindros and Brett Hull. Thanks also to Mike Folga, Jim Ramsey, Michael Cosby, Bob Shank and Howie Wenger for providing us with a wealth of information on conditioning and equipment; Stan Fischler for the terrific books he has written on the game; and Scott Cooper, the world's number one Ranger fan. Finally, we would like to express our appreciation to Mike Myers and Wayne Gretzky for penning the Preface and Foreword.

On a personal level, JD would like to thank both the Fox and MSG networks for putting such quality products on the air, his play-by-play partners Sam Rosen and Mike Emrick, Joe Whalen and Michael McCarthy of MSG, John Shannon of Hockey Night in Canada, and of course, his wife Diana, his daughters Lindsay and Ashley, and his brothers — Wilson, Marshall and Murray — and their families.

As for John Steinbreder, he would like to thank the people who continue to throw such wonderful writing assignments his way, especially Jerry Tarde and his colleagues at *Golf Digest,* Geoff Russell of *Golf World,* Dave Seanor of *Golfweek,* Cindi Crain of *Golf & Travel,* Elaine Armstrong of Rococo International, Robin McMillan of *Met Golfer,* John Walsh and Vince Doria of ESPN, and Duncan Christy of *Sky.* He is also grateful for the support of his mother Cynthia, the friendship of his neighbors Arvid and Pam, the counsel he receives from Bob Carney, the times he gets to talk hockey with Nat, Pete, and JB, and the days and nights he gets to spend with his daughter Exa, a sweet girl who never gets angry when her father switches the television channel from *Rugrats* to a New York Rangers hockey game.

Publisher's Acknowledgments

We're proud of this book; please send us your comments about it by using the IDG Books Worldwide Registration Card at the back of the book or by e-mailing us at feedback/dummies@idgbooks.com. Some of the people who helped bring this book to market include the following:

Acquisitions, Development, and Editorial

Project Editor: Bill Helling

Acquisitions Editor: Sarah Kennedy

Copy Editor: Michael Simsic

Technical Editor: John Halligan, Director of Special Projects of the National Hockey League

Editorial Manager: Mary C. Corder

Editorial Assistant: Donna Love

Production

Associate Project Coordinator: Karen York

Layout and Graphics: Maridee V. Ennis, Jane E. Martin, Deirdre Smith, Michael A. Sullivan

Proofreaders: Kelli Botta, Michelle Croninger, Joel Draper, Nancy Price

Indexer: Steve Rath

Special Help: Dwight Ramsey, Reprint Editor; Ann Miller, Editorial Coordinator

General and Administrative

IDG Books Worldwide, Inc.: John Kilcullen, CEO; Steven Berkowitz, President and Publisher

IDG Books Technology Publishing: Brenda McLaughlin, Senior Vice President and Group Publisher

Dummies Technology Press and Dummies Editorial: Diane Graves Steele, Vice President and Associate Publisher; Kristin A. Cocks, Editorial Director; Mary Bednarek, Acquisitions and Product Development Director

Dummies Trade Press: Kathleen A. Welton, Vice President and Publisher

IDG Books Production for Dummies Press: Beth Jenkins, Production Director; Cindy L. Phipps, Manager of Project Coordination, Production Proofreading, and Indexing; Kathie S. Schutte, Supervisor of Page Layout; Shelley Lea, Supervisor of Graphics and Design; Debbie J. Gates, Production Systems Specialist; Robert Springer, Supervisor of Proofreading; Debbie Stailey, Special Projects Coordinator; Tony Augsburger, Supervisor of Reprints and Bluelines; Leslie Popplewell, Media Archive Coordinator

Dummies Packaging and Book Design: Patti Sandez, Packaging Specialist; Lance Kayser, Packaging Assistant; Kavish + Kavish, Cover Design

◆

The publisher would like to give special thanks to Patrick J. McGovern, without whom this book would not have been possible.

◆

Contents at a Glance

Introduction 1

Part I: Getting Started — Before They Drop the Puck 7
Chapter 1: What Is Hockey? 9
Chapter 2: Pads and Pucks: Gearing Up 17
Chapter 3: Rules of the Game 29

Part II: How the Big Boys Do It 45
Chapter 4: The National Hockey League 47
Chapter 5: The Minors and Other Hockey Leagues 59
Chapter 6: Training 67
Chapter 7: Coaching in the NHL 97
Chapter 8: The Power Play 115
Chapter 9: Intimidation and Hitting 133

Part III: It's Easier from the Stands (A Lot Easier) 143
Chapter 10: How to Watch Hockey on Television 145
Chapter 11: How to Watch Hockey from the Seats 155
Chapter 12: Online, on the Air, and on the Newsstand 163

Part IV: So You're Ready for Your Shift 173
Chapter 13: What You Need to Know to Play Hockey and to Improve 175
Chapter 14: Where to Go if You — and Your Children — Want to Play 189
Chapter 15: What to Do If You Don't Have Any Ice 195

Part V: The Part of Tens 201
Chapter 16: The Ten Best Things about Hockey 203
Chapter 17: The Ten Best Players: NHL and International 209
Chapter 18: The Ten Best Teams 223
Chapter 19: The Ten Best Hitters 227
Chapter 20: The Ten Best Games of All Time 235
Chapter 21: The Ten Best Hockey Personalities 243
Chapter 22: The Ten Best Minor League Players 1
Chapter 23: Ten Timeless Tips for Better Hockey 253

Part VI: Appendixes 257
Appendix A: Hockey Speak 259
Appendix B: Hockey Organizations: From Pee Wees to the Pros 271
Appendix C: Hockey Signals 325
Appendix D: Hockey: The Lists 333

Index 357

IDG Worldwide Registration Card .... Back of Book

Cartoons at a Glance

By Rich Tennant

page 257

page 143

page 7

page 45

page 173

page 201

Fax: 508-546-7747 • **E-mail:** the5wave@tiac.net

Table of Contents

Introduction *1*

About This Book 1
Why You Need This Book 2
How to Use This Book 3
How This Book Is Organized 3
    Part I: Getting Started — Before They Drop the Puck 3
    Part II: How the Big Boys Do It 4
    Part III: It's Easier from the Stands (A Lot Easier) 4
    Part IV: So You're Ready for Your Shift 4
    Part V: The Part of Tens 4
    Part VI: Appendixes 5
Icons Used in This Book 5

Part I: Getting Started — Before They Drop the Puck *7*

Chapter 1: What Is Hockey? 9

The Origins of the Game 9
    Hockey comes to North America 10
    The rise of professional hockey 10
A Typical Hockey Rink 11
How Hockey Is Played: The Positions 12
    Centers 14
    Wings 14
    Goalies 15
    Defensemen 16

Chapter 2: Pads and Pucks: Gearing Up 17

The Modern Hockey Player's Gear 17
    Skates 17
    Sticks 19
    Protection 21
    Goalie protection 22
What They Wore — and Didn't Wear — in Years Past 23
Deciding What Equipment Is Best for You — and Your Kids 25
    Getting the right skates 25
    Getting the right helmet 25
    Padding up: From the shoulders to the hands 25
    From the waist down 26
    Choosing a stick 26
Where to Buy What You Want 27

Chapter 3: Rules of the Game **29**

Scoring 29
Periods 31
Rosters: Who Gets to Play 31
General substitutions 32
Goalie substitutions 32
Infractions 32
Icing 33
Offside 33
Types of Penalties 35
Minors 35
Majors 36
Misconducts 36
How You Get a Penalty 37
Roughing 37
Hooking 38
Charging 38
Interference 39
Slashing 39
High-sticking 39
Checking from behind 40
Fighting 40
Referees and Linesmen: Their Roles and Responsibilities 42

Part II: How the Big Boys Do It *45*

Chapter 4: The National Hockey League **47**

In the Beginning 47
Where the NHL Is Today 49
How the NHL Has Changed over the Years 49
Who's the Boss? 50
The NHL Teams 50
The Conferences and Their Divisions 51
How the Standings Are Determined 53
The Play-off Format 55
Battling for the Stanley Cup 55
The Players 57
Where do the players come from today? 57
Where did the players come from in years past? 58
Player size 58
Player speed 58
Player strength 58

Chapter 5: The Minors and Other Hockey Leagues 59

The Minor Leagues 59

    Minor league franchises — the lowdown 60

    Finding the minor league teams 60

    NHL affiliations 61

    Similarities — and differences — between minor leagues
        and the NHL 62

    Popularity of the minor leagues 62

The College Game 62

    How does Joe College play the game? 63

    The top college teams 63

    College grads who have done well in the pros 63

Women's Leagues and Competitions 64

International Hockey 65

Chapter 6: Training 67

What the Pros Do to Stay in Shape 68

    Running 68

    Cycling 68

    Skating 68

    Stairmaster 69

    Weightlifting 69

Keeping Track of Fitness 70

A Typical NHL Off-Season Conditioning Regimen 71

What You Can Do To Get In Hockey Shape 72

The Need for Exercise Routines 73

Stretching 73

Aerobic Fitness 79

Weight Training 79

    Upper Body: Circuit 1 80

    Upper Body: Circuit 2 82

    Upper Body Variations 85

    Lower Body: Circuit 1 88

    Lower Body Variations 90

    Abdominal Strength Exercises 92

Chapter 7: Coaching in the NHL 97

What a Coach Does before a Season Starts 98

    Training camp 98

    Exhibitions 99

What a Coach Does during the Regular Season 99

A Scotty Bowman Practice 101

    Warm ups 101

    Shooting drills 102

    Practicing the breakout 103

    Practicing the line change 104

    Practicing other skills 104

    Practice: The overall view 105

Different Systems 107
What a Coach Does during a Game 110
    Match-ups 110
    Pre-game versus post-game matching 111
    The home advantage in match-ups 111
Changing on the Fly 112
"Let's Win One for the Gipper"(Locker Room Talks) 112
Coaching during the Play-offs 113
    Avoiding mistakes 113
    Getting mentally ready 114

Chapter 8: The Power Play **115**
    The First Pass 115
    The Second Pass 118
    The Third Pass 119
    The Importance of Passing 119
    The Key to a Power Play: Control 119
    The Half Board Power Play 122
    The Five-on-Three Advantage 123
        The face-off 124
        Retain control 124
        Take your chances close to the net 126
    Penalty Kills (Or: Killing a Penalty) 128
        Different ways to kill a penalty 130

Chapter 9: Intimidation and Hitting **133**
    What Players Say to Each Other on the Ice 133
    What Players Do to Each Other on the Ice (Aside from Talking) 134
    The Five Best Fighters 135
    The Five Best Intimidators 137
    The Five Best Agitators 139

Part III: It's Easier from the Stands (A Lot Easier) *143*

Chapter 10: How to Watch Hockey on Television **145**
    Following the Puck (Sometimes) 145
    Watching the Plays Form 147
    What to Look For from the Top Teams 148
        Philadelphia Flyers 148
        Detroit Red Wings 148
        New Jersey Devils 149
        New York Rangers 149
        Anaheim Mighty Ducks 150
        Edmonton Oilers 151
        Buffalo Sabres 151
    What the Camera Doesn't Show You 152

Chapter 11: How to Watch Hockey from the Seats 155

Paying Attention 155
Watching the Whole Rink 156
Watching an Opposing Player 157
Enjoying the Culinary Delights 158
Keeping Your Cool 158
JD's Five Favorite Arenas 158
Arrowhead Pond at Anaheim 159
Madison Square Garden 159
Maple Leaf Gardens 160
Molson Centre 160
San Jose Arena 161
Honorable Mention: Lethbridge Arena 161

Chapter 12: Online, on the Air, and on the Newsstand 163

Hockey Web Sites 163
nhl.com 163
NHL team sites 164
sportsline.com 165
espn.com 166
Broadcast TV and Radio 167
Fox Broadcasting 167
ESPN 167
CBC 168
TSN 168
SRC 168
RDS 168
Regional Cable Television and International 168
Radio 169
Hockey in Print 169
Magazines 169
Newspapers 170
Books 170
The Hockey Hall of Fame 171

Part IV: So You're Ready for Your Shift 173

Chapter 13: What You Need to Know to Play Hockey and to Improve 175

Wayne Gretzky on Passing 175
Mark Messier on Face-Offs 177
Mike Vernon on Defending the Breakaway 178
Al MacInnis on Shooting from the Point 179
Gary Roberts on Scoring as a Power Forward 180
Eric Lindros on Shooting off the Pass 182
Brett Hull on Getting Free in Front of the Net 183

Ron Hextall on Handling the Puck as a Goalie 184
Mike Gartner on Power Skating 184
Brian Leetch on Playing Defense 185

**Chapter 14: Where to Go if You — and Your Children —
Want to Play 189**

Youth and Adult Leagues in Canada and the U.S. 189
What to look for 190
How to join 190
Leagues in Other Parts of the World 190
Hockey Camps and Schools in Canada and the U.S. 191
Camps and Schools in Other Parts of the World 191
Pond Hockey 191
Knowing when the ice is good — and keeping it that way 192
Holding your own in pickup games 192
Pond-hockey etiquette 193

Chapter 15: What to Do If You Don't Have Any Ice 195

In-line Skating 195
The lowdown on in-line skates 196
In-line skating equipment 197
In-line Hockey and Street Hockey 197
Where and how it is played 197
What is needed for equipment 198
The rules 199

Part V: The Part of Tens 201

Chapter 16: The Ten Best Things about Hockey 203

Speed 203
Passion 204
Check Out Some of Its Fans 204
See It Live 205
Accommodating Players 205
Women Watching and Playing Hockey 206
Great Way to Exercise Up North during the Winter 206
It's an International Game 207
Fun for Everyone 207
The Game Is Growing Big-Time 207

Chapter 17: The Ten Best Players: NHL and International 209

The Best in the NHL 209
Wayne Gretzky — Edmonton Oilers, Los Angeles Kings,
St. Louis Blues, New York Rangers 209
Mario Lemieux — Pittsburgh Penguins 210
Bobby Orr — Boston Bruins, Chicago Blackhawks 211

Gordie Howe — Detroit Red Wings, Hartford Whalers 212
Mark Messier — Edmonton Oilers, New York Rangers,
    Vancouver Canucks 213
Maurice Richard — Montreal Canadiens 213
Doug Harvey — Montreal Canadians, New York Rangers,
    Detroit Red Wings, St. Louis Blues 213
Eddie Shore — Boston Bruins, New York Americans 214
Jean Beliveau — Montreal Canadiens 214
Glenn Hall — Detroit Red Wings, Chicago Blackhawks,
    St. Louis Blues 215
Terry Sawchuk — Detroit Red Wings, Boston Bruins,
    Toronto Maple Leafs, Los Angeles Kings, New York Rangers 216
The Best International Players 217
    Sergei Fedorov 217
    Viacheslav Fetisov 217
    Peter Forsberg 218
    Dominik Hasek 218
    Valeri Kharlamov 219
    Jari Kurri 220
    Jaromir Jagr 220
    Borje Salming 220
    Peter Stastny 221
    Vladislav Tretiak 221

Chapter 18: The Ten Best Teams **223**
    The Ottawa Senators — 1919–1927 223
    The Toronto Maple Leafs — 1947–1951 223
    The Detroit Red Wings — 1950–1955 224
    The Montreal Canadiens — 1956–1960 224
    The Toronto Maple Leafs — 1962–1967 224
    The Montreal Canadiens — 1965–1969 224
    The Montreal Canadiens — 1976–1979 224
    The New York Islanders — 1980–1984 225
    The Edmonton Oilers — 1984–1990 226
    The 1980 United States Olympic Hockey Team 226
    Honorable Mention — The Charlestown Chiefs 226

Chapter 19: The Ten Best Hitters **227**
    Bobby Baun 227
    Barry Beck 227
    Leo Boivin 229
    Bill Ezinicki 229
    Tim Horton 230
    Bryan Marchment 230
    Dennis Owchar 231
    Bob Plager 231
    Denis Potvin 232
    Ulf Samuelsson 232

Chapter 20: The Ten Best Games of All Time 235

    March 24, 1936 235
    May 2, 1967 236
    April 8, 1971 237
    December 31, 1975 237
    February 22, 1980 238
    February 27, 1994 238
    May 25, 1994 239
    April 24, 1996 239
    September 7, 1996 240
    September 12, 1996 241

Chapter 21: The Ten Best Hockey Personalities 243

    Don Cherry 243
    Phil Esposito 244
    John Ferguson 244
    Nick Fotiu 245
    Bernard "Boom Boom" Geoffrion 246
    Bobby Hull 246
    Tom McVie 246
    Red Storey 247
    Dave "Tiger" Williams 247
    Lorne "Gump" Worsley 248

Chapter 22: The Ten Best Minor League Players 249

    Johnny Bower 249
    Jock Callander 250
    Guyle Fielder 250
    Dick Gamble 250
    Fred Glover 251
    Scott Gruhl 251
    Willie Marshall 251
    Dave Michayluk 251
    Willie O'Ree 252
    Len Thornson 252

Chapter 23: Ten Timeless Tips for Better Hockey 253

    Learn to Skate 253
    Wear a Helmet 254
    Don't Skate on Thin Ice 254
    Always Keep Your Head Up 254
    Be a Team Player 254
    Go and See a Game Live 254
    Make Sure Your Equipment Fits 255
    Use Your Stick Properly 255
    Watch Hockey in All the Right Places 255
    Be Free 255

Part VI: Appendixes 257

Appendix A: Hockey Speak 259

Appendix B: Hockey Organizations: From Pee Wees to the Pros 271

Youth Hockey 272
  Alabama 272
  Alaska 272
  Arizona 273
  Arkansas 273
  California 273
  Colorado 275
  Connecticut 276
  Delaware 277
  Florida 277
  Georgia 278
  Idaho 278
  Illinois (Northern) 278
  Illinois (Central) 280
  Illinois (Southern) 280
  Indiana 280
  Iowa 281
  Kansas 282
  Kentucky 282
  Maine 282
  Maryland 282
  Massachusetts 283
  Minnesota (Northern) 286
  Minnesota (Central) 287
  Minnesota (Southern) 290
  Michigan (Northern and Central) 291
  Michigan (Southern) 295
  Missouri 296
  Montana 296
  Nebraska 296
  Nevada 296
  New Hampshire 296
  New Jersey 297
  New York (Central) 300
  New York (Western) 300
  New York (Eastern) 301
  New Mexico 303
  North Carolina 303
  Ohio 304
  Oklahoma 305
  Oregon 305
  Pennsylvania (Eastern) 305
  Pennsylvania (Western) 307

            Rhode Island 308
            South Carolina 308
            South Dakota 308
            Texas 309
            Utah 309
            Virginia 309
            Vermont 310
            Washington 310
            Wisconsin (Northwest) 311
            Wisconsin (Northeast) 311
            Wisconsin (Central: Region 3, Green Bay Area) 312
            Wisconsin (Southeast) 313
            Wisconsin (Southern: Region 5) 314
            Wisconsin (Western Associations) 316
            West Virginia 317
            Wyoming 317
        Canada 317
            Alberta 317
            British Columbia 317
            Manitoba 318
            New Brunswick... 318
            Ontario (Northern) 318
            Ontario (Southern) 319
            Quebec 320
            Saskatchewan 321
        Adult Hockey 322
        NHL: Directory of Addresses 322
            Outside North America 321
            NHL offices 322
            NHL Players Association (NHLPA) 322
            NHL Teams 322

Appendix C: Hockey Signals 325
        Boarding 325
        Butt ending 325
        Charging 325
        Checking from behind 326
        Cross checking 326
        Delayed calling of penalty 326
        Delayed (slow) whistle 326
        Delaying the game 327
        Elbowing.. 327
        Fighting 327
        Goal scored 327
        Hand pass 327
        High-sticking 328
        Holding 328
        Holding the face mask 328

Hooking 328

Icing 328

Interference 329

Kneeing 329

Match penalty 329

Misconduct 329

Offside 329

Penalty shot 330

Slashing 330

Spearing 330

Time-out 330

Tripping 331

Wash-out 331

Appendix D: Hockey: The Lists **333**

The Hockey Hall of Fame 333

Forwards and defensemen 333

Goaltenders 340

Stanley Cup Winners 341

NHL "Mosts" 344

NHL Career Milestones 348

Forwards and defensemen 348

Goaltenders 350

Coaches 352

NHL Single-Season Milestones 353

Forwards and defensemen 353

Goaltenders 355

Index *357*

IDG Worldwide Registration Card .... *Back of Book*

Foreword

My first experience with a pair of skates and a hockey stick happened before I turned three. My coach, also known as "Dad," instructed me from the comfort of our kitchen, while I played on the home-made rink that had once been our backyard. Dad wasn't trying to build a hockey star from our kitchen; he was only trying to stay warm. Even back then, hockey was my life. I lived, breathed, slept, dreamed, and played hockey. Reading John Davidson's *Hockey For Dummies* takes me back to those days growing up in Ontario. It reminds me of all the important lessons I learned, and all the great moments I've experienced as a player.

For those of you who are new to the game I love, *Hockey For Dummies* is the most comprehensive, easily understood source of hockey history and instruction I've ever come across. Not only was "JD" a superb player in the NHL, he is also an extremely skilled commentator sharing his knowledge of the game with fans all over North America. From hat tricks to power plays, *Hockey For Dummies* provides the reader with the wisdom of an expert.

John has also included advice from some of his pals in the NHL (check out my section on passing!). This is the sort of "inside information" you ordinarily get at an expensive hockey camp. But it's all collected here — and I think even my father could pick up one or two new secrets. From cover to cover, you'll get all the basics. If you're a fan or a serious player, I'd bet you can dip into any page and learn. Whoever you are, *Hockey For Dummies* has something for every hockey lover.

— Wayne Gretzky
NHL's All-Time Leading Scorer

Preface

Congratulations! You have chosen to learn about the best sport invented by man. The perfect combination of soccer, basketball and football. The best water sport ever . . . on frozen water, that is.

To those of you who are just getting acquainted with the world of Hockey, it might seem as foreign to you as the movie *Rollerball* and equally as physical. It is a fast-paced, contact game that's played on a hard surface with a hard puck with hard sticks surrounded by hard boards played by hard men — and women.

It's true that hockey has sometimes been referred to as the "fourth sport" in the U.S., but now, the NHL has expansion teams in warm-weather climates like Florida and Arizona — and with the explosive popularity and growth of in-line skating, hockey is now accessible to everyone!

There's nothing like watching Paul Coffey streak down the ice at Mach Two. And there's nothing like the sound of an Al MacInnis slap shot. The perfection of Jaromir Jagr's wrist shot. The balletic grace of a Darius Kaspiritis body check. Or, last but not least, the perfection of a Wayne Gretzky flip pass as it "feathers" though sixteen legs — landing flat onto the stick of a man just as he's crossing the blue line.

Maybe many of you cannot yet grasp what I have described. So, read on, my children and discover a kind of love that myself and others have know all along . . . it's a special love. Why, it's the love of hockey.

Game on!

— Mike Myers
Canadian actor, comedian, and hockey fan

Introduction

$\mathbf{W}$elcome to *Hockey For Dummies,* the book that tells you everything you've always wanted to know — and then some — about the most exciting sport in the world. It's skaters streaking down the ice at breakneck speeds. It's slap shots screaming past goalies. It's deft stick handling, crisp passing, crunching body checks, fantastic playmaking, and even a bit of fighting with the pros. As a sport, hockey has everything — which is why we're writing about it.

About This Book

We want this book to appeal to every level of player and fan, from the eight-year-old boy competing on Saturday mornings in his local youth hockey league to the sixty-five-year-old grandmother who hasn't missed a New York Rangers game at Madison Square Garden in 20 years. We hope the native Floridian who knows next to nothing about the sport will find it easier to watch and understand after perusing this volume; and we'd like it to be as compelling a read for the longtime fan or player who thinks he, or she, knows it all. We even want to give the National Hockey League pros that JD (aka John Davidson) hangs around with something new and different to talk about in the locker room. Perhaps it will be the names they find on his Top Ten lists. Maybe it will be his strategies for penalty kills and power plays. Whatever the attraction, we hope that they, and all our other readers, find *Hockey For Dummies* interesting, useful, and fun.

There has never before been a book like this, one that recounts the workings of the National Hockey League, explains the type of equipment players use, describes the rules of the game and the philosophies of the different coaches, and that gives tips on watching hockey on television and ways to improve your slap shot and board work. It is both history journal and instructional guide. And it might even make you laugh a little, too.

Some of you, we believe, will be hard-core hockey fans who grew up playing on the frozen ponds in your neighborhoods and following your favorite NHL teams. Even if you know and love the game already, you'll find plenty of new information in this book. An equal number of you may be fairly new to the game. You may live in warm-weather places, such as Miami and Phoenix, that only recently have gotten interested in hockey. Many of you may not know the difference between a cross check and a slap shot. You may not understand how many points a team gets for a regular-season win or what makes the play-off system work. You may even think that skates are those strange-looking sting rays that swim in the ocean and that John Davidson, whose name appears on the cover of this book is actually the onetime singer and game show host, not the former standout goalie who is now the game's best-known television analyst. We forgive you for any of these transgressions if you promise to buy this book. And then we'll help you become as knowledgeable and passionate about the sport as your Snow Belt brethren. We might also talk you — and your children — into playing the game yourself. In fact, we can even show you different ways to enjoy the sport, even if it's the middle of summer and there's no ice around. We like hockey so much we'll do anything to play it. Well, almost anything.

Why You Need This Book

Beginners need this book because nothing else will give them as complete an introduction to the game and an understanding as to how it works. Do you know what the left wing does? The right defenseman? Not to worry, we explain both of them. Do you know how to buy hockey equipment for yourself or your children (or for that matter, your grandchildren)? Do you know how many teams now play in the NHL? Do you know how players in that league train or what they practice before a game? Do you have any idea what they say to each other on the ice? Newcomers to the game may ask these and many, many more questions. And we happily answer them.

At the same time, however, we also try to pique the interest of those who know the sport better. And that's the real beauty of this volume. It addresses the needs of the neophyte without talking down to the casual player, or the rabid NHL season ticket holder, or the high school scoring star, or those bangers who earn their keep in the top pro league. It has plenty of good information for everybody.

There are several reasons why JD is the perfect person to write this book — and the one who gets top billing on the cover. A goalie who was born in Ottawa, Ontario, and raised in Calgary, Alberta, he played ten seasons in the NHL, some as a member of the St. Louis Blues but mostly with the New York Rangers. The highlight of his playing career was leading the Rangers to the Stanley Cup Finals in 1979, which they lost in a hard-fought series to the Montreal Canadiens. Back and knee injuries forced JD to retire in 1983, but he didn't just shrink away from the game. He spent a year as an analyst for New York Rangers broadcasts on the Madison Square Garden Network and then moved to a similar position with the wildly popular *Hockey Night in Canada,* which is as big up north as *Monday Night Football* is in the States.

JD stayed there for two years before coming back to MSG, where he still works. He also serves as lead game analyst for Fox Sports. Over the years he has done games for the three other major broadcast networks and covered two Winter Olympics (and will soon cover another Winter Olympics in 1998). In addition, he has won three Emmys and one Cable ACE award. He knows the sport and is as able as anyone to simplify the game and convey its intricacies to fans of all levels and backgrounds as anyone. That's what makes him so good on TV, and a natural to do this book.

How to Use This Book

You shouldn't read this book, as you read a novel, from cover to cover. Pick the different chapters that interest you most and go from there. Beginners may want to start with the glossary so they have a better sense of Hockeyspeak before they start turning the other pages. Parents and kids who play in one of the many recreational leagues, or just on the local rink or pond, may want to turn to Chapters 2, 3, 13, 14, and 15 first, while those more into spectating should enjoy what we have in Chapters 4, 5, 10, 11, and 12. And JD's Top Ten Lists should be of interest to anybody who has followed the game. You may want to read only bits and pieces of the book at a time or sit down for an extended session. However you do it, we want to make sure you are discovering more about the game and having fun in the process.

How This Book Is Organized

We have taken great care in organizing this book. We begin with an explanation of how hockey began and what it's all about, and then describe the equipment needed to play the game and the rules. Later on, we get into the NHL, discuss things like training and coaching, talk about the best ways to watch the game from the stands or in your living room, and outline what you need to know to play hockey yourself. We finish up with JD's Top Ten Lists and the appendixes, which tell you how to talk a good game and where to find a place to play. This book is simple yet comprehensive.

Part I: Getting Started — Before They Drop the Puck

First, we describe how the sport began and where it was originally played. In addition, we explain the various positions on the ice and what each person is responsible for doing so you and your friends don't scurry around like a bunch of maniacs. We also tell you what a hockey rink is and what it looks like. We talk about the equipment hockey players use and the rules they must follow on the ice. We know, it sometimes looks like complete anarchy out there. But it's not. There's rhyme and reason to it all.

Part II: How the Big Boys Do It

Here, we look at the NHL, the premier hockey league in the world, and go over everything from when it was started (1917) to what the Stanley Cup is (hockey's version of the World Series) to how fast the players are (in a word, very). Then we get into the minors, the colleges, and the women's leagues (real women do play hockey). We include a section on training at the professional level and another on coaching that gets into everything from shooting drills to matching lines. We next cover the power play, which is perhaps the most critical test of any hockey team — on offense or on defense. We also tell you how to defend against the power play. Finally, we examine the world of intimidation and hitting in hockey.

Part III: It's Easier from the Stands (A Lot Easier)

Some people prefer to play hockey, while others like to watch. This part clues you in on the best ways to follow the game on television. We also have tips on how to get the most out of a game from the stands and go over the various TV shows, newspapers, magazines, and online services you can turn to if you want to stay informed.

Part IV: So You're Ready for Your Shift

This part is mostly for players, and we have a number of the league's top pros giving tips: Wayne Gretzky on passing; Mark Messier on winning face-offs; and so on. Also, we tell you where to go and what to look for in youth and adult hockey leagues throughout the U.S. and Canada as well as some hockey schools and camps. In addition, we have information on what to do if you haven't any ice (such as street hockey and in-line skating, for example).

Part V: The Part of Tens

This part has the best things hockey has to offer, as compiled by JD himself, and other lists ranging from the top teams of all time to the most ferocious hitters.

Part VI: Appendixes

Hockey has a language all its own, and in Appendix A we give you the terms you'll need in order to talk hockey with the best of them. Appendix B lists the various hockey organizations in the States and Canada, from PeeWees to the pros. In Appendix C, you can find an illustrated list of the hockey referee signals and why they are called. Finally, Appendix D gives you lists of NHL information, from addresses to statistics.

Icons Used in This Book

We lead you through all this information with some icons developed especially for this book. They point you toward valuable advice and alert you to important hazards.

Chateau bow-wow is a standard expression in hockey describing the place players go when they mess up. Read this section, or you'll end up in JD's doghouse.

This icon lets players know when they are getting good advice — and some of this advice comes directly from NHL players.

This information bears repeating. Bears repeating.

Be careful with this stuff; you could hurt yourself.

This icon points out passages that make it easier for fans to watch their favorite sport, either on TV or from the stands.

Hockey coaches really are teachers on skates, so pay attention to these parts. You might learn something important.

Information for the big kids.

Information for the little ones.

Talk like this, and the guys in the cheap seats will understand you.

Words of wisdom from the hockey maven. Read this carefully, or he'll slash you.

Part I

Getting Started — Before They Drop the Puck

The 5th Wave   By Rich Tennant

"This is great! It even comes with a jar of official All-Star sweat for that Stanley Cup Final look."

In this part . . .

*I*n this part, we get you started with an introduction to
hockey and what it's all about, from the origins of the
sport and the way players have dressed and protected
themselves over the years to the rules of the game. We
also tell you what the different players do — and we
explain how you can outfit yourself and your kids in
everything from shoulder pads and skates to sticks
and gloves. We alert you to the things you can — and
cannot — do when you are on the ice.

Chapter 1

What Is Hockey?

. . . .

In This Chapter

▶ Discovering hockey's roots

▶ Figuring out which player does what

▶ Examining a typical hockey rink

. . . .

*H*ockey has been played for longer than any of us has been alive, but we can't tell you exactly when it was invented, or by whom, because no one really knows for sure. We do have some idea of how it got started, however, and we can describe the ways the game has grown and changed over the years. Once a relatively obscure recreation for people who lived in the north country, hockey is now played all over the world and has become one of the most popular winter sports. Frankly, we don't know what we'd do without it, and millions of other people feel the same way.

The Origins of the Game

Most historians place the roots of hockey in the chilly climes of northern Europe, specifically Great Britain and France, where field hockey was a popular summer sport more than 500 years ago. When the ponds and lakes froze in winter, it was not unusual for the athletes who fancied that sport to play a version of it on ice. An ice game known as *kolven* was popular in Holland in the 17th century, and later on the game really took hold in England. In his book, *Fischler's Illustrated History of Hockey,* veteran hockey journalist and broadcaster Stan Fischler writes about a rudimentary version of the sport becoming popular in the English marshland community of Bury Fen in the 1820s. The game, he explains, was called *bandy,* and the local players used to scramble around the town's frozen meadowlands, swatting a wooden or cork ball, known as a *kit* or *cat,* with wooden sticks made from the branches of local willow trees. Articles in London newspapers around that time mention increasing interest in the sport, which many observers believe got its name from the French word *hoquet,* which means "shepherd's crook" or "bent stick." A number of writers thought this game should be forbidden because it was so disruptive to people out for a leisurely winter skate.

Hockey comes to North America

Not surprisingly, the earliest North American games were played in Canada. British soldiers stationed in Halifax, Nova Scotia, were reported to have organized contests on frozen ponds in and around that city in the 1870s, and about that same time in Montreal students from McGill University began facing off against each other in a downtown ice rink. The continent's first hockey league was said to have been launched in Kingston, Ontario, in 1885, and it included four teams.

Hockey became so popular that games were soon being played on a regular basis between clubs from Toronto, Ottawa, and Montreal. The English Governor General of Canada, Lord Stanley of Preston, was so impressed that in 1892 he bought a silver bowl with an interior gold finish and decreed that it be given each year to the best amateur team in Canada. That trophy, of course, has come to be known as the Stanley Cup and is awarded today to the franchise that wins the National Hockey League play-offs.

When hockey was first played in Canada, the teams had nine men per side. But by the time the Stanley Cup was introduced, it was a seven-man game. The change came about accidentally in the late 1880s after a club playing in the Montreal Winter Carnival showed up two men short, and its opponent agreed to drop the same number of players on its team to even the match. In time, players began to prefer the smaller squad, and it wasn't long before that number became the standard for the sport. Each team featured one goaltender, three forwards, two defensemen, and a rover, who had the option of moving up ice on the attack or falling back to defend his goal.

The rise of professional hockey

Hockey was a strictly amateur affair until 1904, when the first professional league was created — oddly enough in the U.S. Known as the International Pro Hockey League, it was based in the iron-mining region of Michigan's Upper Peninsula. That folded in 1907, but then an even bigger league emerged three years later, the National Hockey Association (NHA). And shortly after that came the Pacific Coast League (PCL). In 1914, a transcontinental championship series was arranged between the two, with the winner getting the coveted cup of Lord Stanley. World War I threw the entire hockey establishment into disarray, and the men running the NHA decided to suspend operations.

But after the war, the hockey powers that be decided to start a whole new organization that would be known as the National Hockey League (NHL). At its inception, the NHL boasted five franchises — the Montreal Canadiens, the Montreal Wanderers, the Ottawa Senators, the Quebec Bulldogs, and the Toronto Arenas. The league's first game was held December 19, 1917. The clubs played a 22-game schedule and, picking up on a rule change instituted by the old NHA, dropped the rover and employed only six players on a side. Toronto finished that first season on top, and in March 1918 met the Pacific Coast League champion Vancouver Millionaires for the Stanley Cup. Toronto won, three games to two. Eventually the PCL folded, and at the start of the 1926 season, the NHL, which at that point had ten teams, divided into two divisions and took control of the Stanley Cup.

A Typical Hockey Rink

In the old days, hockey rinks were set up on ponds, lakes, and rivers, with the snow that had been shoveled off serving as the boundaries. But things are very different today. Sure, pond hockey still exists, but the professional game and the vast majority of amateur contests are now played indoors on regulation rinks.

As shown in Figure 1-1, the official size of a rink in the NHL is 200 feet long and 85 feet wide (61m and 26m). Surrounding the playing surface are the boards, which must measure between 40 and 48 inches, with the ideal height being 42 inches (106cm).

Eleven feet (3.35m) from each end of the rink is the goal, the posts of which are four feet high and six feet wide (1.2m and 1.8m). Each goal has a net, in front of which is a semicircular *crease* that has a radius of six feet (1.8m).

Additionally, the areas between the two goals are divided into three parts by a pair of blue lines, each of which is 60 feet (18.3m) from its respective goal. The area between the blue line and the goal line is either the offensive zone or the defensive zone, depending on which team is attacking and who is defending the goal.

 A red line then dissects the playing surface between the two blue lines, and that is called *center ice*. The rink also contains five face-off circles, two in each defensive zone and one at center ice where the puck is dropped between the opposing centermen at the start of each period. There are four other face-off spots, just outside the blue lines, where the puck may also be dropped after various infractions have been called in that area or if the referee stops play for some other reason.

The entire rink is encircled by synthetic glass except for the area just in front of the two player benches. There is glass behind the benches to protect those fans from the puck — and to protect the players from the fans.

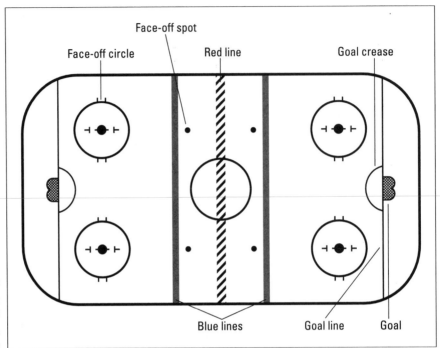

Figure 1-1:
The hockey
rink.

Hockey rinks for international competition, including the Winter Olympics, must be 200 feet by 100 feet (61m by 30.5m). That makes them some 15 feet (4.6m) wider than those used in the NHL, a design characteristic that leads to more open play and gives the game greater flow but also takes away much of the physical play that North American fans seem to appreciate. The majority of hockey rinks in the U.S. are built to NHL specs, but more and more international-sized arenas are being constructed.

How Hockey Is Played: The Positions

Hockey is played on ice with a frozen rubber puck and sticks that are made of wood and space-age materials like graphite, fiberglass, aluminum, and even titanium. Each team is still comprised of six players, all of whom wear skates and various types of padding and protection, depending on their position. Obviously, goaltenders wear the most, and speedy playmakers or scorers the least. The goal of the game is to score goals by putting the puck in the opposing team's net and keeping it out of your own.

In most cases, a hockey team is comprised of a goalie (the *netminder*), two defensemen, and three forwards (one of which is called a center, and the two wings, left and right). (See Figure 1-2 for an approximate placement of these positions.) We say "in most cases" because different game situations may induce a coach to change things up a bit. When looking for more offense, for example, a coach may employ four forwards instead of three.

As we discuss in greater depth in Chapter 3, hockey referees penalize teams and players for infractions by taking a man off the ice and making them play for a period of time, generally two minutes, with one less skater than the other squad (which puts the numerically superior team into a situation called a power play; see Chapter 8 for all the details). So the team that has been penalized has only five, not six players on the ice. Sometimes, late in the game a club that is behind takes out its goaltender and replaces him with another player to create more offense.

As a rule, all hockey teams carry two goalies. Youth hockey clubs generally have enough players to put out three lines (each line consists of a centerman and two other forwards) and three sets of defensemen (each set is made up of one left defenseman and one right). Teams in the NHL are allowed to suit as many as 18 players, excluding goaltenders, for a game; that gives them enough for four lines. Traditionally, professional coaches in the U.S. and Canada have been flexible with the units they put onto the ice, letting different lines play with different sets of defensemen. But more and

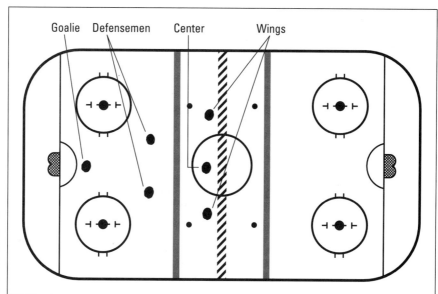

Figure 1-2:
Typical hockey positions.

Goalie   Defensemen   Center   Wings

more, teams follow the European model and skate three units of five, meaning that they keep the sets of forwards and defensemen together all the time. The other players who dress for the game in that system are extras who usually play only when there is an injury or equipment problem involving one of the regulars.

Centers

Centers are the team's quarterback, the ones who direct the play in both the offensive and defensive zones, and they come in all shapes and sizes. You have people like Eric Lindros and Mark Messier, who combine speed, power, and scoring ability, as well as uncanny leadership. Another type is the playmaking center, like Wayne Gretzky and Adam Oates, who can score but also excel at making the good pass and setting up their teammates. And then there are two-way marvels, such as Peter Forsberg who are scoring threats and tenacious defensive specialists as well. Different as they all may be in many ways, good NHL centermen usually have several things in common:

- ✔ They must be good on face-offs.
- ✔ They must be able to pass and shoot well.
- ✔ They must be able to lead the team on both ends of the ice.

The first-line center is generally a team's highest scorer either because he's a great playmaker (passer) or finisher (goal scorer), or both. Most times the second-line center has similar abilities, though they may not be on as high a level as the man anchoring line number 1. Third-line centers are supposed to be good on face-offs and strong on checking; their primary job in most cases is to keep the other team's top line from scoring.

Wings

Traditionally, *wings* (or *wingers*) went up and down the ice on their respective sides, the right wingers on the right and the left wingers on the left. And what determined which side the players played? Their shot. A right-handed shot was positioned on the right wing, and a left-handed winger played the left wing. The most notable exception to this rule was Maurice (Rocket) Richard, one of the greatest players ever, who shot left but played right wing.

But thanks again to the European influence, you now frequently see left-handed shots playing on the right side, for example, because it gives left-handed shots a better chance at *one-timing shots* (shooting right off the pass without breaking stride), which can be very effective ways of scoring a goal. Instead of stopping the puck and practically teeing it up (like Gary McCord, of *Golf For Dummies* fame), you strike the puck on the move. The benefit is that it cuts the release time in half and gives the shooter a better chance of scoring.

Several different types of wingers play in the NHL these days.

- One is a checker like Jere Lehtinen. His primary job is to stay on the other team's good players and make sure they don't score. He doesn't put many points on the board, but he provides an invaluable service to his team by keeping the other guys' big gun at bay.

- Next is the gritty, tough forward who makes plays along the boards and in the corners, plays the body well yet also knows how to score in the trenches, and ideally has a bit of a mean streak in him. Scott Mellanby is a good example of this kind of player, and so are Pat Verbeek and Keith Tkachuk.

- You also have the pure scoring wings, such as Brett Hull, who has a big shot, as well as the speed scorers, like Peter Bondra and Mike Gartner, flashy skaters who seem to fly down the ice.

- In addition, the league has a few wingers, such as Jari Kurri, who can play it both ways, either as a scorer or a checker. And finally, there are enforcers such as Tie Domi and Bob Probert, tough guys who hit and intimidate and are not afraid to drop their gloves and use their fists.

As is the case with centermen, coaches generally put their most talented offensive wingers on the first two lines and keep their defensive specialists for the third line. Many times, the fourth-line wingers are asked to pick up the pace of the game by hitting hard, creating turnovers, and being aggressive. Those who play on the fourth unit don't get nearly as much ice time as the others, so they usually try to do as much as they can during their shifts. They can really ignite a team if they get some good licks in and get the crowd going as well.

Goalies

Years ago, the big kid who couldn't skate was traditionally given the goalie stick, but not anymore. Goalkeepers today must be excellent skaters and first-rate stickhandlers or they won't last very long. Agility is key, and so is athleticism as the men in the net must be able to scramble around with all that equipment. They must also have great hockey smarts and not only read plays as they form but also react quickly to them. In addition, goalies must talk incessantly to their teammates, telling their defensemen who are working behind the net where to go with the puck and barking warnings to their forwards about which of the opponents are bearing down on them. Listen closely the next time you are at a game or watching one on TV, and you can hear the netminder shouting to his fellow players when the puck is deep in their end. (Dominik Hasek, who was voted Most Valuable Player in the NHL for the 1996–1997 season, talks more than any other goalie!)

A goalie gaffe

Consider a 1974 game that our very own JD played with the St. Louis Blues. "One of the opposing forwards, a player named Jerry Korab, wristed the puck down the ice from his own defensive zone, and I went over to stop it," the fearless coauthor and onetime goaltender says. "But I looked up for just one second to see where I was going to put the puck and while I was doing that, it hit off the heel of my stick, went through my legs, and then trickled off the goal post and into the net, before 16,000 people." The reason he messed up? Concentration, pure and simple. He lost his concentration for a moment, and it cost him and his Blues. Fortunately, JD quickly adds, his teammates picked him up, and St. Louis came back to tie the game 6-6.

Great goalies have great instincts, and they must also have a tremendous ability to concentrate and keep focused on what's going on. Remember, in hockey play does not stop very often. It's not like baseball, which seems to have more downtime than action, or football, in which players have time to rest and regroup before each play. Hockey is often continuous, and a goaltender must be able to focus for the entire game. Concentration, in many ways, is the difference between a major league and a minor league goalie. And only a minor lapse can be the difference between a win and a loss.

Defensemen

These players have two jobs, really. *Defensemen* mainly defend their end of the ice and keep the other team from scoring. It's a position in which you must be physically dominating. You have to be able to take the body, to clear men out from the front of the goal, to block shots, and to grapple with the opponent's forwards in the corner and along the boards. But after the defense has been taken care of, defensemen have to then switch to offense. The first pass is key to any successful rush up ice, and the vast majority of the time, the defensemen have to make the first pass. Defensemen often set the tone and get things going on the offensive end.

Occasionally a defenseman can also lead a team's offense, such as the great Bobby Orr, who won the James Norris Trophy for being the league's best defenseman eight consecutive times and captured two scoring titles, or Brian Leetch. And there are some defensemen, such as Leetch, Chris Chelios, and Ray Bourque who can play the position extremely well both ways. But most defensemen are valued mostly for their ability to keep the other team from scoring and are not asked to do much else.

Chapter 2

Pads and Pucks: Gearing Up

● ●

In This Chapter

▶ Understanding what all the major pieces of gear are

▶ Deciding how much armor you need

▶ Searching for the best place to buy equipment

● ●

*L*ike knights going off to battle, hockey players must cloak themselves in armor before heading out to the ice. Players today wear much more equipment than they did in the game's early years, and many players look like modern-day gladiators when they step into a rink. It's a good thing, too, because with the speed of the shots and the power of the checks, they need all the protection they can get.

The Modern Hockey Player's Gear

Hockey gear varies a great deal, depending upon the age, sex, and ability of the player and where he or she is competing. A member of the Vancouver Canucks, for example, is going to have much different gear than a weekend skater involved in a pickup pond game. For this section, we focus on a National Hockey League skater and all that he dons when it comes time to play. He has the most up-to-date equipment — and wears a lot of it when he goes onto the ice (as seen in Figure 2-1).

Skates

Nothing is more important to an NHL player than his skates, and the ones on the market today are marvels of technology. The basic design has not changed that much in 30 years, but instead of using only leather for the boots, manufacturers now employ a combination of materials. The inside of many skates, for example, is made of *clarino,* a synthetic leather that is easier to break in and more water-resistant.

Figure 2-1:
Up-to-date
equipment
and plenty
of it (Sergei
Fedorov).

The heel and lace eyelets are still constructed completely of leather, but the rest of a skate's exterior also includes ballistic nylon; kevlar, which is also used in bullet-proof vests; and graphite to keep it light, stiff (for better support and protection), and durable. As for the old metal runners, they have been replaced by a plastic holder in which a metal blade is inserted. (See Figure 2-2.)

Skate blades have different degrees of shape to them, and the kind a player chooses depends on the type of performance he wants. The bottom of Brian Leetch's blades, for example, have what is known as a *deep hollow* — the area between the two edges has been hollowed out and curves a bit to the inside. Rangers equipment manager Mike Folga sharpens Leetch's blades that way because the smooth-skating defenseman wants to be able to cut on the ice the way Barry Sanders does on a football field; the deeper the hollow, the easier it is to make those types of moves. Another pair of talented defensemen, Ray Bourque and Paul Coffey, have somewhat flatter blades because they are more straight-ahead skaters. Same with center Mark Messier.

While goalies' skates have a somewhat different shape and design, they are made of the same materials. In addition, they have a plastic shell on the outside to provide better protection from pucks banging off their feet, and their blades are a bit wider.

Figure 2-2:
A typical
hockey
skate.

Sticks

Sticks are probably the next most important piece of equipment. Some are made of traditional wood, and others feature aluminum, graphite, kevlar, or titanium shafts into which wooden blades are placed and then sealed with a hot-melt glue. Perhaps half the players in the NHL use stick shafts made of those new materials, in part because they are more durable and cost-effective. The blades go for only $8 or $9 apiece, less than half the price of a complete wooden stick, and the savings can add up after a while. Additionally, some players like the feel of the aluminum or graphite shafts and believe they can get off a better shot with them. Goalies' sticks, which have a wide "paddle" partway down the shaft so that it is easier to block shots, are still made entirely of wood (wrapped with fiberglass).

Sticks come in different degrees of *flex:* medium, stiff, and extra stiff. The stronger player who hits more slap shots will probably want a stiffer stick because a *slap shot* is made with a full windup — and is the most powerful shot. A forward who shoots closer to the net and likes to *snap* his shots (made with a shortened backswing and a quick follow-through) will probably opt for a stick that's more flexible. And all sticks have blades that are curved, even ones used by goalies, because that gives a shot — or pass — more lift and power.

The NHL has very specific regulations on sticks that may be used in league play. According to its rule book, sticks should be no longer than 63 inches (160cm) from the heel to the end of the shaft, and the blade may not be more than 12 $\frac{1}{2}$ inches (32cm) in length. In addition, a blade may be no more than three inches and no less than two inches wide (7.5 and 5cm), and the curve may not exceed $\frac{1}{2}$ inch (1.27cm). For goalies, the widened part of the stick, or "paddle," can be a maximum of 26 inches (66cm), and the blade must not exceed 3 $\frac{1}{2}$ inches (9cm) in width or 15 $\frac{1}{2}$ inches (39.37cm) in length. Figure 2-3 shows some sample sticks.

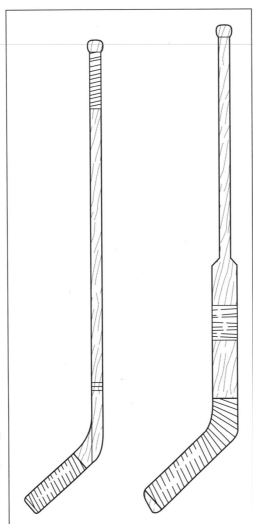

Figure 2-3:
A regular stick and a goalie's stick.

Protection

The rest of a hockey player's equipment is designed primarily to protect him from sticks, pucks, goal posts, and opposing players, while enabling him to maneuver with as much speed and agility as possible. Helmets are a critical piece of gear for players on any level, and some pros like to attach a clear shield in front to protect their eyes. (All amateur players must wear a full face guard on their helmets.) Figure 2-4 shows some typical protection.

Shoulder pads vary in size depending on the position a person plays and his preferences; defensemen usually have heavier pads because they do more checking than other players and take a lot of punishment on the ice; some defensemen look like they should be playing linebacker for the Dallas Cowboys. Also, their shoulder pads often extend all the way to their waists because they often drop to their knees to block shots and need padding across their chests. Some even have a pad that goes down their spines to protect them from slashes across the back. Forwards, on the other hand, might opt for lighter shoulder pads, depending on their role. Some forwards have the shoulder pads extended down their backs for further protection.

A checking wing will want more protection than a *sniper* (a pure goal scorer) who doesn't hit other players or the boards all that much. Wayne Gretzky's shoulder pads not only look as old as he is but offer very little in the way of protection. But as a scorer and playmaker who doesn't mix it up physically very much, he really doesn't need much else.

Figure 2-4:
After skates and a stick, a hockey player's equipment is for protection (Eric Lindros).

© NHL Images/Allsport/Joe Patronite

A pro may also wear padded pants, a protective cup, shin guards, elbow pads, and gloves. Though it doesn't look that different from the gear players were wearing 20 years ago, it has changed a lot in terms of substance thanks to the development of new plastics, foams, and other materials that make it all lighter, stronger, and more durable. Even the *sweaters*, or jerseys, are better. Once made of wool because games were initially played outside, they had all the comfort of a rubber suit on a hot July day. But now they are put together with very lightweight and breathable materials.

Goalie protection

Not surprisingly, goalies have a somewhat different ensemble. In addition to helmets, they wear masks, and many put on extra neck protection as well. Chest protectors are essential, and they all put padding down both their arms to their wrists. Goalies wear quite different gloves from those that their teammates wear. See Figure 2-5 for the goaltender's regalia.

Figure 2-5:
A modern
goalie is
well
protected.

© NHL Images/Ray Grabowski

The puck

Rule 25 of the NHL rule handbook provides a description of that little object known as the "puck" — a word whose origin may be 17th-century French from a verb that means "to poke." The handbook says:

The puck shall be made of vulcanized rubber, or other approved material, one inch (1") thick and three inches (3") in diameter and shall weigh between five and one-half ounces (5 ½ oz.) and six ounces (6 oz.).

The home team shall be responsible for providing an adequate supply of official pucks which shall be kept in a frozen condition. This supply of pucks shall be kept at the penalty bench under the control of one of the regular off-ice officials or a special attendant.

A glove known as a *blocker* goes on the hand that holds the stick, and a glove known as the *catcher,* which looks like a fancy first-baseman's mitt, goes on the other hand. Goalies also have large, pillow-like pads on the fronts of their legs that wrap around the tops of their skates and go up past their knees. Years ago, the outside of the pads were made entirely of leather and the inside was stuffed with deer hair. Those materials are also used to make the more modern version, but manufacturers also include a number of synthetic materials to make the pads lighter and more water-resistant.

What They Wore — and Didn't Wear — in Years Past

It's remarkable how little equipment the hockey players of the past wore and how rudimentary the gear they did have truly was. In the beginning, skates consisted of blades that were attached to shoes, and sticks were made from tree branches. The first goalie shin and knee pads had originally been designed for cricket. The quality of the gear progressed over the years, with true hockey skates being made and players wearing protective gloves. Shin guards eventually came into being, but many times they didn't do much to soften the blow of a puck or stick, and players were known to stuff newspaper or magazines behind them for extra protection. (Compare the players in Figure 2-6 to those you see today.)

For many years the blades on sticks were completely straight, but New York Rangers star Andy Bathgate began experimenting with a curve in the late 1950s. During a European tour of Ranger and Blackhawk players, Bathgate showed his innovation to Bobby Hull and Stan Mikita, and they began playing with one themselves. And it wasn't long before most NHL players had done the same thing.

Amazingly, goalies played without masks until 1959, when Jacques Plante wore face protection at a game in the old Madison Square Garden after he had taken a puck in the cheekbone from Andy Bathgate. Plante's coach, Toe Blake, pressured him to shed the mask later on, and he did for a while. But he started wearing a mask again the following spring, and other goaltenders eventually followed suit. But it wasn't until 1973 that an NHL netminder (journeyman Andy Brown) appeared in a game without a mask for the last time.

It's also surprising to think that players didn't begin wearing helmets with any sort of regularity until the early 1970s; prior to that the only people who wore them did so mostly because they were recovering from a head injury, or, as was the case of one former Chicago Blackhawk forward, because they were embarrassed about being bald. (No, it wasn't Bobby Hull.) The league passed a rule prior to the start of the 1979–80 season decreeing that anyone who came into the NHL from that point on had to wear a helmet. By the early 1990s there were only a few players left who went bareheaded, and the last one to do so was Craig MacTavish, who retired after the 1996–97 season.

Deciding What Equipment Is Best for You — and Your Kids

The best way to buy the right equipment is to find a store or outlet that specializes in hockey equipment and has knowledgeable salespeople that can not only help pick out the best gear for you and your kids but also make sure it all fits properly.

Getting the right skates

Let's start with skates. Most adults should get ones that are a size to a size-and-a-half down from their usual shoe size. For children, they should drop half a size. It's important that the skates fit comfortably and snugly at the time of purchase; it's not like buying a sweater two sizes too big and waiting for a kid to grow into it. The best way to check is to push your toe, or your child's, to the front of the skate and then put a finger down behind the heel. If you can fit more than one in there, the skate is too big. The whole key to good skating ability is support, and you can't get support if the skate doesn't fit.

Getting the right helmet

When looking for a helmet, make sure you have the right width and that it does not wobble. Children should have protection for the ears. A full face guard, either a clear shield or wire cage, is recommended for all levels of play, and so is a chin cup.

Padding up: From the shoulders to the hands

Shoulder pads should be comfortable and not too bulky. You want the cup to fit right on the shoulder and the pad to almost rest against your neck; anything that's looser in that area may jam into you when someone checks you or you fall to the ice. And that will hurt. Defensemen should get shoulder pads with full frontal protection so they can block shots without worry; forwards can get away with a lot less.

Whether you get heavy-duty, football-like equipment or go for lighter-weight wear depends on your abilities and your level of play. Many adult and youth leagues don't allow checking, for example, so there's no reason to get big, expensive pads.

As for elbow pads, you want ones that fit properly on the point of the elbow and won't slip up and down. And you want to make sure that they're not so tight that they constrict the flow of blood. These days, elbow pads come in various lengths; some people prefer to wear a long glove and short elbow pads, while others, Brett Hull of the St. Louis Blues is one that comes to mind, like a shorter glove and longer pads. You should have the forearm covered against slashes and stick checks so it is as well-protected as the elbow.

Gloves used to be all leather, but now they're made mostly of kevlar or nylon or some combination of the two. You want something with a strong thumb, which is an area where you get most of your injuries. For a good fit, you should have a little room at the end of your fingers.

From the waist down

Hockey pants used to be held up exclusively by suspenders, but now they come with belts, so it's not so hard tucking that sweater in the right side, à la Wayne Gretzky. The key is getting pants with good thigh, hip, and tailbone protection.

Shin guards should fit in the center of the kneecap and go down to the top of the skate. They run from 7 inches in length to 17 inches. If you are a defenseman, you want to get ones with lots of padding because you will be blocking more shots than a forward, who should get guards of lighter weight and size. Defensemen often have padding that wraps right around the back of their legs.

Choosing a stick

Sticks are more a question of preference and size. The aluminum shafts are somewhat more expensive, but they do last longer and might not be a bad way to go for the more serious player. Kids, beginners, and very part-time players can get by just fine with wooden sticks.

So what will all this equipment cost? Plenty if you go down and pick it all out at once. Outfitting one child will run anywhere between $300 and $400, while equipment for adults could go from $400 all the way up to $1,000 for top-of-the-line stuff. You should purchase equipment that best suits your level of play and commitment, and the same goes for the kids. Just don't take shortcuts on the critical gear, like helmets and skates. It pays to be safe and comfortable.

Some extra advice for parents outfitting children: Check out area stores for trade-in and swap programs. Many youth hockey leagues and sporting goods stores that supply them allow parents to trade in skates and pads for gear that fits as their children grow up, at minimal cost. Do it if you can.

Where to Buy What You Want

Finding first-rate hockey gear is not always the easiest task. The big sporting goods chains carry some equipment. Unless their primary orientation is hockey, however, they probably won't have the quality and selection you need if you want to buy skates, helmets, and sticks. Check your local Yellow Pages for the name of outlets that might specialize in hockey gear and peruse *The Hockey News,* which often carries advertisements from that sort of store. You may also want to check out the pro shop at the local ice rink; they usually are well stocked with up-to-date equipment and have knowledgeable salespeople.

Sometimes you can find an independent retailer who has everything you need to play the game and offers not only a fair price but also expert help in sizing and selection. Our favorite in that category is Gerry Cosby's, which has a big store at Madison Square Garden in New York City and outlets in Princeton, New Jersey; Westbury, Long Island; and Sheffield, Massachusetts. Gerry Cosby was a Boston native who worked as an office boy at the old Boston Arena and later served as the practice goalie for the Bruins before joining the Rangers' organization. He became so good at the game that he started for the 1933 United States team that won the gold medal at the 1933 World Championships in Helsinki, Finland, the one and only time the U.S. came out on top in that competition.

Cosby stumbled into the sporting goods business in the late 1930s when the president of a minor league hockey organization asked him to get six dozen sticks for one of the teams. Cosby bought some from a company in Pennsylvania that also made washing machine parts, sold the sticks for a slight profit, and built up his business from there, opening his first store on Manhattan's upper east side. It remains a family-owned operation, currently run by Gerry's son Michael, and caters to athletes of all ages and abilities, from Pee-Wees to the pros. Many of the teams in the NHL buy some, if not all, of their equipment from Cosby's, and when Wayne Gretzky started playing for the New York Rangers, he outfitted his young sons in hockey gear at that store.

Whether you want to purchase a pair of Bauer Supreme skates, Eric Lindros's stick, Brian Leetch's jersey or a set of Cooper shoulder pads, the selection and quality of merchandise at Gerry Cosby's is second-to-none, and the salespeople know what they are doing. And worry not if you don't live anywhere near the Big Apple; Cosby's has an extensive mail-order catalog that it is happy to mail out (Gerry Cosby's, 3 Pennsylvania Plaza, New York, New York, 10001, 212-563-6464). In addition, several other national mail-order houses specialize in hockey gear; check the advertising pages of *The Hockey News* for the ones that are best for you.

As for those less athletic fans who are more interested in making a fashion statement than a hat trick, they can buy NHL-licensed merchandise bearing the logo of their favorite team in a wide range of stores from Kmart and Target to Saks Fifth Avenue and Bloomingdale's. The products available span the spectrum, from hockey sweaters and team hats to wallpaper and bedsheets. Most franchises have team stores of some sort in the city in which they are based and also out at the arena, and the big sporting goods chains such as Modell's and Foot Locker have some gear for sale. In addition, the NHL puts out a catalog for all its licensed merchandise goods as well as other items such as autographed collectibles and electronic games.

Chapter 3

Rules of the Game

- -

In This Chapter

▶ Putting the puck where it belongs

▶ Following the rules of the game

▶ Understanding the difference between roughing, slashing, charging, and hooking

- -

Walk into a hockey game that's tied with only a minute to go in the third period, and you're likely to find something resembling one of the street scenes from *A Tale of Two Cities*. (If you haven't read the book, picture torch- and pitchfork-carrying mobs, terrified aristocrats, and a lone, abandoned child, all milling around a very busy guillotine. Put this scene on an ice rink, make a few casting changes, and you have the tail end of a close game.) In other words, absolute chaos — and it appears as if all sense of order has gone. But that's not the case at all. Hockey, like the other major sports, is governed by a strict code of rules, and games are much more controlled than they often seem. This chapter describes the NHL's most important regulations and the roles of the people who must enforce them on the ice.

Scoring

The object of hockey is to score goals, and the club that scores the most wins the game. To score a goal, an attacking player must put the puck between the goal posts and over the red goal line. But how you get the puck over the goal line determines whether you get the point or not:

✔ You can use your stick to get the puck over the goal line.

✔ You can have the puck deflect into the net off any part of your body or skate.

A referee will allow a puck that has been deflected into the goal by a defender's body, skate, or stick to stand as a score as well. However, a member of the attacking team may not deliberately bat the puck into the net with any part of his body or kick it in with his foot. And anything that deflects in off the referee or linesmen doesn't count as a goal, either.

An offensive player who puts the puck into the net is credited with scoring a goal. The player (or players) that made the immediate pass(es) that led to the goal receives an *assist*. No more than two assists can be handed out per goal. Each player gets one point for a goal or assist, and the NHL player who amasses the most points during the season wins the scoring title and the coveted Art Ross Trophy.

The greatest assist and scoring feats

Most goals in a game: 7

Joe Malone

Quebec Bulldogs (1920)

Most goals in a season: 92

Wayne Gretzky

Edmonton Oilers (1981–82)

Most goals in a career (and counting): 862

Wayne Gretzky

Edmonton Oilers, Los Angeles Kings, St. Louis Blues, New York Rangers

Most assists in a season: 163

Wayne Gretzky

Edmonton Oilers (1985-86)

Most assists in a career (and counting): 1843

Wayne Gretzky

Edmonton Oilers, Los Angeles Kings, St. Louis Blues, New York Rangers

Most goals and assists in one game: 6, 4

Darrel Sittler

Toronto Maple Leafs (1976)

Most goals and assists in one period: 3, 3

Bryan Trottier

New York Islanders (1988)

Because this last feat was accomplished against JD's Rangers, JD adds: "I must have been injured that night." (Be sure to check out Appendix D for many more hockey statistics and figures.)

Periods

NHL games are divided into three, 20-minute periods. If the contest is tied at the end of regulation during the regular season, the teams play an additional period of sudden death overtime that lasts no more than five minutes, with the club that scores first winning. If no one scores, the game is declared a tie. During the play-offs, however, the overtime lasts until a goal is scored, with the teams breaking after 20 minutes as they do during a normal contest.

Sometimes, the games go on like an all-night party, such as the time in 1936 when it took the Detroit Red Wings nearly six full overtime periods to score on the Montreal Maroons and win a play-off game 1-0. It was 2:25 a.m. when the winning shot went in, and when it was all over the teams had played more than 175 minutes. That's almost three full games.

Rosters: Who Gets to Play

Teams may dress no more than 18 players, excluding goalies, for each game. A list of all eligible players must be given to the referee or official scorer beforehand, and after that no changes to the roster can be made. There is no such limit on the number of goalies a team can use.

Generally, a club has two goalies ready to go each game, one of whom starts while the other sits on the bench. If both should get hurt, a team is entitled to dress and play any available *netminder* (goalie), provided he is eligible.

Franchises in the NHL often have several players that practice with the team on a regular basis but do not dress for the games. They make up a sort of unofficial *taxi squad*, and play only sporadically during the regular season and hardly at all in the play-offs.

The shoot-out

Some minor and international leagues handle the overtime situation a bit differently. They have their teams play a five-minute sudden death period, and if no one scores, the game is then decided by a *shoot-out*. Each team picks five players, and each one of them takes a penalty shot on the other's goalie, skating in by themselves with the puck from the red line (center ice) and trying to score. Whichever team scores more is declared the winner; and if the squads remain tied after the first shoot-out, they start another. This method is very popular in some hockey circles because of the added excitement it generates. A shoot-out was used to determine the 1994 Olympic gold medal champion at Lillehammer, when Sweden bested the Canadian national team.

General substitutions

Skaters may be rotated from the bench while play is in progress provided that the people coming off the ice are within five feet of their bench and out of the play before the switch is made. That's known as *changing on the fly*. If a player doesn't get to that spot, his team is whistled for having too many men on the ice and loses that man to the penalty box for two minutes.

Once play has been stopped, the visiting team has the option of replacing its players on the ice. The referee gives a reasonable amount of time (5–10 seconds), and then he puts up his hands to indicate no further changes. At that point, the home team may then make its desired substitutions. This set-up gives the home team the advantage as far as matchups are concerned, letting it put out the players it wants to face those on the opposing squad. To counter those, the visiting team often substitutes as soon as play begins again and gets the people it wants onto the ice by quickly changing on the fly. (See Chapter 7 to read about the interesting game of match ups and changes.)

Goalie substitutions

As for goaltenders, they may be substituted at any time (usually after the whistle has blown for a stoppage of play — but not always). The new player coming in after a stoppage is allowed warm-ups only if his team's two goaltenders have already been knocked out of the game and he is goalie #3. In that case, the netminder is allowed two minutes to get ready, unless he is being inserted for a penalty shot. Then he must go to work stone cold.

Infractions

The dictionary tells us that an infraction is a "breach, violation, or infringe-ment" of the rules; hardly a minute goes by in a game without one occurring. At last count, the NHL had 93 "official rules," all of which are laid out in a book that is 148 pages long. We don't have the time or space to go over each one of the rules, but we can describe briefly some of the most common breaches. (You can find the signals for these infractions in Appendix C.)

Icing

Icing is called when a player behind the red line in his end of the rink shoots a puck past the goal line in his offensive zone when both teams are playing at even strength. Play is stopped when an opponent other than the goalie touches the puck. (See Figure 3-1 for an illustration of icing from the defensive zone, from behind the goal line, and from the neutral zone.) Icing is considered an infraction because it can be used by teams to take away legitimate scoring chances from skaters on the offensive.

A club that is a man down, or more, may "ice" the puck as often as it likes in order to kill the penalty.

Offside

A player may not skate into his offensive zone ahead of the puck (see Figure 3-2). If that happens, a whistle is blown, and a face-off is held just outside the zone where the breach — *offside* — occurred. What matters in an offside is the position of the skates: Both skates must be all the way over the blue line for a player to be potentially off-side. The location of the stick does not matter.

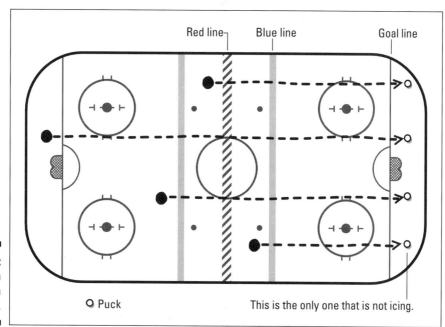

Figure 3-1:
An
illustration
of icing.

Offside is also called if a player makes what is called a *two-line pass.* A defenseman with the puck in front of his own net, for example, cannot snap it to a teammate beyond the red line at center ice because it would have to go over two lines, first the blue and then the red, to get there. For that play to work, the player at center ice would have to skate inside the red line, closer to his own net, to receive the pass. (See Figure 3-3.)

Offside is called to keep players from hanging around the red line at center ice, or all the way down in their offensive zone, and waiting for a pass that will give them a *breakaway* (skating toward the goal with no defenders around except for the goalie) and an easy chance at a goal.

Keep in mind that if you — the receiver of the puck — precede the puck, you are offside.

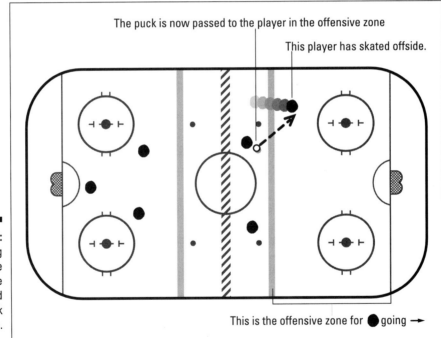

The puck is now passed to the player in the offensive zone

This player has skated offside.

This is the offensive zone for ● going →

Figure 3-2:
Skating into the offensive zone ahead of the puck is offside.

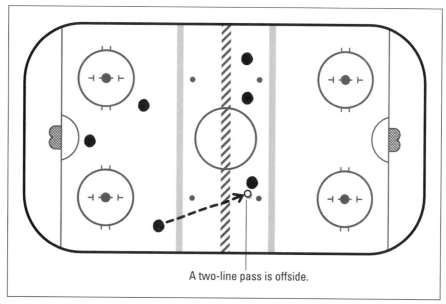

A two-line pass is offside.

Types of Penalties

There are three types of penalties in hockey: *minor, major,* and *misconduct.* The severity of the action determines the kind of penalty handed down. A player who accidentally trips an opponent, for example, faces a less stringent punishment (probably two minutes in the penalty box) than one who punches another player in the mouth or hits him across the face with his stick (at least five minutes in the box, and maybe more). There is bad, and then there is really bad. And the badder a player is on the ice, the longer he will spend watching the game from the sidelines. (Refer to Appendix C for an illustration of the signals for these penalties.)

Minors

Most of the penalties called during an NHL game are minors, in which players are sent to the box for two minutes for things like roughing, slashing, tripping, holding, or hooking an opponent. Misbehave a bit more, and a player might receive a double minor and have to serve two, two-minute penalties consecutively.

Majors

If the violation is even more egregious, such as for fighting, a ref hands out a major penalty, which lasts for five minutes. No substitute is permitted during that time, and the team on which the foul is called will be forced to compete with one less man. A player who is assessed a major for injuring an opponent in the face or head with his stick is automatically fined $100. And a skater who gets three majors in the same game is thrown out.

Misconducts

There are also three kinds of misconduct penalties.

- A *basic misconduct,* which is called for blatant and dangerous rule violations, forces a skater to sit in the penalty box for ten minutes. Bad as that infraction might be, however, it does not lead to the loss of a man, and therefore no one goes onto the power play (see Chapter 8 for details on the power play).

- Get a *game misconduct,* however, and a player is tossed from the ice right away. Violators are also fined and face the possibility of suspension if their infraction, be it a vicious slash or brutal cross-check, is particularly egregious. Any skater who is whistled for a total of three game misconducts during the regular season is automatically suspended for one contest, unless the misconducts involve abuse of officials or stick-related fouls; then it takes only two in the same season to lead to suspension. Two game misconducts in the play-offs of any given year will result in the same action.

- Finally, referees may also call what is known as a *gross misconduct,* which also results in a game suspension, a fine, and the possibility of even more serious league action.

Note: If a player receives a game misconduct penalty, his team does not have to play the rest of the game a man down — the team is only short a player during the penalty time for the player who was tossed from the game. After the penalty time is up, a substitute can take the place of the evicted player.

Sometimes the infraction is so great that a penalty shot is called, and the player who was fouled gets to skate in on the goalie by himself and try to score. Penalty shots come about for a variety of reasons, such as a player deliberately displacing the goal post during a breakaway for the other team, falling on the puck in his *crease* (the area in front of the goal), picking up the puck with his hand in the crease area, and taking a player down from behind on a breakaway. Penalty shots don't happen very often, but when they do, they create one of the most exciting moments in hockey, especially in a big game.

How You Get a Penalty

It's not really that hard to get a penalty. If a player slashes his opponent across his wrist with a stick, he's gone, most likely for two minutes but maybe even longer. Same thing if he knocks down a man from behind. Or holds him up in front of the net. Or mouths off to the referee. If a player breaks one of the league's rules, he'll probably receive a penalty (unless the referee doesn't see him or is inclined to let things go).

Just so you know what your favorite winger or centerman is not supposed to do when he skates onto the ice, we have compiled descriptions of the most frequently called penalties.

Roughing

Roughing is called after a player strikes an opponent in a minor altercation that the referee determines is not worthy of a major. (See Figure 3-4.) For example, if two players push and shove a lot and appear ready to fight but don't actually drop their gloves and start punching each other, then it's

Figure 3-4:
Does this look like roughing to you?

© NHL Images/Al Messerschmidt

considered roughing. They may also be whistled for particularly rough behavior after play has stopped; a good face plant (such as grinding one's palm into an opponent's face) often leads to a roughing penalty, and so might an open-handed slap or an obvious elbow.

Hooking

If a player impedes the progress of another by "hooking" him with his stick and keeping him from making a play, then he is called for *hooking*. Generally that happens when a skater has scooted by the person in charge of guarding him, and the defenseman has no other recourse but to hold the player up by "hooking" him with his stick. Not only does that break up a play illegally, but it can also injure a player, especially if the stick used in the hooking comes up high and hits the opposing player in his face. (See Figure 3-5.) Hooking is also known as *water skiing* — which gives you a good idea of what is involved.

Charging

A minor or major penalty may be imposed on a person who skates or jumps into, or *charges,* an opponent in any way (as shown in Figure 3-6). Whether it's determined to be a major or minor penalty depends upon the seriousness of the infraction; the more dangerous the hit, the more likely it will be a major.

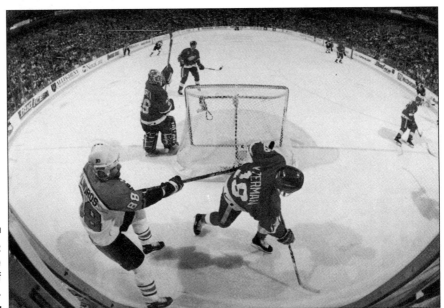

Figure 3-5:
A fish-eye
view of
hooking.

© NHL Images/Allsport/Robert Laberge

Figure 3-6:
Someone is
going to get
called for
charging!

Interference

A common penalty that occurs when a player interferes with or impedes the progress of an opponent who does not have the puck. It happens a lot in front of the net, where players fight for position, and also behind a play as a skater may try to hold up another as he tries to catch up with the puck. In addition, interference is called when a player deliberately knocks the stick out of an opponent's hand or prevents a player who has dropped his stick, or any other piece of equipment, from picking it back up.

Slashing

Players receive this penalty when they smack an opponent with their sticks, or "slash" an opponent, either to hold him up or cause injury. Generally, the slash has to be a fairly strong slash for a referee to call this infraction; the rule book states that "non-agressive stick contact to the pants or the front of the shin pads should not be penalized as slashing."

High-sticking

Any contact made by a stick on an opponent above the shoulders is not allowed, and a minor penalty will be assessed. (See Figure 3-7.) This rule is supposed to protect the players from being hit by a stick in the face, eyes, or head. Also, players cannot bat the puck above the normal height of the shoulders; play is stopped if that happens. In addition, any apparent goal scored as the result of a player striking the puck with his stick above his shoulder is not allowed.

Figure 3-7:
High-sticking (with an elbow thrown in for roughing)!

© NHL Images/Allsport/Robert Laberge

Checking from behind

The officials whistle for this infraction when a player hits an opponent who is not aware of the impending contact and therefore cannot defend himself from behind. It is a very dangerous infraction that can lead to serious injury to the person who has been hit.

Fighting

It's actually called "fisticuffs" in the NHL rule book and is assessed when players drop their gloves and start to act like prizefighters. Players get rid of their gloves because they can hit harder and inflict more pain with their bare knuckles. (See Figure 3-8.) Chapter 9 has more information on fighting.

Figure 3-8:
Fisticuffs in
the NHL.

© NHL Images/Allsport/Al Bello

Hockey and fighting

Fighting has long been an accepted part of professional hockey in the United States and Canada and is considered a natural by-product of a fast and furious game. Years ago, it was not unusual to see entire benches empty during a fight and have every player wrestling their opponents to the ice and throwing punches. But the NHL and other leagues began instituting much stricter rules about fighting, and anyone who leaves the bench to enter or start a brawl these days, or jumps into an altercation as the third man, is treated harshly with penalties and fines.

But unlike college and international hockey organizations, which prohibit fighting, the NHL and other professional leagues in North America still allow it to go on, though not without penalty. That bothers some fans, who would like to see fighting completely banned. But the majority seem to enjoy the occasional scrap between players. And there are those who argue quite sensibly that fighting neutralizes the possibility of smaller players being intimidated by bigger ones, especially if both franchises have a fighter or two on their rosters; no one is going to be able to mess around with one of the smaller skaters if he knows he will then have to answer to one of the fighters. So it actually serves to better keep the peace. Also, the absence of fighting would likely lead to an increase in the number and severity of stick fouls (slashing, high-sticking, and so on), which can be even more dangerous, because players wouldn't have the same outlet for their frustration and rage.

Referees and Linesmen: Their Roles and Responsibilities

Each game in the NHL is officiated by one *referee*, who wears an orange armband, and two *linesmen*. The referee is the one who supervises the entire game and in the case of disputes, his decision is final. He reports any serious infractions to league headquarters and is also in charge of arbitrating any controversial goals or calls. The referee also drops the puck at center ice at the start of each period.

The linesmen have only slightly lesser roles in comparison; they, too, may call penalties and are expected to help out each other, and the referee, should an extra set of eyes and ears be needed. And they are responsible for handling all face-offs after the opening.

Hockey linesmen and referees have a tough job. They must skate up and down the ice to keep up with the play — and it is estimated that they skate up to seven miles per game! They must dodge pucks that fly by at speeds as high as 100 miles per hour. They must avoid getting hit by sticks, skates, and flying bodies as players fight for position and the puck. *Note:* If an official gets hit by the puck, play continues. But if a puck bounces off an official into the goal, that goal is not allowed.

And the officials must deal with a fair amount of verbal abuse as players and coaches argue calls and whine about the penalties that are not assessed. (There is rarely any physical contact between refs and players, à la Roberto Alomar [baseball] or Dennis Rodman [basketball], however, and on the few occasions that physical contact does happen, the leagues act swiftly and sternly.) There is also a tremendous amount of subjectivity involved in the work of the officials; it's not always easy to discern what is and isn't a penalty — or a goal — when things happen as quickly as they do in hockey.

When it comes to calling a penalty, the officials are on their own. But as far as goals are concerned, they have some help. A *goal judge* at the end of each rink decides whether the puck has passed between the goal posts and entirely over the goal line. In addition, a *video goal judge* at each game checks the replays to determine what is and isn't a goal.

What the video goal judge reviews

The video goal judge has the responsibility of reviewing these situations:

- The puck crossing the goal line
- The puck in the net before a goalpost is dislodged
- The puck in the net before or after expiration of time at the end of the period
- The puck directed into the net by a hand or foot
- The puck deflected into the net off an official
- The puck directed into the net after being struck with a high-stick, above the height of the crossbar, by an attacking player
- The correct time on the official game clock (provided the game time is visible on the video goal judge's monitors)

Part II

How the Big Boys Do It

"Hey - at least wait until the puck comes down before you criticize my slap shot."

In this part . . .

This part is where we tell you all about the world's top professional and amateur players, from the big boys of the National Hockey League to the men and women who make up the strongest college teams. Where do they come from? How do they play their games?

We also talk about training and coaching, giving you tips from the best in those fields. And finally, we give you the inside scoop on hitting and intimidating, with JD providing his lists of the greatest fighters, intimidators, and agitators in NHL history.

Chapter 4
The National Hockey League

In This Chapter

▶ Discovering the origins of the NHL

▶ Following the standings

▶ Thinking about the Cup

▶ Wondering at the players' size, speed, and strength

There are hundreds of active hockey associations around the globe, but none has the power, prestige, and players of the National Hockey League. And for that reason, we devote an entire chapter to the international organization that is home to the best teams in the world.

In the Beginning

The NHL was founded in Montreal in November 1917, and the league's first games were played the following month. Initially, there were five franchises: the Montreal Canadiens, the Ottawa Senators, the Montreal Wanderers, the Quebec Bulldogs, and the Toronto Arenas. But Quebec decided not to operate that first season, so its players were allocated to the other teams. The clubs played a 22-game schedule, and Toronto was the only one that had a rink with artificial ice.

Things did not go smoothly in the beginning. Shortly after the season started, the Wanderers began having serious financial problems and got so low on players that the other teams offered to donate some of their own so that the club could continue competing. And then the Montreal Arena, which was home to both the Wanderers and the Canadiens, burned to the ground. That was enough for the owners of the Wanderers, and they withdrew the team from the league, leaving the NHL with only three teams. (The Canadiens moved their home games to the 3,250-seat Jubilee Rink.) Toronto won the championship that first tumultuous season, beating Montreal in a two-game play-off and then went on to capture the Stanley Cup (more about that later) by topping the Vancouver Millionaires of the rival Pacific Coast Hockey Association (PCHA) in a best-of-five series.

Do we mean to say that the NHL was not the only professional hockey league operating at the time? Yes, indeed. In fact, the PCHA had been around for many years, and athletes had been getting paid to play hockey for even longer. Historians believe that several of the men who put together the earliest amateur hockey clubs quietly lined the pockets of their top players and shelled out whatever money they had to in order to get the very best talent. Many believe that the first unabashedly professional hockey team was the Portage Lakers of Houghton, Michigan, which was organized in 1902. And by the end of that decade, two leagues known as the National Hockey Association (NHA) and the Canadian Hockey Association (CHA) employed a number of professional players. In 1911, a pair of those stars, the brothers Lester and Frank Patrick, decided to form a third league, the PCHA. (Unfortunately, we are unable to confirm long-standing rumors that the first player they ever signed was a strapping goalie named John Davidson.)

The seeds for the NHL were planted in the fall of 1917 when the NHA disbanded, partially due to the loss of players, many of whom had gone overseas to fight in World War I, and also because of the disdain team owners felt toward one of their own, Eddie Livingstone, who held the Toronto franchise. They disliked the man so much that they hatched a plan to start a new league without him, and after meeting in Montreal's Windsor Hotel, they agreed to reorganize as the National Hockey League. The first games were played on December 19th, and Livingstone was nowhere to be seen.

The NHL limped through its first several years of operation. Only 700 fans showed up for the Wanderers opening match with Toronto, for example, even though soldiers in uniform were let in free. The 1918–19 Stanley Cup playoffs were halted after five games because of a Spanish influenza epidemic, which sickened many of the players and claimed the life of the Montreal Canadiens' Joe Hall. And the existence of other leagues, such as the PCHA and the Western Canadian Hockey League, which was started in 1921, kept the NHL from dominating the hockey scene. But one by one, the other associations folded, and 1926 marked the last year a team from outside the NHL played for the Stanley Cup. From that point on, the NHL had the professional game pretty much to itself.

A penny for his thoughts

The NHL had its share of colorful players in the early years, and one of the most outrageous was Ken Randall of the Toronto Arenas, who was suspended for a time during the inaugural season of 1917–18 because he owed $35 in back fines for arguing with referees. No problem, Randall said. He brought a bag of pennies to the rink before the start of one game and put it down on the ice as a form of partial payment. One of the opposing players jokingly hit the bag with his stick as he skated by, however, and the pennies spilled all over the rink, delaying the dropping of the puck until the players could pick up all the coins.

Where the NHL Is Today

The NHL has never been more popular or in better financial shape, and at the end of the 1996–97 season, the league boasted 26 franchises and had announced plans to expand to 30 by the year 2000. Each team plays 82 regular-season games, beginning in October, and then a four-round play-off competition for the Stanley Cup begins in mid-April, with the Finals ending in early June.

The NHL employs more than 600 players, and its games are televised all over the world. The Stanley Cup Championship, for example, is broadcast to more than 140 countries, from Albania to Zimbabwe, and watched in more than 300 million homes. (See "Battling for the Stanley Cup," later in this chapter.) Owners of NHL teams include corporate heavyweights like the Disney Co., and the teams now play in sleek new arenas that are modern entertainment centers with laser lights and rock 'n roll music as well as food courts and luxury seating. (Refer to Appendix D for NHL league and franchise contact information.)

How the NHL Has Changed over the Years

The NHL has definitely changed over the years. Let us count the ways.

- The players have gotten bigger, stronger, and better, and so has the equipment.
- The games are faster, and the shots harder.
- The goalies all wear face masks and the forwards and defensemen helmets.
- Sticks are now made out of materials like graphite and aluminum, and most of the players' protective padding is comprised of space-age plastics and fabrics.
- The league has more games, harder hitting, and more play-off action.
- Teams are based all over North America, from Vancouver, British Columbia, to Tampa Bay, Florida, and crowds of 19,000 are not unusual for a regular-season contest.
- And we mustn't forget the money. If a player made $2,000 a year in the early days of the NHL, he was pulling down big bucks. But the fellows today do a whole lot better: The average annual salary after the 1996–97 season was about $1 million.

Who's the Boss?

At the end of the 1996–1997 season, the commissioner of the league was Gary Bettman, and he took office in February 1993. A native of New York City who was associated with the law firm of Proskauer Rose Goetz and Mendelsohn, Bettman worked for the National Basketball Association for 12 years, serving last as senior vice president and general counsel before coming to his senses and joining the *coolest game on earth.*™

Bettman is the top dog, but there are a number of other men and women who help him run the league. Stephen Solomon, a senior vice president and chief operating officer, is number two. Another senior VP is Brian Burke, who directs hockey operations and makes sure that things go smoothly down on the ice: Among his many duties is meting out punishments to players who behave badly. And then there is Rick Dudley, the president of NHL Enterprises and the man in charge of the league's very profitable marketing, licensing, and publishing business, both domestic and international. Glenn Adamo (vice president of broadcasting) does the schedule, Bernadette Mansur is in charge of corporate communications, Arthur Pincus takes care of public relations, and Charlie Schmitt runs the Internet end of things.

Bettman is based in New York, and the league has other principal offices in Montreal and Toronto.

The NHL Teams

As we mentioned earlier, there were 26 teams at the end of the 1996–97 season:

 Anaheim Mighty Ducks   Chicago Blackhawks

 Boston Bruins   Colorado Avalanche

 Buffalo Sabres   Dallas Stars

 Calgary Flames   Detroit Red Wings

 Carolina Hurricanes   Edmonton Oilers

Florida Panthers	Phoenix Coyotes
Los Angeles Kings	Pittsburgh Penguins
Montreal Canadiens	St. Louis Blues
New Jersey Devils	San Jose Sharks
New York Islanders	Tampa Bay Lightning
New York Rangers	Toronto Maple Leafs
Ottawa Senators	Vancouver Canucks
Philadelphia Flyers	Washington Capitals

The Hartford Whalers moved to North Carolina prior to the opening of the 1997–98 season and changed their name to the Hurricanes. An expansion team begins play in Nashville, Tennessee, in 1998–99, and one will start up the following year in Atlanta. Columbus, Ohio, and Minneapolis/St. Paul will join the NHL ranks in the fall of 2000.

The Conferences and Their Divisions

At the end of the 1996–97 season, the NHL was divided into two conferences, Eastern and Western, and each of those had two divisions: the Northeast and Atlantic were part of the Eastern Conference while the Central and Pacific were in the Western. Table 4-1 shows these conferences and their teams for the 1997–1998 season.

Table 4-1	The NHL Conferences

Eastern Conference

Northeast Division	Atlantic Division
Boston	Florida
Buffalo	New Jersey
Montreal	NY Islanders
Carolina	NY Rangers
Ottawa	Philadelphia
Pittsburgh	Tampa Bay
	Washington

Western Conference

Central Division	Pacific Division
Chicago	Anaheim
Dallas	Calgary
Detroit	Colorado
Phoenix	Edmonton
St. Louis	Los Angeles
Toronto	San Jose
	Vancouver

Expansion is changing all that, however, and each conference will add a new division in 1998–1999, for a total of three divisions per conference. Table 4-2 shows how it will all look.

Table 4-2	The NHL Conferences in 1998–1999	

Eastern Conference

Atlantic	Southeast	Northeast
New Jersey	Florida	Boston
NY Islanders	North Carolina	Buffalo
NY Rangers	Tampa Bay	Montreal
Philadelphia	Washington	Ottawa
Pittsburgh		

Western Conference		
Northwest	*Pacific*	*Central*
Calgary	Anaheim	Chicago
Colorado	Dallas	Detroit
Edmonton	Los Angeles	St. Louis
Vancouver	Phoenix	Toronto
	San Jose	

Atlanta will join the Southeast in 1999–2000, while Columbus will go to the Northeast the following season.

Nashville will join the Central in 1998–99, while Minneapolis/St. Paul doesn't enter the Northwest until 2000.

How the Standings Are Determined

Each team gets two points for a win during the regular season, one for a tie, and none for a loss. The teams in each conference with the most points at the end of the season finish highest in the standings. Table 4-3 shows how the standings added up at the end of the 1996-1997 season. (GP=games played, W=wins, L=losses, T=ties, GF=goals for, GA=goals against, PTS=points, PCTG=percentage)

Table 4-3			The NHL 1996–1997 Final Standings					
Eastern Conference (Northeast Division)								
	GP	*W*	*L*	*T*	*GF*	*GA*	*PTS*	*PCTG*
Buffalo	62	32	20	10	181	155	74	.597
Pittsburgh	61	31	25	5	217	199	67	.549
Hartford	61	24	28	9	174	192	57	.467
Montreal	63	23	29	11	195	222	57	.452
Ottawa	61	20	28	13	173	183	53	.434
Boston	62	21	33	8	179	219	50	.403

(continued)

Table 4-3 *(continued)*

Eastern Conference (Atlantic Division)

	GP	W	L	T	GF	GA	PTS	PCTG
Philadelphia	62	36	17	9	206	157	81	.653
New Jersey	61	31	18	12	165	143	74	.607
Florida	63	29	19	15	175	147	73	.579
NY Rangers	63	28	26	9	204	176	65	.516
Washington	61	24	30	7	157	172	55	.451
Tampa Bay	61	24	30	7	170	191	55	.451
NY Islanders	61	20	31	10	165	182	50	.410

Western Conference (Central Division)

	GP	W	L	T	GF	GA	PTS	PCTG
Dallas	64	38	22	4	196	155	80	.625
Detroit	61	30	19	12	195	144	72	.590
St. Louis	65	28	29	8	192	199	64	.492
Phoenix	63	28	31	4	181	197	60	.476
Chicago	63	25	29	9	166	163	59	.468
Toronto	62	23	37	2	181	219	48	.387

Western Conference (Pacific Division)

	GP	W	L	T	GF	GA	PTS	PCTG
Colorado	62	38	16	8	209	150	84	.677
Edmonton	64	29	28	7	199	193	65	.508
Vancouver	62	28	32	2	201	213	58	.468
Anaheim	62	25	30	7	179	187	57	.460
Calgary	63	25	31	7	169	186	57	.452
Los Angeles	64	23	33	8	172	210	54	.422
San Jose	61	21	33	7	157	204	49	.402

The Play-off Format

Basically, there are four, best-of-seven-games series, beginning with the Conference Quarterfinals and then continuing with the Conference Semi-Finals, the Conference Finals, and then the Stanley Cup Championship. The top eight teams from each conference competed in the first round of the 1996–97 playoffs, and the winners of those faced off in Round Two (the semi-finals). Two teams from each conference battled for the Conference titles in the third round, with the winners of each conference going against each other for the Stanley Cup.

Sixteen teams competed in the 1996–97 Cup play-offs, and that same number will be eligible for post-season play after all the expansion teams have entered the league. The first-place team in each of the six divisions will qualify, as will the next five best teams in each conference. The three division winners in each conference will be seeded one through three for the play-offs, and the next five best teams, in order of points, will be seeded fourth through eighth. In each conference, team #1 will play team # 8, #2 will play #7, and so on, in the Quarter-Finals, which will remain best-of-seven series. And the competition for the Cup will continue from there, with each club being re-seeded at the end of each play-off round.

Battling for the Stanley Cup

To many, the *Stanley Cup* is the finest trophy in sports, a glittering cup perched atop a silver barrel bearing the names of the greatest teams and players in professional hockey history. It was donated in 1892 by the English Governor General of Canada, Lord Stanley of Preston, who so enjoyed the game of ice hockey that he bought a silver bowl with an interior gold finish (cost: $48.67 Canadian) and asked that it be given each year to the best team in the Dominion. Initially, it was handed out to the clubs that won the Amateur Hockey Association of Canada championship, and it was their responsibility to defend it against all comers. Challenges came as often as a couple times a season in the early years of the Cup's existence, as teams from other hockey leagues in Canada sought to unseat the reigning champion.

The first winner of the Stanley Cup was the Montreal Amateur Athletic Association team, which seemed appropriate considering it was one of the oldest hockey clubs in the world. For several years, Cup challenge matches pitted amateur, semi-amateur, and professional teams against each other. But then the pros took over, and in 1910, the forerunner to the NHL, the National Hockey Association, took control of the trophy and began accepting challenges issued by teams from other professional leagues. From 1914 through 1916, the Stanley Cup winner was decided in a play-off between the team that captured the NHA title and the club that finished first in the Pacific Coast Hockey Association. And when the NHL came into being in 1917, it began battling the Western League's champs for the Cup. That rivalry lasted through the 1926 season. But then the PCHA folded, and the Stanley Cup became the official championship trophy of the NHL. (See Appendix D for a list of Stanley Cup winners — and also-rans — through the years.)

There are many things about the Cup that makes it unique in professional sports. None of the other major leagues has a trophy as old or as steeped in tradition, for example. And they certainly don't allow players from the winning team to take it home during the off-season. That's a wonderful custom that lets athletes truly savor their hard-fought victory and share their triumph with their fans. It also has meant that Lord Stanley's Cup has ended up in some very strange places and been put to some odd uses. Players have lugged it into horse stables as well as nursing homes and day care centers. One year it sank to the bottom of Mario Lemieux's swimming pool. The Cup has been used as an ash tray and a planter for geraniums. Dogs have drunk water from it, horses have eaten oats out of it, and fans have sipped fine champagne from the bowl as players toted it from bar to bar. And in the summer of 1997, the Stanley Cup even made a trip to Russia — where 75,000 people were able to cheer it as it was paraded around a soccer stadium in Moscow!

My Cup disappeareth

The Montreal Canadiens won the Stanley Cup in 1924, and not long after their big win, they were honored by the University of Montreal at a dinner. Not surprisingly, the team members that attended the fete brought the trophy with them, and when the gala was over, four of them decided to go to the home of one of the team owners, Leo Dandurand, to drink some more champagne from the Cup. So they all piled into a Model T Ford and drove away. Partway there, the car started to struggle with the load of players as it climbed up a steep hill. The driver stayed put, but the passengers climbed out of the car and began pushing. One of those was Sprague Cleghorn, a tough player who had been holding the Stanley Cup in his arms but decided to put it down on the curb so he could help out. It took some time and sweat, but the men were able to get the car to the top of the hill. And then they hopped back into the Model T and puttered off to Dandurand's home. But shortly after they arrived, the owner looked around the living room and asked, "Where's the Cup?" Suddenly, Cleghorn remembered he had left it by the side of the road. But when they rushed back there in the car, they were relieved to find the trophy sitting just where he had left it.

Battling for the Stanley Cup (after the season)

The Stanley Cup is the only trophy in professional sports that has its own bodyguards. That's right. A team of five men who work for the Hockey Hall of Fame serve as a sort of Secret Service force for the Cup, following it wherever it may go. For example, if a player wants to take the Cup home for a day in the summer, one of those fellows goes with him. It doesn't matter if the player lives overseas; the guardians of the Cup are obliged to follow as they did after the Colorado Avalanche win in 1996: The team's star forward, Peter Forsberg, took the trophy home to Sweden for its first-ever visit to Europe. The same thing happens if a team wants to use the Cup for a fan festival or in a charity event. An escort clad in a Hall of Fame blazer is always there to keep track of the trophy for the Hall of Fame — to ensure that nothing happens to it and to answer any questions that people may have about the cup and its rich history.

The Players

There are many reasons why the NHL has realized so much success over the years, but none is as important as the players who fill the rosters of all its teams. We can't think of another league in the world that has so many talented athletes competing against each other on a regular basis — and they are responsible for giving the NHL the speed, power, and finesse that make it the best place to see the game played.

Where do the players come from today?

They come from all over. Consider a chart the NHL compiled during the 1995–96 season that recorded the birthplace of each of the 640 players who competed in the league one week that fall. There were 389 Canadians (60.8 percent), 108 Americans (16.9), 42 Russians (5.6), 34 Swedes (5.3), 26 Czechs (4.1), 17 Finns (2.7) 6 Ukrainians (.9), 5 Slovaks (.8), 3 Germans (.3),

2 Englishmen (.3), 2 Latvians (.3), and 1 each (.2) from Northern Ireland, Poland, Scotland, South Africa, Belarus, and Lithuania. We do not have any information, however, on how many of the aforementioned players, or their coaches, needed translators or Berlitz lessons.

Where did the players come from in years past?

For decades, Canada has been the home of most of the NHL's players. In fact, it was big news in the 1960s and '70s when an American, or an athlete from another country, made it to the NHL.

Player size

The average NHL player for the 1996–97 season was 6 feet 1 inch tall and weighed 198.1 pounds; 25 years before the numbers were 5 feet 11 inches and 184.2 pounds "The players now are a lot bigger than they used to be," says Jim Ramsey, who has served as head medical trainer for the Winnipeg Jets (now Phoenix Coyotes) and New York Rangers. "Take a guy like Kevin Lowe, who joined the Edmonton Oilers as a defenseman in 1979. At 6 feet 2 inches and 190 pounds, he was one of the biggest guys on the team. But not any more. Now you have people like Eric Lindros, who's 6 feet 4 inches and 220 pounds, and players his size are becoming more and more the norm."

Player speed

Amazingly, NHL players have gotten faster even as they have gotten bigger. Although we cannot measure players' speed as precisely as we can their height and weight, we can safely say that there has never been so much speed in the game.

Player strength

As players have gotten bigger, faster, and more international, they have also gotten stronger, thanks mostly to off-season strength and conditioning regimens and regular weightlifting during the year. "These guys are much more educated about conditioning, and most of them come to training camp at the start of the season in fantastic shape," Ramsey says. "I've been in the league for almost ten years, and they just keep getting stronger and stronger." (See Chapter 6 for information on conditioning and training.)

Chapter 5

The Minors and Other Hockey Leagues

In This Chapter

▶ Examining the differences between the college and professional games

▶ Watching out for women's hockey

▶ Taking a peek at the international game

*T*he NHL may be the biggest fish in the organized hockey pond, but it's certainly not the only one. From Worcester, Massachusetts, to Helsinki, Finland, to Johannesburg, South Africa, to Tokyo, Japan, hundreds of amateur and professional hockey teams, comprised of both men and women, compete in leagues and tournaments. Some battle for Olympic gold and the World Championship, while others merely strive for a city or district title. And their numbers are growing each year as the game of hockey attracts not only more spectators but also more participants.

The Minor Leagues

Some of the most popular professional hockey teams in the world are in the United States minor leagues. Generally speaking, the people on those clubs are either up-and-comers who are about to break into the NHL or marginal players who aren't quite good enough to land a full-time job there. However you categorize them, they play a hard-nosed brand of hockey that is good fun to watch and gives fans many of the same thrills an NHL game does, but only on a lower skill level.

Minor league franchises — the lowdown

It's hard to come up with an exact number on them because the teams and leagues change a lot and what's valid this year may not be so 12 months down the road. At the end of the 1996–97 season, there were seven leagues in the U.S.:

✔ the American Hockey League

✔ the International Hockey League

✔ the East Coast Hockey League

✔ the Colonial Hockey League

✔ the Central Hockey League

✔ the West Coast Hockey League

✔ the Western Professional Hockey League

The **American** and **International** have the highest quality of play and, like Triple A in baseball, are considered just one step below the majors. Each of them boast 18 teams.

The **East Coast** league is more like Double A baseball, a couple of notches down from the NHL, and it has 23 teams.

The **Colonial** and **Central** leagues have ten and seven franchises respectively and are comparable to Single A baseball.

And finally, the **West Coast** and **Western Professional** leagues, both of which have six teams, feature the youngest and most inexperienced players you can find in professional hockey.

Finding the minor league teams

The minor league teams are all over. The American Hockey League is based in West Springfield, Massachusetts, and has clubs from St. John's, New Brunswick, and Portland, Maine, to Syracuse, New York and Hershey, Pennsylvania, while the International League, which has its headquarters in Bloomfield Hills, Michigan, includes teams from Cincinnati, Kansas City, Houston, and Salt Lake City.

The franchises in the East Coast League, which has its home office in Princeton, New Jersey, range from the Baton Rouge Kingfish to the Knoxville Cherokees. And the Colonial League, which changed its name to the United League in the summer of 1997 and moved its base of operations to Lake St. Louis, Missouri, features the Quad City Mallards, the Dayton Ice Bandits, the Muskegon Fury and the Madison Monsters.

The Central League runs its operations out of Tulsa and counts among its franchises the Forth Worth Fire and the San Antonio Iguanas. Then, of course, there are the two West Coast organizations, one of which is based in Reno and the other in Phoenix.

Canada has three primary leagues, known as the *juniors,* for 16- to 20-year-old players that is considered the top feeder system for the NHL:

- ✔ The Ontario Hockey League, which had 17 clubs at the end of the 1996–97 season
- ✔ The Quebec Major Junior Hockey League (14 teams)
- ✔ The Western Hockey League (18 franchises)

Technically, these leagues are stocked with amateur players, most of whom have left their homes to compete on teams in different parts of Canada. The players go to school wherever they play and receive lodging and living allowances. One drawback, however, is that any kid who plays in one of the junior leagues automatically loses his college eligibility in the U.S.

Where do those Canadian youngsters come from? Many of them are drafted out of the midget leagues as 14- or 15-year-olds by the different teams. Or they are selected at open tryouts.

NHL affiliations

Affiliations vary. Some have straight affiliations similar to what goes on in baseball, in which a team works directly with one NHL club that supplies most of the players. But, unlike baseball, there also are a lot of split arrangements in the minor leagues, with two NHL teams providing players to one franchise. Consider the Adirondack Red Wings, an American Hockey League club based in Glen Falls, New York. Both Detroit and Tampa Bay are responsible for stocking that roster, and both probably put six or seven guys there every year. But they don't fill all the spots. Why? Because NHL clubs have a habit of calling up a minor league team's best players during the season and inserting them in their own lineups. That's fine for the parent franchises, but it deprives the minor league squads of their top players. So no matter what their arrangement with the majors, many minor league teams also go out and get a few players on their own to ensure that they aren't left high and dry if the big league clubs run into a lot of injuries, for example, and have to deplete their affiliates.

In addition to the direct and split affiliations, a number of independent clubs have no arrangements with NHL franchises and fill their rosters with whatever players they can find.

Similarities — and differences — between minor leagues and the NHL

Most teams in the minor leagues do not play the same number of games that NHL teams do. Although the teams in American and International Leagues play roughly the same amount of games the NHL does (82), the East Coast teams play about 70, the Colonial and Continental play about 60, and those in the two Western Leagues, closer to 50. (As a rule, the lower the league level, the shorter the schedule because they all work off each others' players; those that are cut by the American and International Leagues often go to play in the East Coast, while those who don't make the East Coast go to the Colonial or Central, and so on.)

And, of course, the minor league players just aren't as good as those in the NHL. The skill level in the NHL is quite a bit higher than what you find in even the upper minor leagues. The general speed of play is probably the biggest difference, and even the top American and International minor leaguers that make it to the NHL have a hard time adjusting to that change.

Popularity of the minor leagues

Minor league hockey is more popular than ever before. Crowds in the International or American Leagues may average 7,000. Though they bring in fewer fans for their regular-season contests, the East Coast draws as many as 10,000 for its All-Star Game. Additionally, the number of teams and leagues in the minors has grown dramatically in recent years (only the American and International leagues existed a decade ago). Hockey used to be considered strictly a cold weather sport, but now there are franchises throughout the Sun Belt. And people there are finding out just what a cool game hockey is.

In Canada, there is a tremendous minor league tradition. Of course, the game has been popular there for eons and has achieved more commercial orientation than its American counterpart. Some Canadian minor league franchises have existed for more than half a century.

The College Game

College hockey in the U.S. has undergone a tremendous revival in recent years and is enjoying a fantastic surge in popularity and interest. In the mid-1990s, 51 schools were playing Division I hockey, 13 competing in Division II, and another 60 playing in Division III. Arenas are generally full, and many of the programs are doing quite well financially. One reason for all this success is that more college players are making it to the NHL than ever before. In fact, 26 percent of all NHL players in 1996–97 played some hockey at an American college, and the presence of so many former college players in the NHL has made scores of people more aware of the college game and the way it is played. (As you may recall, much the same thing happened with college basketball and the NBA.)

The college game has also benefited from the general increase in enthusiasm for hockey; as more people have gotten interested in the sport, more have been exposed to the college game. In addition, many of the youngsters who are playing in town and school leagues are looking to stay involved with the game as they get older and view college hockey, whether on an intercollegiate or club level, as a viable option. And to the very best players, college hockey can now be used as a much more realistic avenue to the NHL.

Finally, the quality of the college programs has increased, and fans are seeing more good hockey than ever before. Ten years ago, there were maybe five really strong programs, but today there may as many as 20.

How does Joe College play the game?

The rinks are roughly the same as those in the NHL, and so are most of the rules. The big difference is that there is no clutching and grabbing, which you see a lot of in the pros these days, and no fighting, which leads to an automatic ejection. Many fans say those differences make the game more fluid and open, and therefore more fun to watch. As for the talent on the ice, the NHL teams simply have more quality players. But the gap has narrowed considerably.

The top college teams

A number of colleges have done very well in the 1990s. Lake Superior State won two NCAA titles, in 1994 and 1992, while North Dakota, Michigan, Boston University, Maine, Northern Michigan, and Wisconsin all captured titles in the same decade. The rest of the best include the University of Vermont, the University of New Hampshire, Colorado College, and the University of Minnesota.

College grads who have done well in the pros

College players didn't do a thing for years in the NHL, and it wasn't until 1961, when Red Berenson joined the Montreal Canadiens from the University of Michigan, that a U.S. collegiate player made it to the NHL. Now, however, the floodgates are open, and the university boys are highly prized. Over the years, some great NHL players have come from the college game. Hall of Famer goalie Ken Dryden (Cornell) obviously did very well, and so did another pair of net minders, Mike Liut (Bowling Green) and Chris Terreri (Wisconsin).

There hasn't been a shortage of top defensemen, either: Ken Morrow, of Bowling Green, played for 10 years and won four Stanley Cups with the New York Islanders; Chris Chelios of the Chicago Blackhawks and the University of Wisconsin has been a perennial All-Star; and Bruce Driver (also Wisconsin) has done a steady job with the New Jersey Devils and the New York Rangers. As for forwards, how about these for an all-college team: Tony Amonte (Boston University), Paul Kariya (Maine), and Doug Weight (Lake Superior State).

Canadian college teams play some good hockey, but they can't compete with the U.S. colleges. One reason is the great influx of Canadian athletes at U.S. schools; an estimated 45 percent of all collegiate players on American teams come from Canada. Not surprisingly, that has sapped a lot of Canada's talent pool, and fewer than 5 percent of all NHL players come from universities up north, which is significantly less than the U.S. schools provide.

Women's Leagues and Competitions

Women have been playing ice hockey for more than a century, but it has never been widely played or wildly popular on either a professional or amateur level until the 1990s. And suddenly, it is all the rage. Women's hockey will be a medal sport at the 1998 Winter Olympics in Nagano, Japan, and it is now being played in 29 countries. A sanctioned world championship for women has been held since 1990, and 16 teams competed in the 1997 event.

No checking is allowed in women's hockey, and no clutching, grabbing, or fighting either, which makes it more of a speed and finesse sport.

Canada and the United States have the most players, as well as the most talented ones, and their numbers continue to grow. In 1990, for example, the U.S. had about 5,500 registered women hockey players; by 1997, the number had more than quadrupled.

By the mid-1990s, two women goalies, Erin Whitten and Manon Rheaume, had played in some of the men's minor league games, and Rheaume had actually tended the net in a couple of exhibition contests for the NHL Tampa Bay Lightning. Some 65 colleges in the U.S. now have sanctioned women's teams, either on a club or varsity level. And there is talk of starting a professional women's league in North America (some already exist in Europe), sometime in the not-too-distant future.

International Hockey

Hockey truly is an international game, and according to the world governing body, the International Ice Hockey Federation, or IIHF, the game is now played in more than 50 countries. That includes obvious nations such as Sweden, which has 80,000 registered amateur and professional players and approximately 4,000 teams, and some more surprising countries, such as Mexico, which has 400 players, and Turkey, which has 270.

The IIHF oversees the sport as it is played around the world, puts on the various world and continental championships (for men, women, and juniors), and runs national tournaments for a number of nations. "All told, we put on as many as 30 events a year," says Kimmo Leinonen, the director of marketing and public relations for the federation. Contact the IIHF at the following address and check out their Web site at `www.iihf.com` (see Figure 5-1).

International Ice Hockey Federation
Parkring 11
8002 Zurich
Switzerland
Phone: 0041 1 289 86 00
Fax General Secretary: 0041 1 289 86 20
Fax PR/Info/EHL/InLine: 0041 1 289 86 22

Figure 5-1:
The IIHF
Web site
is your
gateway to
international
hockey.

Not surprisingly, hockey is biggest in Canada, which has 1.5 million registered players, and the U.S., which has 350,000. But it is loved in so many other places. The people of India and Hong Kong have ice hockey clubs, for example, and so do people in Thailand and Brazil. And then there is Ecuador, which has only one rink in the entire country, and at last count, four teams.

"Hockey is growing so much overseas," Leinonen says. "And its popularity has spread far beyond the cold-climate countries and cities that used to be the only domain of the sport." Leinonen is especially excited about the potential growth in Asia. "Japan has a very good league, and nations such as Korea are getting more into it," he says. "Then, of course, we have the Winter Olympics in Nagano, Japan, in 1998. And in 1997 the Mighty Ducks of Anaheim and the Vancouver Canucks opened their NHL regular-season schedules by playing a pair of games in Tokyo. It's going to be big over there." Correction: It seems like it is going to be big everywhere.

Chapter 6

Training

In This Chapter

▶ Knowing what the pros do to stay in shape

▶ Examining a typical off-season training program

▶ Working yourself into playing shape

*E*lite hockey players are among the best-conditioned athletes in the world. Whether they compete in the NHL, in the minor leagues, in college, or for one of the international teams, they must be in excellent shape in order to hold their own. To do that, they work with personal trainers and team personnel throughout the year, following strict fitness regimens so they may perform up to their highest levels. It wasn't always that way, and like athletes in other professional sports, hockey players didn't really begin to understand the value of sophisticated exercise programs until the mid-1970s. But now, extensive training and conditioning routines are part of every player's life.

To give you a sense of what hockey players do to get and stay in shape, we again turned to some experts for help. One is Jim Ramsey, who has been a medical trainer in the NHL since the mid-1980s, first for the Winnipeg Jets (now the Phoenix Coyotes) and more recently for the New York Rangers. Another is Dr. Howie Wenger, a physical education professor at the University of Victoria in British Columbia, Canada, and an exercise physiologist with the Rangers. He has also worked with the Edmonton Oilers, Vancouver Canucks, and Los Angeles Kings. In addition, he has helped develop conditioning programs for several Canadian Olympic teams. And our third source is Charles Poliquin, a strength and conditioning coach who counts among his individual clients 120 athletes from the NHL, the National Basketball Association, the National Football League, and a number of Canadian Olympic squads. No one understands the whole concept of training and conditioning better than they do.

What the Pros Do to Stay in Shape

NHL players work out a lot, as you will see. These guys are constantly working on their conditioning and never seem to let up. "Players will usually take a couple of weeks off at the end of the season," says Jim Ramsey, "but then they get right back into it." And they keep at it until the end of the year.

Running

Running used to be a part of every athlete's regimen, but not anymore. Very few hockey players ever run during the season, and those that do use it mainly as a warm-up. It's not very popular in the off-season either, and that's because it is such a high-impact exercise that can lead to knee and back problems. And there are very few NHL players who haven't had knee or back problems during their career. Still, some do find it an effective training tool, especially when it comes to building speed and endurance.

Cycling

Many more players prefer to cycle, especially on exercise bikes, because it has a lower impact on knees, backs, and so on. Some players bike during the season to build or maintain aerobic condition and enhance leg strength. (Power comes from the legs in hockey, and when a player is skating, he is using his legs all the time.) During the season, many NHL teams like their players to get on an exercise bike a couple of times a week for up to half an hour a pop. Also, they have them use it as a cool-down after a game and as a way to rid their bodies of lactic acid and other by-products of strenuous exercise that can delay recovery. As for the off-season, most clubs want their players to ride bikes, both stationary and regular, fairly often, perhaps five or six days a week for about 30 to 45 minutes each time.

Skating

Not surprisingly, skating is a huge part of a hockey player's conditioning program, and your average NHLer is on the ice most every day during the season, either for practice or a game. What he does when the season ends is often a different story. Some get together and rent ice time at a local rink during the summer and meet regularly for informal workouts and scrimmages. Others hardly touch the ice until the following season, but they do a lot of in-line skating and/or play roller hockey. Those are very sports-specific exercises that use the same muscles a player employs on the ice and gives him a chance not only to work on conditioning but also to keep honing his hockey skills (stick handling, shooting, passing, and so on). The only problem is that it's much harder to stop on those off-ice skates.

Stairmaster

Players use Stairmasters both in- and off-season the same way they use exercise bikes. Again, they use these machines to build and enhance aerobic fitness. Players generally spend anywhere from 30 to 45 minutes working in one-to-three-minute intervals, building up the intensity as they go. "Interval training is important to elite hockey players because they go on and off the ice so frequently," says Ramsey. "We want them to work hard for 45 seconds and then have some time to recover because that's the way they play during the season, with shifts lasting just under a minute, and then they have some time to rest. Recovery is essential so that they can be 100 percent on the next shift."

The types of exercise we have described so far are all considered aerobic and are needed by hockey players for a number of reasons. According to Howie Wenger, who has written a splendid book on the subject entitled *Fitness for High Performance Hockey* (Trafford Publishing, Victoria, B.C., 1-888-232-4444), aerobic fitness is an athlete's ability to take oxygen into his lungs, deliver it to his muscles via the heart and blood, and then use that oxygen in his muscles to generate energy. Athletes who are aerobically fit, Wenger explains, can recover faster between sprints, between shifts and periods, and also between games. They can recover more quickly from soft tissue and bone injuries, do more strength and power training, and handle jet lag and heat stress more effectively. In addition, their immune systems are enhanced so they can better withstand minor infections and colds and also build a resistance to lactic acid, which causes fatigue. Given all that, is it any wonder that players today listen to what their trainers and physiologists have to say?

Weightlifting

Strength fitness is another important consideration for hockey players. Dr. Wenger points out that strength means bigger muscles, which translates into better injury protection for joints and soft tissue. It also makes players stronger around the puck and helps establish position against opponents. More specifically, abdominal strength allows players to transfer momentum from the lower body to the upper body and protect the lower back, while leg strength is the first step in improving leg power and explosiveness.

Obviously, the best way to improve strength fitness is through weightlifting, and most hockey players in the NHL lift weights at least once a week during the season. Trainers tailor individual programs to each player so that the players can maintain their strength throughout the year. The New York Rangers have 12 different weight machines, and a player might do about 15 mid-range *reps* (or repetitions) on each one, working on everything from leg extensions to bicep curls. Some players, say those nursing knee or shoulder injuries, may spend extra time trying to build those areas up as they try to recover, perhaps lifting weights two or three times a week.

As for the off-season, players increase their time with the weight machines; at a minimum they lift three times a week; some do it as often as six. Generally, they alternate body parts each time, working on the legs one day, the lower back and chest on another, and so forth until they have done their whole body in one week.

Keeping Track of Fitness

It's remarkable to see how closely both professional and top amateur teams now monitor the physical fitness of their players. Players are given a series of tests at the start of the season and then put on monthly conditioning programs, which are customized for their various needs. "We try to handle everything from workouts to nutrition, taking into account our game days and travel schedule," says Jim Ramsey. "We also look at how much ice time a player gets during a game and what he needs to do to stay in shape with that. An athlete such as Brian Leetch, who plays anywhere from 30 to 40 minutes a game, needs less fitness maintenance than a fourth-liner who may only get onto the ice for five minutes a game." Other considerations are injuries, which would certainly affect the extent to which players can work out, and days off. "Say we have three days between games," Ramsey explains. "The coach might give the players that first day off but work them real hard the second day so nobody has a chance to fall out of condition. And the third day would be a light practice, or recovery day, with some work but not too much."

Players are tested again at the end of the season and given workout programs by their trainers for the summer. "It used to be that the younger guys came to training camp the following fall in terrific shape, and the veterans were the ones who needed to get in shape," Ramsey says. "But now, it's the other way around. The vets are the ones who are most fit, and the younger kids coming out of college and the Canadian junior leagues aren't conditioned for the NHL." Hockey clubs are trying to change this situation by bringing their draft picks in at the start of the summer for fitness tests and then giving them programs to work on so they come to camp in better shape than they otherwise might.

Something special for the goalies

Ask anyone in hockey and they'll tell you that goalies are an odd bunch who seem to do everything differently. Even with their conditioning. They do many of the same aerobic exercises a forward or defenseman performs but are not as likely to be found in the weight room. "It's not necessary for a goalie to lift and be strong in his upper body," Ramsey explains.

"Obviously, flexibility is very important, so you want them to do a lot of stretching. They also need to work on ways to enhance their speed and balance as well as their hand-eye coordination." Some goalies, JD among them, have used a variety of eye exercises to improve their ability to see the puck through all the traffic in front of the net. Anything for an edge.

A Typical NHL Off-Season Conditioning Regimen

Charles Poliquin helps out a number of NHL athletes in the off-season, and among his most recent clients is Al MacInnis, a hard-shooting defenseman who played his first league game in 1981 and has been selected for seven All-Star teams. "We train three days out of five," Poliquin says, "and we work out twice each of those days. Some people believe in working out more frequently over a period of time, but I think having plenty of rest days and doing more concentrated work brings better results."

- On **Monday** morning, MacInnis spends about an hour in the weight room working on his chest and back. "We divide the body into three parts for weights," Poliquin says, "and take care of each one on a specific day." After taking a four-hour break, which he does between every workout, MacInnis spends almost an hour Monday afternoon on various abdominal and spinal exercises.

- **Tuesday** morning, the plan calls for 60 minutes of weightlifting for the legs, and in the afternoon he runs for the same amount of time, either sprints (perhaps 30 yards) or longer distances (up to 600 yards). "I call it energy system work," Poliquin explains, "And what we do depends on what time of the summer it is. I like to do sprint work early on to build speed and then distance as we get closer to the start of the season."

- **Wednesday** is a day off, but MacInnis is back at it on **Thursday**, spending an hour in the morning on his shoulders and arms in the weight room and then another hour in the afternoon running.

> ✔ The defenseman takes **Friday** off, and then starts the cycle over again on **Saturday**. "I modify programs every six workouts to maximize adaption so Al gets stronger faster," Poliquin says. "It also helps to keep boredom from setting in."

"I try to create each program specifically for the athlete involved and his needs," he continues. "A lot also depends on his position as well. As a defenseman, Al has different needs than a forward. He needs to be stronger in the abs, for example, because he has to clear players out from in front of the net all the time, and that uses those muscles a lot. We also need to look at the style of the player involved. A guy like Doug Gilmour, for example, never stops skating, so he needs to be really fit aerobically — while someone else may stand around more and not be so active."

What You Can Do to Get In Hockey Shape

"The most important thing adults need to know is that most of us can change our physiology quite a bit," says Dr. Howie Wenger. "It's simply a question of how much a person is willing to challenge himself and genetics. But the fact is, we can get most people fit. Making them elite athletes is another thing altogether, but from a fitness point of view, we can make you better."

So there is hope for all us weekend warriors after all. But only if we take care of three primary needs. The first is stretching. "Static stretches relax the stretched muscles," Dr. Wenger explains. "This allows more blood flow, which enables you to supply more fuel to muscles before and after workouts, remove wastes that cause fatigue after exercise, and cool down the muscles after hard work."

In addition, relaxed muscles offer less resistance to powerful contractions, which should allow athletes to be more explosive. And there is some evidence that soft tissue injuries are reduced when the muscle is relaxed.

Secondly, people need some level of aerobic and cardiovascular fitness. That's what you get from jogging, cycling, swimming, and rowing, for example. It helps your recovery system so that you can exercise, rest, and then go out and do it again. "It's very important in a sport like hockey because it is not continuous but full of lots of stops and starts," says Wenger.

And finally, those of us looking to get fit need to work on our strength. "There is no question that leg strength is very important to the elite hockey player," says Dr. Wenger. "But it's less critical to the recreational athlete who will likely get what he needs from jogging or cycling. But strength fitness is important to the upper body, especially with regards to the abdominal muscles and the shoulders. If those aren't strong, that leaves you suscep-tible to lower back strains and groin pulls. To protect yourself from those, you need reasonably good abdominal strength. Shoulders are critical, too, because of all the banging and shooting that takes place in a game."

The Need for Exercise Routines

After Dr. Wenger identified the three primary areas a recreational hockey players needs to work on to get into better shape, he gave us some exer-cises that can help you get there. The stretches and exercises we are about to discuss are geared toward people from the ages of 15 to 50. But it's important that anyone interested in starting a workout program get clear-ance from a physician before taking one step on a treadmill or lifting a weight. Also, you should start easy and work your way up to more strenuous circuits; 'tis better to err by doing too little than too much.

Stretching

Stretching should be done before and after every workout, practice or game. The most important thing to remember is to go to where you feel the stretch and not where you feel the pain. Don't worry if you feel limited by a lack of flexibility in the beginning; keep doing these and you should get more limber. Here is a stretching circuit designed by Dr. Wenger, reprinted with permission from his book *Fitness for High Performance Hockey* (illustrated by Kelley Dukeshire). The following stretching circuit is designed to incorpo-rate the major muscles used in hockey. The exercises progress from lying to sitting to kneeling to standing.

1. *Relax* with your knees bent and the soles of your feet together. This comfortable position stretches your groin. You can give added stretch by putting outward pressure on the inside of your knees using your hands.

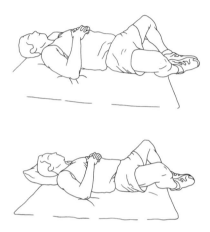

2. Next, straighten both legs and relax; then pull your left leg toward your chest. Keep the back of your head on the mat. Repeat, pulling your right leg toward your chest.

3. With your opposite hand, pull that bent leg over your other leg toward the floor. Turn your head the opposite way until you get the right stretch feeling in your lower back and hip. Do the other leg.

4. From the bent knees position, use the left leg to pull your right leg toward the floor until you feel a stretch along the side of your hip and lower back. Turn your head the opposite way. Repeat for the other side.

5. Sit with your feet a comfortable distance apart. To stretch the inside of your upper legs and hips, slowly lean forward from the hips. Keep your quadriceps relaxed and feet upright. Keep your hands out in front of you for balance and stability. Concentrate on keeping the lower back flat as you do this stretch. Do not strain.

6. To stretch your left hamstrings and the right side of your back, slowly bend forward from the hips toward your left foot. Repeat on the other side.

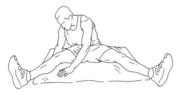

7. Move one leg forward *until the knee of the forward leg is directly over the ankle.* Your other knee should be resting on the floor. Now, without changing the position of the knee on the floor or the forward foot, lower the front of your hip downward. This stretch should be felt in front of the hip and possibly in your hamstrings and groin. Do both sides.

8. Hold on to something that is about shoulder height. With your hands shoulder width apart, keep your arms straight, your chest moving downward, and *your feet remaining directly under your hips.* Keep your knees slightly bent.

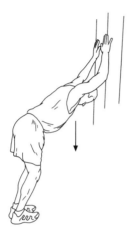

9. With arms overhead, hold the elbow of one arm with the hand of the other arm. Keeping knees slightly bent, pull your elbow behind your head as you bend from your hips to the side. Do both sides. Keeping your knees slightly bent gives you better balance and helps protect your back.

10. In a standing or sitting position, interlace your fingers above your head. Now, with your palms facing upward, push your arms slightly back and up. Feel the stretch in arms, shoulders, and upper back. Do not hold your breath.

11. Hold the top of your left foot with the right hand and gently pull the heel toward your butt. The knee bends at a natural angle in this position and creates a good stretch in knees and quads. Do both legs.

12. To stretch your calf, stand a little ways from a solid support and lean on it. Bend one leg and place your foot on the ground in front of you, leaving the other leg straight behind you. Slowly move your hips forward until you feel a stretch in the calf of your straight leg. Be sure to keep the heel of the foot of the straight leg on the ground and *your toes pointed straight ahead.* Do not bounce. Stretch both legs.

Aerobic Fitness

It's good to do aerobic activities, whether it's cross-country skiing, skating, running, or cycling, three or four times a week. Ski machines and stair climbers are fine as well. Ideally, people should get up to 40–45 minutes of continuous aerobic workouts on those days. "If you can talk comfortably while you are working out, then you are probably just below the level you need to be at," says Dr. Wenger. In the beginning, it may be better to start with 25 minutes, move up to 30 after a week, and then increase your time by 5-minute intervals after that until you get up to 45 minutes. At that point, Howie suggests intensifying the pace, reducing the program to 25 minutes, and then working your way back up again.

Weight Training

The big question here is: How much weight do you lift? Dr. Wenger says it is best to start with a "load" you can do 15–20 times without stopping, no more and no less. Keep with that for three or four months before even thinking about moving to a higher weight that you will likely not be able to do as many times in a row.

As for frequency, Dr. Wenger suggests two times a week. You can do one of your upper body circuits (see sketches) on one of the days you do aerobic fitness (because your aerobic exercises won't usually put a lot of pressure on the upper body) and then do the lower body and abdominal strength exercises on one of the days you are not running, cycling, or whatever. Again, Dr. Wenger provides some upper- and lower-body exercises for weight training from his book *Fitness for High Performance Hockey*.

Upper Body: Circuit 1

Note: You can do these as ***successive sets:*** 3–4 sets at each before moving to the next. Be sure to take a 1–2 minute rest between each set.

Or . . .

You can do these as ***alternating sets:*** 1 set of each exercise, then go back through the circuit 3 or 4 times. You don't rest between sets or circuits.

1: BENCH PRESS

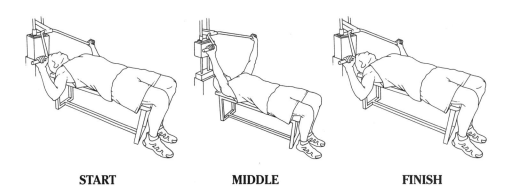

START   **MIDDLE**   **FINISH**

2: TRICEP EXTENSIONS

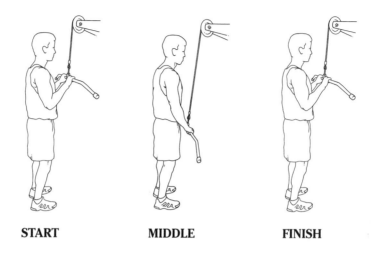

START   **MIDDLE**   **FINISH**

3: LAT PULL-DOWNS

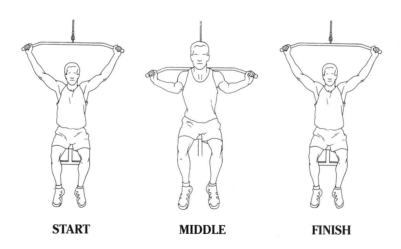

START   **MIDDLE**   **FINISH**

4: SHOULDER EXTENSION

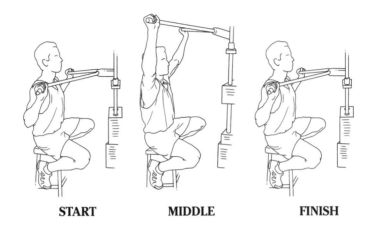

START **MIDDLE** **FINISH**

5: BICEP CURLS

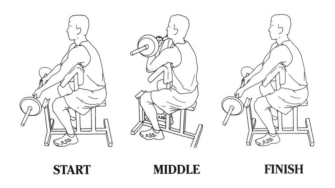

START **MIDDLE** **FINISH**

Upper Body: Circuit 2

Note: You can do these as ***successive sets:*** 3–4 sets at each before moving to the next. Be sure to take a 1–2 minute rest between each set.

Or . . .

You can do these as ***alternating sets:*** 1 set of each exercise, then go back through the circuit 3 or 4 times. You don't rest between sets or circuits.

1: BENCH FLYS WITH DUMBBELLS

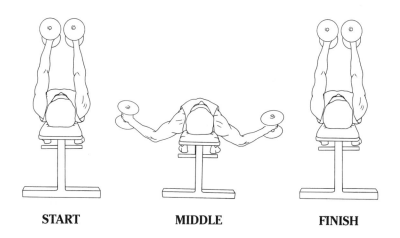

START **MIDDLE** **FINISH**

2: SEATED TRICEP EXTENSION WITH BARBELL

Option: seated alternating tricep extensions using 2 dumbbells.

3: DUMBBELL ROW

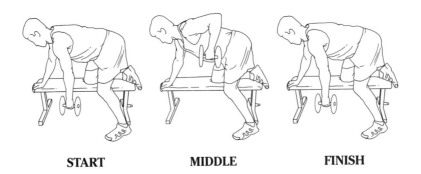

START   **MIDDLE**   **FINISH**

4: ALTERNATING SEATED BICEP CURLS WITH DUMBBELLS

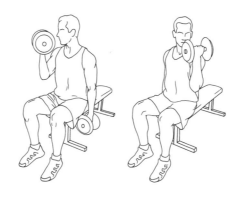

5: STANDING UPRIGHT ROW

START   **MIDDLE**   **FINISH**

Upper Body Variations

You can use these exercises as substitutes in the Upper Body Circuits.

CHEST

You can substitute the *inclined bench press* for the bench press.

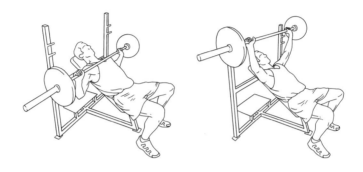

FOREARMS

Do *wrist curls* with palms up and down.

UPPER ARMS

These are *bicep curls*.

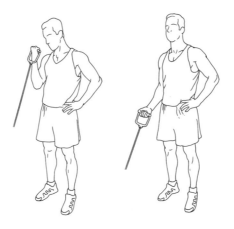

Do *tricep extensions* with the palms down.

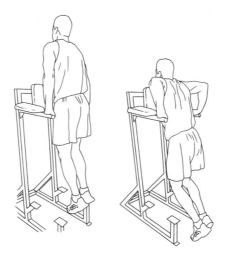

SHOULDERS

These are *palm-down/palm-up arm extensions.*

This is called a *shoulder abduction.*

These are *pec-deck flys.*

| **START** | **MIDDLE** | **FINISH** |

Lower Body: Circuit 1

Note: You can do these as ***successive sets:*** 3–4 sets at each before moving to the next. Be sure to take a 1–2 minutes rest between each set.

Or . . .

You can do these as ***alternating sets:*** 1 set of each exercise, then go back through the circuit 3 or 4 times. You don't rest between sets or circuits.

1: SLIDING DOUBLE LEG PRESS

For thighs and calves.

Note: It's preferable to do this as alternating single leg pushes. You should also push off the toes at the end of each push. (You can also do this exercise lying on your stomach.)

2: DOUBLE LEG HAMSTRING CURLS

Note: It's preferable to do this as alternating single leg curls.

| START | MIDDLE | FINISH |

3: HIP ABDUCTION

Note: Do one set with the left leg and then one set with the right leg.

4: HIP ABDUCTION (GROINS)

Note: Do one set with the left leg and then one set with the right leg. Then move on to Station 1.

Lower Body Variations

You can use these exercises as substitutes in the Lower Body Circuit.

THIGHS

These are *alternating lunges with dumbbells.*

These are *alternating lunges with barbells.*

Squats (or seated leg press).

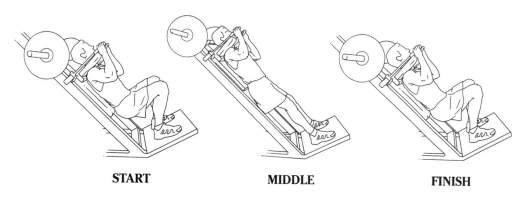

START **MIDDLE** **FINISH**

This routine is for the *quads.*

START **MIDDLE** **FINISH**

And this lower body variation is a *leg extension.*

These exercises are *calf extensions.*

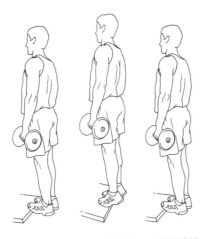

START   **MIDDLE**   **FINISH**

Abdominal Strength Exercises

  ✔ Select one circuit.

  ✔ 20 times through each circuit, then 3 minutes rest, then repeat.

  ✔ You may wish to use an abdominal roller apparatus as a substitute in Circuit 3.

Circuit 1

#1: FLEXED   #2: TWIST RIGHT   #3: FLEXED   #4: TWIST LEFT   #5: STRAIGHT

Circuit 2

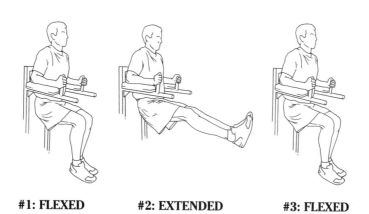

#1: FLEXED   #2: EXTENDED   #3: FLEXED

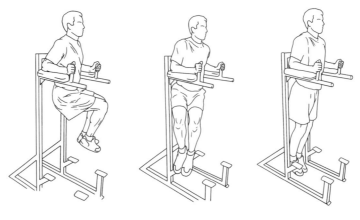

#4: TWIST LEFT   **#5 TWIST RIGHT**   **#6: STRAIGHT**

Circuit 3

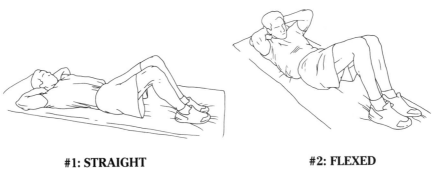

#1: STRAIGHT   **#2: FLEXED**

#3: STRAIGHT   **#4 TWIST LEFT**

#5: STRAIGHT   **#6: TWIST RIGHT**

Note: You can vary Circuit 3 by substituting the following two movements for #3 and #4 or #5 and #6.

Chapter 7

Coaching in the NHL

. . . .

In This Chapter

▶ Preparing for the season

▶ Practicing till it hurts

▶ Coaching during a game

▶ Changing on the fly

▶ Handling the play-offs

. . . .

*P*erhaps the only thing as difficult as playing hockey on a championship level is coaching it. It takes a special person to organize, teach, and tend to a top team. There are practices to run and games to oversee, different systems to employ and various tactics to pursue, video tapes to break down and game plans to create. A good coach not only has to understand how to match his club up against the opposition but also what to say to his players before a contest and how to handle things after the regular season ends and the play-offs begin. In short, he has to know a lot about people and the sport. His good work and judgment can often be the difference between a great team and one that is merely very good.

To help you better understand the many nuances of coaching and the different systems and drills an NHL team uses, we asked two of the league's best — Scotty Bowman, a future Hall of Famer who has won seven Stanley Cups and more games (1,000-plus) than anyone in NHL history, and Colin Campbell, coach of the New York Rangers — to share their ideas and experiences on running a hockey team and explain what they do.

What a Coach Does before a Season Starts

During the off-season, a coach usually rests up a bit from the previous year, plays a little golf, does some fishing, makes a few speeches, and maybe even runs a summer hockey camp. But mostly he works on the upcoming season because the game of hockey has become as much a year-round occupation for the coach as it is for the players.

- ✔ He must evaluate talent, help make trades, and invite promising players to training camp.
- ✔ He has to apply new wrinkles to practices and introduce the players to different offensive and defensive systems.

A coach does all this in hopes of building a winning franchise and being able to put the puck into the net more than any other club in the league.

Training camp

NHL training camps, which are held at various sites throughout the U.S. and Canada, usually open the second week of September. Most years, Campbell asks 50 to 60 players to attend his. During the first few days, he puts the players through a battery of medical tests, mostly to make sure the players are fit and don't have any major health problems. After that's taken care of, the practices begin. "Generally, we have one scrimmage and one practice each day for the first week of camp," Campbell says. He wants to get a good look at the young people trying to make the team, as well as the older players the club acquired in the off-season, and assess the talent he has on hand. "We do lots of drills, from penalty killing and power plays to face-offs and neutral-zone checking," Campbell says. "And I also like to have the scrimmages because it gives me and my two assistants a chance to see how the new players hold up against our core of starters who have come back."

Three decades ago, players used training camp as a time to get into shape for the season. But not anymore. "Athletes today take terrific care of themselves," Campbell says. "They are fit when they show up for camp, and that means we really only have to concern ourselves with maintaining their condition during pre-season, not getting them in shape. And that allows us to spend more time rating the players we have and figuring out which ones will make the team."

Why are NHL players showing up for training camp in such good shape?

NHL players keep in shape for money, for the most part. Competition is fierce, and an athlete who is not in top shape can very easily lose out to a colleague who is. Also, players earn such big salaries in hockey these days that it behooves them to stay in the league as long as possible and keep collecting those hefty paychecks. "It used to be that players retired when they hit 32 or 33," Campbell says.

"But thanks to expansion, we have more teams, and more opportunities, than ever before, and if they stay in shape, they can play for another four or five years. That enables them to generate a lot of additional income, and by doing so, they can virtually ensure themselves of never having to work another day in their lives."

Exhibitions

After a week or so of practice, the exhibition season begins. All NHL teams play perhaps ten pre-season games over a three week period. Again, that's a good time for the coaches to get a feel for the talent they have on their squad, and eventually they start paring down their roster. "We'll get to 30 or 32 players after a period of two weeks or so," Campbell says, "and then we'll drop to 23 or 24, which will be the club we have during the season, barring injury or subpar performance." The last cut is the hardest. It comes a few days before the season begins in early October and usually involves 6 or 7 players that are right on the bubble but don't quite make it. After that's done, the teams get ready to play for keeps.

What a Coach Does during the Regular Season

Coaches do a variety of things during the season. "Obviously, our main focus during the regular season is on winning games," Campbell says. "But while we are concentrating on the team we are playing on a particular day, we are also trying to prepare for our next game and correcting the things we might not have done so well in the past."

Like many clubs in the NHL, the Rangers use a lot of video tape in their preparation. Campbell and his two assistant coaches pore over replays of their opponents' most recent games and look for weaknesses and tendencies.

They also scrutinize tapes of their own play to see where they may be struggling. If his players are not scoring many goals on the power play, for example, Campbell might institute special drills to bolster that part of their game. If the penalty-killing squads aren't doing very well or his centermen are losing a lot of face-offs, he also may have those players perform special drills.

"We have a video coordinator who goes back to our practice facility at the end of each game and breaks down the tape," Campbell says. "He'll be up until three or four in the morning, and when the coaching staff shows up the following day for work, he will have prepared a stat package that describes our scoring chances, details the job we did on face-offs and explains how both teams scored their goals. We'll look over that information, and it'll help us decide what sort of practice to run."

 A team's health may also have a lot to do in determining what sort of practice a coach runs; if a lot of his players are hurt, he may cut back some. And he may do the same thing if the game schedule has gotten busy. There are 82 games in the NHL's regular season, and many times teams have to play back-to-back contests, or as many as three games in four days. "When that happens, we don't seem to have time to do much of anything in practice," Campbell says.

Fatigue can also be a factor, and no coach wants to run his players ragged while they are in the midst of a very busy week or two. But he must be careful not to let too much slide either. "We have to move quickly on breakdowns in the system and take care of them right away so they don't become real problems," Campbell says. He also has to make sure that everybody stays fit; the men who play the most don't have to do as much in terms of conditioning as those who hardly get off the bench during a game and need a strenuous workout to keep in shape.

Soupy's assistants, and what they do

"Soupy" is Colin Campbell's nickname, and like all NHL coaches, he has a pair of assistants that help him run his team. In 1996–97, his assistants were Dick Todd and Bill Moores. Todd stood behind the bench with Campbell during the games and dealt mostly with the defensemen, making sure the right pairings were on the ice and dealing with any adjustments those players might have to make. He also was the guy who went over the tapes from the previous game with the team's video coordinator. Moores worked mostly with the younger players, teaching them different things after practice. Campbell scouted the opposition himself, went over the match-ups for a game, and decided what strategy the team employed. Craig MacTavish, the last player to play without a helmet, has been added as an assistant for the start of the 1997 season. "We don't have a lot of specialized coaches like Major League Baseball or the National Football League," Campbell says. He and his assistants handle many different tasks, and their job descriptions are very broad.

Age is also a consideration when it comes to practice. "If you have an older team, you probably want to run a shorter practice," he explains. "You don't want to wear your veteran players out, you don't want them standing around a lot, and you don't want them bored. A younger team, for example, will probably need more ice time during practice to improve their techniques. And their bodies can better handle more intensive workouts."

A Scotty Bowman Practice

Every coach has a different practice system for his team, and we decided to get one of the best, Scotty Bowman (shown in Figure 7-1), to relate how he runs his. He is arguably the finest hockey coach who ever lived, the winner of seven Stanley Cups, and a brilliant strategist who knows what it takes to make a club succeed. So pay attention.

Figure 7-1:
Coach
Scotty
Bowman.

Warm ups

"Generally, the players all stretch before they come onto the ice, and then we might do a little end-to-end skating warm-up before we really get going," Bowman says. "I'll divide the group up in two, putting half the players in one end of the rink and half in the other. Now, one of my biggest concerns with a practice is making sure the ice on which we'll be handling the puck is in good condition, and most warm-up drills that incorporate skating can tear up the playing surface pretty good. So I get my guys to start skating from behind the goal line, which we won't use for any other part of practice, and only make their stops and turns on that part of the ice. I don't have them going full speed at that point, maybe only 50 to 75 percent. Usually, they'll skate forward to the blue line, then turn around to skate backwards across center ice to the next blue line and then they go forward again."

Most of the players take pucks with them as they glide up and down the ice, handling the puck themselves or passing to teammates. "I think it's a good idea to have them use the puck as much as they want, and I also like them working in groups, perhaps three forwards and two defensemen who usually play together," Bowman says. "I try to do that as much as possible so that players who'll be together on the ice during games will have even more opportunities to get to know each other's moves. I also think it's good to work in units like that because it keeps people from standing around a lot. I want practice to be high tempo, and I try to use as many players as I can at one time in a drill. Doing it that way, we can get a lot done in an hour or so."

Shooting drills

The warm-ups take about ten minutes, and then Bowman may organize a few shooting drills. "I have four or five good ones that will get my forwards and defensemen, as well as my goalies, warmed up," he explains. A favorite of his puts three lines of players — one near the right boards of the rink, another in the middle of the ice, and a third close to the left boards — about 40 feet from the net. The man at the head of each line, beginning with the one on the right, takes a shot at the goalie before giving way to the next one. "I have two groups doing that at the same time," Bowman says, "one in each end of the rink. It gets both goalies working and gives everybody a chance to practice their shot for a bit." (See Figure 7-2.)

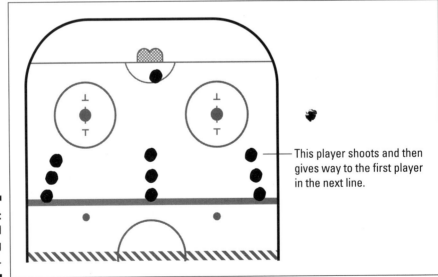

This player shoots and then gives way to the first player in the next line.

Figure 7-2:
A typical shooting drill.

Bowman also uses another drill that begins with a player standing close to the boards at center ice. "I ask him to head out to the far side and make a quick turn toward the goal," he says. "Then I have a guy standing on the left side pass to him, and he'll take a shot from a wide angle near the face-off circle. Right after that, the guy who made the pass will take another puck and make a shot himself, from a similar position on the near side." (See Figure 7-3.) Bowman likes that drill because it forces the goalie to make quick saves from opposite ends of the net. "It's a good way for him to work on his lateral movement," he says. As with the first shooting drill, this one can also be run in both ends of the ice.

Practicing the breakout

Generally, the skating and shooting drills take about 15 minutes. "After that, we'll do whatever needs work at that time of the season," Bowman says. Oftentimes, he works on what is known as the *breakout,* in which a team of three forwards and two defensemen take the puck from behind their net and bring it down to the other end of the ice. "The first time I do this in a practice, I don't put anybody on my players," he says. "It's a five-on-zero rush, and I let them just skate and pass up the ice. But then I'll put a pair of defensemen out for some opposition, to make it a five-on-two. After that, I'll add a forward, and it becomes a five-on-three. And finally, we'll have two more defensemen join them so it becomes a five-on-five and sort of a controlled scrimmage."

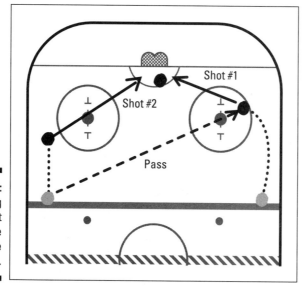

Figure 7-3:
A shooting drill that keeps the goalie moving.

Practicing the line change

Occasionally, Bowman will have his players practice their line changes during those five-on-fives. "I'll let everybody go for 35 or 40 seconds, and then we'll blow a horn," he says. "That tells the players on the ice that it's time for them to get off. So the ones on the attack will try to dump the puck into their offensive zone and then hustle over to the bench and change in favor of some fresh players. People on the ice get tired quickly, and they need to be replaced."

Switching players is known as *changing on the fly* because the play is still in progress. It happens all the time in hockey, even at the youth level, and is one of the things that gives the sport so much speed and intensity. See the section, "Changing on the Fly," later in this chapter for some more details. (Can you imagine professional basketball or football players substituting for their teammates in the middle of a play?)

"We try to get all our players disciplined so they know that after 45 seconds or so on the ice that it's time to get off," Bowman explains. "This drill helps remind them of that and improves their skills at dumping the puck into the offensive zone." How difficult can that really be? Well, it takes work to put that rubber disk in the right spot. "I tell my people to make sure the puck ends up on the side of the rink where the benches are situated so the people coming out don't have so far to go to make the defensive play," he says. "Otherwise, there could be a breakaway, or an *odd-man rush* (either three offensive players against one defenseman — known as a three-on-one — a three-on-two, or a two-on-one) if they aren't able to cover the other team in time." (See Figure 7-4.)

Practicing other skills

Speaking of odd-man rushes, Bowman often incorporates them into drills to give his goalies work and his forwards more chances to pass the puck together and try to score off those situations. In addition, the coach frequently has his team practice face-offs, not only to win control of the puck after a referee or linesman drops it but also to do something productive with it after that.

And Bowman often makes them practice their *forechecking*, which happens when the forwards from one team confront players from the opposing team as that team goes on the offensive and skates up ice with the puck. Forecheckers are supposed to disrupt that club's offensive flow and keep them from skating in on the forechecker's goalie. They should hurry the other team, forcing it to make mistakes and, they hope, creating turnovers that will allow them to go on the offensive and have a chance to score. In addition, he also runs drills that help his players work on ways to beat teams that forecheck them.

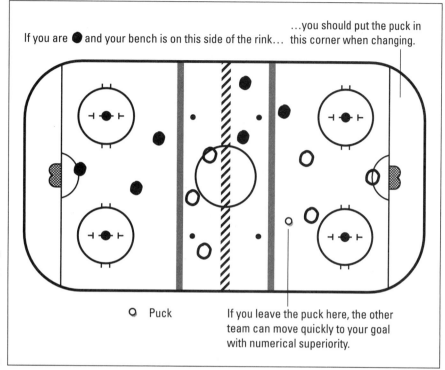

If you are ● and your bench is on this side of the rink...

...you should put the puck in this corner when changing.

Figure 7-4:
A poor line
change can
lead to an
odd-man
rush.

○   Puck

If you leave the puck here, the other team can move quickly to your goal with numerical superiority.

Practice: The overall view

Generally, Bowman runs three drills after warm-ups, each of them taking 10 or 15 minutes apiece. Then the team splits up for a spell, with the defensemen going to one end of the ice to work with the assistant coach in charge of that unit, and the forwards to the other, with the other assistant. And for the next 10 minutes or so, the players work on things specific to their positions. The defensemen, for example, may go over ways to play the point better during a power play, while the forwards may practice their *cycling,* a system that has them moving in a sort of circle around one corner of the ice in the offensive zone with the puck, looking to shed one of their defenders and open a clear path to the goalie for a scoring chance. After that, the players stretch on the ice for a couple of minutes, and then they go home. Occasionally, some players stay after for some extra work, usually guys coming back from injury who haven't been playing or those who haven't been getting into a lot of games. In this day and age, conditioning is such a priority that many players spend up to an hour after practice to do extra work.

The left-wing lock

Scotty Bowman's teams are famous for a type of controlled forechecking known as the *left-wing lock*. In that system, the coach sends his center and right wing into the opposition's defensive zone as the other team gets ready to take the puck out. The idea is to disrupt the other team before it has a chance to develop its offense. Here's how it works.

Your players try to force — funnel — the puck to the open side of the ice (see the first diagram). The left wing, right defenseman, and left defenseman all back up toward center ice. The center and right wing clog up the middle and right side of the ice, forcing the puck up the left side.

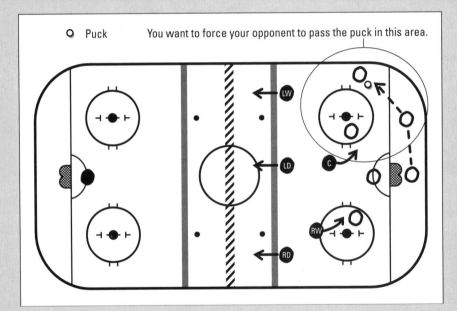

With the left wing, left defenseman, and right defenseman all backing up no further than the red line, and with the center and right wing coming back to help, the team with the puck — your opponent! — has a hard time making a play.

When your opponent tries to move up the ice, he has no where to go with it if you effectively funnel the puck where you want. This is the turnover point (where you can regain control of the puck), shown in the next diagram.

- If the opponent tries to pass within that restricted area where you forced it into, you have a chance to take the puck (1).

- If the opponent dumps the puck deep into your zone, it could be a case of icing if the puck was sent on its way from before the red line. (2). See Chapter 3 for an explanation of icing.

(continued)

(continued)

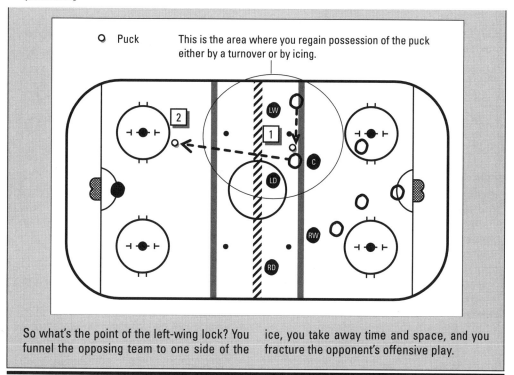

○ Puck   This is the area where you regain possession of the puck either by a turnover or by icing.

So what's the point of the left-wing lock? You funnel the opposing team to one side of the ice, you take away time and space, and you fracture the opponent's offensive play.

Different Systems

It's said that there is more than one way to skin a cat. That same theory applies to hockey coaches and the wide range of approaches they use to win championships. Some teams of the 1990s, such as the Florida Panthers and New Jersey Devils, employ what are known as *traps,* defensive formats designed to minimize the opposition's scoring opportunities and keep its offensive firepower at bay. "It's a system that doesn't call for a lot of aggressive forechecking," says Colin Campbell. "Instead, the goal is to 'trap' the puck in the neutral zone, halting the offensive rush of the other team and taking over possession of the puck at the same time."

According to Campbell, the Panthers like to line up three players at the blue line bordering their offensive zone in an effort to stop their opponents before they have a chance to move very far up ice (as shown in Figure 7-5). On the other hand, the Devils have more of a neutral-zone trap that is put into operation around the red line (as shown in Figure 7-6). Different as they may be in certain areas, the two systems work very well: The Devils, you might recall, won the Stanley Cup in 1995, and the Panthers reached the finals in 1996. But there is one similarity in these traps: The players move as one, like a school of fish. The opponents with the puck feel like they've skated into a spider's web — with nowhere to escape.

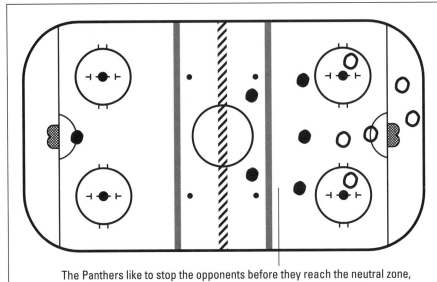

Figure 7-5:
The Florida
trap:
stopping
opponents
before they
move up
the ice.

The Panthers like to stop the opponents before they reach the neutral zone, creating a turnover somewhere near the blue line.

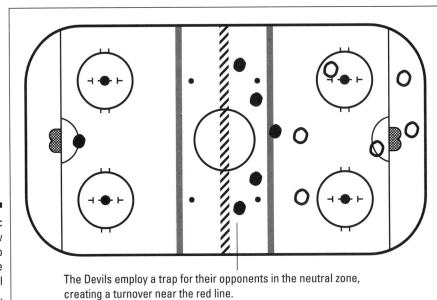

Figure 7-6:
The New
Jersey trap
in the
neutral
zone.

The Devils employ a trap for their opponents in the neutral zone, creating a turnover near the red line.

Perfecting the line change

Changing on the fly is such an important procedure that it deserves a closer look. Here it is, broken down into three main stages.

1. Gain the center ice (red line) so that you are in position to send the puck into the other end without being called for icing (see Chapter 3 for the details on icing).

2. Dump the puck into the corner of the rink that is on the same side of the ice as your team bench.

3. Get to the bench quickly — knowing that the puck is in the opposite end of the ice

and you can safely get fresh players in the ice to replace the tired ones.

The reason you dump the puck into the opposite end of the ice on the same side as your bench is simple: By the time the opposing team gains control of the puck, your fresh players are on the ice and in position to prevent the opponents from moving unobstructed with the puck toward your goal. If you don't dump the puck into the right place while changing on the fly, your players coming onto the ice would have to travel all the way across the rink in order to prevent the opponents from moving freely up ice.

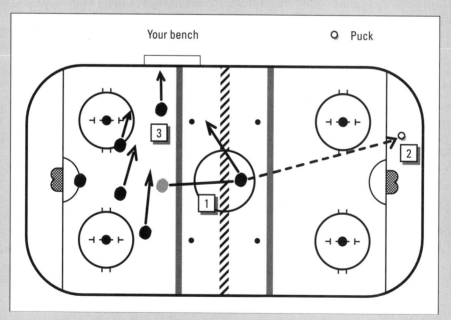

Another team that has done well with a defensive format is Detroit. As we mentioned earlier in this chapter, the Red Wings use their left-wing lock, which is really a variation of a trap, and it has served them very well. No team won as many regular season games during the mid-1990s, and the club captured the 1997 Stanley Cup in four straight games.

But not everybody relies on a trap. The New York Rangers and Edmonton Oilers, for example, employ a *speed* and *pressure* game that is more aggressive and wide open. It's also more entertaining. They usually give up more goals than a team like the Panthers, but they are likely to score more, too. So will the Philadelphia Flyers, who are built on power and toughness, and the Mighty Ducks of Anaheim, who rely mostly on speed. The system a team uses all depends on the philosophies of its coaches and the types of players on its roster. Like Sly Stone used to sing, different strokes for different folks.

What a Coach Does during a Game

Some coaches chew gum during the game, while others munch on ice. They work the referees and chastise the players who aren't performing up-to-snuff. They change lines, match up units, and plot strategies — analyzing their players night after night. They have to think and react very quickly because hockey is the fastest game on earth, and it waits for no one.

Match-ups

Perhaps the most important thing a hockey coach does from the bench is matching his lines and defensive sets against those of his opponents. As a general rule, teams have four lines of three players each, and three pairs of defensemen. The first three lines usually take regular shifts lasting from 30 seconds to one minute, while the fourth line makes only occasional appearances. (Some clubs don't use a fourth line at all, but some do use four lines evenly) As for the defensemen, most teams rotate them in on a regular basis as well. In most cases, the first two lines are offensive threats, while the members of the third line take on more of a defensive, or *checking*, role. The fourth line acts as another third line and is often counted on to provide some good hits against the opposition and lift the tempo for their club.

Pre-game versus post-game matching

Oftentimes, a coach puts together the match-ups he wants before a game. Say, for example, that his opponent has a particularly good checking forward who specializes in harassing the big guns on the other team and keeping them from scoring. The coach may devise a way to keep his best scorer off the ice when that other guy is out.

"It's fine to have a plan beforehand," says Colin Campbell, "but you also have to be prepared to adjust as the game goes on. I like to see what the other guy wants to do and what's working for us on the ice. I need to feel the game out. Sometimes you just need to let guys play, and then there are games where you definitely want certain people out on the ice against specific guys from the other team."

"The key," explains Campbell, who also played 11 years in the NHL, "is being able to adapt to the other guy's system. Only teams that are very deep or very strong can play the way they want and not worry so much about matching up with their opponents. But there's so much parity these days that you don't have one club, like the old Canadiens or Islanders or Oilers, that really stands above all the rest. I remember the great Islander teams of the 1980s, and they could beat you any number of ways. If you tried to fight them, they'd fight you. Hit them, and they'd hit you. Finesse them, and they'd finesse you right back. And usually, they won."

The home advantage in match-ups

It's easier for a coach to get the match-ups he wants when he's at home because the home team always makes the last change before a face-off. If the visitors want different people on the ice after the home coach has made his last move, they have to wait for play to start and change on the fly. (More on that in the next section.)

Scotty Bowman loves to take advantage of a situation if he's playing a team that wants to match his players. "I'll never give him the match he wants on a whistle," he says, "because the moment the puck is dropped, he wants to change and sends another line onto the ice. That will help him get his match, but it also takes time and causes him to lose some forechecking opportunities because his people are going on and off the ice instead. And that means he may not have as many offensive chances because good forechecking can lead to goals."

Changing on the Fly

Another of the coach's primary duties during a game is making *changes on the fly* (illustrated earlier in this chapter), which means he is switching players while the game is going on. Usually, he does that to get a specific match-up on the ice after the puck has been dropped or to replace the players that have been skating hard with a fresh group. "It's important for the guys on the bench to be ready," says Colin Campbell. "They need to pay attention and know when it's time for them to go out there." The coaches are the ones who orchestrate the changes, telling which players to get ready to go. In the NHL, they often don't have to say a word to the individuals; just a look and a nod to the centerman of the line that's going out next does the trick.

Usually, the coaches don't want their players out on the ice for any longer than a minute, and they prefer to keep the shifts down to about 45 seconds. To make sure that goes according to plan, Scotty Bowman has a stopwatch on the bench, which he uses to time his players' shifts. And he wants them to get off the ice right away. "A player's job is not done when he comes toward the bench for a change," he says. "It's over only when he gets himself off the ice."

"Let's Win One for the Gipper" (Locker Room Talks)

What does go on in the locker room before a game, be it a regular season contest or the play-offs? It varies from coach to coach. Some are big on pregame speeches, while others are not. People who run a veteran team on almost any level often defer to the players who are the team leaders and let them get the club ready for big games. Conversely, a coach who is in charge of a younger squad often needs to take the leadership role himself.

"You need to check the temperature of the room to see what needs to be done, if anything," says Colin Campbell. "Sometimes it's quiet, but that's okay. Sometimes it's too quiet, and maybe you need to do something about that. Deciding what to do, whether to give a talk or not and what to say, is really a matter of feel and knowing your team and what it needs when it comes to that."

As a general rule, Campbell always meets with his club before a game, but it's mostly to talk strategy. "Sometimes we get together in the morning and sometimes just before the game begins, to go over things that we need to do," he says. When Mike Keenan was the Rangers' head coach in 1994, the year they won the Stanley Cup, he gave a little talk every night. "But we don't do that anymore," says Campbell, who was one of Keenan's assistants that year. "We've changed it up, which is good. Change is important to guys around here because if you keep doing the same thing, they stop listening after a while. It all becomes too regimented, too predictable, and too boring."

Scotty Bowman says he also gets together with his team before every game. "The first meeting before a 7:30 p.m. game will start at 5:45," he says. "We'll sit down with our top six forwards (the first and second lines) and go over the videotape on the other team's tendencies. What's their forechecking like? Do they crash the net in the offensive zone? What are their defensive zone plays? That will last about ten minutes, and then my coaches and I will meet with the next six forwards and then our defensemen. It's all a part of our preparation."

Coaching during the Play-offs

Colin Campbell loves coaching during the play-offs. "Everything is heightened so dramatically," he says. "The wins are much more fun, and the losses much harder to take. It's much more intense, and I like that."

It's also totally different from the regular season. "In the play-offs, the biggest thing is winning the games," he explains. "As a coach you have to take much more of a short-term attitude in many ways because you don't have much time. There are all sorts of things you might be trying to achieve during the regular season in addition to getting as many wins as possible. Maybe it's playing some of your younger players to see how they do. Perhaps it's resting some of your veterans so they have plenty left at the end of the year. But all that goes out the window in the play-offs. A team has one objective, and that is to win. And it will do whatever it takes to accomplish that."

Avoiding mistakes

As for coaching in the play-offs, Campbell says the most important thing for a team is not making mistakes. "In a short series, which is what you have in the play-offs with the best-of-seven format, you don't want to give the other team any games," he says. "One shift or one shot can make an enormous difference, and a win can tie things up at two games apiece or put you down three games to one, which is a very hard hill to climb. So we work very hard on minimizing mistakes. It's a little like tennis; keep the ball in play, don't hit a ball wide or long, let the other guy make the mistake."

Getting mentally ready

When the play-offs come, Campbell says he has to shut down everything else around him. "That includes my family," he adds. "You have to be able to bring everything down as soon as the game ends, to analyze what your team and the other club have done and figure out ways to do things better. It's very important in the play-offs to be prepared when you go in, so we put together an in-depth booklet on each team we play. But it is also critical that you adjust as the situation demands, and you have to be able to make quick assessments and changes."

Chapter 8

The Power Play

In This Chapter

▶ The first three power-play passes

▶ Remaining in control

▶ The half board power play

▶ Using the five-on-three advantage

▶ Thwarting the power play

A player from the opposing team has just received a penalty for tripping, and for the next two minutes your squad has a man advantage. Congratulations, you're about to go on a power play!

Few things are as important to the success of a hockey team on any level than its ability to score goals during a power play. A *power play* occurs when the opposing club is whistled for a penalty and one of their players is sent to the penalty box (see Chapter 3 for the rules of the game). Thus, one team has the numerical superiority during the penalty time. Coaches employ a variety of plays to try to score during that time, and the power play often creates some of the game's most exciting moments — whether it's a flurry of slap shots from the *point* (that area on the rink just inside the blue line) or a scramble for rebounds in front of the net.

A good power play is a deadly weapon, and no team can win a championship without one.

The First Pass

A power play begins with a face-off in the area around which the penalty occurred. Assume in this case that your team has the man advantage, and the face-off takes place in the circle to the left of your goaltender. The idea is to take control of the puck immediately, bring it up ice to your offensive zone, and then set up so you can take the best possible shots on goal.

Say your centerman wins the face-off and sends the puck back behind your own net. You generally want the defenseman who is your best puck handler to pick up the puck. He becomes the *quarterback* (the QB, to borrow a term from football) for your power play. He can do one of the following things:

✔ Pass to one of the wingers, each of whom should be along the side boards near the tops of the face-off circles (as shown in Figure 8-1)

✔ Slide the puck over to the other defenseman, who should be waiting along the goal line to either his right or left (as shown in Figure 8-2)

The QB also could let the center swing behind the net and pick up the puck himself (see Figure 8-3). Or the QB can carry it up ice. Ideally, the first pass should be to one of the wingers along the boards.

Kids probably shouldn't go up the middle just yet or pass anywhere near the mouth of their own goal; the pros can get away with it, but they've been handling hockey pucks since before you were born.

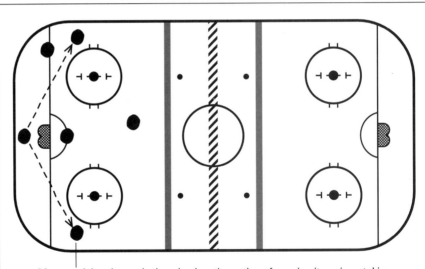

Figure 8-1:
The wingers can take the pass along the boards.

After receiving the puck, the wing has the option of passing it again or taking it toward the opponent's goal.

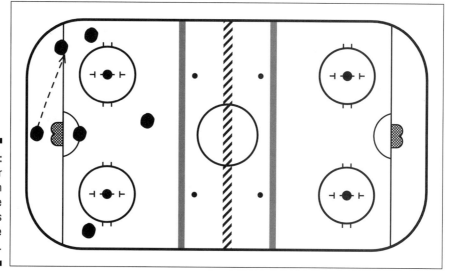

Figure 8-2:
The other
defenseman
can take
the pass
near the
goal line.

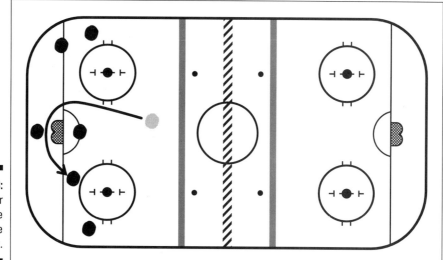

Figure 8-3:
The center
can come
back to take
the puck.

If you're the QB and the last person on your team coming up ice, don't try to beat a player with stick handling in your own defensive zone. You goof, and he's on your goalie in a second. It's the sort of move that lands players in the doghouse. And if the other team scores as a result, you'll probably get sentenced to some time on the end of your bench. How long that lasts depends on your coach's mood. If he's having a bad day, you could be there awhile.

Studies in the power play:
The Pittsburgh Penguins

The 1996–97 Pittsburgh Penguins possessed the widest power play in the NHL — and one of the most effective. In this setup, the key is to get the puck to Mario Lemieux (#1). Once he has it, he tries to suck a defender over to his side, which sets up a two-on-one in front, and

Mario's passing options are either Ron Francis (#4) or Jaromir Jagr (#5). If he wants, #5 can circle around behind the net and give Mario another option. Jason Wooley (#3) and Kevin Hatcher (#2) are out near the blue line.

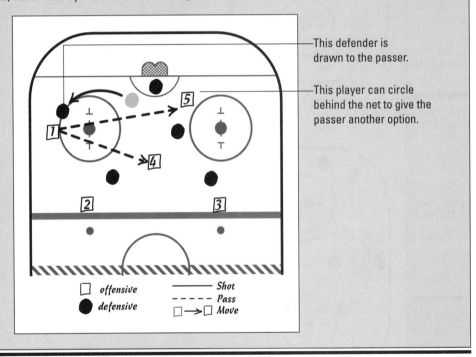

This defender is drawn to the passer.

This player can circle behind the net to give the passer another option.

□ offensive   —— Shot
● defensive   - - - - Pass
              □→□ Move

The Second Pass

The second pass should take the puck from your defensive zone into the neutral zone around the red line. The key there is speed, and that pass should spring the players on the power play and get them moving quickly down the ice.

The Third Pass

Now for the third pass, which can take three primary forms. If the player bringing the puck into the offensive zone is not checked, he can stop and begin setting up a play. If an opponent comes up to him, he can

✔ Fire the puck along the boards, hoping it will scoot behind the net and around to one of his wingers or defensemen — or shoot it high along the glass so the goaltender can't get it. (In either case, make sure you overload the other side with players who can get the puck.)

✔ Dump it cross-corner deep into the offensive zone (to the boards on either side of the net) for either a winger or centerman to pick up.

✔ Pass to the open man.

However the puck gets into the offensive zone, after it's there, the team needs to set up a play. It has the extra man, and it must use that advantage to score.

The Importance of Passing

Before you get into set plays, however, you need to know a little bit about passing. Passing makes or breaks power plays, and it can't be practiced enough.

Youngsters should remember that short passes are better than long ones, and the puck should always go tape to tape, that is, from the tape of your stick blade to that of your teammate's. (Players use tape to protect their blades, which are usually made of wood, and make it easier to handle the puck because the tape acts as a cushion.) The idea is to be accurate and put the puck right on the tape.

You should treat the puck like you treat an egg in an egg toss. If you just hold out your hand and keep it there when someone throws you an egg, the egg will probably break because there's no give. Same thing with a puck and stick. You need to catch the puck with your stick blade and cradle it, so you have maximum control. And if you accept your passes with some give in your stick, you will put yourself in perfect position to pass or shoot right away.

The Key to a Power Play: Control

Control is a key word when it comes to setting up the power play. Control and patience. Most National Hockey League teams employ what is known as the *umbrella* (see Figure 8-4). In the middle of the ice, just inside the blue line of the offensive zone, is the shooter (#2), the player on the power play

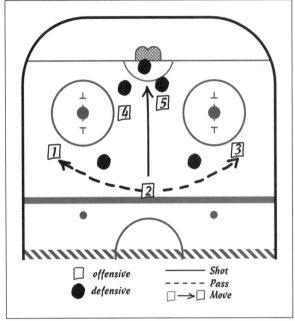

Figure 8-4:
The
umbrella in
action.

team who fires the puck at the net best. To his right, farther down the ice and along the boards, is another forward (#3). And on the opposite side of the zone, perhaps a bit closer to the blue line, is another teammate (#1). Parked in front of the net is another forward (#4), usually a tough guy who can muscle his way around the opposing defensemen, screen the goaltender, punch in rebounds, and deflect in shots. A little bit higher up, but still in the middle, is the center (#5).

The basic idea is to move the puck among the five offensive players until one of them has an opening and can shoot. Crisp passes are essential, and so is making use of the man advantage.

✔ Get the two-on-one situations.

✔ Get the puck to the open man.

✔ Get off the shots.

And be sure to take what the other team gives. If a defender comes to you, that means a teammate is open somewhere. Try to find him. And even if you don't have the puck, make something happen.

✔ Get in the goalie's way.

✔ Look for rebounds.

✔ Keep the puck in the zone if a defender tries to shoot it out.

The high triangle

The *high triangle* is essentially the same power play setup as the umbrella. Remember, the key with the power play in the offensive zone is to create two-on-ones with puck and/or player movement. In this example, the team on the power play has lots of options. If offensive player #2 has the puck, he can shoot it, or if there's lots of traffic in front of the net, he can pass it to #3, thereby creating a two-on-one with defensive player #4. If that defensive player goes after #3, #3 can then pass the puck into the corner to #5, creating a two-on-one with defensive player #2. This passing can happen all over the offensive zone until the players find an opening to shoot — and, they hope, score.

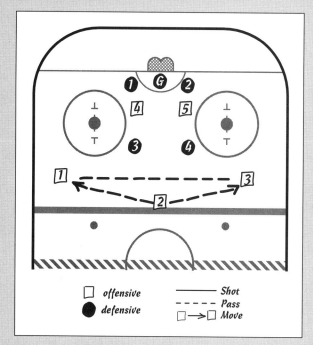

☐ *offensive*   ──── *Shot*
● *defensive*   - - - *Pass*
                ☐→☐ *Move*

FOR KIDS

A good professional team can work a power play like magic, but kids don't have to be quite so sophisticated. Forget about slap shots, for example. The big windups look flashy but are far too difficult for younger players to translate into good shots. Kids should concentrate instead on basic wrist shots, which can be even more effective, not only in scoring goals but also in setting up deflections and rebounds.

The Half Board Power Play

When we talk about *half board,* we mean halfway down the boards in the offensive zone, approximately halfway through the face-off circle. In Figure 8-5, if #4 and #5 are right-handed shots, your playmaker, #1, tries to set up on the right side. If he passes to #4 or #5, they can shoot the puck off the pass because they are facing the passer and don't have to stop the puck to get the shot away. It gives them a quicker, more accurate, and more powerful shot. Also, in the top of Figure 8-5, if #1 has the puck and the defensive players are on #4 and #5, then #3, the pointman, can sneak down low from the back side. In Figure 8-6, if #1 has the puck, he can hit #4 or #5, and hopefully they'll be lefthanded shots and able to shoot off the pass. If they're covered, #3 can sneak down as he did in Figure 8-5 — only on the opposite side.

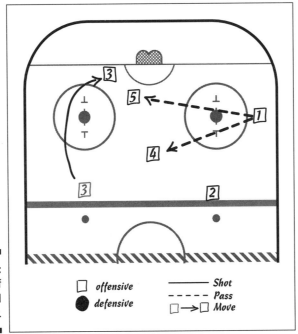

Figure 8-5:
The half board power play.

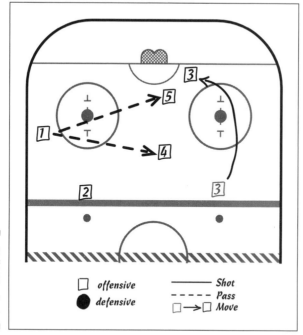

Figure 8-6:
The half
board
power play,
version 2.

□ *offensive*   ——— *Shot*
● *defensive*   - - - - *Pass*
                   □→□ *Move*

The Five-on-Three Advantage

Sometimes when you're on the power play, the opposing team commits a second foul and loses another player — giving your squad a five-on-three advantage! Your chances of scoring go up dramatically in that situation, but you must change your tactics a bit to make sure that happens.

Figure 8-7 shows the basic setup for a five-on-three power play. A lot of teams use four forwards and only one defenseman in a five-on-three situation, hoping to generate as much offense as possible. The defenseman (#2) is in the middle, back at the point. The forwards (#1, #3, #4, and #5) are situated as indicated, their sticks all facing the middle so that they are better able to shoot quickly. Players #1 and #4 should be right-handed shots; players #3 and #5 should be lefties.

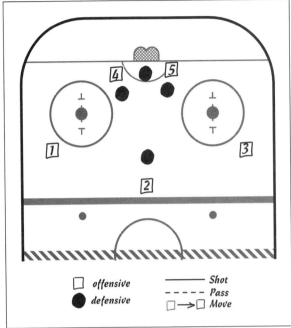

Figure 8-7:
Setting up
for a five-
on-three
power play.

The face-off

First off, you don't want to lose a face-off with a two-man advantage because you want to get control of the puck right away. Two people should always be open, so the centerman should try to get the puck to one of those men when it is dropped.

Retain control

After you get the puck, you should not lose control of it. A two-man advantage means there should always be at least two people open. Try to get the puck as close to the net as possible before you shoot. Be patient in a five-on-three situation, and don't take a lot of shots from the point, or a lot of *one-timers* (shots off the pass) up high in the zone. Try to make the perfect play, to get the puck down low, and get it in. Even if the goalie makes a good save on a shot, all is not lost. With its two-man advantage, your team should be able to snatch the rebound before the opposition.

Goalies often go down when they make the initial save. On the rebound, try to shoot the puck high up and over them.

The best power-play unit(s) in hockey today

Plenty of National Hockey League skaters excel on the power play today, but only ten of them are good enough to be selected to JD's All-Star team. We have put together two units for that squad from current NHL players, and they are so closely matched that we'd be hard pressed to say that one is definitely better than the other. So we'll call them Team I and Team I-A.

Team I has defenseman **Brian Leetch** of the New York Rangers on the left point, just inside the blue line, and Colorado Rockies defenseman **Sandis Ozolinsh** on the right. They are both creative players who do a great job carrying the puck up ice or passing to teammates breaking toward the offensive zone. They also move well without the puck and are good at finding openings where they can take passes and shots on goal.

Up front, the lineup has the Detroit Red Wings' **Brendan Shanahan** on the left side and the Rangers' **Wayne Gretzky** on the right. Shanahan shoots the puck off the pass well, and he's very strong in the corners. Gretzky is simply the best passer in the history of the game.

In the slot in the middle is **Paul Kariya**, the Anaheim Mighty Ducks forward. He, too, is an excellent digger who is good at recovering the puck. He also shoots off the pass as well as anyone.

(continued)

(continued)

Team I-A has **Ray Bourque** of the Boston Bruins and **Al MacInnis** of the St. Louis Blues on the point. MacInnis has one of the hardest shots in the NHL, and he learned the power play from one of the great coaching innovators of all time, the late Bob Johnson. Bourque can do it all: shoot, pass, carry the puck. He's a very accurate shooter and is good at keeping the puck in the offensive zone.

Down lower on the left side and near the face-off circle is Pittsburgh Penguins captain **Mario Lemieux**. A tall, powerful centerman, he can shoot and pass with the best of them. And Mario has the unique ability to control the tempo of the power play, perhaps better than anyone in history. He also has great vision and always seems to know where everybody is. In addition, his strength and long reach enables him to keep the puck away from defenders. On the right side is Lemieux's teammate, winger **Jaromir Jagr**, a great shooter who is also strong and can dig the puck out of the corners. He's also big and can shield the puck from defenders with his body. **Brett Hull** of the St. Louis Blues occupies the slot. Hull is best known for his shot, which comes in hard and fast. He has a lightning-quick release and always seems to find a hole.

Take your chances close to the net

Create your opportunities closer to the net in a five-on-three, and make the goalie move a lot laterally by passing side-to-side. That strategy creates more openings and more chances to score. Remember that a lot of teams use four forwards and only one defenseman with a two-man advantage in order to get more offense. The defenseman is usually positioned at the center point, while two of the forwards stand just above the face-off circles and the other two position themselves on either side of the goal crease.

Teams like to use forwards on their *off* sides, meaning a left-handed shot playing on the right; that puts their sticks toward the middle of the ice and gives them their best chance to get off a quicker shot, firing the puck off the pass for maximum power.

Another thing about the five-on-three: Even the best teams aren't always able to score with a two-man advantage. So don't become discouraged if you don't score every time you have a two-man advantage. Keep working hard, and you should be able to create plenty of scoring opportunities, whether or not you're on the power play.

All-time power-play unit

JD's all-time power-play unit is anchored by a pair of fast-skating defensemen, **Bobby Orr** and **Paul Coffey**. Orr, who spent most of his career with the Boston Bruins, was one of the best to ever play the game, a brilliant stick handler and passer who could take over a game. And no defenseman was better at bringing the puck up ice. Coffey, who broke in with the great Edmonton Oilers teams of the 1980s, was a magnificent passer who moved beautifully with the puck. Both had quick, fast, and accurate shots.

A pair of familiar names, **Wayne Gretzky** and **Mario Lemieux**, are positioned on the right and left side on this team for the same reasons they are on JD's current squad; no one has ever played these positions better. The Great One is the NHL's all-time assists leader, and Mario is among the best scorers and passers the league has ever known. In the slot is **Gordie Howe**, the Detroit Red Wings Hall of Famer who played major-league hockey in five different decades. He was tougher and stronger than most and possessed a wicked shot.

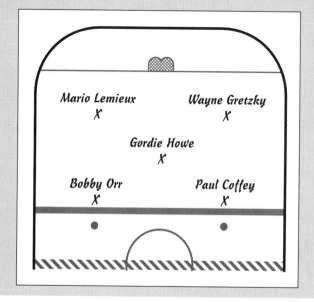

(continued)

(continued)

It wouldn't be right to compile an all-time team without listing a few Honorable Mentions.

✔ **Doug Harvey**, the Montreal Canadien, was the NHL's first super offensive defenseman.

✔ **Brad Park** toiled for both the Bruins and Rangers. Though not particularly quick, he was as smart as they come on the power play; Brad knew when to shoot, pass, and skate.

✔ New York Islanders forward **Mike Bossy** was a pure shooter.

✔ **Phil Esposito**, also of the Rangers and Bruins, was an immovable force in front of the net. His sweeping wrist shot from the slot was deadly.

✔ Winger **Cam Neely**, a fierce competitor for the Boston Bruins, was great at battling the opposing defensemen in front of the net. He had great hand-eye coordination and could deflect slap shots from the point into the net with remarkable proficiency. He also had a tough, accurate shot of his own.

Penalty Kills (Or: Killing a Penalty)

Effective penalty killing is as important to a team as a productive power play, and hockey clubs are constantly trying to devise better ways to stave off the opposition when their opponents have the man advantage. (By the way, coaches call their power play and penalty killing units "special teams" and put an enormous amount of practice time into making them work properly.)

Clubs that had a man in the penalty box used to take a passive approach and let their opponents penetrate their defensive zone before putting up much of a fight. Also, they put their more defensive-oriented players onto the ice to kill penalties, oftentimes positioning two skaters on either side of the net and up the ice a bit and then two more closer to the blue line in a formation known as the *box* (as shown in Figure 8-8). Or they arranged them in a *diamond,* which puts one man in the slot in front of the goalie, another up top near the blue line and two teammates in between them latitude-wise and a bit wider on either side (see Figure 8-9).

But a lot of that has changed in recent years. The box and diamond are still used, but players for the most part have become much more aggressive. Many coaches now prefer a pressure game when it comes to penalty kills, and they are working harder at stopping the other team before it even has a chance to get into the offensive zone or set up. In addition, they use a lot more skill players on those units, guys with speed and goal scoring ability, who can skate well and anticipate.

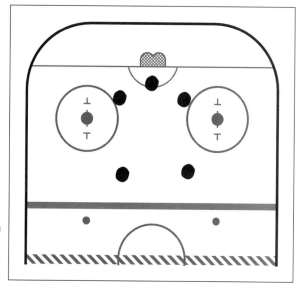

Figure 8-8:
The box.

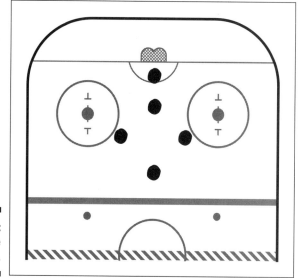

Figure 8-9:
The
diamond.

Many teams of the 1990s have penalty-killing systems that employ pairs, or *tandems,* of forwards. Generally, they use three sets, giving each one perhaps 40 seconds of ice time. As for their defensemen, they often put their biggest regulars together for a shift so they can clear out the front of the net and keep the forwards from the opposing team from screening the goalie and having good position for tipping any shots or stuffing in rebounds.

Different ways to kill a penalty

REMEMBER

There are several things a team needs to be aware of as it gets ready to kill a penalty.

- First of all, the team that is trying to kill a penalty needs to adapt to the club that's on the power play and how it sets up. If the opponent utilizes a lot of diagonal passing, for example, with the left defenseman sending the puck to the right wing and vice versa, then the diamond system will most likely work best. But for a team that uses a more traditional power play format and takes a lot of shots from the point, the box will likely be better.

- Whatever system is employed, the primary objective of the penalty killers remains the same: Take possession of the puck as often as possible and "ice" it down to the opposite end of the rink, which the rule book says you can do (see Chapter 3 for the details on icing). Icing eats up precious seconds of time and keeps the puck away from those players on the power play.

- In addition, a team should never let more than one of its penalty killers get caught inside the opposition's blue line; that can easily lead to the kinds of odd-man rushes that score goals.

- Also, a team must make sure to have a good face-off man on the ice at all times. Taking possession, and keeping it away from the other team, is critical to good penalty killing, and winning face-offs is one of the best ways to take possession of the puck. Of course, good goaltending also is an obvious key to any club that's down a man.

- The team killing penalties should think about its offense every now and again. If the team works hard and anticipates passes and shots well, it can often create scoring chances for itself, and few things can swing the momentum of a game quicker than a short-handed goal.

The best penalty-killers of all time

Two guys deserve special mention for the work they did as penalty killers in the NHL. One is Bob Gainey, who played 16 years with the Montreal Canadiens and won the Frank J. Selke Trophy each of the first four years it was awarded to the NHL forward who "best excels in the defensive aspects of the game." Gainey scored 239 goals in his career and played on five Stanley Cup teams, but he is best remembered as a fierce defender who combined power and speed and was considered by many coaches to be one of the most complete hockey players to ever lace up a pair of skates. The other is Doug Jarvis, who played in the league for 13 years, some of those as Gainey's teammate in Montreal and the rest for the Washington Capitals and the Hartford Whalers. He scored fewer goals than Gainey (139), won only one Cup, and captured the Selke Trophy only once. But he, too, was a tough defender, especially on the penalty kill, and a diligent worker who understood the game and played with a lot of smarts.

Interestingly, Gainey and Jarvis found themselves reunited in the mid-1990s as both of them held jobs with the Dallas Stars; Gainey was the team's general manager, and Jarvis, one of the assistant coaches.

Chapter 9

Intimidation and Hitting

● ●

In This Chapter

▶ Talking on the ice

▶ Things that players do to each other besides talking

▶ The best fighters, intimidators, and agitators of all time

● ●

Championship hockey isn't only about good skating and shooting. The top clubs must also have people who can throw hard checks, agitate opponents so completely that they get off their games, intimidate the other team with their speed and power, and have a physical presence on the ice that keeps the other squad from beating up on their star players. Any professional, international, or collegiate team that both hits and intimidates well can greatly increase its chances of winning.

You want proof of that? Okay, consider the Philadelphia Flyers of the mid-1970s, the Broad Street Bullies who won two Stanley Cups and so terrified their opponents that players sometimes, and quite suddenly, got "sick" before games against them and insisted on taking a day off. But there was really nothing wrong; they just had a case of what came to be known as the Philly Flu. No one liked facing the 1996 Stanley Cup Champion Colorado Avalanche either, and that's partially because they had one of the greatest agitators in the game's history, Claude Lemieux, and a number of other scrappers and hitters who made life miserable for the other team.

What Players Say to Each Other on the Ice

Players don't say much to each other on the ice that we can repeat here, that's for sure. At least not verbatim. But speaking in generalities, we can tell you that NHL players often question one another's lineage and wonder how each other's mother/sister/wife/girlfriend is doing. In most cases, they don't ask about each other's kids or pets, and they're not exchanging stock tips or pasta recipes as they dig for pucks along the boards. In short, the language and the innuendo are as blue as a clear winter sky and as spicy as a bowl of five-alarm chili. Nothing is sacred, and invariably each team, whether it's a high school club or the Boston Bruins, has a couple of guys who are particularly good at one-liners, and they are constantly throwing barbs at the opposition. Why? To get them angry. To get them thinking about something other than the game. To get them to take a bad penalty. To intimidate them. The idea is to get an edge, any edge, and players are always looking to gain some sort of advantage. Sometimes talking does the trick.

Jawing with the opposition is not the only way to achieve that. Many times, players talk to the referees and linesmen, in much gentler ways, about the things a person from the other team might be doing. That guy is having a good night. He's scored a goal, assisted on another, and is making hits all over the ice. Perhaps he's also working the player's teammates over with his stick and getting away with a bunch of slashing fouls. He might consider going up to the ref during a time-out and complaining. "That guy's had his stick up all night," he'd say. "You've got to start calling that, or someone's going to get hurt." Maybe the player points that out to the official two or three times in the early part of the game. And by doing that, maybe he plants a seed that will blossom later on in the contest when the ref finally does call the guy for slashing.

Teammates talk to each other all the time on the ice. Usually, they're asking for the puck, or telling one another what to do, or warning about where players from the other team are coming from and what they are about to do to them. The most vocal players on most teams are the goalies, who act as a sort of cruise director when the puck is in their end. They scream at their defensemen to get out of their way; they tell their forwards what to do with the puck as they skate behind the net or into the corners; and they alert their teammates to any opponents who may be bearing down on them for a check. Like catchers in baseball, goalies have the best view of the playing surface, and they are constantly directing traffic.

What Players Do to Each Other on the Ice (Aside from Talking)

Players do a number of things other than speak to each other on the ice. Hard body checks can work wonders, not only in making a player a little nervous about flying into the corner for a puck and standing in front of the goal looking for a rebound but also wearing him out some; hitting wears a skater out. Slashes are illegal, but they are often employed, especially in the pros, in order to slow down good players and make them a bit more leery about coming down ice with the puck. Some guys use their elbows a lot when they hit. Whatever the tactics, the aims are the same: to keep the opposing players from being too confident on the ice, to upset their rhythm, to beat them up with a lot of physical contact, and to get them mad so they are more concerned about getting even than they are about scoring goals and winning games.

But hard-hitting and chippy play are not the only ways one team can intimidate another. Speed is just as useful an approach. It's dangerous, it's scary, and it works. Speed forces players to make mistakes. It gives them less time and space in which to work the puck, and that can often lead to turnovers. A team with a lot of players who can move around the opposition's defensemen with apparent ease, get to the loose pucks, and work it back up ice faster than the other team is going to frighten a lot of clubs.

Sheer talent can also have an effect. What rookie hasn't been intimidated by Wayne Gretzky, a slightly built man who rarely throws a check and hardly ever gets sent to the penalty box? It is his special skill as a hockey player, his unique ability to score and pass so deftly, that terrifies the opposition and makes him as ominous an opponent as some big gorilla. Same with a great team. Ask players who competed against the top Montreal teams of the 1960s and '70s, or the Edmonton Oiler and New York Islander squads of the '80s, and they'll tell you about the pit they often felt in their stomachs as they looked across the ice at a Stanley Cup championship club doing its pre-game warm-ups. How could they not have the slightest bit of trepidation?

And then, of course, there are arenas, which can sometimes be the most intimidating of all. The old Montreal Forum with all its championship banners, its knowledgeable fans, and its great history was probably worth at least a goal to the Canadiens some nights. Old Chicago Stadium and Boston Garden had similar feels. They were smaller arenas that had a more intimate atmosphere than their successors that made the hometown crowds seem twice as big. "I don't think we're in Kansas anymore," Dorothy said in the Wizard of Oz. Some out-of-town rinks can make players feel just as lost.

The Five Best Fighters

Fighting is only an option in the NHL and the North American minor leagues; it is punished by ejection everywhere else, from the Pee-Wees to the Olympics, and therefore is rarely used at those levels. Most NHL teams have at least one player who is good with his fists. In most cases, his presence — on the bench and on the ice — is enough to keep the peace. But if his team needs a lift, or if the opposition has been beating up on one of his top players, he goes after one of the other squad's tough guys. The scrap usually starts with a check or maybe a slash, and the next thing you know, the two fellows have dropped their gloves and started wrestling with each other while standing on their skates, looking for a chance to land a punch or two before the linesmen come in to break it up.

If the fight is between two tough guys and the officials feel it will help settle the game down, the officials often let them go at it for a spell. But if it seems like a mismatch or threatens to get out of control, they try to step in right away.

The NHL has had its share of good fighters over the years, and the following pugilists made our list of the top five:

- **Bob Probert.** At 6 feet 5 inches and 225 pounds, this right winger is the best heavyweight scrapper ever to play the game. He led the NHL in penalty minutes while with the Detroit Red Wings in 1987–88, spending the equivalent of almost seven full games in the box. Probert has a nasty temperament and a deadly punch, but he can play a little bit as well, scoring 29 goals one season and adding 20 and 19 tallies during two others.

- **John Ferguson.** Mr. Intensity. The longtime Montreal Canadien left wing played 500 games in the NHL, won five Stanley Cups and amassed more than 1,200 penalty minutes. He also scored 145 goals during his career, showing that he could handle the puck almost as well as he could handle his fists. A tough competitor who used to get irate with his teammates if they so much as talked to members of the opposition during warm-ups.

- **Dave Brown.** Another bruiser with size (6 feet 5 inches, 225 pounds) who understood his role as a fighter and represented his team well. While in the minors he led the American Hockey League in penalty minutes with 418 one season, and he racked up over 270 on two occasions in the NHL. Brown wasn't much of a scorer, and he never amassed more than 12 goals in an NHL campaign. But very few could match him when the gloves came off.

- **Joey Kocur.** Smaller than Probert and Brown but just as ferocious, Kocur led the league in penalty minutes (377) in 1985–86. He has a deadly right and is known as a one-punch guy; if he lands that one punch, he can really do some damage. A native of Calgary, Kocur has had a lot of injury trouble with his hands over the years from all the punches he has thrown, many of which have bounced off the helmets of his many foes.

- **Marty McSorley.** Another big boy, at 6 feet 1 inch, 225 pounds, who won the penalty minutes crown in 1992–93 while with the Los Angeles Kings. McSorley is an excellent fighter who served for a time as the Kings' enforcer and made sure no one messed with then-teammate Wayne Gretzky. He can play either forward or defense, and he frequently participates in the power play, something that generally only a club's best offensive players do. McSorley has scored ten or more goals in a season five times during his career.

These guys may not merit being in the top five, but they deserve some kind of honorable mention:

- ✔ **Orland Kurtenbach.** The 13-year veteran didn't like to fight, but when he did, there wasn't anybody tougher. He also had great reach, which enabled him to slip in a few good punches while keeping his opponent at bay. Kurtenbach played for four teams over his career, scoring 119 goals and piling up 628 penalty minutes.

- ✔ **The Hanson Brothers.** They wrapped aluminum foil around their knuckles before each game, to give their punches extra zing, and then they took on all comers in the classic George Roy Hill movie *Slapshot.* The Hansons pummeled their opponents on the ice, they battled fans in the stands, and they did time in the slammer. "These guys are folk heroes," Paul Newman said to a desk sergeant as a teammate bailed the brothers out of jail. "They're not folk heroes, they're criminals," the cop replied. "Well," Newman countered, "most folk heroes started out as criminals." Real cementheads. But real good. And they knew how to take care of themselves.

The Five Best Intimidators

Intimidation has been a part of organized hockey from the beginning, and the pros who have been best at it over the years make their point without always having to drop their gloves. They use their sticks, their elbows, their speed, or their power to create a sense of fear and forboding in the athletes they play against and make them a bit more cautious as they skate around the ice. And why is that good? Because it can create scoring chances for their club and give them a better chance of winning.

- ✔ **Gordie Howe.** Mr. Hockey was best known for his uncanny scoring ability, his six Most Valuable Player Awards, and his 21 selections to the NHL All-Star squad. But he was also the best intimidator the sport has ever seen, a mean guy who liked to go into the corners with his stick and elbows up. Howe liked getting back at people who did him — or one of his teammates — wrong, but he was a patient man who didn't have to act right away. In fact, he was happy to wait five or six weeks before getting his revenge, and when he did, look out. Most players were peeking constantly over their shoulders when Howe was out on the ice. (See Figure 9-1.)

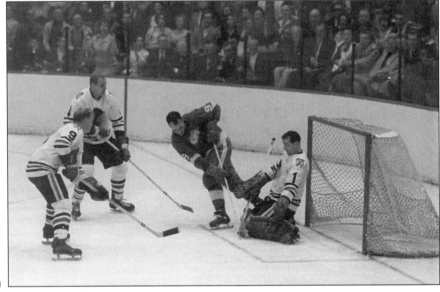

Figure 9-1:
Known for
his scoring,
Howe could
intimidate
with the
best.

✔ **Mark Messier.** Like Howe, Messier is an immensely talented player with a nasty streak who will do whatever it takes to win. His intensity is unsurpassed, and he is famous for "the Look," a glare that emanates toughness, confidence, and abandon. He lifts up his teammates with that and uses it to rattle the opposition as well. Messier also intimidates with his speed; he is a fast skater who often puts defensemen back on their heels because they are so worried about his quickness.

✔ **Ted Lindsay.** He is a smallish man, only 5 feet 8 inches and 160 pounds, but you wouldn't know it from the way he battled during his 17 years with the Detroit Red Wings and the Chicago Blackhawks. Lindsay became known as "Terrible Ted," and that was no reflection on the playing ability of a man who scored 379 NHL goals; he helped his teams win four Stanley Cups, and played on nine All-Star teams. He simply competed in a very ill-humor. A left winger who played on Detroit's renowned "Production Line" with Gordie Howe and Sid Abel, he also carried the moniker "Scarface" and accumulated more than 700 stitches during his NHL career. In addition, Lindsay piled up more than 1,800 penalty minutes in his time.

✔ **Eddie Shore.** The stellar defenseman last played in the NHL in 1940. His reputation survives after all these years as one of the toughest to ever play the game. A four-time MVP, he was the sort of player who had the whole arena standing whenever he had the puck. A prolific scorer, he could also throw a body check as well as anyone, and he never backed down from a fight.

Terrible Ted

Some players can never get the game of hockey out of their systems, and Ted Lindsay is still one of those people. Initially, he retired at the end of the 1960 season, when he was 35 years old, ancient by hockey standards back then. Four years later, however, he attempted a comeback with the Red Wings, and to most everybody's surprise made the team and went on to play one more season. The Terrible One scored 14 goals and ended the year as one of the league leaders in penalties. He dazzled his hometown fans all year with his bone-crunching checks and reckless spirit. In one game, Lindsay received a penalty for spearing a Montreal defenseman who was seven inches taller and 40 lbs. heavier. Another Canadien came over to settle matters with Lindsay as his friend was helped off the ice, but the future Hall of Famer gripped his stick with both hands and slashed the Montrealer, who was nearly 20 years younger, across the legs. All that player could do after that was limp away.

As he entered his 70s, Ted Lindsay still had a locker at the Detroit Red Wings practice facility and went out there to work out most every day. He does a variety of activities to keep in shape but rarely plays in NHL old-timer games anymore. It's not that he can't get it done physically; it's just that he gets too intense on the ice and starts knocking people around.

✔ **Eric Lindros.** A big brute (6 feet 4 inches, 235 pounds) who uses his stick a lot and is not afraid to run people over. Lindros is very talented and very tough. Not many want to mess with him.

The Five Best Agitators

Sometimes there is a fine line between agitating and intimidating, but we think the difference is clear: Intimidators frighten other players while agitators simply bother them. And the five men we have listed in this section were as bothersome as anyone who ever played the game.

✔ **Esa Tikkanen.** A chatterbox who never stops talking, Tikkanen works over his opponents in his native Finnish, English, and some bizarre combination of the two in a tongue his teammates call "Tikkanese." He has a terrific shot, and his five Stanley Cups show that he's a winner. And remember, he will do anything to win. His coaches have always put him out against the other team's top player, and with good reason. Wayne Gretzky says he is the best checker he has ever faced.

✔ **Claude Lemieux.** A big talker who drives opponents crazy with his chippy play, Lemieux rarely fights but does whatever else he can to take players off their game, using his stick, his elbows, and his mouth. He loves to goad people into taking bad penalties and often does. Another winner, he has played for three Stanley Cup champs.

✔ **Ulf Samuelsson.** He agitates so well that most fans in the league think of him as a villain, a hard-hitting player who rarely fights but will gladly take out an opponent. But his teammates love his tough play and the way he battles. And he's been a fan favorite wherever he's played. A native of Sweden who entered the NHL in 1984, Ulf has often been among the league leaders in penalty minutes.

✔ **Bobby Clarke.** The career-long Philadelphia Flyer who was a member of those brutal Broad Street Bullies teams in the 1970s, Clarke was as antagonistic as they came. A prolific goal scorer and a great leader, he also racked up more than 1,400 penalty minutes of his own and certainly induced players on the teams he played to take as many themselves. Fiercely competitive, he never stopped looking for an edge. Clarke was elected to the Hockey Hall of Fame in 1987. (See Figure 9-2.)

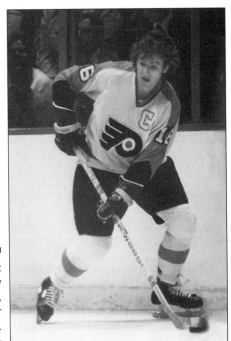

Figure 9-2:
Bobby
Clarke,
agitator par
excellence.

✔ **Dave "Tiger" Williams.** He played on five teams over 14 seasons, and at the end of the 1996–97 campaign, he still held the NHL title for the most penalty minutes in a career — 3,996 during the regular season and 4,421 including the play-offs. Tiger got many of those from working over the top players on the opposing team and getting under their skin. A great agitator, he also liked to drop his gloves. But it would be unfair to categorize Williams, who retired in 1988, solely as a fighter; he also tallied 241 goals during his career, an average of 17 a season.

Honorable mention: Tony Leswick, the former New York Ranger, Detroit Red Wing, and Chicago Blackhawk, may not have been one of the five best agitators, but he sure was a hell of a troublemaker. He played for 12 years during the 1940s and 1950s and spent much of his career driving the opposition crazy with his antagonistic play. Future Hall of Fame coach Scotty Bowman says he was "a real pest," which might account for all the time he spent in the penalty box; when Leswick retired in 1958 he had piled up 900 minutes.

What about goalies?

You usually don't think of goalies as agitators, but the New York Islanders' Billy Smith and Ron Hextall, most recently of the Philadelphia Flyers, were two of the best in that regard. Scrappy, competitive, and incredibly possessive of the area in front of the goal, they fought for position outside of the crease and often did things like smack the backs of their opponents' ankles with their sticks to keep them at bay.

The goalies racked up more than their share of penalty minutes each season and were not averse to dropping their gloves on occasion and mixing it up on the ice. Loved by their teammates, they were loathed by the opposition, who considered them real pains. And you know what? They were.

Billy Smith, shown here, proved goalies can be agitators, too.

Part III

It's Easier from the Stands (A Lot Easier)

In this part . . .

Hockey is one of the greatest spectator sports around, so in this part we give you advice on how to enjoy it even more as you watch on television or from an arena seat. In addition, we let you know where you can keep up with your favorite game — in newspapers, in magazines, on radio, on television, and (of course) on the World Wide Web.

Chapter 10

How to Watch Hockey on Television

In This Chapter
▶ Following the puck
▶ Not following the puck
▶ Watching the top teams
▶ What you can't see on television

Television technology has made tremendous advances over the years, and so has the way that networks produce hockey games. It has often been said that the sport doesn't translate well to the little screen, but we think talk like that is so much nonsense. Thanks to great camera work and a rich selection of replays, most of the excitement, speed, and hitting of the game can be captured by TV and brought inside a fan's living room. It really is the next best thing to being there. Even during intermissions, hockey offers something special that none of the other major sports (baseball, basketball, and football) have: live interviews with players and conversations with coaches on what happened on the ice during the previous period and how things might change for the next one.

Following the Puck (Sometimes)

Perhaps the best way to watch a hockey game is simply to follow the puck. Much of the action is centered around that rubber disk, and if you have your eyes on it, you won't miss the big plays.

But plenty happens on other parts of the ice, whether it's a center back checking, a winger battling for position in front of the net, or a defenseman streaking deep into the offensive zone for a pass (see Chapter 1 for an explanation of the positions). If you want to see more than just what's going on around the puck, we recommend that you let the play-by-play man keep you apprised of where it is and allow your eyes to focus on other aspects of the game, whether it's a play forming down ice or a matchup between one team's big scorer and the other club's top checker.

You can back away from the game for a bit and see what is going on away from the puck, which can be a lot of fun. If Mark Messier skates onto the ice, who does the opposing coach put out against him? Same with a player like Paul Kariya or Joe Sakic. And don't worry if you miss a great goal; you can watch the instant replay, and the producers will likely show you the play from several different angles. Listen, too, to the color analyst, the person in the television booth who tries to explain to the fans exactly how and why a good play happened and describe the things that caused a mistake. That's JD's job when he takes to the air for either Fox Broadcasting or the Madison Square Garden Network. A good analyst can make even the least experienced fan understand what's going on.

The FoxTrax puck

Fox Broadcasting developed the innovative FoxTrax puck for use in NHL games and unveiled it in 1996 in order to make it easier for fans to watch the hockey puck move during a game. People have complained for years about how difficult it can sometimes be to try to watch a hockey puck dart around the ice; to many television viewers, the puck is simply too small and too fast to make any sense at all. So Fox came up with a computerized puck that takes on a glow when it appears on the television screen and develops a comet-like tail; it's blue until it reaches 65 miles per hour, at which point it turns to red.

The FoxTrax puck is actually a traditional NHL puck which has been sliced in half and then partially hollowed out so that a small circuit board and a series of diodes can be installed inside before it is put back together and re-sealed with epoxy. Sensors the size of cigarette packs are then installed above the rinks in the arenas in which the pucks are used. These sensors feed information from the puck to computers, which transmit that data to what is known as the Fox "Puck Truck," a mobile production vehicle that eventually sends the information out for home reception. Many purists hate the blue and red innovation, but it does seem to make the game more understandable to the newer fans.

Watching the Plays Form

One of the best things to watch at a hockey game is how the plays form. They frequently start behind their own net with an offensive-minded defenseman such as Brian Leetch surveying the setup before him and then beginning to work his way up ice with the puck. Some of his teammates might circle and curl trying to get open, while others crisscross. Passes are made, shots are taken, and when the other team regains possession, the whole thing starts over again, this time from behind the opposite goal.

Video replays give viewers at home a whole range of options when they tune into a hockey game. Watch how the puck got where it did when play has stopped. Who gave it away, and why? Was it the result of sloppy stick handling? A strong hit? You can learn a lot just by looking carefully at what happened along the way.

It's also fun, whether the action is live or taped, to focus on the one-on-one battles in a hockey game, to see who's winning the face-offs, the scrambles in front of the net, the struggles for the puck along the boards even when they are away from the puck. It's like keying on one player in football; hone in on a particular skater and watch how he moves around the ice, how he handles the puck, and how he deals with his opponents and offensive and defensive tactics. You can see a more individual side of the sport and get a better sense of all that goes on during a hockey game.

Old-time television viewing

In the old days, hockey fans at home didn't get to see many plays form because the camera work and coverage was not so advanced. But that isn't a problem today, thanks to vast improvements in production technique and capability. A television network may employ 35 workers, ranging from the announcers and statisticians to the cameramen and directors, and use eight or more television cameras for regular-season games. Twenty years ago, the television networks may have used only four cameras. For an important play-off game, the networks may use as many as 14 cameras. In addition, they employ six instant replay tape machines for a regular-season contest and as many as 11 for the play-offs, up from two or three just two decades ago. That enables them to provide replays to viewers from many more angles than they could in the days when JD played. Viewers can see shots from inside the goal net and in places along the boards that show heart-pounding aspects of checking and scoring in ways that television viewers could have only dreamed about in the 1960s and '70s. And then there is the overhead camera that is suspended from the ceiling of the arena; it provides a picture of the entire rink and finally lets the fans at home watch the important plays form. It's now almost as good as being there.

What to Look For from the Top Teams

Hockey teams, like people, have their own personalities, and many of them play the game quite differently. Understanding a team's character makes it easier to watch them on the tube because you have a sense of what they like to do and know what to look for when they take the ice. Here is a list of some of the top teams of the mid-1990s and the style of hockey they play.

Philadelphia Flyers

Toughness is what sells in the City of Brotherly Love, and that's one of the main traits of its hockey club. Eric Lindros (Figure 10-1), John LeClair (Figure 10-2), & Co. are big, fast, tough players who have both the talent to score and the ability to deal out punishment in the corners and in front of the net. A team that relies a great deal on brute force.

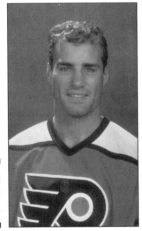

Figure 10-1:
Eric
Lindros.

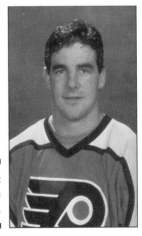

Figure 10-2:
John
LeClair.

Detroit Red Wings

Coach Scotty Bowman employs what is known as a *left-wing lock,* in which his left wing seldom forechecks in the offensive zone but stays back to help out defensively (see Chapter 7 for all the details on the left-wing lock). The winningest coach in NHL history with more than 1,000 victories to his credit, Bowman believes in defense first. And to get to the Red Wings' goalie, a team often has to crash through a wall of defenders.

New Jersey Devils

Coach Jacques Lemaire (shown in Figure 10-3) played in Montreal when Scotty Bowman was in charge there, so it's not surprising that he, too, is big on defense. His Devils employ what is known as a *neutral zone trap,* which essentially puts most of his players in the area on the rink between the two blue lines when the opposing team starts to come down ice. The goal is to keep the opposition from getting into the offensive zone by cutting off the second pass out of its own end, and it often works. It's as if they have put out a spiderweb of players (see Chapter 7 for more information on the neutral zone trap). The Devils are a tough team that likes to hit. The Devils also rely heavily on the awesome skills of goaltender Martin Brodeur. All of this means that the Devils play an effective but often boring style of play, especially when they have the lead.

Figure 10-3:
Coach
Jacques
Lemaire.

New York Rangers

With Wayne Gretzky (see Figure 10-4), Adam Graves, and other ex–Edmonton Oilers, the Rangers prefer a speed and pressure game that is more wide-open and offensive than the way New Jersey or Detroit plays. They learned the method from Glen Sather (shown in Figure 10-5), and they brought it with them to New York. The team can play it tough when it has to, and thanks to the skills of goalie Mike Richter, the Blueshirts also win their share of 1-0 games. But speed and pressure is the way they like to go.

Figure 10-4:
The Great
One: Wayne
Gretzky.

Figure 10-5:
General
Manager
Glen
Sather.

Anaheim Mighty Ducks

An up-and-coming club built mostly on speed and the remarkable talents of its big scorers, Paul Kariya (shown in Figure 10-6) and Teemu Selanne. Watch them whenever possible. With those two snapping pucks into the net, the Ducks will only get better and better.

Figure 10-6:
Paul Kariya.

Edmonton Oilers

Glen Sather doesn't coach this franchise anymore, but as general manager, his hockey influences are still felt. Consequently, the Oilers remain a speed team that likes to pressure the puck. As is the case with the Rangers, Edmonton often gives up a lot of shots because it is always on the attack. But the Oilers score more than their share of goals, which makes them an exciting team to watch.

Buffalo Sabres

Young and brash describes this team best. The strongest player is eccentric goalie Dominik Hasek (see Figure 10-7), and he's one of the best in the league. (Actually, that description is redundant; we have yet to meet a goalie, former or otherwise, who isn't a bit odd.) A very physical, in-your-face team, the Sabres are free-spirited and have a sort of us-against-the-world attitude. The Sabres may not be overly talented, but they are tough, hardworking guys who give their all.

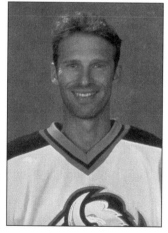

Figure 10-7:
Dominik
Hasek.

What the Camera Doesn't Show You

With all the equipment the television networks have set up around a hockey rink, you don't miss very much, whether it's a coach shouting at the referee from the bench or a pair of forwards from opposing teams hacking at each other with their sticks behind the play. And if the producers can't get the shot live, they almost always come up with a replay. They are especially good at isolating cameras on big-time players. A director may trail a scorer like Tony Amonte (shown in Figure 10-8) for a couple of shifts to see how he works the ice and what he is doing. And if he puts the puck in the net, assists on a goal, delivers a big hit, or just misses on a shot, the crew has him on tape and can play it over and over again for the fans.

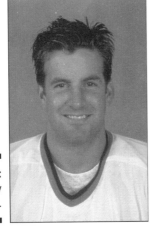

Figure 10-8:
Tony
Amonte.

But still, the cameras don't show you everything. They can miss the action that goes on away from the play, and you can only imagine what really happens there. Perhaps two skaters begin battling for the puck at one end of the rink, keep mixing it up even as the play moves toward the opposite net, and then continue going at each other as they finally head up ice them-selves. The live camera feed usually won't pick that up, and you can only hope that one of the replay cameras does. Chances are, however, it won't.

Television viewers also don't have the opportunity to hear or see the coaches during a game and aren't given much of a sense of what goes on behind the bench as the game progresses, which is too bad because there is so much happening — from the coach sending certain players onto the ice for their shifts to his talking strategy with one of his assistants to his telling his defensemen how to handle certain players from the other team.

Occasionally, you can "hear" what's going on while you are watching a game on television, so listen carefully. The "ping" the puck makes when it hits one of the goalposts but doesn't go in the goal is one of the most distinctive sounds of hockey. (Any puck that hits a goalpost and continues into the net is a goal; any puck that bounces away is not a goal and is still in play.) No matter how loud an arena — or living room — may be, that noise of rubber hitting metal at such a high speed can silence the fans for an instant as they try to figure out exactly what has happened. It's an extreme emotion for both sides; the fans of the squad that has taken the shot are frustrated and can't believe the puck didn't go into the net, and those on the other side are relieved that they survived such a close call and a little nervous about the next shot going in.

The "crunch" against the boards of a player who has just received a solid body check is another sound to listen for. The impact of a great hit can echo throughout an arena, and it is one of the things that gives hockey its special intensity.

Chapter 11

How to Watch Hockey
from the Seats

. . . .

In This Chapter

▶ Keeping your eyes on the ice

▶ Picking the best seat

▶ Finding the best food

▶ Touring JD's favorite arenas

. . . .

*H*ockey is a great game to watch on television, and an even better one to see in person. In fact, we don't think there's another sport that comes close to matching the speed, excitement, and finesse of a live NHL game or a game played by top international, minor league, or college teams. So do yourself a favor this season: Buy some tickets and get out to see a game. And make sure you remember some of the tips we give in this chapter.

Paying Attention

Hockey is a fast sport, so the key to good watching is paying attention. While you're looking down to squeeze some mustard on your hot dog, your team could score a goal. Or give one up. Eat before or after the game, or between periods when the only action on the rink is the Zamboni resurfacing the ice or some puck-shooting contest for fans from the stands. Thumb through the program during stoppages of play. Chat with your neighbor during the time-outs. But when the puck is dropped and the skating begins, keep your eyes peeled on the ice.

Watching the Whole Rink

There are so many subplots to a hockey game and different things to watch. One of the things we like to do is to follow the matchups on the ice, to see what skaters the coaches put out to play against each other. That's an important consideration in every game, especially during the play-offs when the stakes are highest. Who's checking Gretzky? Or Forsberg? Or your nine-year-old son? Who does coach Scotty Bowman send onto the ice against Paul Kariya and Teemu Selanne? It's a chess game between the two clubs and great fun to watch.

These days, most seats in a hockey arena are good. But we recommend that you get a seat in one of the corners because you can see the entire rink from there (see Figure 11-1). You should get down close to the ice, where you can really get a sense of the hitting, speed, and athleticism of the players. You don't get quite as good a view from that level of the ice (a higher position enables you to see more of the action unfold), but you're right there during a game and can see how amazingly talented these people are.

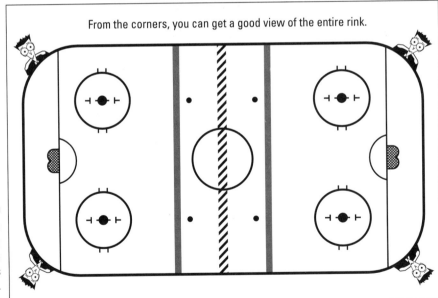

From the corners, you can get a good view of the entire rink.

Figure 11-1:
Viewing
from the
corners is
ideal.

What exactly is a Zamboni?

A *Zamboni* is a four-wheel-drive vehicle that scrapes, cleans, and floods the surface of a hockey rink before each period of a game. Invented by a California rink operator named Frank Zamboni, it grew out of an experiment he conducted with a tractor pulling a sled across the ice at his rink. The one-driver Zamboni made its debut in 1949 and soon became a fixture at rinks all over the world. Basically, it scrapes the snow off an ice rink that has had heavy skating activity and lays down a fresh coat of hot water, which creates a new surface of ice in about ten minutes. The procedure improves the quality of the ice and enhances the speed and finesse of the modern game of hockey.

© NHL Images/Diane Sobolewski

Watching an Opposing Player

Focus on the opposing team's star player when he comes to town. Like Eric Lindros or Brett Hull. Or maybe it's the centerman on the team your son's high school is playing who has just been named all-state. Keep your eyes on him for a few shifts, and only him. See what he does without the puck. See what the other team does to him without the puck. See how he gets himself in position to shoot, pass, or check.

If the members of a hockey team don't work together on the ice, they won't win. So as a fan, you should enjoy the effort the players expend each and every night. When you watch players at the NHL level, or even those in a minor league game or collegiate and international competitions, take time to appreciate their ability to perform ballerina-like moves while skating at some 30 mph and carrying a stick. It really is remarkable what these guys can do. The power, strength, and finesse they all possess is truly something to behold.

Enjoying the Culinary Delights

Anyone who goes to more than a few games a year should get to know where the freshest popcorn is made in his or her home arena and where to find the best hot dogs. (Or perhaps you'd prefer gourmet ice cream, freshly made Chinese food, or other fancier eats, which most facilities sell along with more traditional fare.) Each arena has those culinary hot spots, and it pays to discover where they are. Vendors will get to know you and are sure to treat a good fan well, especially if they get a few extra dollars along the way.

Keeping Your Cool

One more thing if you see a game in person: Don't be abusive to the players, officials, security people, ushers, or fans around you. The language at some hockey arenas is as salty as anything you'd find in the locker rooms after the game, and that's not always comfortable when you have your six-year-old daughter and a couple of her friends in tow. Remember, it's a family game, and a fun game.

  ✔ Behave.

  ✔ Don't drink too much.

  ✔ Don't throw things.

  ✔ Don't swear.

  ✔ And don't ruin it for everybody else.

JD's Five Favorite Arenas

Our man in the television booth spends more time in hockey rinks during the winter than he does at home, so he knows his way around these buildings pretty well. Here are his top five, in alphabetical order, and one honorable mention, for purely sentimental purposes. It wasn't the classiest place JD ever played, but it was certainly the most memorable.

Arrowhead Pond at Anaheim

It's down the street from Disneyland, so you can take your family there before the ref drops the puck. It's also close to where the Angels play. The arena is beautiful, with palm trees on the outside (you don't see those around the Calgary Saddledome in mid-February) and lots of granite and marble inside. An impressive building that feels almost like a palace. The workers are clean, very polite, and pleasant, all of which you would expect from Disney.

Madison Square Garden

"The World's Most Famous Arena," its history is one of the things that makes it so special, even though the Garden has changed addresses several times over the years. The current edition has been operating on the west side of Manhattan since 1968, and it's one of the loudest in the league. The fans there are among the most passionate and knowledgeable in the game, and when the building roars, it roars. Oddly located, the rink is actually on the fifth floor of a building that sits atop busy Pennsylvania Station. Great fans who love hockey and know the game well fill the Garden, shown in Figure 11-2. The food is pretty good, too, since the concession stands were renovated a few seasons ago.

Figure 11-2:
Madison
Square
Garden
atop Penn
Station.

Maple Leaf Gardens

Known as the Old Lady of Carlton Street, this building celebrated its 65th anniversary in 1997. No other arena in the NHL has been around so long. The seats are too small (at least for us), the concession lines intolerably long, and you need a road map to get from one part of the building to another. But it is still one of the best venues in the league. (See Figure 11-3.) It has been the site of some of the greatest games in hockey history and has the venerable feel of a church. Old pictures lining the hallway walls add a nice touch.

Molson Centre

It's tough to replace a legend like the old Montreal Forum, but this building comes close. It opened in 1997, but somehow it manages to carry on much of the tradition and ambiance of the Canadiens and their former arena. All the old championship banners and retired jerseys hang from the rafters, the fans still dress up, and something special remains about going to a game in Montreal. Stop by the concession stands for the best hot dogs in the league, and the buns are toasted, too!

Figure 11-3:
Maple Leaf
Gardens in
Toronto.

San Jose Arena

The home of the Sharks has had terrific mood and atmosphere from day one. The arena contains excellent facilities for players, broadcasters and fans alike. The home team comes onto the ice at the start of the game through the mouth of a shark, and the fans all move their arms back and forth like a shark's jaw when their players go on the power play. It's a simple but great place to see a game.

Honorable Mention: Lethbridge Arena

JD was a 17-year-old goalie on the Lethbridge Sugar Kings in Alberta, Canada, when they faced off against the Edmonton Maple Leafs in a junior league play-off game back in 1971. The Sugar Kings were losing 2-1, 19 seconds into the third period when the smallish, wooden building suddenly caught fire. The place was packed with some 1,800 fans at the time, and they quickly filed out, as did the players who didn't have time to take off their skates or retrieve their clothes from the locker room. With most everybody standing across the street on the sidewalk in amazement, the arena burned to the ground in 90 minutes. The game was finished the next night in a nearby arena, with Lethbridge tying the score in the third period and then going on to win 3-2 in overtime. Later that same evening, the Sugar Kings also beat Edmonton in the scheduled game and went on to win the series.

Chapter 12

Online, on the Air, and on the Newsstand

In This Chapter

▶ Surfing the Web for hockey stuff

▶ Flipping through TV and radio stations for the big game

▶ Scouring books, magazines, and newspapers for hockey coverage

Keeping up with your favorite sport is, thankfully, not hard to do. Hockey is everywhere, and you can find news about the sport ranging from player profiles and trades to game summaries and analysis on your computer or television screen, in the newspapers and magazines, and on the radio. You just need to know where to look.

Hockey Web Sites

There is no shortage of hockey in cyberspace, and a few taps on the mouse can land you on some fascinating and fun-filled sites. Strap on your helmet, and we'll show you some.

nhl.com

This is the league's own Web site, www.nhl.com, which by the end of the 1997 season was enjoying more than one million hits a day (see Figure 12-1). It provides fans with live game information as well as good video highlights, daily stats that are updated instantaneously, and access to the league's vast information database. In addition, nhl.com offers features such as the 1996–97 series "A Long Way Home," which profiles some of the league's greatest international stars including Pavel Bure of the Vancouver Canucks, Mats Sundin from the Toronto Maple Leafs, Washington Capital center Michal Pivonka, and Colorado Avalanche defenseman Uwe Krupp.

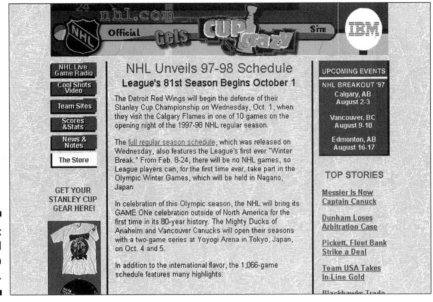

Figure 12-1:
The official
NHL Web
site.

Fans can skate the Web and find other treats like "Grab the Mike," a program that allows one person each week to interview his or her favorite player. Or there's "In the Crease With JD," which enables people to take part in weekly roundtable discussions with our favorite NHL broadcaster and his celebrity guests.

Fans can also vote players onto the All-Star team through nhl.com and buy league-licensed merchandise for Christmas, birthdays, and other special occasions through the NHL's Cyber Store.

NHL team sites

The league isn't the only hockey organization that has entered the computer age in a big way; many of the NHL's 26 franchises have developed their own Web sites that offer reams of information that enables fans all over the world to keep up with their favorite clubs like never before (see Table 12-1).

Table 12-1	NHL Team Web Sites
Team	**Site**
Anaheim Mighty Ducks	www.mightyducks.com
Boston Bruins	www.bostonbruins.com
Buffalo Sabres	www.sabres.com
Calgary Flames	(no site yet)

Team	Site
Carolina Hurricanes	(no site yet)
Chicago Blackhawks	www.chiblackhawks.com
Colorado Avalanche	www.coloradoavalanche.com
Dallas Stars	www.dallasstarshockey.com
Detroit Red Wings	www.detroitredwings.com
Edmonton Oilers	(no site yet)
Florida Panthers	www.flpanthers.com
Los Angeles Kings	www.lakings.com
Montreal Canadiens	www.nhl.com/teampage.mon
New Jersey Devils	(no site yet)
New York Islanders	www.xice.com
New York Rangers	www.newyorkrangers.com
Ottawa Senators	www.ottawasenators.com
Philadelphia Flyers	(no site yet)
Phoenix Coyotes	www.nhlcoyotes.com
Pittsburgh Penguins	www.pittsburghpenguins.com
St. Louis Blues	(no site yet)
San Jose Sharks	www.sjsharks.com
Tampa Bay Lightning	www.tampabaylightning.com
Toronto Maple Leafs	www.torontomapleleafs.com
Vancouver Canucks	www.orcabay.com/Canucks/index.shtml
Washington Capitals	www.washingtoncaps.com

sportsline.com

Another big player on the Internet is CBS Sportsline, or
www.sportsline.com, which has a wealth of information on a number of
sports, including hockey (see Figure 12-2). You can find up-to-the-minute
news on games and trades, analysis of playoff series and draft choices, the
most-recent standings and statistics of NHL teams, and renowned broadcast
and print journalists, including our own JD, debating and speculating on the
hockey issues of the day. Sportsline also has skill competitions such as NHL
Picks, which is sort of a Rotisserie League on ice, and features Wayne
Gretzky's own World Wide Web site. Fans can go through a comprehensive
bio of the Great One, review his accomplishments as a pro, chat with the
perennial All-Star through scheduled e-mail sessions, and be like Wayne in
an interactive, 3-D hockey game using Shockwave software.

Figure 12-2:
Sportsline
covers
hockey,
too!

espn.com

Then there is the ESPN Sportszone (www.espn.com), the most visited destination site on the World Wide Web (see Figure 12-3). It offers a host of information for the hockey fan, including news and scores, highlights, player profiles, statistics, previews, analysis, contests, chats with some of the sport's top personalities, on-site reporting from important games, and the weekly NHL Break Away, which has players, coaches, and journalists answering questions for fans.

Figure 12-3:
The ESPN
Sportszone
is a great
place to go
for hockey
info.

Broadcast TV and Radio

All you need is a TV or radio to take advantage of many hockey resources. The kind of coverage you want is there.

Fox Broadcasting

Not so long ago hockey fans could not even find a game on national broadcast television, but all that changed in 1994 when Rupert Murdoch's Fox Broadcasting signed a five-year, $50 million contract to televise NHL contests. As a result of that deal, the network carries the All-Star Game each January and then a Game of the Week through the end of the regular season eleven weeks later. After the play-offs get started, it airs a Game of the Week for the first three rounds and then presents three games during the Stanley Cup Finals, including Game Seven, if necessary.

Fox has done a lot for hockey in just a few short years. Putting the game back on broadcast TV on a regular basis has helped get more people excited about the sport, and the network has not been afraid to innovate. One example of that is the FoxTrax puck, which Fox uses in all the games it televises. The puck contains a computer chip that makes it glow on the TV screen. The network spent some $2 million researching the puck and hopes the thing will help attract more viewers by making the game easier to watch for novices.

ESPN

The Bristol, Connecticut, cable network carries 26 regular-season NHL contests during the year and then televises a game every night in the play-offs except for Wednesdays and Sundays (which are its days for Major League Baseball, one of those "other" sports). ESPN's sister channel, ESPN2, does three games a week during the regular season, which comes to a total of 75 when all's said and done. And "the Deuce" also has a hockey game a night through the first round of the play-offs, when available.

ESPN also covers hockey in a number of other ways, whether it's through clips and commentaries on "Sportscenter" or the guys on Sunday morning's "Sports Reporters" debating some critical issue. You can find the game on ESPN in many different shapes and forms.

CBC

As you might suspect, hockey is very big in the north country, and the Canadian Broadcasting Corporation has the biggest show there, *Hockey Night in Canada,* in which the network airs a doubleheader every Saturday evening during the regular season. It's as much a TV happening as *Monday Night Football* in the States. CBC also does a game a night during the play-offs, if possible — preferably one that includes a Canadian team.

TSN

The Sports Network is Canada's version of ESPN, and it does 31 NHL contests a year, carrying either one or two games a week during the regular season. It, too, does a game a night in the first round of the play-offs and may present as many as 14 play-off games in one year.

SRC

The French-language arm of CBC also airs a Game of the Week for the entire season as well as one series per round for the first two playoff rounds. It also carries the Stanley Cup Finals, and possibly the Conference Finals if it involves two Canadian clubs.

RDS

Réseau Des Sports is the French arm of TSN, and it, too, has a Game of the Week during the regular season and covers one playoff match up during the first round. It may carry another series in round two if the series pits a pair of Canadian teams against each other.

Regional Cable Television and International

There are plenty of other places to find hockey on television, both in and out of North America. More than 160 countries carry NHL games during the regular season and play-offs, for example, and a sizable number air competitions within other professional and amateur leagues throughout the year. And what viewers cannot find on the major broadcast or cable channels, they can often locate on one of the many regional cable networks, such as Madison Square Garden or Sports Channel in the metropolitan New York area or Prime in Los Angeles, that may cover all a team's games live and provide daily news on the team.

Radio

Sports radio has hit the big time, and there are plenty of stations throughout North America on which you can listen to fans, commentators, players, coaches, and team executives talking hockey. One of our favorite shows is hosted by The Fabulous Sports Babe on ABC Radio. We also like the way ESPN Radio covers the game as well as the attention countless local stations give hockey across the U.S. and Canada.

Hockey in Print

The best place to start with the print media is the NHL, which publishes the *Official Guide and Record Book* before the start of each season. It's a can't-miss for the rabid fan and has everything you'd ever want to know about the league and its players and teams.

Other super NHL publications include the league's official yearbook and its annual *All-Star Game Program,* both of which are wonderful sources of information. In addition, the NHL and the Players Association publish *Power Play Magazine* together, a youth hockey volume that covers the NHL for youngsters. Finally, the individual franchises each sell official team journals at the arenas that are full of great photos, statistics, and stories about the club and its players.

Magazines

The Sporting News provides terrific week-to-week coverage, and *Sports Illustrated* (800-992-0196) does a good job as well, especially around play-off time. And the major newsweeklies, *Time* and *Newsweek,* devote a story to the game every now and again.

But the best publication for the sport is *The Hockey News* (416-340-8000). Based in Toronto, it looks at the game at both a professional and amateur level like no one else. And in addition to its regular weekly edition, *The Hockey News* also publishes some first-rate special issues.

Other magazines of note include:

- *Sports Illustrated for Kids* (800-992-0196)
- *American Hockey Magazine* (719-881-7679) out of Colorado Springs
- *USA Hockey In-Line Magazine* (719-599-5500) out of Colorado Springs
- *Hockey Illustrated* (212-780-3500) based in New York City

> ✔ *The Hockey Digest* (847- 491-6440) in Evanston, Illinois
> ✔ *The Beckett Hockey Monthly* (972-991-6657) out of Dallas — for trading card enthusiasts
> ✔ *Let's Play Hockey* (612-729-0023) in Minneapolis

Newspapers

The local newspapers in each NHL city provide good coverage of the local team, and so do the newspapers in towns that have minor league or college hockey. On a national basis, *USA Today* does better than most, bringing solid information from around the league together in one spot; it contains great box scores and goes to print very late so the morning edition has all the finals.

Books

Hockey fans also have a terrific selection of books from which to choose. The NHL put out a great coffee-table publication on the occasion of its 75th anniversary in 1991, appropriately titled *The Official National Hockey League 75th Anniversary Commemorative Book* (McClelland & Stewart, 1991), and it is a classic. So is the *Stanley Cup Centennial* book (Firefly), the NHL-produced book about the Stanley Cup a year later. Read it if you want a colorful and complete history of the league and the greatest trophy in sports.

Another good buy is *A Day in the Life of the National Hockey League* (Harper Collins, 1996), which brilliantly recounts in words and pictures all that went on in the league one March day in 1996.

We recommend you browse your local bookstore or library for any of the countless treatments writers have given the game over the years. You may want to check out the work of veteran broadcaster and journalist, Stan Fischler, who has been writing about the sport for more than 40 years and has written some 65 books that discuss everything from the history of the game to its all-time great players.

Two other authors of note are Dick Irvin (son and namesake of the Hall of Fame coach and the play-by-play analyst for *Hockey Night in Canada*) and broadcast journalist Brian McFarlane. Both have written several good volumes on the sport.

And then there is our top choice, former Montreal Canadiens goaltender and Hall of Famer Ken Dryden, whose book *The Game* (Times Books in the U.S., Macmillan in Canada, 1983) is considered by many, including us, to be the best ever written about hockey (except for this one, of course).

The Hockey Hall of Fame

Located in Toronto, this is a must-see for anyone interested in the sport. It was established in 1943, and members were first honored two years later. Originally, the Hall was housed in a building on the grounds of the Canadian National Exhibition in Toronto. It moved to its current spot, on the corner of Front and Yonge Streets, in 1993. At the start of the 1996–97 season it boasted 304 members. The Hall is a fascinating shrine to the coolest game on earth, with some wonderful interactive facilities and countless exhibits on the greatest players, games, and coaches the sport has ever known. Nothing captures the history — or excitement — of hockey so well. Visit their Web site at www.hhof.com (see Figure 12-4).

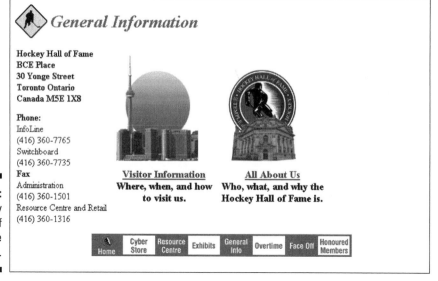

Figure 12-4:
The Hockey
Hall of
Fame on the
Web.

Part IV
So You're Ready for Your Shift

The 5th Wave   By Rich Tennant

"Shoot! I thought that thing would finally keep the Red Wings out of the alfalfa!"

In this part . . .

This section is for those readers who want to play the game themselves — or for those who are looking to get other members of their families involved. We start off with playing tips from pros like Wayne Gretzky and Brett Hull, and then we tell you where to go if you and your children want to play, whether you have any ice or not. Hockey without ice? Read on . . .

Chapter 13
What You Need to Know to Play Hockey and to Improve

. . . .

In This Chapter

▶ Passing advice from Gretzky

▶ Messier and face-offs

▶ Defending the breakaway, according to Vernon

▶ MacInnis discusses shooting from the point

▶ Power forward scoring, by Roberts

▶ Lindros and shooting off the pass

▶ Hull's method to get free in front of the net

▶ Hextall and handling the puck as a goalie

▶ Gartner and power skating

▶ Leetch explains playing defense

. . . .

The best way to pick up any sport, and to get better, is to listen to the professionals and learn what they do. So we got in touch with several of the NHL's better players and asked for their advice on different aspects of the game. So just listen up.

Wayne Gretzky on Passing

"There are two primary kinds of passes," the Great One explains. "One is solid and hard, and the other is known as the feather. If the player you are passing to is standing still, use the *firm pass.* And if he's going at a good rate of speed, use the *feather,* and make sure you get it out ahead of him so he can skate into it." (See Figure 13-1.)

Figure 13-1:
Gretzky
prepares
to pass.

© NHL Images/Allsport/Elsa Masch

"I think it's important to practice the backhand pass as much as the fore-hand one," Gretzky continues. "And you want to do that as much as possible at a young age so you grow up feeling comfortable with it, especially if you want to be a centerman. Some youngsters ignore the backhand and don't feel relaxed with it as a result."

Number 99 is famous for skating behind the net with the puck in his offensive zone and looking for teammates to get open in front of the net. (He camps out there so often, in fact, that commentators refer to that part of the ice as *Gretzky's office*.) "When I get back there, I prefer to use a backhand pass to get the puck out front," he says. "I like to use the net as a sort of screen, to buy time from the opposing defensemen who may be trying to get me, and to buy some time back there. I try to keep the puck away from them as long as possible so I can hopefully make a play."

One final tip: Use plenty of tape on the blade of your stick. "It gives you more control on your passes and shots, and it enables you to pass the puck *flatter* (meaning not lifting it) when you have a decent amount of tape on your blade," Wayne says. "I tried doing it like Bobby Orr, with only a couple of pieces on the blade, but I couldn't do it."

Mark Messier on Face-Offs

"A centerman should always watch the linesman's hands when the puck is about to be dropped," says the perennial All-Star, shown in Figure 13-2. "Forget about the other player, but keep your eyes on the linesman because he's the one who actually has the puck. In the defensive zone, the best thing to do is try and adjust to what your opponent is doing. Read him. Look at his eyes, where his stick is facing, how his body is turned, how he's holding the stick and where he's telling his teammates to line up. All that should give you some idea of what he is going to do with the puck, whether he's going to shoot off the draw, pass the puck to one of his defensemen behind him, or over to one of his wingers. And then you should react accordingly.

"Probably the best thing you can do with the puck in your defensive zone is bring it back behind you so one of your defensemen can pick it up and try to get it outside the zone. To do that, turn the hand you put on the lower part of the stick into a backwards position, which will give you more power as you bring the stick back when the puck is dropped."

Figure 13-2:
Mark
Messier.

© NHL Images/Allsport/Glenn Cratty

"We work on set plays off the face-off all the time in practice," Messier says. "And we also practice things that we might do when time is running out and there may be only a minute or so left in the game. It's sort of like the two-minute drill in football, and we have a little bit different way of doing things then. Also, many times in practice, a coach will take a dozen pucks or so and drop them for two centermen so they can work on their face-offs. Your best position for that is having your legs spread for balance and your stick down, so you are set up almost like a tripod."

"Remember, in a power play situation especially, the centerman is the quarterback, and he should know where every player on the ice is," Mark continues. "It is his job to set everybody up and know what he will do with the puck when the linesman drops it. And he should also be aware of the tendencies of the opposing centermen he will face on a particular night and watch them closely from the bench to see what they are doing with the puck after a draw (another name for face-off). That way, he will be better prepared when he steps onto the ice."

Mike Vernon on Defending the Breakaway

"The first thing I try to do is recognize the person that's coming in as soon as he hits the blue line," says the goalie for the 1997 Stanley Cup champion Detroit Red Wings and now member of the San Jose Sharks. "Is he a shooter? A *deker* (someone who will first make a move to get the goalie out of position and then shoot)? Or maybe a third- or fourth-line center (who usually don't have the best hands or shot on the team)? Then I adjust my position. I don't want to be too far out of my net, especially if the guy coming down is a Swede or Russian because they generally have a lot of speed and move in very, very quickly. If I go out too far, they'll be on me in a hurry." (See Figure 13-3.)

"If I had my choice, I'd rather face a shooter than a deker," explains Vernon. "I believe I have a better chance of stopping him. How do I tell if a guy is going to shoot or deke? Well, the best way is to look at where the puck is on his stick as he's coming down ice. If he's holding it right out in front of him, then I can expect a deke because it's impossible to shoot with your stick that way. If, however, he's carrying it on the side, he can do either, shoot or deke. I believe that if the puck is cocked to one side, I should get ready for the shot first. But at the same time, I need to stay still because if I open up, the guy coming down on me will stick the puck in the five hole (the area between a goalie's legs). I expect most people on a breakaway to fake a shot, try and deke me and put the puck between my legs. Mario Lemieux did that well. In fact, he did that better than anybody else."

The different holes

Hockey coaches and players have designated seven *holes* in a net guarded by a goalie as a way of communicating where pucks should be shot (and what areas a goalie should be careful to defend). Holes number one and two are above the shoulders of the netminder, and three and four are in the lower corners of the goal, on either side of his ankles. And as mentioned in the preceding text, the five hole is right between the legs while six and seven are underneath the armpits. We also think there's an eighth hole, right between the eyes, which is where a person who decides to be a goalie, or a writer, instead of going to law or medical school, deserves to be hit with the puck.

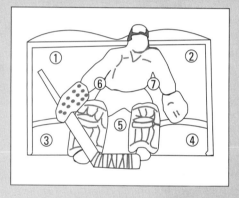

Al MacInnis on Shooting from the Point

This rangy defenseman (shown in Figure 13-4) has won the fastest-shot contest during the NHL All-Star Weekend three times, and his shot from the point was clocked as high as 98 miles per hour. Not surprisingly, goalies don't like to see him wind up.

The winner of the Conn Smythe Trophy as the most valuable player in the play-offs for the Calgary Flames when they won the Stanley Cup in 1989, MacInnis grew up on a farm in Nova Scotia and practiced his slap shot whenever he could. He put a sheet of plywood against the barn and shot buckets of pucks against it all summer long. "I would do as many as 300 a day," he recalls. "It helped me build up my strength and work on my timing." When he takes a shot from the point today, MacInnis tries to keep his hands close together, which means that when he takes his windup for a shot, he creates a bigger arc, which in turn gives him more power. At 6 feet 2 inches and 200 pounds, he is a big player who stands upright when he skates and uses a curved stick with a bit of a wedge to it, giving him added lift.

Figure 13-3:
Vernon
goes down
for the
save.

© NHL Images/Allsport/Al Bello

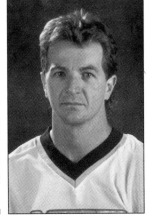

Figure 13-4:
Al
MacInnis,
perennial
fast-shot
champ.

Gary Roberts on Scoring as a Power Forward

Scoring as a power forward requires a set of special talents. A player must not only be big and strong and able to overpower his opponent on either end of the ice, but also have legitimate goal-scoring ability. Gary Roberts is one of those rare athletes who fills both those bills and is one of the best power forwards in the NHL. (See Figure 13-5.)

"Body position is really important," Roberts says. "I like to keep my back to the goalie and be as close to him as I can without being in the crease so the defenseman can't get in behind me and throw a cross check. One of the key things that a power forward who wants to score should do is keep his stick loose so he can knock in rebounds or deflect pucks. Someone on the other team may be all over you, they may be checking you from behind, whacking you across the ankles with their sticks, grabbing your jersey. But no matter what they do, try and keep your stick free so you can somehow get it on the puck should it come by, even if you're tied up.

"For rebounds, I like to use a stick that's fairly straight with maybe a little toe curve. The straightness will help you put it on your backhand shots better than a sharply curved blade, and the toe curve will let you flick the puck upstairs, 'roofing it' we call it, into the one or two hole. I also believe it's best to have a stick with a stiff shaft because so much of your shooting at that position comes in close, and you really have to bear down on those two- and three-footers. You don't have much time with those, only an instant, and a stiffer shaft will help you get those types of shots off faster and harder."

Figure 13-5:
Power
forward
Gary
Roberts.

Eric Lindros on Shooting off the Pass

"I like to keep both my hands high on the stick when I'm getting ready to shoot off the pass," says the Philadelphia Flyer centerman. "Why? Because it's easier and quicker to move your lower hand down on the stick where it has to be when the pass comes than to try and move it up. Also, it's important to keep my center of gravity low and my legs spread apart just enough so I can adjust to the pass. The idea is to get yourself in the best possible position to shoot because the thing that makes a shot like that work is its quickness and speed. You want to surprise the goaltender, and to do that you need to shoot as quickly as possible. I work on shooting off the pass a lot after practice because it can be so effective. I always have, though it was a problem in junior hockey because I broke so many sticks working on it, and it cost the team money." But clearly the practice paid off, and Lindros shoots off the pass as well as anybody. (See Figure 13-6.)

Who's the best at setting up the shot off the pass? "Paul Kariya," Lindros says without hesitation. "We played together during the World Championships in 1993, and he was unbelievable."

Figure 13-6:
Eric
Lindros.

© NHL Images/Allsport/Rick Stewart

Brett Hull on Getting Free in Front of the Net

"A lot of it is developing the proper state of mind," says one of the NHL's most prolific scorers of the 1990s. "One thing that's important is learning to take a lot of abuse from the opposition without retaliating or yapping back. And sooner or later, they forget about you."

"When I'm in the slot trying to score, I try to move around a lot," says Hull. "If I get knocked down by a cross check, I stay down for a bit and then get right up, the hope being that the defensman thinks he has taken you out of the play and forgets about you. Then I try to get up real quick and get open."

The All-Star right winger (shown in Figure 13-7) goes out of his way not to show up an opponent when he scores a goal. "Usually, I try to go to the bench right away," he says. "I don't pump my arms too much or raise them high because I don't want to embarrass people. I actually think it's better if you can slip in and out without drawing too much attention to yourself. If you make people get emotional about you, then they make it their business to know where you are every second you are on the ice. They are always looking to see where you are. It's much better to be out of sight, out of mind."

Figure 13-7:
Brett Hull knows how to slip in and out of the action.

ST. LOUIS

"I always try to keep my stick free whenever I am getting tied up in front of the opposition's net," Hull continues. "Just in case I can somehow get to the puck, whether for a deflection, a redirection or a rebound. I've played with some amazing centermen, Wayne Gretzky and Adam Oates to name but two, who had a terrific knack of putting the puck on my stick. Somehow, they would find it. Another guy who was really good at that was Peter Zezel."

"All scorers need good centermen," Hull says, "and it's possible to develop a really strong relationship with one. It's like in football, where a quarterback can throw a pass to a receiver before he even breaks out of his cut. A good centerman knows his wings, and he can move the puck to a spot before you even turn to go there."

Ron Hextall on Handling the Puck as a Goalie

Hextall's grandfather (Bryan Sr.) and father (Bryan Jr.) both played in the NHL, so he's been hanging around hockey rinks as long as he can remember. "I used to watch Eddie Giacomin when my father played in Detroit," Ron says. "He handled the puck as well as anybody, and I watched him all the time when he was with the Wings. And then, when I started playing goalie as a kid, I used to get really bored just standing around. So I started to move with the puck a little bit during games. As I grew up, I began spending lots of time shooting pucks with a forward's stick, maybe two or three hours each day. Also, I played a lot of pond hockey and always tried to work on my shooting and puck handling."

Learning how to handle the puck well is critical for a goalie who wants to get good. "But don't try to do too much with it," says Hextall, shown in Figure 13-8. "Overhandle the puck, and you can get in trouble fast. In addition, be careful when you pass it off to one of your teammates in the defensive zone; move it out from the boards or net and give him the chance to swoop in and take it clean."

Hextall, who in 1989 became the first netminder in NHL history to score a goal in a play-off game, uses a blade that he says has "more of a bend to it than a curve. If a blade has a big curve to it, then you could have trouble stopping the puck. I use a stick that looks more like an eight-iron because it's bent backwards a little bit. With it tilted that way, I can shoot the puck harder and higher. And I think it helps me get rid of rebounds more quickly."

Mike Gartner on Power Skating

"It was my dad's idea for me to work on my skating at an early age," says the veteran forward. "He put me in a power skating school when I was eight or nine years old, and I remember having to cruise around the ice for an hour and a half at a time without the puck. I hated it, but it made me a much better skater." In fact, it made Gartner one of the strongest in the NHL, and he's won the league's fastest man competition during All-Star Weekend each of the three times he has entered.

Figure 13-8:
Ron Hextall
pouncing
on the puck.

"Technique is very important," Gartner says. "Most players don't bend their knees enough, which means they don't get low enough. That provides the power they need when they finish their strike. It's important to take a full, elongated stride. You also have to remember to use your arms, to pump them like a sprinter does to build up speed. And don't stop moving your legs when you go into a turn; that's the time you want to accelerate." (See Figure 13-9.)

Brian Leetch on Playing Defense

"One of the key things to remember is never look at the puck when an opposing forward is coming down on you," says the perennial All-Star defenseman. "Look at his chest instead, the logo on his sweater, so you won't get mesmerized by the puck." If your opponent is bigger than you, Leetch explains, positioning is critical. "If you're positioned properly, then he will have a harder time trying to outmuscle you," he says. "If your opponent gets even a little position on one side of you, he can use his strength to outmuscle you and get by. If, however, it's a smaller player who relies more on his speed than his strength, you want to give him room to the outside. Let him go to the outside, but be smart with your angle and don't let him beat you to the net."

Figure 13-9:
Mike
Gartner is
one of the
NHL's
fastest
skaters.

© NHL Images/Allsport/Glenn Cratty

Leetch, shown in Figure 13-10, has twice won the NHL's Norris Trophy, given each year to the league's top defenseman, and one of the reasons he is so successful is that he prepares. "It helps to know each player that you face," he explains. "Know what their tendencies are, their strengths and weaknesses. That will help you react quicker and figure out the best way to play them. And if there's a new guy on the ice, a player you have never seen before, watch from the bench to see how he does stuff, to understand what his moves are."

It's tough trying to clear out a big, strong guy from the front of your net, and if you can't outmuscle him, Leetch suggests that you resort to timing. "Try to get to the player just as the puck is about to arrive," he says. "Don't let him take a clear shot or pass if you can help it."

And if your team gets caught in a *two-on-one* situation (two opposing forwards coming down on your goalie with only one defenseman back), the man defending must give the goalie the shooter and make sure the person with the puck doesn't pass it across to his teammate. If that happens, the goalie will most likely be out of position, and the other team will have a very good scoring chance.

Figure 13-10:
Brian
Leetch, a
top
defenseman.

© NHL Images/Allsport/Nat Butler

Chapter 14

Where to Go if You — and Your Children — Want to Play

In This Chapter

▶ Making contact with youth and adult leagues

▶ Getting back to basics: pond hockey

ockey isn't only for professionals, and it doesn't matter if you aren't good enough to compete on your country's national amateur team. Men and women of all ages and abilities play and enjoy the sport, and so do boys and girls as young as kindergartners. They participate in various youth and adult leagues around the world, they go to hockey schools and camps during summer vacations and they organize pickup games on frozen lakes and ponds during winter's icy grip. In fact, there is no shortage of opportunities for people who want to play the game, and the number of hockey leagues and associations has been growing steadily in recent years as the sport has become more and more popular.

Youth and Adult Leagues in Canada and the U.S.

You can find hundreds of leagues in North America that offer organized competition for players of all ages. Most leagues run from late fall to early spring, though some leagues operate all year round. Wherever they may be and however they are organized, hockey leagues are fun and a great way for people to enjoy the game.

What to look for

The important thing in finding the right league is determining what caliber of play is best suited for you and/or your children, for there are leagues designed to accommodate a wide range of aspirations and abilities. According to Darryl Seibel, media and public relations director for USA Hockey, the sport's national governing body, there are two primary types of leagues:

- Recreational (or house) leagues
- Competitive (or travel) leagues

"The recreational leagues usually play all their games in the same arena, hence the nickname 'house,'" Seibel explains. "They are less serious and not as advanced skill-wise as the travel leagues, in which each team represents a city or region and plays half of its games in out-of-town rinks." Within those two categories, there are several subsets. Some leagues don't allow checking of any kind while others encourage it. "Take a look at what's available in your area and see how they fit your wants and needs as a player, or those of your children," Seibel says. "Don't get involved in a competitive checking league, for example, if you're just looking for a non-contact recreational game. The idea is to find what works best for you and your level of talent."

How to join

There are a couple of ways to join a good league. One way is simply to contact the local ice rink and see what league, or leagues, operate out of that facility. The other way is to call USA Hockey if you are in the States (719-599-5500), or the Canadian Hockey Association if you are in Canada (403-777-3636). Both those groups are clearinghouses for information on amateur hockey and can not only tell you how to find different leagues all over North America but also advise you on which ones might best meet your needs and those of your children. (See Appendix B for more information on these — and other — organizations.)

Leagues in Other Parts of the World

As we mention in Chapter 5, hockey is played in over 50 countries, and each one of those has some sort of amateur association that promotes youth and/or adult hockey. The best way to find out what different nations have to offer outside North America is to call the International Ice Hockey Federation, which is based in Zurich, Switzerland, at 41-1-289-8600. The IIHF has a wealth of information on the game as it is played everywhere from Finland and Spain to South Africa and Japan and knows how to contact any of the different international leagues (see Chapter 5 for more info on the IIHF, and visit their Web site at www.iihf.com).

Hockey Camps and Schools in Canada and the U.S.

It has been a time-honored tradition in parts of Canada and the United States for youngsters to head off to hockey camp or school at the start of their summer vacation and work on their games for a few weeks, many times with coaches and players from the NHL. And as the sport has grown in popularity, so have the number of camps and schools that cater to boys and girls. The best way to get information on those camps and schools is to check out the annual Summer Hockey School Guide that *The Hockey News* puts out each spring. It is chock-full of school and camp listings for North America and includes details on each one, such as age groups attending, hours spent on the ice, sleeping accommodations, specialized programs and entertainment facilities.

Other good sources are USA Hockey and the Canadian Hockey Association, which also have comprehensive directories of hockey schools and camps, and your local ice rink.

Camps and Schools in Other Parts of the World

There is no shortages of camps and schools in other parts of the world, especially in northern Europe, and players can find plenty of opportunities abroad. The two best sources for these are *The Hockey News* annual directory and the International Ice Hockey Federation.

Pond Hockey

For those who grew up in ice hockey country — and we both did — there is nothing quite like playing the sport on a frozen neighborhood pond or lake. The air is cold and clear, the ice hard and fast, the pickup games spirited and fun. We remember shoveling snow off the ice after evening blizzards, looking for pucks that had been inadvertently shot into the woods around the pond, and building our own goalie nets out of two-by-fours and chicken wire. We loved the sounds our skates made as we cut across the ice, and the joy of passing a puck back and forth with a best friend as we scampered up and down the pond. We recall spending the better part of a winter weekend on the ice, of getting so cold some days that we couldn't feel the freezing wind against our faces anymore and had trouble untying our skates when the sun went down. And who can forget walking back into the warmth of our parents' homes later on and thawing out in front of the fireplace with a mug of hot chocolate?

Knowing when the ice is good — and keeping it that way

Oftentimes, the best ice of the year is the first ice, which comes to Canada and the northern U.S. in late fall and hasn't been marred by snow. It is clear and smooth, so much so that in most bodies of water you can see right through to the bottom. This is known as black ice, and it's as good as anything you'll find in a rink. Actually, it's better.

Black ice lasts only for the early stages of the outdoor hockey season, however, and after a while the skating surface gets whiter, thicker, and in most cases rougher. We never had Zambonis to resurface our ponds and lakes, but many times we tried the next best thing, and that was either hauling buckets of water out to the ponds, which we would pour down on the ice at the end of the day, or running a hose out there. The idea was to use the water to clean off the excess snow from all the skating and put a new layer of water on the surface, which would freeze by morning and make our makeshift rink good as new.

One note of caution about pond hockey: Always make sure that the ice is safe before you skate on it. The best way for youngsters to do that is have a parent come down and take a look at the place where they want to play, or better yet, a local policeman or fireman. If you aren't sure about its thickness, then wait. You can never be too careful when it comes to ice strength.

Holding your own in pickup games

There is something special about pickup hockey, and it provides the same sort of innocent fun as touch football or sandlot baseball. You go down to the pond, see who shows up, pick up sides, and drop the puck. Usually, there are no forwards, no defensemen, and no goalies — just people playing together and having a good time. It doesn't take much to hold your own in games like those; just skate hard and do the best you can. If you get tired, you can slack off a bit and play defense or goalie. And when you get your second wind, you can glide back down ice and battle for the puck in front of your opponents' goal. The beauty of the game as it is played with that attitude is there is no pressure to perform.

All anyone should care about is having fun. And skating around a pond with a bunch of friends in the middle of winter is good fun.

Pond-hockey etiquette

These are the essential rules for pond hockey:

✔ No lifting

✔ No checking

✔ No slap shots

✔ No fighting

Lifting the puck is prohibited strictly as a safety measure because typical pond hockey attire doesn't include mouth guards, shin guards, thigh pads, shoulder pads, or cups. And since everybody takes a turn at playing goalie whenever the other team skates into the offensive zone, the net minder is without proper protection as well.

Checking is frowned upon for much the same reason, though it is also banned because the ages and sizes of players in a pond hockey game can vary greatly, and no one wants to see a chiseled 18-year-old beat up on a middle-aged skater. Or vice versa.

Slap shots are not allowed because of the danger that their speed presents, and fighting is strictly taboo, though there are still times when we drop our gloves, as players in the NHL often do, and wrestle each other to the ice, trying to pull jerseys over each others' heads and throwing mock punches.

Pond hockey has certainly been around for a long time and will be around for years to come (see Figure 14–1).

Figure 14-1:
An early
game of
pond hocky
at McGill
University
in Montreal.

Chapter 15

What to Do If You Don't Have Any Ice

In This Chapter

▶ In-line skating

▶ Playing in-line and street hockey

*I*ce is nice, but you can still skate and play hockey without it. Back when we were kids, we shot plastic pucks at nets in the driveway and used tennis balls in the five-on-five games we played on our lawns. But today, we can do so much more off the ice, thanks to the development of "in-line" skates, which allow us to glide across paved surfaces such as driveways and parking lots as easily as hockey players streak down a stretch of ice. In fact, in-line skating and hockey have exploded in recent years and are now two of the fastest-growing sports in North America. In-line hockey leagues have sprouted up all over the world, and old-time street hockey, still being played in sneakers, has also never been bigger.

The development in in-line skates has made it possible for people in the Snow Belt to enjoy skating and hockey all year round and allowed those who live in more temperate climes to play, watch, and experience different versions of the game that may not be exactly what is found in an NHL arena, but still are pretty close. And it has also helped build hockey's popularity, both as a spectator and participatory sport, even further.

In-line Skating

Originally designed as a form of cross-training for ice hockey players, in-line skating now provides exercise, recreation, and transportation for millions.

The lowdown on in-line skates

In-line skates differ from the old roller skates in that they utilize four wheels in a straight line while the roller skates employ two wheels in front and two in back (see Figure 15-1). Basically, the boot used in the in-line skate is very similar to the one on an ice hockey skate, with thick padding on the ankles, strong support in the front, and a good heel cup to keep the feet in place. Their exterior is made of leather and nylon, and the inside is generally comprised of a synthetic leather known as *clarino*. Models that are designed mostly for outdoor use have hard plastic toes for protection.

As for price, in-line skates start at $150 and run as high as $500. The major variable in price has to do with the type of track, or *chassis,* that is used to hold the wheels. The less expensive ones are made of plastic or nylon, and those that cost more are comprised of aluminum. Different sizes of wheels are employed, with the outside diameter ranging from 56 millimeters to 80 millimeters. The smaller wheels allow skaters to turn more quickly while the larger wheels let them go faster. Manufacturers include traditional ice skate makers CCM and Bauer, as well as Nike, which has gotten into both the ice hockey and in-line hockey games in a big way.

Figure 15-1:
A typical
in-line
skate.

In-line skating equipment

Aside from their footgear, in-line skaters generally wear a sort of bicycle helmet, wrist guards, elbow pads, and knee pads. The best place to get all this gear is from the pro shop at your local ice rink or a sporting goods store that specializes in hockey equipment.

In-line Hockey and Street Hockey

In-line hockey is just what you would expect it to be: hockey played on in-line skates. *Street hockey,* on the other hand, is played on foot, using sneakers instead of skates. We often hear of roller hockey, and that's usually just another way of describing in-line skating. (Part of that confusion comes from the fact that the first brand of in-line skates to make any sort of splash were known as "Rollerblades.") But roller hockey can also refer to a sport played with the old quad roller skates, which have two wheels in front and two in back. That sport, however, represents only a small percentage of the off-ice hockey universe, so for the purposes of this section, we cover only the in-line and street hockey versions of the game.

Where and how it is played

Both in-line and street hockey are played all over the world. There are several hundred youth and adult in-line leagues in the U.S. and Canada alone, and a similar number overseas. There are professional leagues, national amateur events, summer in-line hockey camps and an annual world championship. The sport got so big in America, for example, that in 1994 USA Hockey started a special organization, USA Hockey InLine, whose mission is to promote the growth of the game and administer the sport as it is played in this country. And three years later it boasted 85,000 members. (Check out the Web site of USA Hockey InLine at `www.usahockey.com/inline`, as shown in Figure 15-2.)

"The focus on in-line hockey right now is more recreational than competitive," says USA Hockey spokesman Darryl Seibel. "It has been enjoying a tremendous amount of growth, and in many ways answers the biggest challenge we have as hockey's national governing body, and that is access to facilities. The game has grown so quickly that people sometimes have trouble finding ice time. So in-line hockey is a terrific alternative. There is no dependence on an ice rink to play, or on cold weather."

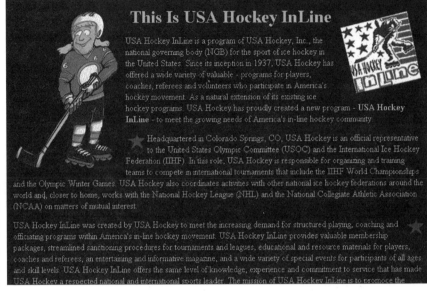

Speaking of rinks, in-line and street hockey can be played in any number of locales. Parking lots are popular venues as are driveways or the concrete floors of ice rinks that haven't been flooded and frozen. That's one of the beauties of those sports: they don't require very fancy or extensive facilities.

What is needed for equipment

Obviously, the key component for in-line hockey is a pair of skates. Helmets are also essential, and if you are playing in a youth league, you will also need a cage to protect your face. Shin guards are worn, and so are elbow pads and gloves. Those items are all similar to the equipment that ice hockey players wear, though they are generally lighter and better ventilated (because in-line hockey is often played in warmer weather, and there's a greater need for the equipment to breathe).

People playing at a higher level of the sport will don additional gear, including a sort of girdle with pads for the thighs, hips, and tailbone as well as an athletic supporter and cup and shoulder pads. Their hockey pants, which will fit over their shin guards like sweat pants, generally have a special material called *cordura* over the knees to prevent skidding. The sticks feature hard plastic blades, and some of the hard plastic pucks that are used for in-line hockey have nylon pegs on each side to help them slide more easily on rink surfaces.

The gear needed for street hockey is not much different, the two primary exceptions being that sneakers are used instead of skates and hard plastic balls rather than pucks. Additionally, street hockey players don't usually wear shoulder pads and some of the other gear such as girdles.

As for prices, the people at Gerry Cosby's in New York say that helmets for kids run about $55, gloves $45, shin and elbow pads $40, and sticks $15. If a person starts playing competitively, he or she will need to spend more money on higher-quality gear and will have to buy things such as girdles ($50–$90), pants ($40–$60), and an athletic supporter and cup ($11).

Competition gloves for adults can run from $130 to $140, and shin and elbow pads can go as high as $60. Total cost to outfit a competitive in-line hockey player (forward or defenseman) is about $400 to $500, while a goalie may go as high as $1,000.

The rules

Well, the rules for in-line hockey and street hockey are more or less the same as ice hockey — with one major exception: there is *no* checking.

The Swoosh makes its mark

Nike has very quickly become a major player in the on- and off-ice hockey world. In addition to signing up star NHL players such as Detroit Red Wings forward Sergei Fedorov as spokesmen, manufacturing skates with its own logo for both ice and in-line hockey, developing an athletic shoe specifically for street hockey, and buying up equipment makers such as Canstar (which produced Bauer skates and Cooper protective gear), the Oregon-based company has begun cosponsoring a youth street hockey program with the NHL that allows more than 250,000 boys and girls ages 6-16 to play street hockey at more than 1,000 program centers across North America — at no cost. Organized at the league level, NHL franchises invite schools, communities, and park and recreation centers to receive a turnkey, comprehensive street hockey curriculum, which includes distribution of quality NHL-licensed street hockey equipment, program training materials, manuals, premiums, and affiliations with their local NHL teams. In addition, participants receive instruction on the fundamentals of the game from NHL coaches and players. At the start of the 1997–98 NHL season, 22 team markets were involved in the program, including Calgary, Vancouver, Toronto, Los Angeles, Tampa Bay, Dallas, Phoenix, and New York. Nike is also involved with the league's popular Breakout program, a traveling off-ice hockey tournament and festival that stopped in 20 North American cities in 1997 and watched about 100 local teams compete in street and in-line hockey events. Look out, Michael Jordan. The NHL is hot.

Part V

The Part of Tens

The 5th Wave   By Rich Tennant

"In an astonishing discovery, the body of a 3½ million year old hockey player was found frozen beneath the ice of this hockey rink today. 'Hockey-Man', as the remains will be known as is being shipped to the NHL's Museum of Historical Artifacts."

In this part . . .

*J*ohn Davidson is a man of many opinions, and following
are his opinions on the greatest games ever played
and the best personalities the sport has known. But
that's not all. JD has also put together lists of his all-time
players and compiled a collection of tips for better
hockey. It's a revealing and exclusive look at the sport
from its number one broadcaster.

Chapter 16

The Ten Best Things about Hockey

. . . .

In This Chapter

▶ Speed, passion, fans

▶ Live action, neat players, women participating

▶ Cold-weather exercise, international appeal, fun for all

▶ It's getting big!

. . . .

There's so much to like about hockey, and as our friends at the NHL like to say, it is the coolest game. Here are ten reasons why.

Speed

Hockey is the fastest team sport on earth, and speed is what separates it from all others. Speed creates action. It creates hard hitting and scoring chances, and as a result it creates unbelievable excitement. Speed creates time and space, and it allows the greatest to be the greatest. And when we talk about speed, we are not just talking about how fast people skate. Speed relates to how players react to certain situations and how they think on the ice. Wayne Gretzky, for example, has never been anywhere near the fastest skater in the NHL, but he is one of the best at reading plays, at seeing them in his mind, at reacting quickly and making things happen, all in an instant. (See Figure 16-1.) It's about speed.

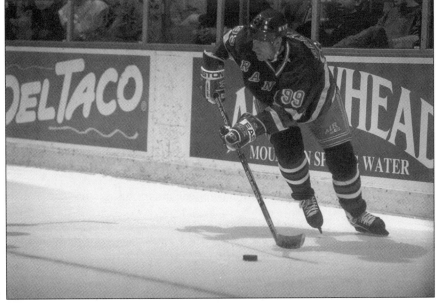

© NHL Images/Allsport/Elsa Masch

Passion

Hockey is also about passion. The players, the coaches, the fans, and even most of the news media who cover it on a regular basis have a deep-rooted passion for the game. *The Random House College Dictionary* defines passion as "any powerful or compelling emotion or feeling" and "a strong or extravagant fondness, enthusiasm or desire." It could also read "What one sees and feels during a well-played hockey game in a sold-out arena."

Check Out Some of Its Fans

What's not to love about a sport that includes Susan Sarandon, Goldie Hawn, Cheryl Tiegs, and Carol Alt among its devotees? And don't forget Michael J. Fox, Christopher Reeve, and Matthew Perry.

See It Live

Thanks to its combination of speed, finesse, hitting, and non-stop action, no game translates better for the fan in the stands than hockey. And if you don't believe us, consider what William Faulkner wrote in *Sports Illustrated* after going to his first game in 1955: "The vacant ice looked tired . . . then it filled with motion, speed. To the innocent, who had never seen it before, it seemed discorded and inconsequent, bizarre and paradoxical like the frantic darting of the weightless bugs which run on the surface of stagnant pools. Then it would break, coalesce through a kind of kaleidoscopic whirl like a child's toy, into a pattern, a design almost beautiful, as if an inspired chore-ographer had drilled a willing and patient and hard-working troupe of dancers."

Sounds like he had a good time.

Accommodating Players

Ask anybody who deals with professional athletes on a regular basis, and they'll tell you that hockey players are *the* best to be around. They're pleasant, friendly, and unlike some of their brethren in other sports, actually seem to like what they're doing and feel lucky to be making a good living at it. Hip-Hip-Hooray.

Women Watching and Playing Hockey

Check out the stands at any professional hockey game, and the split be-tween men and women is close to 50-50. Also, more and more women are playing at the high school, college, and professional levels. And at the 1998 Winter Olympics in Nagano, Japan, women's ice hockey will be a medal sport for the first time.

Check out the USA Hockey, Inc., home page on the Web at www.usahockey.com for links to hockey activities for women of all ages. (See Figure 16-2.) USA Hockey is the national governing body for ice hockey in the U.S.

A STORIED PAST PROVIDES THE FOUNDATION FOR A BRIGHT FUTURE IN WOMEN'S ICE HOCKEY

Most people are surprised to learn that women's ice hockey has a history that dates back to 1892, when the very first organized and recorded all-female ice hockey game was played in Ontario, Canada. Over the span of more than a century, girls and women have pursued their interest in the sport, and today that sector continues to be one of the fastest growing among USA Hockey membership registration. A look back at the last several years reveals greater changes and growth in ice hockey, with the best yet to come for women and girls involved in the sport.

Great Way to Exercise Up North during the Winter

It may not be a problem for hockey fans living below the Mason-Dixon line, but for folks up north, hockey gives them one of their best chances to exercise outside in the winter months and get some fresh air. In addition, there's something special about heading down to the neighborhood pond on a Saturday morning with your skates slung over your stick and cruising around the ice with your friends as you all wait for enough players to show up for a pickup game. Norman Rockwell couldn't paint a better north country scene.

It's an International Game

Like other great sports, hockey is played all over the world. To be sure, Canada and the United States are still the top two, but consider some of the other countries that boast pro leagues and/or strong amateur programs: Russia, Finland, Sweden, Norway, Germany, Lithuania, Japan, Switzerland, Australia, South Africa, England, Scotland, Spain, Slovakia, the Czech Republic, Italy, Austria, and the Netherlands. The game has universal appeal and brings people of all nationalities together.

Fun for Everyone

Hockey has leagues for all ages and levels of talent. From the eight-year-old traveling teams to old-timer divisions (where JD competes these days), from girls' leagues to squads for young men, people can learn to play the game and keep on enjoying it for years to come. Even if there's no ice around, the game can still be played; witness the huge growth in street hockey throughout the U.S.

The Game Is Growing Big-Time

Even bigger than our waistlines. What once was primarily a snow-belt phenomenon and a big hit across the frozen Canadian prairies is now played and watched throughout the U.S. And perhaps the strongest evidence is that there are more professional hockey teams in Texas than any other state in the union. And not all kids want to be Michael Jordan or Troy Aikman when they grow up, anymore. More and more of them would rather be Wayne Gretzky, Mario Lemieux, or Brian Leetch.

Chapter 17

The Ten Best Players: NHL and International

In This Chapter

▶ The best NHL players

▶ The best international players

The Best in the NHL

The NHL has had some terrific players over the years, but none better than the fellows we have listed in this chapter. We tried to limit our roll to the top ten, but we couldn't quite pare it down. So we give you, faithful reader, eleven, beginning with the greatest of them all and working our way down from there.

Wayne Gretzky — Edmonton Oilers, Los Angeles Kings, St. Louis Blues, New York Rangers

Many regard Gretzky as the best of all time. He is not big (6 feet, 185 pounds.), not fast, and not particularly strong, but no one has ever been smarter (see Figure 17-1). He has an uncanny ability to think faster and react quicker than anyone else. He was 18 years old when he made his NHL debut, scoring 51 goals in 79 games and winning the MVP trophy. He also played in the All-Star Game that year and captured the Lady Byng Trophy for sportsmanship and clean play. Not a bad start, and Gretzky hasn't slowed down much since then. At the end of the 1997 season, he owned or shared more than 60 NHL records, had won the MVP trophy nine times, had collected ten scoring titles, and had received two play-off MVP awards. All told, Wayne has scored more than 2,700 points in his career, far more than anybody else. Truly, he is the Great One.

Figure 17-1:
Gretzky: not big, fast, or strong — but great.

© NHL Images/Bruce Bennett

Mario Lemieux — Pittsburgh Penguins

Lemieux, a big, rangy center, burst upon the NHL scene in 1985 and wasted no time in making a name for himself. He scored 43 goals and recorded 57 assists that season on his way to being named Rookie of the Year. In 1988, he won the first of three MVP trophies and the first of five scoring titles while being named to the NHL's starting All-Star team. Mario made hockey a big hit in Pittsburgh and helped the Penguins win two Stanley Cups. He controlled the pace of play better than anyone in the game, shooting and passing the puck with tremendous skill and grace. Scotty Bowman, the only coach to record more than 1,000 wins in NHL history, says Mario was the best player he ever had. Robbed of a full career due to back injuries and a heroic bout with Hodgkin's disease, he retired after the 1996–97 season.

Bobby Orr — Boston Bruins, Chicago Blackhawks

Bobby Orr was one of the smoothest skaters and puck handlers of all time and arguably the best defenseman to ever play the game. His end-to-end rushes were a thing of beauty. He won the Norris Trophy for best defensemen in the NHL eight straight years. Boston won two Stanley Cups while he was there. Orr had terrible knees and was able to play only eight full seasons, but he still managed to score 270 goals and 645 assists and capture the league scoring title twice, in 1970 and 1975. He also won the Rookie of the Year award in 1967, the regular season MVP award in 1970, 1971, and 1972, and most valuable player for the play-offs in 1970 and 1972. A fan favorite and great drawing card during his peak years, Orr saw his game drop off noticeably by the time he joined the Blackhawks in 1976, and he retired three years later. Shortly afterwards, he was voted into the Hall of Fame. (See Figure 17-2.)

Figure 17-2:
Bobby Orr
in action at
Madison
Square
Garden.

Gordie Howe — Detroit Red Wings, Hartford Whalers

What more can you say about the man known as Mr. Hockey? A big (6 feet 1 inch, 200 pounds) right winger who joined the NHL in 1946 and went on to play 26 seasons in the league, Howe won the league's MVP trophy six times and scored 1,846 points in his career. Only Gretzky has more. A tough guy as well, Gordie did not put up with a lot of foolishness on the ice and amassed a total of 1,675 penalty minutes. He was the original intimidator. His career nearly ended in 1950 when as a 22-year-old he suffered a skull fracture. But he bounced back to win the scoring title the next year. Initially retired in 1971, he staged a comeback two years later and began playing with the Houston Aeros of the World Hockey Association at age 45. Along with his sons Marty and Mark, Gordie played for the Whalers when that franchise joined the NHL in 1979, and he finally stepped down the following year when he was 51. (See Figure 17-3.)

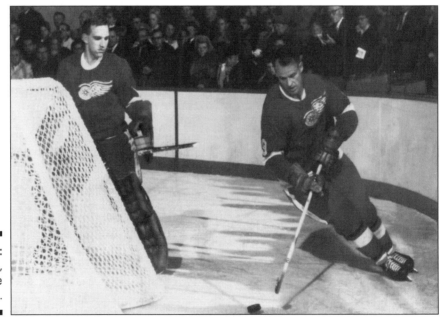

Figure 17-3: Mr. Hockey, Gordie Howe.

Mark Messier — Edmonton Oilers, New York Rangers, Vancouver Canucks

One of the greatest leaders in the history of the sport, he helped the Rangers capture their first Stanley Cup in 54 years in 1994. Messier believes that a combination of speed and toughness is critical for a great team, and he possesses both himself. He has won two MVP trophies for his regular season play and one for the 1984 play-offs. Messier stood fifth on the list of all-time NHL point scorers at the start of the 1996–97 season, behind Gretzky, Howe, Marcel Dionne, and Phil Esposito. In addition, he has played in 12 All-Star Games and on six Stanley Cup champions. A winner, pure and simple, and a great clutch player. The late Bob Johnson, who coached at Calgary and Pittsburgh in the NHL after a distinguished career at the University of Wisconsin, once said that Messier was to hockey what Jim Brown was to football.

Maurice Richard — Montreal Canadiens

The right winger known as the Rocket was the first player in NHL history to score 50 goals in 50 games. All told, he put the puck in the net 544 times over his 18-year career and recorded 421 assists. Richard became known as one of the best big-game scorers of all time, and his teams won eight Stanley Cups. Fast and strong, he had a deadly shot and was famous for the intense look he used to get in his eyes as he played. The Rocket was a first-team All-Star eight times and made second team on six occasions. He won the MVP award in 1947 and entered the Hall of Fame in 1961.

Doug Harvey — Montreal Canadians, New York Rangers, Detroit Red Wings, St. Louis Blues

Harvey played his first NHL game in 1946 and for 20 seasons set the standard for NHL defensemen. Many observers think he was the best ever to play that position, even after Bobby Orr came onto the scene in the late 1960s. He won seven Norris Trophies, given to the top defenseman in the league each year, and played on six Cup-winning teams. Named first-team All-Star ten years in a row. A deft skater and passer, Harvey was also a hard-hitting defender and played both ways as well as anybody. He was elected to the Hall of Fame in 1973. (See Figure 17-4.)

Figure 17-4:
The great
defenseman
Harvey.

Eddie Shore — Boston Bruins, New York Americans

The NHL's first superstar, defenseman Eddie Shore, aka "the Edmonton Express," is credited with putting the professional game on the map in America. He joined the Boston Bruins in 1926 and played in the league for 14 years, winning the regular season MVP trophy four times. A great skater, Shore became the first defenseman in the league to carry the puck up ice with regularity, and teams often based their entire game plans on how to stop him. Shore helped Boston win two Stanley Cups and is regarded as one of the toughest men to ever play. He once took the laces out of his skates and whirled his way around the ice, tap dancing and skating backwards with his ankles his only real form of support. He also played nearly an entire game in Montreal one night during the 1928–29 season, sitting down only to serve a two-minute penalty. Otherwise, he never left the ice. And he scored the game's only goal.

Jean Beliveau — Montreal Canadiens

Beliveau (shown in Figure 17-5) was a tall, graceful center who played 20 seasons in the NHL, all for the Habs. He looked and acted like royalty on ice. He won two Hart Trophies (Most Valuable Player during the regular season), was a first-team All-Star six times, and played on a remarkable ten Stanley Cup Championship teams. In 1956 he captured the NHL scoring title, and nine years later he received the Conn Smythe Trophy as the most valuable player in the play-offs. The team captain for much of his time in Montreal, Beliveau remains one of Canada's most popular athletes ever.

Glenn Hall — Detroit Red Wings, Chicago Blackhawks, St. Louis Blues

Glenn Hall was a stellar netminder known to this day as "Mr. Goalie." He played 18 years in the NHL, amassing 407 wins, 84 shutouts, and a lifetime goals-against average of 2.51. Though he competed on only one Stanley Cup team, Hall distinguished himself in many other ways. He was named to the All-Star squad 11 times, won the rookie-of-the-year award in 1956, took home the Vezina Trophy for being the season's best goaltender three times, and was elected to the NHL Hall of Fame in 1975. Famous for his acrobatic goaltending style and durability, Hall once played in 552 straight games. And he didn't wear a mask for any of them.

Terry Sawchuk — Detroit Red Wings, Boston Bruins, Toronto Maple Leafs, Los Angeles Kings, New York Rangers

Sawchuk played 21 years in front of the goal in the NHL, recording a remarkable 103 shutouts and retiring in 1970 with a career 2.52 goals-against average. (See Figure 17-6.) He played on four Stanley Cup winners and won Rookie of the Year honors in 1951 and the Vezina Trophy for best goaltender in 1952, 1953, and 1955. Emile Francis, the former coach and general manager of the New York Rangers and a one-time goaltender himself, has described Sawchuk as the greatest netminder of all time. Unfortunately, his career was plagued with injuries and ailments, and he died in the spring of 1970 from a pulmonary embolism shortly after playing his last game.

Figure 17-6:
Sawchuk
pursuing a
loose puck.

The Best International Players

Hockey truly is an international sport, and many of the game's greatest players have come from faraway lands. In recognition of that, we have put together a compendium of the best international players we've ever seen. Some made it to the NHL, and others didn't. But they all possessed remarkable talent.

Sergei Fedorov

Born in the former Soviet Union, he began playing for the Detroit Red Wings in 1990. Originally a high-scoring forward who recorded more than 200 goals his first six seasons in the league, he started playing defense in 1997 and has handled that transition so well that pundits are predicting he'll one day win the Norris Trophy, which is awarded to the NHL's top defenseman. Fedorov has already won the league's MVP award (1994), has twice been honored as its best defensive forward (1994 and 1996), and is a four-time All-Star. (See Figure 17-7.)

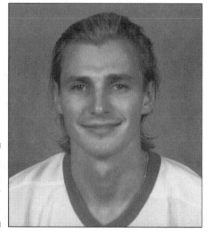

Figure 17-7: Fedorov is known for his defense.

Viacheslav Fetisov

A Moscow native, Fetisov is recognized as one of the best Russian players of all time. He played 13 years for the Central Red Army Team and then came to the New Jersey Devils at the start of the 1989–90 season, becoming one of the first athletes the former Soviet Union leadership allowed to compete in the NHL. A defenseman, he captained the formidable Red Army team, won the coveted Gold Stick Award as Europe's top player three times, was thrice

Soviet Player of the Year, and took home two Olympic gold medals and one silver over his career. He has already been inducted into Russia's Hockey Hall of Fame. In his prime, he was a top offensive and defensive player who knew how to throw a check. He spent six seasons with the Devils before moving to Detroit. (See Figure 17-8.)

Figure 17-8: Festiov is an internationally recognized superstar.

Peter Forsberg

Just three years into his NHL career, the young Swedish center already had people around the league anointing him the NHL's next great best player. A member of the Colorado Avalanche (formerly the Quebec Nordiques), Forsberg won the Rookie of the Year award in 1995. A year earlier, he helped his home country win the hockey gold medal at Lillehammer by scoring the game-winning goal in a shoot-out. Sweden honored him by putting his likeness on a stamp. A brilliant player at both ends of the ice, he has that rare combination of power and finesse — and can bull his way around the ice with the puck.

Dominik Hasek

Known as the Dominator for his stellar goaltending, Hasek was Czech goalie of the year from 1986–1990 and Czech player of the year from 1988–1990. He started off with Chicago in the NHL and then went to Buffalo. He became the first European-trained netminder to lead the league in goals-against average. He has won the Vezina Trophy twice (1994 and 1995) and captured the league MVP award in 1997 — a first for a goalie. In April 1994, his Sabres beat New Jersey 1-0 in a four-overtime game that went on past midnight. At 10 a.m. the next day, the man who had recorded the shutout was back on the ice practicing. The James Brown of the NHL. (See Figure 17-9.)

Figure 17-9:
Hasek
makes
another
save.

Valeri Kharlamov

Valeri Kharlamov was a forward with the Red Army team who flourished in the 1970s (see Figure 17-10). He possessed a rare combination of raw speed and exceptional control and had an amazingly high skill level. Kharlamov came in on JD during an exhibition game in the late 1970s and snapped off a wrist shot so smooth and fast that the fearless author didn't even know the Russian had fired the puck — let alone scored. He never played in the U.S. and died much too young a man in an automobile accident.

Figure 17-10:
Kharlamov
was a rare
talent.

Jari Kurri

This Finnish right winger (shown in Figure 17-11) was part of the great Edmonton Oiler teams of the 1980s. He has also played for the New York Rangers, Los Angeles Kings, and Anaheim Mighty Ducks. Kurri was the first European to lead the NHL in goals scored (68 in 1985–86) and has put more than 600 pucks in the net over his career. He is a seven-time All-Star, and many consider him to be one of the finest defensive wingers in the history of the game.

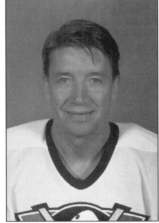

Figure 17-11:
Kurri made his presence felt around the NHL.

Jaromir Jagr

The super-strong forward from the Czech Republic has shone as Mario Lemieux's linemate on the Pittsburgh Penguins. Jagr, shown in Figure 17-12, led the league in scoring in 1994–95. His goal total after six NHL seasons exceeded 200. He is a very dedicated, powerful winger who is brilliant at keeping his body between the puck and the defenseman. Moving him is like trying to uproot a redwood. As a kid, he put car tires on either end of an iron bar and used that for weightlifting. He did thousands of squats to build his legs, which is one reason he's so strong.

Borje Salming

The Hall of Fame defenseman from Sweden played 17 years in Toronto and Detroit, retiring after the 1989–90 season. Salming was the first Swedish player to play regularly in the NHL, paving the way for several of his countrymen. He was smart, competitive, and a great shot-blocker. He rang up almost 800 points in his career and more than 1,300 penalty minutes. The Toronto fans loved him.

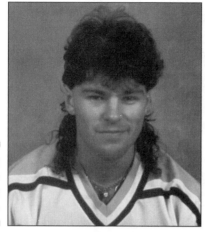

Peter Stastny

Peter Stastny defected from what was then Czechoslovakia in 1980 and then started playing in the NHL, first with the Quebec Nordiques (see Figure 17-13) and later with the New Jersey Devils and St. Louis Blues. He was Player of the Year in his native land in 1979 and 1980. He scored 109 points his first year in the NHL and was named Rookie of the Year. A six-time All-Star, Stastny played with tremendous passion and energy, scoring 450 goals and 789 assists during his NHL career.

Vladislav Tretiak

Tretiak was one of the greatest goalies of all time, though he never played in the NHL. As a member of the famed Red Army team, he helped win 13 Soviet League Championships and ten World Championships. Tretiak was Soviet Player of the Year on five occasions and absolutely unbeatable at times. In 19 Olympic hockey games, he allowed only 33 goals, for a 1.74 goals-against average. He was the first Soviet player inducted into the Hockey Hall of Fame. As goalie coach for the Chicago Blackhawks, he tutored the superb Ed Belfour, who decided to wear Tretiak's old number, 20, when he was traded to San Jose during the 1996–97 season.

Figure 17-13:
Stastny in
his Quebec
days.

Chapter 18

The Ten Best Teams

- -

In This Chapter

▶ Ottawa Senators, Toronto Maple Leafs, Detroit Red Wings

▶ Montreal Canadiens, New York Islanders, Edmonton Oilers

▶ 1980 United States Olympic Hockey Team, Charlestown Chiefs

- -

There have been so many great teams through the years that we had a hard time picking out the top ten, especially when we began to look closely at some of the dynasties that have ruled in the NHL since its inception. How, for example, could we say that the 1956 Canadiens were better than the squad that played in 1957? Both won Stanley Cups. Both were coached by Toe Blake. Both had superstars Jean Beliveau, Maurice Richard, Bernie "Boom Boom" Geoffrion, and Doug Harvey. We came across the same problem with the great Islander teams of the early 1980s, which won four Cups in a row, and the Edmonton Oilers team that captured five titles in a seven-year period later that decade. So instead of selecting only individual teams, we decided to include dynasties as well. The list is done in chronological order, with some help from the NHL.

The Ottawa Senators — 1919–1927

The Senators finished first seven times during this stretch and won four Stanley Cups, thanks to the fine play of future Hall of Famers King Clancy, Punch Broadbent, Cy Denneny, and Alex Connell.

The Toronto Maple Leafs — 1947–1951

The Maple Leafs won four Cups in five years and had a dazzling playoff record of 35-11. Their top players included Syl Apps, Turk Broda, Ted Kennedy, and Al Rollins. Amazingly, the Leafs didn't finish first once in the regular season during this period. But they knew how to handle the big games.

The Detroit Red Wings — 1950–1955

Just as Toronto was peaking, a dynasty rose in Detroit, led by Gordie Howe, Sid Abel, tough guy Ted Lindsay, Red Kelly, Terry Sawchuk, and Alex Delvecchio. And they went on to capture four titles (1950, 1952, 1954, and 1955) in six campaigns while finishing first in the regular season each year.

The Montreal Canadiens — 1956–1960

Again, the mantel was passed from one powerhouse to another. Montreal dethroned Detroit in 1956 and won Lord Stanley's Cup five years in a row, losing only five play-off games during that stretch. Amazing when you first think about that streak, but then consider the future Hall of Famers who were on the team. And don't forget coach Toe Blake.

The Toronto Maple Leafs — 1962–1967

The Leafs came back in the mid-'60s to win four Cups in that six-year period. Punch Imlach coached a squad that boasted Johnny Bower, Terry Sawchuk, Allan Stanley, Red Kelly, Frank Mahovlich, and Tim Horton, all of whom ended up in the Hall of Fame.

The Montreal Canadiens — 1965–1969

The Habs were never down for very long, and they rivaled the Leafs for sheer domination of the hockey world in the 1960s. Montreal won the Cup in '65, '66, '68, and '69, and they came very close to making it five in a row again but fell to the Leafs in the 1967 Stanley Cup Finals, four games to two. Their playoff record during those years was 46-14.

The Montreal Canadiens — 1976–1979

Again, the Canadiens rose to the top, capturing four Stanley Cups in a row (including one particularly hard-fought series in 1979 against the New York Rangers, who were anchored by some goaltender named Davidson). Scotty

Bowman was the coach, and his roster featured goalie extraordinaire Ken Dryden (see Figure 18-1), Guy Lafleur, Jacques Lemaire, Mario Tremblay, Bob Gainey, and Yvan Cournoyer. The Canadiens had a stunning playoff record during those years of 48 wins to only 10 losses. They were practically unbeatable in the big games.

Figure 18-1:
Ken Dryden won the Vezina Trophy as the NHL's top goalie five times.

The New York Islanders — 1980–1984

The storied Montreal Canadiens seemed to disappear all of a sudden, and the new kids on the block took over. Once an expansion laughingstock, the Islanders became one of the greatest dynasties in NHL history, winning four straight Cups from 1980 through 1983. Al Arbour, the coach, and Bill Torrey, the general manager, put together an All-Star laden crew that included Mike Bossy, Bryan Trottier, Billy Smith, and Denis Potvin.

The Edmonton Oilers — 1984–1990

This team took over from the Islanders and reigned supreme for the next seven years, winning five Stanley Cups. Given their lineup, it's not surprising they did so well. Wayne Gretzky played for all but one of those teams, and other key Oilers included Mark Messier, Jari Kurri, Paul Coffey, Kevin Lowe, Jeff Beukeboom, Glen Anderson, and Esa Tikkanen.

The 1980 United States Olympic Hockey Team

They believed in miracles, and after a while they had us believing in them, too. Their victory over a far superior Soviet Union squad (on paper, at least) in the semifinal round at Lake Placid was of Biblical proportions, and their gold medal win over Finland added a great chapter to an improbable story. Herb Brooks never matched these heroics as a coach on the professional level, but he was masterful here, and so were such players as Mark Pavelich, Mark Johnson, Mike Eruzione, Ken Morrow, and Jim Craig. Forget about hockey, this was one of the great teams in the history of sports. Listen closely and you can still hear the Olympic arena echoing with the chants, "USA! USA! USA!"

Honorable Mention — The Charlestown Chiefs

No list of epic franchises would be complete without the great minor league squad coached by the immortal Reggie Dunlop and manned by the incomparable Hanson Brothers in the George Roy Hill film *Slapshot*. Fabulous team, fabulous movie. "Old-time hockey, coach?" The best.

Chapter 19
The Ten Best Hitters

● ●

In This Chapter

▶ Baun, Beck, Boivin

▶ Ezinicki, Horton, Marchment

▶ Owchar, Plager, Potvin, Samuelsson

● ●

Checking is not allowed in the youth leagues, and you don't see a lot of it during pond hockey pick-up games. But it's a big part of the NHL, and some pros have built careers on their ability to take the body and take out the opposition. Here is our list of the ten players who were best at that, in alphabetical order.

Bobby Baun

Not a big guy (5 feet 9 inches, 180 pounds), but he was tough as iron, and fearless to boot. Baun was an open-ice checker who liked to cut low to get his man. He played 17 seasons for Toronto, Oakland, and Detroit, retiring after the 1972–73 campaign. He played on four Stanley Cup champion teams. He even played a game and a half during the 1964 Finals with a broken leg numbed by painkillers and didn't have it set until after the Leafs won the series. (See Figure 19-1.)

Barry Beck

Beck was a defenseman who was built like a linebacker (6 feet 3 inches, 215 pounds) and hit like one, too. He competed for ten years with Colorado, the New York Rangers, and Los Angeles. He liked to use his shoulders on his checks, but they couldn't take the punishment after a while, and Beck had to retire early. Sometimes reckless with his hitting, he would sometimes miss his man completely and go crashing into the boards — or into one of the team benches instead. (See Figure 19-2.)

Figure 19-1:
The man
who played
on a broken
leg: Bobby
Baun.

Figure 19-2:
Barry Beck
in action.

Leo Boivin

Another defenseman, Boivin played 1,150 games over 19 seasons for the Boston Bruins, Toronto Maple Leafs, Detroit Red Wings, Pittsburgh Penguins, and Minnesota North Stars, retiring in 1970. A hard hitter, he perfected the hip check. And he did it cleanly, amassing more than 100 penalty minutes in only 1 of his 19 seasons. (Figure 19-3 shows Boivin trying to keep Gordie Howe from scoring.)

Bill Ezinicki

Known as "Wild Bill," he broke in with the Toronto Maple Leafs in 1944 and was one of the first real hitters in the game. He played on three of the Leafs' Stanley Cup teams and then went to Boston and New York before retiring from hockey in 1955.

Figure 19-3:
Leo Boivin harasses Gordie Howe.

Tim Horton

Horton played 24 years in the NHL and was part of four Stanley Cup champions. Strength and power were the keys to his game. Horton wasn't very big (5 feet 10 inches, 180 pounds), but he could hit as hard as anyone, and for that reason he commanded a lot of respect. Emile "The Cat" Francis remembers watching Horton stop the powerfully-built Bobby Hull in his tracks by simply sticking out his arm as he streaked down his wing in a game one night. A six-time All-Star, Horton scored 115 goals and recorded 403 assists in his years with the Toronto Maple Leafs, New York Rangers, Buffalo Sabres, and Pittsburgh Penguins. He also spent 1,611 minutes in the penalty box. Tragically, he died in a car accident in the winter of 1974 when he was with the Sabres. He was 44 years old.

Bryan Marchment

Marchment is a sturdy defenseman who has played for the Winnipeg Jets, Chicago Blackhawks, Hartford Whalers, and Edmonton Oilers. He is a head-on hitter who can loosen fillings with his checks. Some of his peers say he takes the occasional cheap shot, and they don't like him for that. He is not a big goal or assist man, but he can rack up the penalty minutes; he had 1,154 at the start of the 1996–97 season. And that was the beginning of only his sixth full season in the league. (See Figure 19-4.)

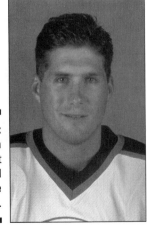

Figure 19-4:
Bryan
Marchment
can hand
out the
punishment.

Dennis Owchar

"Who?" you might ask, and we would understand if his name didn't ring a bell with even the most rabid hockey fan. Owchar played only six seasons in the NHL and scored a mere 30 goals. But he was an All-Star when it came to hitting. A defenseman who competed for Pittsburgh and Colorado in the 1970s, he used to explode at opposing players who came into his zone, knocking them down and sometimes knocking them out. They may not have known who Dennis Owchar was either when the game started. But after one of his checks, they had a very good idea of what he was all about. (See Figure 19-5.)

Figure 19-5: Dennis Owchar let his opponents know he was there.

Bob Plager

A former member of the St. Louis Blues and New York Rangers, Plager spent 14 seasons in the league and became well-known for laying hefty hip checks on his opponents. (See Figure 19-6.) A tough player, Plager wasn't afraid to drop his gloves, either. Perhaps his most famous fight was with his brother Barclay when the two of them faced off against each other in a Junior Hockey game. It started on the ice with sticks and ended up in the arena hallway with fists.

Figure 19-6:
Bob Plager
knew how
to take
out his
opponents.

Denis Potvin

Potvin was a longtime New York Islander captain and a brilliant defenseman who helped his team secure four consecutive Stanley Cup titles in the early 1980s. He put up more than 1,000 points in his career and over 1,300 penalty minutes. Tough checker. If you played against him and took just a second to admire your shot or pass, WHAM! And then you'd be picking yourself up off the ice. If you hadn't lost consciousness, that is. (See Figure 19-7.)

Ulf Samuelsson

Samuelsson (shown in Figure 19-8) is a controversial Swede who has played for the Hartford Whalers, Pittsburgh Penguins, and New York Rangers. He has never scored many goals (only 43 by the start of his 11th season), but he has piled up the penalty minutes (2,036). Like Marchment, Ulfie is a straight-ahead hitter who knows how to catch a player who's not paying attention.

Figure 19-7:
WHAM!
Denis
Potvin hit
you.

Figure 19-8:
"Ulfie"
Samuelsson
knows how
to hit.

Chapter 20

The Ten Best Games of All Time

In This Chapter

▶ Games, games, games

▶ More games

▶ And even more games

*T*here have been some classic contests over the years, hard-fought games that filled arenas with tension and energy and produced superior passing, shooting, hitting, and goaltending.

This chapter contains a list of our top ten games, which we have arranged chronologically. They were all so good that people still feel the excitement when they talk about them.

March 24, 1936

The Montreal Maroons faced off against the Detroit Red Wings in this semifinal play-off game that would become the longest played in NHL history. The teams battled to a 0–0 tie for an incredible 176 minutes and 30 seconds — nearly three hours — before Modere "Mud" Bruneteau of Detroit took a pass from Hec Kilrea in the sixth overtime period and scored. It was 2:25 a.m. when the red light finally went on.

The Wings ended up winning the series and then beat Toronto for the Stanley Cup. (Figure 20-1 shows Bruneteau in action.)

Figure 20-1:
"Mud"
Bruneteau
in the mid-
1940s.

May 2, 1967

Game Six of the Cup Finals pitted the Maple Leafs against the Canadiens at a time when both teams dominated the NHL. Montreal's Gump Worsley and Toronto's Terry Sawchuk were brilliant in goal, but the Leafs held on to win the game 3–1 — and the championship — sealing the victory with an empty-net goal in the final minute. Toronto hasn't won the Cup since, and it was the last game for the traditional six-team NHL as the league expanded to 12 franchises the following season. Recognizing this, Leafs coach Punch Imlach sent out his older players — Marcel Pronovost, Allan Stanley, George Armstrong, and Bob Pulford — so they could be on the ice as the final seconds of that era ticked away.

April 8, 1971

This was Game Two of the first round series between the powerhouse Boston Bruins, who had set an NHL record for wins that year with 57, and the Montreal Canadiens, who had finished 24 points behind. The Bruins had won the first game in the Boston Garden and were up 5–1 late in the second period of Game Two when Henri Richard made a nifty move around Bobby Orr and scored to make it 5–2. The Habs suddenly caught fire and ended up winning that contest 7–5 and then upsetting the Bruins in a dramatic seventh game. Their ace in the hole was a rookie goaltender named Ken Dryden, who had played in only a handful of regular season games. Buoyed by that win, the Canadiens went on to take the Cup.

December 31, 1975

The Canadiens battled the Central Red Army team in a tense exhibition contest that ended in a 3–3 tie. Many consider it to be the greatest game ever played. Ken Dryden was spectacular in net, turning away 13 shots; Vladislav Tretiak (shown in Figure 20-2) was even better for the Soviets, making 39 saves. Many say they had never seen so much emotion in the old Montreal Forum. When Steve Shutt (Figure 20-3) scored a goal, his agent Alan Eagleson got so excited that he hustled down from the stands and hugged him on the bench.

Figure 20-2:
Central Red Army goalie Vladislav Tretiak.

Figure 20-3:
Steve Shutt
of the
Canadiens.

February 22, 1980

The Miracle on Ice, when the U.S. Olympic Team stunned the Soviet Union, and the rest of the sporting world, with their improbable 4–3 upset. Coach Herb Brooks had told his charges before the game, "You were meant to be here. This moment is yours," and they played as if they actually believed him, forcing Tretiak out of the game after one period and going on to win on a Mike Eruzione goal in the third period.

February 27, 1994

The Canadian and Swedish Olympic teams met in the gold medal game at Lillehammer and battled to a tie at the end of regulation in a gritty contest. Then came the shoot-out. Canada's goaltender Corey Hirsch (shown in Figure 20-4) sat on his bench and looked away as his teammates took their penalty shots on Sweden's netminder Tommy Salo. Both men played valiantly, but the Swedes prevailed when Peter Forsberg (Figure 20-5) put the puck past Hirsch. The win meant so much to Sweden that a group of ten Air Force fighters met the team's plane as it entered that country's airspace and escorted it home.

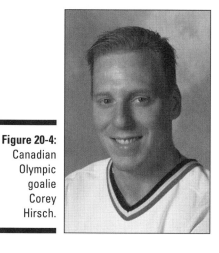

Figure 20-4:
Canadian
Olympic
goalie
Corey
Hirsch.

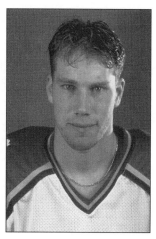

Figure 20-5:
Swedish
Olympic
forward
Peter
Forsberg.

May 25, 1994

The Rangers, facing elimination in their Eastern Conference Finals match-up with the New Jersey Devils, skated into the Meadowlands Arena that night down three games to two. Captain Mark Messier had guaranteed victory the day before in practice, but he didn't seem like much of a seer when his Rangers fell behind 2–0 after one period. The Blueshirts closed the gap to 2–1 after the second, and then Messier took over, scoring a hat trick in the final period to deliver a 4–2 win. His final goal was short-handed and came with less than two minutes left. "No one man wins a hockey game," he said in the locker room afterwards. Maybe not. But he had come close.

April 24, 1996

The Pittsburgh Penguins and Washington Capitals met in Game Four of the Conference Quarterfinals in Landover, Maryland. The score was tied 2–2 after regulation, and the teams headed into overtime. In the second frame, Penguins defenseman Chris Tamer knocked his own net off its moorings during a wild scramble in front of the crease, and a penalty shot was called, the first time in Stanley Cup history that that had happened in overtime. Joe Juneau took the shot but was stopped by Pittsburgh's Ken Wregget. The Pens went on to win in overtime period number four on a Peter Nedved goal after almost 140 minutes of hockey. (Nedved is pictured in Figure 20-6.)

Figure 20-6:
Peter
Nedved in a
more
relaxed
setting.

September 7, 1996

Canada and Sweden met in Philadelphia in the semifinal round of the 1996 World Cup. The game had everything: hard hitting, great passing and playmaking, fine goaltending. Sweden was the better team, but Canada's grit won it. Up 2–0 after two periods even though they were outshot 26–14, Canada let Sweden tie it up in the third. But Theo Fleury (shown in Figure 20-7) put the puck in the net 12 seconds from the end of the second overtime period, and Canada went on to the finals.

Figure 20-7:
Canadian
World Cup
participant
Theo Fleury.

September 12, 1996

Days later, Team USA wins the third and final game of its play-off for the World Cup against Canada at the Montreal Forum. This game had hard hitting throughout, great end-to-end action, and was closer than the score of 5 to 2 might indicate; the U.S. scored two empty-net goals at the end. Mike Richter played brilliantly, recording 37 saves, while John LeClair had two goals. It was the biggest international win for the United States since the 1980 Olympic Team's gold at Lake Placid. Afterward, veteran referee Kerry Fraser and linesmen Gord Broseker and Ray Scapinello said it was the best game any of them had ever been a part of.

Chapter 21

The Ten Best Hockey Personalities

In This Chapter

▶ Cherry, Esposito, Ferguson

▶ Fotiu, "Boom Boom" Geoffrion, Hull

▶ McVie, Storey, "Tiger" Williams, "Gump" Worsley

*L*ike any sport, hockey has more than it share of personalities. Some do and say outrageously funny things while others simply play the game with great style and flair. Then, of course, there are combinations of both. After searching far and wide, we came up with this collection of characters, all involved in some way with the game of hockey and all just a little bit out of the ordinary.

Don Cherry

Brash, controversial and opinionated, the one-time Boston Bruins and Colorado Rockies coach now makes his living in television, offering his opinions in the "Coach's Corner" on the CBC's popular *Hockey Night in Canada.* Don Cherry has been a fan favorite since his coaching days, and his blue-collar style and a nationalist tilt make him enormously popular in his homeland. He loves a good brawl and is known to watch hockey fights on his VCR. He is tough on European players and others not born north of the border, as well as those who decry violence in the sport. His nickname is "Grapes." During his first game back in Boston after leaving the Bruins, he called time-out with his Rockies ahead in the final minute and started signing autographs for the fans around his bench while his former bosses stewed. He is also an eccentric dresser who fancies high-collared, custom-made shirts. (See Figure 21-1.)

Figure 21-1:
Cherry in
his
coaching
days.

Phil Esposito

One of the great scorers in NHL history, Esposito played 18 seasons for the Chicago Blackhawks, Boston Bruins, and New York Rangers, recording 717 goals and 873 assists. He was a passionate and superstitious member of two Stanley Cup championship teams. He donned a black turtleneck underneath his Bruins jersey one night for a game against Toronto because he had a cold and scored three goals. So he wore it every game after that. He always dressed right to left, putting his right sock on before his left, and so on. Famous for his collection of good luck charms, his locker looked like something from a gypsy's caravan with beads, rabbits' feet, and other trinkets hanging all over the place.

John Ferguson

During his eight years with the Montreal Canadiens (in which he won five Cups), Ferguson scored 145 goals, but he was much better known for his fighting, compiling more than 1,200 penalty minutes in his career. He retired in 1971 and then went on to serve as coach and general manager of the New York Rangers and general manager of the Winnipeg Jets. In his autobiography, *Thunder and Lightning,* Ferguson wrote "When you get right down to it, I made it my business to be an absolutely miserable SOB on the ice, all of the time." He was. At the opening face-off of his first NHL game, he got into a fight with Boston Bruins badboy Ted Green, who thumped him soundly. He was scheduled to fight heavyweight boxer — and Canadian champion — George Chuvalo in a three-round bout, but he had to back out when his bosses in Montreal objected.

Nick Fotiu

Nick Fotiu, a Staten Island, New York, native, grew up playing roller hockey and managed to stick in the NHL for 13 seasons. He was a big Rangers fan as a kid and wormed his way into Madison Square Garden whenever he had the chance to see them play. (See Figure 21-2.) He never caught a puck in the stands, so he made it a point to give away as many as he could to fans as a pro. It was not unusual for Fotiu to be the last person to leave the ice after pre-game warm-ups; he'd skate around the rink and toss up pucks to kids in different parts of the stands. Sometimes he'd sit up in the cheap seats in Madison Square Garden with a cup of coffee and think about the good old days. After leaving the Rangers, Nick went on to play for Hartford, Calgary, Philadelphia, and Edmonton, retiring in 1989. He scored 60 goals and amassed nearly 1,400 penalty minutes.

Famous for practical jokes, he once swiped a lobster from a hotel restaurant and put it on his sleeping roommate Bill Golsdworthy's chest. But only after taking the rubber bands off its claws.

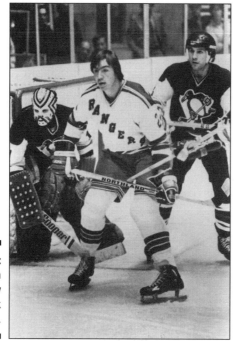

Figure 21-2:
Fotiu with the New York Rangers.

Bernard "Boom Boom" Geoffrion

The longtime Montreal Canadiens star, who also played for a time with the New York Rangers, scored 393 goals and recorded 429 assists over 16 seasons. He won six Stanley Cups as well. He helped to popularize the slap shot, hence his nickname. A Hall of Famer, Geoffrion won the Rookie of the Year Award in 1952 and the Most Valuable Player Award in 1961, and twice led the league in scoring. He hurt his knee during the 1961 season and had it set in a cast. But as the Stanley Cup play-offs heated up, he began to get antsy. So he called over teammate Doug Harvey one night as they traveled by train to their next game and said, "Let's get this thing off." The two of them went into the women's room and hacked the plaster off with a borrowed knife. Geoffrion also coached NHL teams in Atlanta, Montreal, and New York, giving memorable pre-game speeches, including one in Atlanta that went, "There are three things we must do tonight, and that is shoot and pass."

Bobby Hull

The Golden Jet brought great glamour to hockey in the 1960s and helped popularize the game like no one before him. He became famous for his blonde hair and Greek god-like physique as well as for his slap shot, which other players began imitating, and his all-around abilities. He killed penalties. He anchored the power play. He scored goals. And he signed every autograph. Many believe that Hull's magnetism was one of the main reasons why the league decided to expand from six to 12 teams after the 1967 season. He was also a major factor in the creation — and six-year survival — of the World Hockey Association; Hull jumped to the Winnipeg Jets of the upstart league in 1972, signing a deal that paid him the then enormous sum of $2 million over five years and giving the league instant credibility. If any injury kept him out of a game, attendance figures were down 5,000 fans or so. Hull won three scoring titles and started nine All-Star Games. In 1966 he became the first NHLer to score more than 50 goals in a season. All told, he put the puck in the net 610 times during his 16-year career.

Tom McVie

The longtime minor league player finally made it to the NHL in 1991 when he became head coach of the New Jersey Devils. He played for a spell in the old Western League for Hal Laycoe, a former NHL defenseman and a stickler for punctuality. One day before a game in Los Angeles, Laycoe called a team meeting by the hotel swimming pool for 12 noon. All players were in attendance at one minute of, except for McVie. All of a sudden, however, he stepped out to the balcony of his room three stories high and dove into the pool, clothes and all. "Coach," he shouted when he came out of the water, "You can't fine me for being late."

He would sometimes stuff a regulation-size hockey puck into his mouth to amuse his teammates and skate around practice that way.

Red Storey

Storey was an NHL Hall of Fame referee who also handled games in the Canadian Football League, sometimes doing both in the same day. A big man with flame-red hair, he is still revered as an after-dinner speaker in Canada. He is also quick-witted and self-effacing, as evidenced by his encounter with a fan at the old Boston Garden some years ago. A freak snowstorm had held up Storey's arrival, and the game didn't start on time as a result. When he finally skated onto the ice, a fan yelled down: "Hey Storey, what time are you going to get going?" Not breaking stride, he said: "If I could tell time, do you think I'd still be a referee?"

Dave "Tiger" Williams

Anyone who racks up just under 4,000 regular season penalty minutes and spends more than 66 games in the box has to have personality, right? A 14-year veteran who played for five teams, Williams was a fearless player who liked to use his fists — and anything else — to intimidate his opponents. He was an incessant talker who spewed insults and other indelicacies during games. However, he used his hands for more than just fighting, scoring 241 goals. After he'd put a puck in the net, Tiger would skate to center ice with his stick between his legs and ride it like a witch's broom, waving to the fans as he glided by, driving the other team crazy. He also had a fierce temper; he once became so enraged that he threw chairs out of the penalty box and onto the ice. Another time he slammed the door to the box so hard that the glass fell out.

Lorne "Gump" Worsley

Nicknamed after the cartoon character Andy Gump, Worsley was a rotund Hall of Fame goaltender who played 861 NHL games, only six of them with a mask (see Figure 21-3). He had a real fear of flying, yet he survived the NHL travel regimen for 21 seasons. He also won four Stanley Cups. When asked by a reporter after a particularly tough game what team was hardest on him, Worsley answered, "The Rangers." And that was the team he played for at the time. He had some difficult moments in New York, thanks in no small part to his coach Phil Watson. One day after the Rangers had suffered a bad loss, the coach met the press and said "How can we win when our goalie has a beer belly?" When reporters informed the Gumpster what Watson had said, he replied "That just shows what a dope we have for a coach. Everybody knows I don't drink beer; just whiskey."

Figure 21-3: "Gump" Worsley during his time with the Montreal Canadiens.

Chapter 22

The Ten Best Minor League Players

▶ Bower, Callander, Fielder

▶ Gamble, Glover, Gruhl

▶ Marshall, Michayluk, O'Ree, Thornson

*M*ost hockey fans have never heard of them, and many of their biggest moments as players occurred before sparse crowds in cities like Hershey, Portland, Muskegon, and Providence. Like thousands of athletes throughout Europe and North America, they hoped to play regularly in the NHL, but in most cases weren't quite good enough to make much of a mark when they did get the call. But they were dedicated players who loved the game and never gave up on their dreams.

We talked to hockey mavens across the U.S. and Canada and came up with a list of the top minor league players of all time. One, goalie Johnny Bower, went on to star in the NHL. But the rest didn't have much more than a cup of coffee there, if even that. All of them, however, did big things in the minors.

Johnny Bower

Bower was a dominating goalie who played for Providence and Cleveland in the American Hockey League before starting a 15-year NHL career that brought him four Stanley Cup Championships, a Vezina Trophy as the league's outstanding goaltender, and a hallowed spot in the Hockey Hall of Fame. At one point in the minors, Bower had a shutout streak of nearly 250 minutes, which adds up to four-plus games. He spent eight years there before getting his chance with the New York Rangers in 1953. He had won many of the AHL's performance awards, but he still had a hard time breaking into the NHL. Problem was, there were only six big-league teams in those days, and not many jobs for netminders, no matter how good they were.

Bower recorded five shutouts his first season in New York and unseated Gump Worsley as the starter. He went on to play until 1970, spending most of his years with the Maple Leafs. No one was ever sure about his age, but Bower was said to be 46 years old when he finally retired.

Jock Callander

Callander played center in 800-plus games in the International Hockey League with Toledo, Muskegon, Atlanta, and Cleveland. He also competed in the Central Hockey League in Utah and Montana. His lack of speed kept him in the minors for most of his career, but he was a brilliant playmaker who did a great job on the power play. He spent parts of five years in the NHL with Pittsburgh and Tampa Bay but only played in 109 regular season games, scoring a total of 22 goals and chalking up 29 assists. He did, however, earn a Stanley Cup Championship ring with the Penguins in 1992.

Guyle Fielder

Fielder was not very smooth, but he was one of the smartest centermen to ever lace up a pair of skates. He played mostly for Seattle in the Western League. He got called up to Detroit in the 1950s and was put on a line with Hall of Famers Gordie Howe and Ted Lindsay. But Fielder didn't like it there and eventually asked to be sent back to Seattle. He spent parts of four seasons with the NHL Wings, Blackhawks, and Bruins, but only played in nine regular season games and never recorded a goal or assist. He is still considered one of the best to ever play in the minor leagues.

Dick Gamble

The left winger scored 468 goals in 898 minor league games during the 1950s and '60s, mostly for teams in Buffalo and Rochester. He had 30 goals or more in 11 seasons. He was a good up-and-down winger who possessed a tremendous shot. Played at various times for Montreal, Chicago, and Toronto in the NHL and competed on two Stanley Cup winners. When he left the game in 1967, he had scored 41 goals in 195 NHL contests.

Fred Glover

Glover scored 20 goals or more in 16 AHL seasons at Indianapolis and Cleveland. He was a tough forward and a never-give-up style of player. His team in Cleveland once won three consecutive championships. He made it to the NHL in 1948 and played 92 games over five seasons for the Red Wings and Blackhawks, netting 13 goals and adding 11 assists.

Scott Gruhl

Gruhl was another longtime minor leaguer who did not skate well but was able to do everything else — be it scoring, checking, or passing — and do it well. In 13 International Hockey League seasons, Gruhl recorded 596 goals, 703 assists, and nearly 2,300 penalty minutes. He played with a lot of energy and passion. He was an abrasive sort who was a real pain to play against. But you loved him if he was on your team. He played in only 20 games over three seasons in the NHL for the Los Angeles Kings and Pittsburgh Penguins in the mid-1980s. His NHL career stats include three goals and three assists.

Willie Marshall

Marshall played 20 seasons in the AHL for teams like the Pittsburgh Hornets and the Hershey Bears. He was a tough, heady forward who made beautiful passes. He played in 33 games with the Toronto Maple Leafs in the mid-1950s, scoring one goal. He was another victim of the league being very small and full of great players in those days. With today's pay scale, Marshall would make $4 million a year. And be worth every penny.

Dave Michayluk

The hardworking forward scored 100 or more points in nine consecutive seasons in the minors, playing in cities such as Kalamazoo, Springfield, and Portland. Michayluk made it to the NHL in 1981 and played a total of 14 games over three years for the Philadelphia Flyers and Pittsburgh Penguins scoring just two goals. However, he got his name on the Stanley Cup in 1992 when the Pens won their second consecutive title.

Willie O'Ree

A legend with the San Diego Gulls of the Western League, he became the first player of African descent to compete in the National Hockey League, breaking the so-called color barrier in 1958 when he joined the Boston Bruins. The right winger played a total of only 45 games over two seasons in the NHL, scoring just 4 goals and recording 10 assists. But he made a huge contribution just by getting there. He played professional hockey for 11 teams over a 21-year career and is regarded as one of the fastest skaters in the history of the game, even though he lost sight in his right eye after a puck hit him there when he was 18 years old. He twice led the Western League in goals, tallying 38 for both the 1964–65 and 1968–69 seasons. He retired in 1980 but is still an active supporter of the game. The Willie O'Ree All-Star Weekend celebrates diversity in hockey and promotes the sport to minority youngsters across North America.

Len Thornson

The high-scoring forward with the Fort Wayne Komets of the International Hockey League during the 1960s led the league in scoring three different seasons and posted more than 100 points a year seven times. He wasn't a great skater, but he was a very deceptive puck handler and knew how to shoot.

Chapter 23

Ten Timeless Tips for Better Hockey

In This Chapter

▶ Learn to skate, use a helmet, keep off thin ice

▶ Keep your head up, be a team player, watch a live game

▶ Make your equipment fit, use your stick correctly

▶ Watch hockey in the right places

▶ Enjoy yourself

*H*owever you look at it, hockey is a great game. But we think that players and fans can enjoy it even more if they just follow some simple advice. You didn't ask for it, but we're going to give it to you, anyway. After all, it's our book.

Learn to Skate

You can't run before you walk, and you can't play hockey before you know how to skate. It will make the game more enjoyable, and make you a better player if you figure out how to scoot around the ice long before you start working on slap shots and no-look passes. Take lessons if need be, read books of instruction (like ours). But make sure you spend some time learning how to skate well before you do much else with the game.

Wear a Helmet

Ice is slippery stuff, and it's easy to fall down the wrong way during a hockey game, even if you are a pro. So don't take any foolish chances. Wear a helmet, no matter how old you are. Even if you're just gliding quietly around a pond or rink, you never know what could happen. Always be on the safe side.

Don't Skate on Thin Ice

Speaking of ice, make sure the stuff you decide to skate on is thick enough. We know, it's not a problem for the people that use rinks full of refrigeration equipment. But playing on ponds is still big throughout Canada and the northern United States, and people there need to make sure that the surface they're playing on is secure.

Always Keep Your Head Up

There's nothing a hulking defenseman likes to see more than some unsuspecting forward carrying the puck up ice with his head down. OUCH! Get used to handling the puck with your head up. It's also best to keep it that way when you go into the boards; that will lessen the chance of a serious neck injury should you fall or be checked into them.

Be a Team Player

Hockey's not like tennis or golf. It's a team sport, and the best teams are the ones that play together. Pass the puck. Get open in front of the net. Cover for your teammates. Work hard for them. And don't let opposing players mess with anyone on your squad. It's important to stick up for each other.

Go and See a Game Live

No sport in the history of the world is more fun to watch in person than hockey. Whether it's your brother's high school game, a big-time college contest, the minor leagues, or the NHL, get some tickets and check it out. A Stanley Cup play-off game is the best, what with the forwards whirling around, the defensemen throwing solid body checks, the goalies kicking out hard, low shots from the point, and the crowd building itself into a near frenzy. It's hard to beat a good game.

Make Sure Your Equipment Fits

Few things are worse than a pair of skates that are either too tight or too loose. And a stick that doesn't fit isn't going to produce as many goals. So take the time to get the proper gear and make sure it fits. Also, take care of what you have. Hockey equipment can be expensive, but it will last (as long as you aren't growing a couple of inches every year) for quite a while. So wipe down your skate blades and dry out your pads after every game and practice.

Use Your Stick Properly

Shoot with it, pass with it, use it for balance. You can scratch your nose with it for all we care. Just don't flail it around like some martial arts weapon.

Watch Hockey in All the Right Places

Our favorites are the Madison Square Garden Network and Fox Broadcasting, which is where JD works when he's not pretending to be William Faulkner. What a surprise, right? Also, check out the '98 Olympics on CBS. Hey, we're not above making a few shameless plugs.

Be Free

Organized leagues are great fun, but sometimes it's nice to get away from all that structure and just play. We played pond hockey as kids and shot tennis balls off our driveways into nets set up by the garage doors. We played with plastic pucks and sticks in dormitory hallways and scrambled around parking lots in the midst of a street hockey game. Street hockey is the sport in one of its purest forms, and well worth trying. Just be careful not to break any windows.

Part VI
Appendixes

The 5th Wave   By Rich Tennant

"I don't know who you are, kid, but goalie practice was over 2 hours ago! You can't show up late! Get in here! I'm not through with you!"

In this part . . .

*1*n this part, we show you how to talk hockey like a pro, and after reading this section you should be able to hold your own with even the most knowledgeable players, fans, or coaches. We then provide the names of various hockey organizations around the world, from Pee Wees to the Pros, so that you can track down whatever information you may need to know about watching and playing this wonderful game. We also introduce you to the signals you see the officials make at a hockey game, whether it be ice hockey or roller hockey. We finish with a set of lists that range from Hockey Hall of Fame members to statistics showing you the some of hockey's greatest accomplishments.

Appendix A
Hockey Speak

Altercation

Any physical interaction between two or more opposing players that results in a penalty (or penalties) being assessed.

Assist

An assist is credited to a player who helps set up a goal. Assists are awarded to the last man to handle the puck immediately preceding the goal. There is a maximum of two assists per goal.

Attacking zone

When you are on the attack, your attacking zone is between your opponent's blue line and goal line.

Back check

Forwards in their offensive zone skate back quickly to their own defensive zone to protect their goal and keep the opponent from shooting.

Blocker

For the goalie, the glove that goes on the hand that holds the stick.

Blue line

Two lines running across the width of the rink, one on either side of the red line. The area between the blue lines is called the neutral zone. (See Chapter 1 for a diagram of the rink.)

Boarding

Violently checking an opponent into the boards from behind. Boarding is illegal and merits a penalty.

Boards

The wall around a hockey rink (which was at one time really made of wood but which is now usually of fiberglass) measuring about 42 inches high and topped off by synthetic glass to protect the spectators while giving them a good view of the action.

Body check

A body check is where you use your body against an opponent who has possession of the puck. Legal body checking must be done only with the hips or shoulders and must be above the opponent's knees and below the neck. Unnecessarily rough body checking is penalized.

Box

A defensive alignment (similar to the *diamond*) often used by a team defending against a power play. (See Chapter 8 for all the details.)

Breakaway

A player in control of the puck has a breakaway when the only opponent between him and the opposition's goal is the goalie (and a reasonable scoring opportunity exists).

Breakout

The play used by the attacking team to move the puck out of its own zone and up the ice toward the opponent's goal.

Butt ending

Using the shaft of the stick to jab or attempt to jab an opposing player. Known in Quebec as "donner six pouces" (to give six inches).

Catcher

For the goalie, this is a glove (which looks like a fancy first-baseman's mitt) that goes on the non-stick hand.

Center

In a traditional alignment with three forwards, the center plays between the left and right wings. (See Chapter 1 for information on the positions.)

Changing on the fly

When players from the bench substitute for players on the ice, while the clock is running. (See Chapter 7 for how an NHL coach approaches this task.)

Charging

Taking more than three strides before deliberately checking an opponent.

Château Bow-Wow

The "doghouse" — where hockey players go when they mess up.

Clearing the puck

When the puck is passed, knocked, or shot away from the front of the goal net or other area.

Crease

The semi-circular area in front of each goal is called the crease. (See Chapter 1 for a diagram of the rink.) If any offensive player is in the goal crease when a goal is scored, the goal is not allowed. The crease is painted blue. The goal crease is designed to protect the goalies from interference by attacking players. The area marked on the ice in front of the penalty timekeeper's seat is for the use of the referee.

Cross checking

Hitting an opponent with the shaft of the stick while both hands are on the stick and no part of the stick is on the ice.

Defending zone

When the other team is on the attack, the defending zone is the area between your goal line and your blue line.

Defensemen

Two defensemen usually try to stop the opponent's play at their own blue line. The defensemen block shots and also clear the puck from in front of their goal. Offensively, defensemen take the puck up the ice or pass the puck ahead to the forwards; they then follow the play into the attacking zone and help keep it there. (See Chapter 1 for the lowdown on positions.)

Deke

A deke is a fake by a player in possession of the puck in order to get around an opponent or to make a goalie move out of position. To deke, you move the puck or a part of your body to one side and then in the opposite direction. ("Deke" is taken from "decoy.")

Delay of game

This is called when a player purposely delays the game. Delay of game is commonly called when a goalie shoots the puck into the stands without the puck deflecting off a skater or the glass. Delay of game also occurs when a player intentionally knocks a goalpost out of its stand (usually in an attempt to prevent a goal from being scored).

Delayed off-side

In this situation, an attacking player has preceded the puck into the offensive zone (normally a case for off-side), but the defending team has gained possession of the puck and can bring it out of their defensive zone without any delay or contact with an opposing player.

Diamond

A defensive alignment (similar to the *box*) often used by a team defending against a power play. (See Chapter 8 for all the details.)

Dig

An attempt to gain possession of the puck in the corners of the rink.

Directing the puck

Changing the course of the puck in a desired direction by using the body, skate, or stick.

Dive

When a player exaggerates being hooked or tripped in an attempt to draw a penalty.

Elbowing

Using the elbow to impede or disrupt the opponent.

Empty net goal

A goal scored against an opponent that has pulled the goalie.

Face-off

The action of an official dropping the puck between the sticks of two opposing players to start play.

Fisticuffs

When a player throws a punch (closed fist) and makes contact with an opponent.

Five-hole

The area in the opening between a goalie's leg pads. (See the sidebar "The different holes" in Chapter 13 for a description of all the holes.)

Flat pass

A pass where the puck remains on the surface of the ice.

Flex

Hockey sticks come in different degrees of *flex* — medium, stiff, and extra stiff. A stronger player, who hits more powerful shots, usually wants a stiffer stick.

Flip pass

A pass where the puck is lifted so that it goes over an opponent or his stick.

Forecheck

Forwards forecheck by hurrying into the opponent's defensive zone to either keep the puck there or take it away.

Forward

The center and the wings are traditionally considered to be the forwards. Refer to Chapter 1 for information on these positions.

Freezing the puck

A player freezes the puck by holding it against the boards with the stick or skates. A goalie freezes the puck (when the opposition is threatening to score) by either holding the puck in the glove or trapping it on the ice. *Note:* A delay-of-game penalty can be called if the goalie freezes the puck when the opposition is not threatening.

G

An abbreviation for "goals."

Game suspension

When a player, coach, or manager receives a game suspension, that person can't participate in the next scheduled game.

Goal

A goal is achieved when the entire puck crosses the goal line and enters the net. You can't deliberately kick it in or bat it in with a glove, although a goal is counted when a puck deflects off a player (but not off an official). A goal is worth one point.

Goal judge

A goal judge sits behind each goal (off-ice!) and signals when the puck has crossed the red goal line by turning on a red light above his station. The referee can ask the goal judge's advice on disputed goals, but the referee has final authority and can overrule the goal judge.

Goaltender

The goaltender's main job is to keep the puck from entering the goal net. The goaltender is also know as the goalie, the goalkeeper, or the netminder.

GP

An abbreviation for "games played."

Great One

The Great One is none other than Wayne Gretzky.

Habs

A nickname for the Montreal Canadiens. The word comes from the French "habitant" (those who live here).

Hat trick

A player who scores three goals in one game achieves a "hat trick."

Head butting

Using the head while delivering a body check (head first) in the chest, head, neck, or back area; or using the head to strike an opponent.

Heel of the stick

The point where the shaft of the stick and the bottom of the blade meet. (See Chapter 2 for a diagram of a stick.)

High sticking

Carrying the stick above the shoulder to use against the opponent.

Holding

Using your hands on an opponent or the opponent's equipment to impede your opponent's progress.

Hooking

Applying the blade of the stick to any part of an opponent's body or stick and pulling or tugging with the stick in order to disrupt that opponent.

Icing

An infraction called when a player shoots the puck from his side of the red line across the opponent's goal line (as diagrammed in Chapter 3). Play is stopped when an opponent (other than the goalie) touches the puck. The face-off is held in the offending team's end of the ice. A team that is short-handed can ice the puck without being penalized.

Injury potential penalties

Injury potential penalties include butt ending, checking from behind, head butting, spearing, board checking, charging, cross checking, elbowing/kneeing, high sticking, holding the face mask, slashing, and roughing. A linesman may report these infractions occurring behind the play to the referee (following the next stoppage of play) if the referee did not see them.

In-line hockey

Hockey played on in-line skates. See Chapter 15.

Interference

Making body contact with an opponent who does not have possession of the puck. Interference is also called when a player is standing in the crease or otherwise makes contact with the goaltender.

Kneeing

Using the knee in an effort to impede or foul an opponent.

Left-wing lock

Coach Scotty Bowman often uses this formation in which his left wing seldom forechecks in the offensive zone but stays back to help out defensively. (See Chapter 7.)

Linesman

Two linesmen are used to call offside, offside passes, icing, and handle all face-offs not occurring at center ice. Although they don't call penalties, they can recommend to the referee that a penalty be called.

Neutral zone

The central ice area between the two blue lines (neither the defending nor the attacking zone). Chapter 1 has a diagram.

Off-ice (minor) official

These officials include the official scorer, game timekeeper, penalty timekeeper, and the two goal judges. The referee has full control of all game officials and final decision.

Offside

A team is offside when a player crosses the attacking blue line before the puck does (as diagrammed in Chapter 3). A face-off then takes place just outside that blue line (in the offending player's defensive zone). The determining factor in most offside situations is the position of the skates: Both skates must be completely over the blue line ahead of the puck for the play to be offside.

Offside pass

An offside pass (also known as a "two-line" pass) occurs when a member of the attacking team passes the puck from behind his own defending blue line to a teammate across the center red line. (See Chapter 3 for a diagram.) If the puck precedes the player across the red line, the pass is legal. Also, an attacking player may pass the puck over the center red line and the attacking blue line to a teammate if the puck precedes that teammate across the blue line. The face-off after an offside pass takes place at the spot where the pass originated.

One-timer

Shooting the puck immediately upon receiving it without stopping it first. A one-timer is an effective way to beat the goalie before he can slide from one side of the crease to another.

Penalty

A penalty is the result of an infraction of the rules by a player or team official. A penalty usually results in the removal of the offending player (or team official) for a specified period of time. See Chapter 3 for more info on the rules of the game, and check out Appendix C for the signals used to indicate penalties. In some cases, the penalty may be the awarding of a penalty shot on goal or the actual awarding of a goal.

Penalty killing

When a team is shorthanded and attempts to prevent the opposition from scoring, this activity is known as "penalty killing." (See Chapter 8 for more details on penalty killing.)

Penalty-killing unit

The group of players brought in by a shorthanded team in order to defend against a power play.

Penalty shot

A penalty shot is awarded to an offensive player who — on a breakaway — is illegally checked or impeded. The puck is placed at the center face-off spot, and the player has a free try at the opposing goal with no other defenders on the ice besides the goalie.

PIM

An abbreviation for "penalties in minutes" (penalty minutes accumulated).

Pipe

The pipe is the goalpost, and if you hit a puck "between the pipes" you score a goal!

Point

The point is the area just inside the opposition's blue line close to the boards on either side of the rink. A defenseman usually occupies this area when his team is in control of the puck in the opposition's defensive zone.

Poke check

Trying to knock the puck away from an opponent by stabbing at it with the blade of the stick.

Possession of the puck

The last player or goalie to make contact with the puck is the one who has possession. This definition includes a puck that is deflected off a player or any part of his equipment.

Power play

When a team has more players on the ice than the opposition due to one or more penalties against the opposing team. Chapter 8 has all the details about the power play.

Pts.

An abbreviation for "total points."

Pulling of the goalie

A team that is losing will sometimes take their own goalie off the ice and use another forward. This situation occurs most frequently near the end of the game when a team is behind and needs some emergency offense.

Red line

The line that divides the rink into two equal parts. This area is center ice. (Chapter 1 has a diagram.)

Referee

The referee supervises the game, calls the penalties, determines if goals are scored, and handles face-offs at center ice at the start of each period and after goals. The referee has the final decision over all other officials.

Roughing

Engaging in fisticuffs (fighting) or shoving. Chapter 9 is full of information on this type of hitting.

Save

A shot blocked by the goalie — a shot that otherwise would have gone into the net!

Shadow

When a player covers an opponent one-on-one everywhere on the ice in order to limit the effectiveness of this opponent.

Shoot-out

Some minor and international leagues refine the overtime situation by having their teams play a five-minute sudden death period, and if no one scores, the game is decided by a *shoot-out*. Each team picks five players, and each one of them takes a penalty shot on the other team's goalie, skating in by themselves with the puck from center ice and trying to score. Whichever team scores more wins.

Shorthanded

A shorthanded team is below the numerical strength of its opponents on the ice. When a goal is scored against a shorthanded team, the penalty that caused the team scored against to be shorthanded is terminated, and both teams are again at equal strength.

Slap shot

A slap shot occurs when the player swings the stick back and then quickly forward, slapping the puck ahead with a forehand shot.

Slashing

When a player swings the stick at an opponent. Slashing merits a penalty, whether contact is made or not. Tapping an opponent's stick not slashing.

Slot

The prime scoring area up the middle of the ice, between the face-off circles. When you "clear the slot," you shove an opposing player out of the area in front of your goal.

Smothering the puck

When a goalie or other players fall on the puck. Smothering is legal when done by the goalie or *accidentally* by another player.

Sniper

A player who is a pure goal scorer and who doesn't hit other players or the boards all that much.

Spearing

Poking or attempting to poke an opponent with the tip of the blade of the stick while holding the stick with one or both hands.

Splitting the defense

When a player in possession of the puck goes between two opposing defenders while attacking.

Stanley Cup

The trophy awarded annually to the NHL champion after a best-of-seven Stanley Cup Championship Series.

Stick checking

Using the stick or its blade to poke or strike an opponent's stick or puck in an attempt to get possession of the puck.

Stickhandling

A term for carrying the puck along the ice with the stick.

Street hockey

Hockey played without skates of any kind. See Chapter 15.

Sweater

The term used to designate a hockey jersey.

Sweep check

Using the entire length of the stick with a sweeping motion along the surface off the ice in order to dislodge the puck from an opponent. A team that is shorthanded on a power play often employs a sweep check.

Team official

A person responsible for the operation of a team, such as a coach, manager, or trainer.

Trap

Traps are defensive formations designed to minimize the opposition's scoring opportunities and keep its offense from functioning. The idea is to trap the puck in the neutral zone, halting the opponents and regaining control of the puck. (Chapter 7 has some more information on different kinds of traps.)

Tripping

Using a stick, arm, or leg to cause an opponent to trip or fall.

Turnover

Just as in basketball or in football, you can make a turnover in hockey by losing control of the puck to the opposing team.

Two-line pass

An offside pass (that actually crosses two lines). (See Chapter 3.)

Umbrella

A formation — resembling an open umbrella — used by a team that is on the power play to take advantage of its numerical superiority. See Chapter 8 for an explanation and a diagram!

Wings

The left wing and the right wing (also known as forwards) move up and down the sides of the rink. Offensively, they skate on each side of the center, exchanging passes with him, while trying themselves for a shot on goal and/ or a rebound of a shot from the point. Defensively, they watch the opponent's wings. (See Chapter 1 for a description of the positions.)

Wrist shot

A wrist shot is used to shoot the puck off the blade of the stick with a flicking motion of the wrist.

Zamboni

The vehicle used to prepare the rink's ice surface before the game and after each period. The Zamboni scrapes a thin layer off the ice, heats the ice, and puts down a fresh layer of heated water that freezes to form a new layer of ice. (See Chapter 11 for a picture of this wonderful machine.)

Appendix B

Hockey Organizations: From Pee Wees to the Pros

• •

*T*wo organizations should be at the head of any list for hockey information: USA Hockey and the Canadian Hockey Association.

USA Hockey is the governing body for the sport of ice hockey in the United States. And for in-line hockey enthusiasts, USA Hockey sponsors USA Hockey Inline. If you want to join USA Hockey, you can reach it at the following address (and their Web site has links to everything you need to know about this organization):

USA Hockey
4965 N. 30th Street
Colorado Springs, CO 80919
800-872-4759
www.usahockey.com

The Canadian Hockey Association links players, coaches, officials, volunteers, and anyone else involved in local hockey associations across Canada to other provincial, national, and international hockey bodies. This organization represents every part of the country and covers hockey levels up to the National Hockey League. Here's how to reach the Canadian Hockey Association:

Canadian Hockey Association
1600 James Naismith Drive
Gloucester, ON K1B 5N4
Canada
613-748-5613
www.canadianhockey.ca

Youth Hockey

Youth hockey is booming in North America, and nowhere is that more evident than in the number of hockey organizations catering to our younger players in recent years! Here is a listing of tons of North American and other youth hockey organizations. These groups are quite varied in their levels and their approaches; for further information, contact them. We tried to include Web site information, if possible. For further details on such organizations, as well as listings of youth hockey camps, schools, and tournaments, be sure to visit the Youth Hockey Network home page at www.youthhockeynetwork.com, which prides itself on being the best place to get information on youth hockey.

Alabama

Huntsville Amateur Hockey Association
Phone: 205-830-2595
250 Smith Dr.
Harvest, AL 35749
Home Rink: Wilcoxson Iceplex
Rink Location: Huntsville
www.hsv.tis.net/hockey

USA Hockey, Inc.
Phone: 770-419-0349
E-mail: mccaig@bellsouth.net
5852 Fairwood Knoll
Acworth, AL 30101

Fond Du Lac Blueline Club
Phone: 414-921-2057
E-mail: blueline@fdldotnet.com
68 N. Butler Street
Fond Du Lac, AL 54935-3138

Alaska

Peninsula Hellfighters Jr. Hockey
Phone: 907-783-0180
E-mail: heisler@aonline.com
538 Arena Drive
Soldotna, AK 99669
Home Rink: Central Peninsula Sports Center
Rink Location: Soldotna

Anchorage North Stars
Phone: 907-243-6470
E-mail: scoob@alaska.net
4641 Sandy Beach Drive
Anchorage, AK 99502
Home Rink: Ben Boeke Arena
Rink Location: Anchorage

Alaska All Star Hockey Assoc.
Phone: 907-344-1378
E-mail: kevin@alaska.net
1830 Commodore Drive
Anchorage, AK 99507
Home Rink: Dempsey Anderson Arena
Rink Location: Anchorage

Alaska Firebirds
Phone: 907-248-5625
E-mail: landeru@arctic.net
4011 Turnagain Blvd. E. #6
Anchorage, AK 99517

Arctic Lions Hockey Association
Alaska Hockey League
Phone: 907-451-9886
E-mail: empower@polarnet.com
401 Driveway Street
Fairbanks, AK 99701
arcticlions.yhn.com

Alaska State Hockey Association
Phone: 907-278-0720
E-mail: techsupgrp@micronet.net
2254 Forest Park Drive
Anchorage, AK 99517

Big Lake Amateur Hockey Association
Phone: 907-892-7567
E-mail: styers@matnet.com
Box 520124
Big Lake, AK 99652
Home Rink: Brett Memorial
Rink Location: Wasilla

Arizona

Desert Youth Hockey Association
Phone: 602-994-9119
E-mail: admin@dyha.org
1520 N McClintock Dr.
Tempe, AZ 85281-1643
Home Rink: Oceanside Ice Arena
Rink Location: Tempe
www.dyha.org

Tucson Hockey Club, Inc.
Phone: 520-885-2265
8765 E. Placita Bolivar
Tucson, AZ 85715
Home Rink: Tucson Convention Center
Dowtown Tucson
Rink Location: Southern AZ

Old Pueblo Youth Hockey Association, Inc.
Arizona Amateur Hockey Association
Phone: 520-296-2478
E-mail: fdhealy@aol.com
7625 E. Calle Los Arboles
Tucson, AZ 85750
Rink Location: Iceoplex
opyha.yhn.com

Valley of the Sun Hockey Association
Phone: 602-251-0531
P.O. Box 15333
Phoenix, AZ 85060
Home Rink: Phoenix Coliseum
Rink Location: Central Phoenix

Arkansas

NorthWest Arkansas Amateur Hockey
Association
E-mail: vview@cswnet.com
Rt. 4 Box 150
Huntsville, AR 72740
Home Rink: Jones Center For Families
Rink Location: Springdale

Arkansas Ice Hockey Association
Phone: 501-771-1985
E-mail: jacebedo@aristotle.net
1311 Bowman Road
Little Rock, AR 72211
Home Rink: Little Rock Skating Arena
Rink Location: West Little Rock

California

Southern California Amateur Hockey
Association
Phone: 562-928-1127
Fax: 562-928-1127
9911 Paramount Blvd. #320
Downey, CA 90240
Home Rinks: 20+ rinks in Southern CA
scaha.yhn.com

San Diego Stars Hockey Club
Phone: 619-695-8829
E-mail: sdshc@aol.com
9974 Scripps Ranch Blvd. #285
San Diego, CA 92131
Home Rink: San Diego Ice Arena
Rink Location: San Diego

Marina Cities Hockey Club
Phone: 213-549-8456
8721 Santa Monica Blvd. #307
Los Angeles, CA 90069
Home Rink: Culver City Ice Arena
Rink Location: Culver City

Stockton Jr. Colts Hockey Association
Phone: 209-461-4761
E-mail: ab04@inreach.com
P.O. Box 946
Valley Springs, CA 95252
Home Rink: Oakpark Ice Arena
Rink Location: Stockton

South Coast Sabers Midget AA
Phone: 714-557-8929
E-mail: liebich@aol.com
Home Rink: Glacial Garden Ice Arenas
Rink Location: Lakewood & Anaheim
www.hb.quik.com/~mize

Team California South Squirt "A" team
Phone: 818-773-7416
22011-11 Hiawaha
Chatsworth, CA
Home Rink: Lakewood
Rink Location: Lakewood

Beach City Lightning Hockey Association
Phone: 714-377-9649
E-mail: shootout@themall.net
17052 A Sims Street
Huntington Beach, CA 92649
Home Rink: Surf City Skate Zone
Rink Location: Huntington Beach

Beach City Lightning
Phone: 714-314-5158
E-mail: EChandler@worldnet.att.net
9182 Pioneer Dr.
Huntington Beach, CA 92646
Home Rink: Surf City Skate Zone
Rink Location: Huntington Beach

Team California 19 & Under
Phone: 415-694-7470
E-mail: mlaw@canuq.ang.af.mil
P.O. Box 463
Moffett Fed Afld, CA 94035

Marina Cities "Sharks" Hockey Club
Phone: 310-996-1968
E-mail: MCsharks@aol.com
4545 Sepulveda Blvd.
Culver City, CA 90230
Home Rink: Culver City Ice Rink
Rink Location: Los Angeles

Team California Girls Pee Wee
Phone: 714-855-1132
E-mail: takazaki@aol.com
22671 Dunkenfield
Lake Forest, CA 92630
Home Rink: Glacial Gardens
Rink Location: Lakewood

Sacramento Junior Ice Hockey Association
Phone: 916-556-5185
E-mail: boltman@elkgrove.net
Home Rink: Sacramento & Stockton

Santa Clara Valley Hockey Association
E-mail:
rosenberg_bill@mm.rdd.lmsc.lockheed.com
820 Bruce Drive
Palo Alto, CA 94303
Home Rink: Ice-O-Plex
Rink Location: Fremont

Thunder Youth Hockey Club
Phone: 805-988-1100
E-mail: Waynel@concentric.net
2170 Eastridge Loop
Oxnard, CA 93030
Home Rink: Easy Street Arena
Rink Location: Simi Valley
www.tyhc.com/thunder.html

South Coast Sabers Hockey Association
Phone: 310-430-9454
4601 Ironwood Ave
Seal Beach, CA 90740
Home Rink: Glacial Garden Ice Arena
Rink Location: Anaheim

San Diego Storm
Phone: 619-549-6688
E-mail: docgreg@flash.net
10928 Waterton Rd.
San Diego, CA 92131
Home Rink: Iceoplex Escondido
Rink Location: Escondido

San Jose Blades Hockey Club
Phone: 408-226-4445
E-mail: Sk8r10@ix.netcom.com
6292 Mahan Drive
San Jose, CA 95123
Home Rink: Ice Centre of SJ
Rink Location: San Jose

Pasadena Maple Leafs
Phone: 818-351-0895
1205 N. Michillinda Ave.
Pasadena, CA 91107
Home Rink: Pasadena Ice Center
Rink Location: Pasadena

Pasadena Maple Leafs Midget AA
Phone: 714-281-8665
E-mail: hokyman@SoCa.com
1019 Road Runner Road
Anaheim, CA 92807
Home Rink: The Garden
Rink Location: Lakewood

Pasadena Hockey Association
Phone: 818-351-0174
E-mail: greyfox4@ix.netcom.com
1205 N. Michillinda Ave.
Pasadena, CA 91107-1707
Home Rink: Pasadena
Rink Location: Pasadena
www.netcom.com/~greyfox4/PHA.html

Bay Harbor Minor Hockey Association
Phone: 310-378-5676
E-mail: puckwgn@aol.com
E-mail: pucktruck@aol.com
28382 S. Western Ave., Suite 367
Rancho Palos Verdes, CA 90732
Home Rink: Skating Edge Ice Arena
Rink Location: Harbor City

West Valley Wolves
Phone: 805-297-4733
E-mail: glh@thevine.net
20801 Franwood Dr.
Saugus, CA 91350
Home Rink: Iceoplex
Rink Location: North Hills

Long Beach Jr. Ice Dogs
Phone: 310-202-8859
E-mail: jricedogs@aol.com
11038 Braddock Drive
Culver City, CA 90230
Home Rink: Glacial Gardens Ice Arena
Rink Location: Lakewood

Lake Arrowhead Hockey Association
Phone: 909-336-5759
E-mail: Mitesmom@aol.com
P.O. Box 4092
Blue Jay, CA 92317
Home Rink: Ice Castle at Blue Jay
Rink Location: Lake Arrowhead/Blue Jay

Westminster Wave
Phone: 714-899-7900 ext. 14
13071 Springdale Ave.
Westminster, CA 92683
Home Rink: Westminster Ice Palace
Rink Location: Westminster

Aliso Viejo Ice Palace
Phone: 714-643-9648 ext. 17
9 Journey
Aliso Viejo, CA 92656
Home Rink: Aliso Viejo Ice Palace
Rink Location: Aliso Viejo

Los Angeles Youth Hockey Association
Home of the Los Angeles Wildcats
Phone: 310-945-3228
E-mail: LAWildcats@aol.com
14271 Galy Street
Tustin, CA 92680
Home Rink: Glacial Gardens Ice Arena
Rink Location: Lakewood/Long Beach

Colorado

Pikes Peak Amateur Hockey Association
Phone: 719-536-0596
E-mail: ingram@pcisys.net
7690 Calloway Court
Colorado Springs, CO 80909
Home Rink: Numerous
Rink Location: Colorado Springs

Steamboat Springs Youth Hockey
Association
Phone: 970-879-1785
E-mail: 75712.1541@compuserve.com
P.O. Box 776010
Steamboat Springs, CO 80477
Home Rink: Howelsen Ice Arena
Rink Location: Steamboat Springs

Foothills Hockey Association
Phone: 303-984-1409
E-mail: ras@carbon.cudenver.edu
11098 W. Jewell Ave., #A3, Box 1172
Lakewood, CO 80232
Home Rink: Foothills Ice Arena
Rink Location: Lakewood

Littleton Hockey Association
Phone: 303-798-7935 ext. 205
6580 S. Vine St.
Littleton, CO 80122
Home Rink: South Suburban Ice Arena
Rink Location: Littleton

P.H.Y.A.
Phone: 719-545-9002
100 N. Grand
Pueblo, CO 81003
Home Rink: Pueblo Plazza Ice Arena
Rink Location: Pueblo

Connecticut

Central CT Youth Hockey Association Inc.
Phone: 860-529-9090
E-mail: pssobin@mail.snet.net
16 Straddle Hill
Wethersfield, CT 06109-2720
Home Rink: South Windsor Arena
Rink Location: South Windsor

Junior Blades of New Haven
Phone: 203-934-6935
E-mail: srblade85@aol.com
7 Noble Street
West Haven, CT 06516
Home Rink: Ed. L. Bennett Rink
Rink Location: West Haven

Wallingford Hawks Youth Hockey
Phone: 203-269-0397
E-mail: rtsv62a@prodigy.com
P.O. Box 644
Wallingford, CT 06492
Home Rink: Choate-Rosemary Hall
Rink Location: Wallingford
pages.prodigy.com/hawks

Middlesex County Youth Hockey
Association, Inc.
Phone: 860-344-0470
P.O. Box 461
Middletown, CT 06457
Home Rink: Wesleyan University
Rink Location: Middletown

Connecticut Hockey Institute
Phone: 860-675-7703
19 Cliff Dr.
Avon, CT 06001
Home Rink: International Skating Center
Rink Location: Simsbury

New Milford Youth Hockey
Phone: 860-210-PUCK
E-mail: puck210@aol.com
37 Maplewood Dr.
New Milford, CT 06776
Home Rink: Canterbury School
Rink Location: New Milford

Stamford Youth Hockey Association
Phone: 203-352-4391
E-mail: david.morrissette@us.ms.philips.com
59 Judy Lane
Stamford, CT 06906
Home Rink: Terry Connors Rink
Rink Location: Stamford

Souteastern Connecticuit Youth Hockey
E-mail: secyh@uconect.com
New London, CT
Home Rink: Norwich Ice Rink
Rink Location: Norwich

Griffin Youth Hockey Association
Phone: 860-546-6606
E-mail: Redlead@aol.com
232 Barstow Rd.
Canterbury, CT 06331-1104
Home Rink: Brown Memorial Rink
Rink Location: Pomfret

Washington-Gunnery Hockey Association
Phone: 860-355-3566
E-mail: Pyers@nai.net
12 Crescent Lane
New Milford, CT 06776
Home Rink: The Gunnery
Rink Location: Washington

East Haven Youth Hockey Association
Phone: 203-467-8425
E-mail: gcelone@juno.com
P.O. Box 12073
East Haven, CT 06512
Home Rink: East Haven Memorial Rink
Rink Location: East Haven

Ridgefield Youth Hockey Assn.
Phone: 203-762-5356
E-mail: KLudwig@Prodigy.net
20 Silver Spring Rd.
Wilton, CT 06897
Home Rink: Winter Garden
Rink Location: Ridgefield

Delaware

Elsmere In-Line Skating Center
Phone: 302-654-5520
E-mail: dberger@aidi.nemours.org
215 New Road
Wilmington, DE 19805
Home Rink: Elsmere Skating Center
Rink Location: Wilimington

Wilmington Typhoon
Phone: 302-656-5005
E-mail: dotg@magpage.com
1301 Carruthers Lane
Wilmington, DE 19803
Home Rink: 302-656-5005
Rink Location: Wilmington

Delaware Junior Blue Hens
Phone: 302-453-9824
E-mail: delhawk@ix.netcom.com
13 Van Sant Rd.
Newark, DE 19711
Phone: 302-831-1350
E-mail: dannyb@udel.edu
Home Rink: University of Delaware Ice
Arena—South College Ave.
Rink Location: Newark

Delaware Ducks
Phone: 302-234-1042
E-mail: gargoyl@concentric.net
608 Frenchtown Road
New Castle, DE 19720
Home Rink: The Pond
Rink Location: Newark

Florida

Gold Coast Minor Hockey
Phone: 954-943-2123
F.G.C.M.H.L.
4601 N. Fed. Highway
Pompano Beach, FL
Home Rink: Gold Coast Ice Arena
Rink Location: Pompano Beach

Southernmost Hockey Club
Phone: 305-296-8056
E-mail: rwm@mpgn.com
800 Eisenhower Dr. #1
Key West, FL 33040
Home Rink: SoMost Hockey Club
Rink Location: Key West
members.aol.com/KWhockey/index.html

Seminole Flames Hockey Club
E-mail: ocsocid@sundial.net
1720 Crown Point Woods Cir.
Ocoee, FL 34761
Home Rink: Tampa Skating Academy
Rink Location: Oldsmar

Tampa Bay Thunder MHC
Phone: 813-535-5399
1529 Hunter Lane
Clearwater, FL 34624
Home Rink: TBSA
Rink Location: Oldsmar

Tampa Bay Junior Lightning
Phone: 800-872-2992
E-mail: stike@trcinc.com
12320 Racetrack Road
Tampa, FL 33626
Home Rink: Sun Blades
Rink Location: Clearwater

Jackonsonville Storm Youth Hockey
Association
Phone: 904-287-1453
E-mail:minebur@aol.com
1217 Creekwood Way
Jacksonville, FL 32259
Home Rink: Skateworld
Rink Location: Jacksonville

South Florida Youth Hockey Association
Phone: 954-452-8537
E-mail: slapshot@icanect.net
8161 S.W. 29th Court
Davie, FL 33328
Home Rink: Pembroke Pines Twin Rinks
Rink Location: Pembroke Pines

Planet Ice Youth Hockey Association of the
Palm Beaches, Inc.
Phone: 561-694-2908
E-mail: goalermom@aol.com
P.O. Box 33148
Palm Beach Gardens, FL 33420
Home Rink: Planet Ice
Rink Location: Palm Beach Gardens

South Florida Youth Hockey Association
Phone: 954-452-8537
E-mail: slapshot@icanect.net
P.O. Box 452198
Sunrise, FL 33345
Rink Location: Pembroke Pines
sfyha.yhn.com

Orlando Youth Hockey
Phone: 407-397-9747
E-mail: oyha@florida-emall.com
Home Rink: Rock on Ice
Rink Location: Orlando

Florida Sunshine Ambassadors
Phone: 561-477-3102
E-mail: interwld@msn.com
P. O. Box 3472
Boca Raton, FL 33427
Home Rink: Gold Coast Ice Arena
Rink Location: Pompano Beach: Florida
Panthers NHL Practice Facility

Georgia

Georgia Amateur Hockey Association
Phone: 770-513-2310, 404-816-3303
Home Rink: Atlanta Ice Forum
Rink Location: Duluth

G.A.H.A.
Phone: 770-736-0085
Duluth, GA 30155
Home Rink: Ice Forum Duluth
Rink Location: Duluth

Idaho

Idaho Falls Youth Hockey Association
Phone: 208-523-7679
E-mail: gregory.hackett@anl.gov
1384 Terry Drive
Idaho Falls, Idaho 83404
Home Rink: Joe Marmo/Wayne Lehto Arena
Rink Location: Tautphaus Park
www.srv.net/~ifhockey

Illinois (Northern)

Wolves Amateur Hockey Association
Phone: 630-778-6969
E-mail: moynihc@mcs.net
1611 Abby Drive
Naperville, IL 60563
Home Rink: All Seasons Ice Arenas
Rink Location: Naperville
www.mcs.net/~moynihc/home.html

Joliet Jaguars Youth Hockey
Phone: 815-744-9810
3000 W. Jefferson St.
Joliet, IL 60431
Home Rink: Inwood Ice Arena
Rink Location: Joliet

Team Illinois 1983
Phone: 708-383-6786
E-mail: creticos@interaccess.com
141 S. Humphrey Avenue
Oak Park, IL 60302
Phone: 847-465-8550
E-mail: s0404@aol.com
95 Fox Hill Drive
Buffalo Grove, IL 60089
Home Rink: Seven Bridges
Rink Location: Woodridge

Chicago Rebels
E-mail: rebels@mcs.net
Home Rink: Southwest Ice Arena
Rink Location: Crestwood

Zion Atoms Hockey Association
Phone: 847-249-4195
P.O. Box 277
Wadsworth, IL 60083
Home Rink: Zion Ice Arena
Rink Location: Zion

Barrington Redwings Hockey Organization
Phone: 847-381-4191
E-mail: blf@concentric.net
168 Whitney Drive
Barrington, IL 60010
Home Rink: Barrington Ice Arena
Rink Location: Barrington

Danville Jr. Wings
Phone: 217-442-3414
E-mail: mpowers3@ix.netcom.com
110 E. 3rd Street
Tilton, IL 61833
Home Rink: David S. Palmer Civic Center
Rink Location: Danville

Homewood-Flosmorr Cardinals
Phone: 708-687-0900
E-mail: pvh16@aol.com
6020 West 151st Street
Oak Forest, IL 60452
Home Rink: H-F Ice Rink
Rink Location: Flosmorr

Flames Hockey Club
1N450 Highland Ave.
Glen Ellyn, IL 60137
Phone: 630-736-8060
Fax: 630-736-8076
E-mail: cidflames@aol.com
Home Rink: Center Ice of DuPage
Rink Location: Glen Ellyn

Kings Hockey League
E-mail: cntr01@mot.com
Phone: 630-837-4320
P.O. Box 68342
Schaumburg, IL 60168-0342
Home Rink: Polar Dome
Rink Location: Dundee
kings.yhn.com

Springfield Youth Hockey Association
Phone: 217-544-9190 ext. 1215
E-mail: umedia@earthlink.net
P.O. Box 9264
Springfield, IL 62791
Home Rink: Nelson Recreation Center
Rink Location: Springfield

Danville Jr. Wings Youth Hockey
Phone: 217-442-2010
Danville, IL 61833
Home Rink: David S. Palmer Civic Center
Rink Location: Danville

Team Illinois Pee Wee Minor Girls
Phone: 708-848-2414
E-mail: doug.gengler@landmark.com
1122 S. Oak Park
Oak Park, IL 60304
Home Rink: Seven Bridges
Rink Location: Woodridge

Oak Lawn Saints
Phone: 708-422-3729
9320 S. Kenton
Oak Lawn, IL 60453
Home Rink: Oak Lawn Ice Arena
Rink Location: Oak Lawn

Peoria Youth Hockey Assoc.
Phone: 309-686-0634
E-mail: pzkelton@iaonline.com
1904 East Knox Street
Peoria, IL 61614

Peoria Youth Hockey Association
Phone: 309-697-0800
8 Stahl Place
Bartonville, IL 61607-1868
Home Rink: Owens Center
Rink Location: Peoria

Downers Grove Huskies
Phone: 708-972-1230
E-mail: MaonTek@ix.netcom.com
617 N. Pinecrest
Bolingbrook, IL 60440
Home Rink: Downers Grove Ice Arena
Rink Location: Downers Grove

Evanston Youth Hockey Association
Phone: 847-332-2217
1701 Main Street
Evanston, IL 60202
E-mail: micor@mcs.net

Chicago Blues
Phone: 312-409-0000
E-mail: mika620010@aol.com
1215 W. Sherwin
Chicago, IL 60626
Home Rink: McFetridge
Rink Location: Chicago

Danville Jr. Wings Youth Hockey
Phone: 217-442-3414
110 E. 3rd Street
Tilton, IL 61833
Home Rink: David S. Palmer Civic Center
Rink Location: Danville

Metro West High School Hockey League
Phone: 630-357-6238
819 Lockwood Circle
Naperville, IL 60563
Home Rink: Several

Vikings Youth Hockey
Phone: 708-802-0054
E-mail: yhn@mc.net
P.O. Box 1104
Tinley Park, IL 60477
Home Rinks: Orland Park Ice Arena
Rink Location: Orland Park

Chicago Hawks
Phone: 773-233-0111
E-mail: tecwfm@aol.com
P.O. Box 1915
Bridgeview, IL 60457
Home Rink: Bridgeview Ice Arena Saints
Spectrum
Rink Location: Bridgeview

Crystal Lake Hockey Club
Phone: 815-455-2379
P.O. Box 671
Crystal Lake, IL 60039-0671
Home Rink: Crystal Ice House

Saints Hockey Club
Phone: 708-857-2427
E-mail: txsr88a@prodigy.com
P.O. Box 45
Oak Lawn, IL 60454-0001
Home Rink: Oak Lawn Ice Arena
Rink Location: Oak Lawn

Illinois (Central)

Danville Jr. Wings Youth Hockey
Phone: 217-442-2010
Danville, IL 61833
Home Rink: David S. Palmer Civic Center
Rink Location: Danville

Pekin Youth Hockey, Inc.
Central Illinois Hockey League
Phone: 309-925-3947
E-mail: calvert@dpc.net
18066 Red Shale Hill Road
Pekin, IL 61554
Rink Location: Pekin
pekinyouthhockey.yhn.com

Champaign-Urbana Youth Hockey
Association
Phone: 217-344-8297
E-mail: aart@uiuc.edu
P.O. Box 262
Champaign, IL 61824
Home Rink: Univ. of Illinois Ice Arena
Rink Location: Champaign

Illinois (Southern)

M.V.A.I.H.A.
Phone: 618-281-3655
E-mail: ldstou@bpcbbs.com
320 Longview Drive
Columbia, IL 62236
Home Rink: Cahokia
Rink Location: Cahokia

Indiana

Irish Youth Hockey League
Phone: 219-277-7519
E-mail: brian_mielock@cmi.com
P.O. Box 49
Notre Dame, IN 46556
Home Rink: Notre Dame Ice Box
Rink Location: Notre Dame

Indianapolis Youth Hockey Association
Phone: 317-815-0499
E-mail: mike@dgtech.com
P.O. Box 24
Carmel, IN 46032
Home Rink: Carmel Ice Skadium
Rink Location: Carmel

Portage Roller Hockey Association
Phone: 219-947-7131
E-mail: HYsticking@aol.com
1207 W. Old Ridge Road
Hobart, IN 46342
Home Rink: Sports Plex
Rink Location: Portage
members.aol.com/HYsticking/
index.html

Fort Wayne Youth Hockey
USA Hockey
E-mail: coachockey@aol.com
P.O. Box 13122
Fort Wayne, IN 46867
Rink Location: Fort Wayne
fortwaynehockey.yhn.com

Indy Blues-Pee Wee AA
Phone: 317-842-1198
E-mail: IndyBlue1@aol.com
13061 New Britton Drive
Fishers, IN 46038
Home Rink: Pan Am Plaza
Rink Location: Indianapolis

Iowa

Quad-City Hockey Association
Phone: 319-359-4512
516 Brown Street
Bettendorf, IA 52722
Home Rink: Quad-City Sport Center
Rink Location: Davenport

Dubuque Youth Hockey Association
Phone: 319-556-3831
E-mail: hockey89@mwci.net
221 Southgate Dr
Dubuque, IA 52002
Home Rink: Five Flags
Rink Location: Dubuque

Mason City Youth Hockey
Phone: 515-424-1816
E-mail: brandenshank@willowtree.com
Hwy 18 West
Mason City, IA 50401
Home Rink: North Iowa Ice Arena
Rink Location: Mason City

Ames Minor Hockey
Phone: 515-292-3606
E-mail: kkennick@iastate.edu
Ames, IA 50010
Home Rink: Ames/ISU Ice Arena
Rink Location: Ames

Siouxland Youth Hockey
Phone: 712-258-8973
E-mail: redraly@pionet.net
3113 Harris St.
Sioux City, IA 51103
Home Rink: S.C. Auditorium
Rink Location: Sioux City

Dubuque Youth Hockey Assn.
Phone: 319-583-3747
E-mail: rrassman@mwci.net
2151 Concord Ct.
Dubuque, IA 52003
Home Rink: Five Flags Center
Rink Location: Dubuque

Hawkeye Youth Ice Skating Association
Phone: 319-363-8281
E-mail: Rustyd@netins.net
616 D Ave. N.W.
Cedar Rapids, IA 52405

Old Capitol Youth Hockey Association
Phone: 319-337-6518
E-mail: jerald-moon@uiowa.edu
55 Brunswick Ct.
Iowa City, IA 52240
Home Rink: Mercer Park Ice Plex

Waterloo Youth Hockey Association
Phone: 319-233-9560
E-mail: trobbin@kirkwood.cc.ia.us
3612 Cadillac Drive
Waterloo, IA 50701
Home Rink: Young Arena
Rink Location: Waterloo

Greater Des Moines Youth Hockey
Association
Phone: 515-278-9757
E-mail: pdephillip@aol
2408 71st Street
Des Moines, IA 50322
Home Rink: Metro Ice Arena
Rink Location: Urbandale

Kansas

Lawrence Amateur Hockey Association
Phone: 913-865-4305
E-mail: schwaby126@aol.com
373 Woodlawn Dr.
Lawrence, KS 66049
Home Rink: The Rinks
Rink Location: Shawnee

Kentucky

Northern Kentucky Youth Hockey
Association
Phone: 606-344-1994
E-mail: ken.handley@sdrc.com
2638 Anderson Rd.
Cresent Springs, KY 41017
Home Rink: Northern Kentucky Ice Center
Rink Location: Cresent Springs

Northern Kentucky Junior Hockey (NKJHA)
Phone: 606-344-1994
E-mail: ken.handley@sdrc.com
2638 Anderson Rd.
Cresent Springs, KY 41017
Home Rink: Northern Kentucky Ice Center
Rink Location: Cresent Springs

Louisville Youth Hockey Association
E-mail: lyha@rocketmail.com
Louisville, KY
Home Rink: Iceland Ice Arena
Rink Location: Anchorage, KY
www.ntr.net/~rstastny/lyha.html

Maine

Central Maine Youth Hockey Association
E-mail: janlmoore@aol.com
18 Hudon Road
Lisbon, ME 04250
Home Rink: Pettingill Ice Arena
Rink Location: Auburn

Penobscot Valley Hockey Club
Phone: 207-989-0449
13 Rockland Ct.
Brewer, ME 04412
Home Rink: H.O. Bouchard Sports
Complex
Rink Location: Brewer

Dover Youth Hockey
Phone: 207-384-3221
E-mail: dh2309@mail.rscs.net
53 Oldfields Rd.
So. Berwick, ME 03908
Home Rink: Dover Arena
Rink Location: Dover, NH

PVHC
Phone: 207-989-0449
E-mail: Nanook5782@aol.com
13 Rockland CT
Brewer, ME 04412
Home Rink: H.O. Bouchard Arena
Rink Location: Brewer

BYHA Liberty Mutual Squirts
Phone: 207-282-3144
E-mail: hocpuk@lamere.net
Biddeford, ME 04005
Home Rink: The Arena
Rink Location: Biddeford

Portland Jr. Pirates
Phone: 207-797-3851
E-mail: marsh@mainelink.net
Home Rink: Cumberland City Civic Center
Rink Location: Portland

Casco Bay Hockey Association
Phone: 207-829-4159
E-mail: a37kolzig@aol.com
135 Longwoods Rd.
Cumberland, ME 04021
Home Rink: North Yarmouth Academy/
Portland Ice Arena
Rink Location: Yarmouth Portland

Maryland

Nelson Hockey
Phone: 301-953-0200
E-mail: nburton@erols.com
13800 Old Gunpowder Road
Laurel, MD 20707
Home Rink: The Gardens Ice House
Rink Location: Laurel

Magruder High School Ice Hockey Club
Phone: 301-977-7385
E-mail: mmccary@sysnet.net
18420 Gardenia Way
Gaithersburg, MD 20879
Home Rink: Ice Gardens
Rink Location: Laurel

Easton Ice Hawks
Phone: 410-643-1036
E-mail: ptorre@friend.ly.net
124 Tennessee Road
Stevensville, MD 21666
Home Rink: Talbot Cty. Comm. Ctr.
Rink Location: Easton

Baltimore Junior Bandits
Phone: 410-695-0310
E-mail: pr10036@aol.com
759 Pine Drift Way
Odenton, MD 21113
Home Rink: Ice World
Rink Location: Abingdon

Bowie Hockey Club Mite "B"
Phone: 410-765-1646
E-mail:
bunting.r.l@postal.essd.northgrum.com
2908 Crystal Place Lane
Pasadena, MD 21122
Home Rink: Bowie
Rink Location: Bowie

Howard County Youth Hockey
Phone: 410-730-3865
E-mail: ocsrdo@nmaa.org
5876 Thunderhill Road
Columbia, MD 21044
Home Rink: Columbia Ice Rink
Rink Location: Columbia

Washington Little Capitals AA
Phone: 301-460-3617
1620 Woodwell Road
Silver Spring, MD 20906
Home Rink: Piney Orchard, MD
Rink Location: Metro DC area
www.mnsinc.com/bry/litlcaps/htm

Bowie Hockey Club
Phone: 410-757-3217
E-mail: russ.poisson@cop.mts.dec.com
1553 Star Pine Drive
Annapolis, MD 21401
Home Rink: Bowie Ice Arena
Rink Location: Bowie

Chesapeake Bay Chiefs
Phone: 410-849-5438
E-mail: mdbancroft@aol.com
159 Friar Tuck Hill
Sherwood Forest, MD 21405
Home Rink: Piney Orchard Ice Forum
Rink Location: Odenton

Washington Junior Capitals
Phone: 301-774-1327
Home Rink: Piney Orchard
Rink Location: Odenton

Washington Little Capitals
Phone: 301-774-1327
Home Rinks: Various
Rink Locations: Wash, DC Metro Area

Frederick Area Hockey Club "Phantoms"
Phone: 301-253-9656
E-mail: fahcmom@aol.com
12617 Finger Board Road
Monrovia, MD 21770
Home Rink: Frederick Sport and Ice Arena
Rink Location: Frederick

Mt. Hebron Viking High School Hockey
E-mail: pooty@erols.com
Home Rink: Laurel Ice Gardens
Rink Location: Laurel

Massachusetts

Lakers Youth Hockey
Phone: 508-389-2675
E-mail: lowell@neesnet.com
86 Lee Street
West Boylston, MA 01583
Home Rink: Buffone Rink
Rink Location: Worcester

MBJHL
Phone: 617-279-0859
E-mail: mbjhl@usa1.com
P.O. Box 80480
Stoneham, MA 02180
Home Rink: Marlboro, Wilmington
Rink Location: Marlboro, Wilmington

Hyde Park Youth Hockey
Phone: 617-323-1324
E-mail: chynes2000@aol.com
208 Temple Street
West Roxbury, MA 02132
Home Rink: Bajko Rink
Rink Location: West Roxbury

Needham Youth Hockey
Phone: 617-444-8551
E-mail: meditype@erols.com
1480 Central Avenue
Needham, MA 02192
Home Rink: St. Sebastian's
Rink Location: Needham

Boston Jr. Terriers
Phone: 617-696-2292
E-mail: Jrterrier@aol.com
138 Highland St.
Milton, MA 02186
Home Rink: Walter Brown Arena
Rink Location: Boston University

South Boston Youth Hockey
Phone: 617-268-8915
E-mail: zopmac@ix.netcom.com
895 East Broadway
South Boston, MA 02127
Home Rink: Murphy
Rink Location: South Boston

Arlington Hockey & Figure Skating Club
Phone: 617-643-3483
E-mail: fitz954@aol.com
204 Renfrew Street
Arlington, MA 02174
Home Rink: Veterans Memorial Sports Center
Rink Location: Arlington

Peabody Youth Hockey
Phone: 508-532-9469
E-mail: mmg606768@msn.com
Peabody, MA 01960
Home Rink: Mcvann-Okeefe
Rink Location: Peabody

Assabet Valley Minor Hockey Association
Phone: 508-670-2744
E-mail: dazuka@aol.com
P.O. Box 1022
Billerica, MA 01821
Home Rink: Valley Sports Arena
Rink Location: Concord

South Shore Seahawks
E-mail: senatore@massmed.org
P.O. Box 699
Marshfield, MA 02050
Home Rink: Hobomock Arenas
Rink Location: Pembroke

Hetland Panthers Youth Hockey
Association District 5
Phone: 508-763-9803
E-mail: retrotek1@aol.com
18 Ashley Brook Lane
Rochester, MA 02770
Home Rink: Hetland Stephan Memorial
Rink Location: New Bedford

SWS Youth Hockey
Phone: 508-672-7777
E-mail: mcnaughton.jim@gtefsd.com
Fall River, MA 02720
Home Rink: Driscoll
Rink Location: Fall River

Barnstable Youth Hockey
Phone: 508-428-7117
E-mail: poberlander@whoi.edu
P.O. Box 1075
Marstons Mills, MA 02648
Home Rink: Kennedy
Rink Location: Hyannis

Ash-West Youth Hockey Warriors
Phone: 508-874-0352
E-mail: rrogers@tiac.net
156 West Princeton Rd.
Westminster, MA 01473
Home Rink: Iorio Arena
Rink Location: Cushing Academy, Ashburnham

District 7 Girls Hockey Bandits
Phone: 508-297-0912
E-mail: stger@tiac.net
126 Glenallen St.
Winchenden, MA 01477
Home Rink: Iorio Arena
Rink Location: Cushing Academy,
Ashburnham

Franklin County Hockey Association
Phone: 413-863-4008
E-mail: cjacobs@k12.oit.umass.edu
10 Nadeau Ave.
Turners Falls, MA 01376
Home Rink: Greenfield
Rink Location: Greenfield

Bay State Youth Hockey
Phone: 508-949-0441
E-mail: M_LeBlanc@delni.enet.dec.com
18 Sunrise Shore Road
Dudley, MA 01571
Home Rink: Daniel Horgan
Rink Location: Auburn

Twin City Youth Hockey Association
Phone: 508-537-1486
E-mail: brandimarte@mail.dec.com
P.O. Box 143
Leominster, MA 01453
Home Rink: Wallace Civic Center
Rink Location: Fitchburg
world.std.com/~porourke/tcyh/
tcyh.html

Central Mass Outlaws
Phone: 508-874-0352
E-mail: rrogers@tiac.net
156 West Princeton Road
Westminster, MA 01473
Home Rink: New England Sports Center
Rink Location: Marlboro

Demons Youth Hockey
Phone: 508-435-9269
E-mail: kenr@osf.org
289 Elm St.
Hopkinton, MA 01748
Home Rink: Northstar, Navin
Rink Location: Westboro

Danvers Youth Hockey Assoc.
E-mail: mjones@nextwavetel.com
46 Manning Park Rd.
Billerica, MA 01821
Home Rink: McVann Rink
Rink Location: Peabody

Charlestown Youth Hockey Assoc
Phone: 617-241-5566
E-mail: Lawnwood@aol.com
46 Union Street
Charlestown, MA 02129
Home Rink: Emmons-Horrigan-O'Neil
Rink Location: Charlestown

North Andover Youth Hockey League, Inc
Phone: 508-688-5533
E-mail: wjkeogh@aol.com
P.O. Box 253
North Andover, MA 01845
Home Rink: Brooks School
Rink Location: North Andover

Greater Boston Jr. Bruins
Phone: 617-241-5566
E-mail: Lawnwood@aol.com
253 Main Street
Charlestown, MA 02129
Home Rink: Quincy Youth Arena
Rink Location: Quincy

Westwood Youth Hockey
Phone: 617-326-7476
E-mail: Mfitzpatrick@warrenpubcorp.com
144 Colburn Street
Westwood, MA 02090
Home Rink: Babson
Rink Location: Wellesley

Reading Youth Hockey
Phone: 617-492-2777 ext. 3807
E-mail: phil_mccabe@wgbh.org
8 Bear Hill Road
Reading, MA 01867
Home Rink: Burbank Ice Arena
Rink Location: Reading

Valley Jr. Warriors Bantam
Phone: 508-532-5224
E-mail: playhock@aol.com
4 Roland Rd.
Peabody, MA 01960
Home Rink: Valley Forum
Rink Location: Lawrence

Barnstable Youth Hockey
E-mail: poberlander@whoi.edu
P.O. Box 1075
Marstons Mills, MA 02648
Home Rink: Kennedy
Rink Location: Hyannis

Plymouth Youth Hockey
Phone: 508-999-0072
E-mail: rokhok@ma.ultranet.com
19 Richfield Circle
Carver, MA 02330
Home Rink: Armstrong
Rink Location: Plymouth

UMass Jr. Minutemen
Phone: 860-875-5663
E-mail: chapdel@hsd.utc.com
48 1/2 Egypt Rd.
Ellingtion Ct., MA 06029
Home Rink: Mullins Center
Rink Location: Amherst
www.ecs.umass.edu/ece/looze/TM/
TMPage.html

Boston Junior Bruins
Phone: 508-366-2007
E-mail: Rivhok@aol.com
P.O. Box 460
Lexington, MA
Home Rink: Kasabuski Arena
Rink Location: Saugus

Lynnfield Youth Hockey
Phone: 617-344-6174
E-mail: econway1@geocities,com
P.O. Box 192
Lynnfield, MA 01940
Home Rink: Peabody Rink
Rink Location: Peabody

Minnesota (Northern)

Mesabi East Youth Hockey
Phone: 218-865-6752
E-mail: ldusing@northernnet.com
6277 Red Pine Road
Gilbert, MN 55741
Home Rink: Arena
Rink Location: Hoyt Lakes

Fairmont
Phone: 507-235-9031
Fairmont, MN 56031
Home Rink: Martin Co. Arena
Rink Location: Fairmont

Long Prairie Hockey Association
Phone: 320-732-2162
E-mail: johntoft@rea.com
103 2nd St. So., P.O. Box 238
Long Prairie, MN 56347
Home Rink: Todd Co. Expo. Arena
Rink Location: Long Prairie

Minnesota Hockey Showcase
Phone: 612-920-8826
5608 Vermont Street
St Louis Park, MN 55416
Home Rink: Mpls/St Paul

Bemidji Youth Hockey Assn
Phone: 218-759-2229
E-mail: elliott@northernnet.com
4403 Sherman Dr. NE
Bemidji, MN 56601
Home Rink: Nymore Gardens
Rink Location: Bemidji

Annadale/Maple Lake Youth Hockey
Association
M.A.H.A.
8704 Japser Ave. NW
Annadale, MN 55302

Anoka Area Hockey Association
M.A.H.A.
14279 Vintage St. NW
Andover, MN 55304

Elk River Hockey Association
M.A.H.A.
11080 190-1/2 Ave. NW
Elk River, MN 55330

Forest Lake Youth Hockey Association
M.A.H.A.
9889 N. Shore Trail
Forest Lake, MN 55025

Goodview-Winona Hockey Association
M.A.H.A.
562 Kerry Drive
Goodview, MN 55987

Blaine Youth Hockey Association
M.A.H.A.
230 159th Ave. NE
Ham Lake, MN 55304

Hanover Youth Hockey Association
M.A.H.A.
8900 Trail Haven Rd.
Hamel, MN 55340

Chicago Lakes Hockey Association
M.A.H.A.
13030 4th Ave. N
Lindstrom, MN 55045

Orona Youth Hockey Association
M.A.H.A.
2905 Fox St.
Long Lake, MN 55356

Crow River Youth Hockey Association
M.A.H.A.
6476 Fogelman
Maple Plain, MN 55359

Monticello Youth Hockey Association
M.A.H.A.
13986 Duffield Ave. NW
Monticello, MN 55362

Pine City Youth Hockey Association
M.A.H.A.
620 9th St.
Pine City, MN 55063

Buffalo Youth Hockey Association
M.A.H.A.
10125 Ebert Rd.
Rogers, MN 55374

St. Cloud Youth Hockey Association
M.A.H.A.
1568 Cypress Rd.
St. Cloud, MN 56303

Waseca Hockey Association
M.A.H.A.
40296 160th St.
Waseca, MN 56093

Minnesota (Central)

Youth Association Hockey, Inc.
Phone: 612-653-8253
E-mail: pharvey@isd.net
2407 Ronald Ave.
White Bear Lake, MN 55110-4863
Home Rink: Ramsey Co.
Rink Location: Ramsey County

Blaine Youth Hockey Association
Phone: 612-434-5112
230 159th Ave. NE
Ham Lake, MN 55304
Home Rink: Fogerty
Rink Location: Blaine

Orono Hockey Boosters, Inc.
Phone: 612-473-2521
E-mail: wayzjac9@skypoint.com
P.O. Box 205
Long Lake, MN 55356
Home Rink: Pond Arena
Rink Location: Mound

Southwest Hockey Association
Phone: 612-922-4211
E-mail: youthhockeydad@hotmail.com
4715 Ewing Ave. S.
Minneapolis, MN
Home Rink: Parade Ice Garden
Rink Location: Minneapolis

Anoka Area Hockey Association
Phone: 612-427-9919
E-mail: yhn@mc.net
P.O. Box 112
Anoka, MN 55303
Home Rink: Anoka Area Ice Arena
Rink Location: Anoka

Champlin Park Youth Hockey Association
Phone: 612-969-2543
Champlin, MN 55316
Home Rink: Ice Forum at Champlin
Rink Location: Champlin

Kennedy Hockey Booster Club
Phone: 612-881-2136
E-mail: art69@mail.idt.net
10316 Clinton Ave So.
Bloomington, MN 55420
Home Rink: Bloomington Ice Gardens
Rink Location: Bloomington

Bloomington Jefferson Hockey Booster Club
M.A.H.A.
10532 Zion Ave. South
Bloomington, MN 55437

Bloomington Athletic Association
M.A.H.A.
5023 Overlook Circle
Bloomington, MN 55437

Brooklyn Center Hockey Association
M.A.H.A.
4113 Joyce Lane
Brooklyn, MN 55429

Brooklyn Park Hockey Association
M.A.H.A.
3266 Berwick Knoll
Brooklyn Park, MN 55443

Coon Rapids Hockey Association
M.A.H.A.
9716 Zilla St.
Coon Rapids, MN 55433

Cottage Grove Hockey Association
M.A.H.A.
8324 69th St. South
Cottage Grove, MN 55016

Eagan Hockey Association
M.A.H.A.
889 Curry Trail
Eagan, MN 55123

Mora Area Youth Recreation Association
M.A.H.A.
RR 1 Box 125D
Brook Park, MN 55007

Chaska Community Hockey Association
M.A.H.A.
7255 159th St.
Carver, MN 55315

East River Hockey Association
M.A.H.A.
1840 Fairway Drive
Columbia Heights, MN 55421

Benilde/St. Margaret
M.A.H.A.
5135 Lincoln Dr. #107
Edina, MN 55436

Edina Hockey Association
M.A.H.A.
7224 Tara Rd
Edina, MN 55439

Hutchinson Hockey Association
M.A.H.A.
1240 7th Ave. NW
Hutchinson, MN 55350

Inver Grove Heights Hockey Association
M.A.H.A.
8430 Carvin Ct.
Inver Grove Heights, MN 55076

Tartan Area Youth Hockey Association
M.A.H.A.
9023 N. 9th St.
Lake Elmo, MN 55128

Osseo-Maple Grove Hockey Association
M.A.H.A.
9139 Quantico Lane
Maple Grove, MN 55369

Mahtomedi Youth Hockey Association
M.A.H.A.
214 Shamrock Dr.
Mehtomedi, MN 55115

Edison Youth Hockey Association
M.A.H.A.
1317 3rd St. NE
Minneapolis, MN 55418

Henry Youth Hockey Association
M.A.H.A.
38245 Aldridge Ave. N
Minneapolis, MN 55432

Southwest Hockey Association
M.A.H.A.
2016 Laurel Avenue West
Minneapolis, MN 55405

Washburn Area Hockey Association
M.A.H.A.
4200 Fremont Ave. S.
Minneapolis, MN 55409

Minnesota Girls & Womens Hockey
Association
M.A.H.A.
5500 Wayzala Blvd.
Minneapolis, MN 55416

Hopkins Youth Hockey Association
M.A.H.A.
3730 Plymouth Rd.
Minnetonka, MN 55343

Mound/Westonka Hockey Association
M.A.H.A.
4100 Enchanted Lane
Mound/Westonka, MN 55364

Irondale Youth Hockey Association
M.A.H.A.
2373 LaPont Dr.
Mounds View, MN 55112

North St. Paul Hockey Association
M.A.H.A.
2202 Buhl Ave.
St. Paul, MN 55109

Armstrong Youth Hockey Association
M.A.H.A.
9645 28th Ave. N.
Plymouth, MN 55441

Wayzata Youth Hockey Association
M.A.H.A.
3440 Urbandale Lane N.
Plymouth, MN 55447

Richfield Hockey Association
M.A.H.A.
7526 14th Ave. South
Richfield, MN 55423

Cooper Youth Hockey Association
M.A.H.A.
3713 Regent Ave. N.
Robbinsdale, MN 55422

Roseville Hockey Association
M.A.H.A.
2701 Dale
Roseville, MN 55113

South St. Paul Hockey Association
M.A.H.A.
1 Apfleridge Ct.
South St. Paul, MN 55075

St. Louis Park Hockey Association
M.A.H.A.
2842 Salem Ave. S.
St. Louis Park, MN 55416

Como Area Hockey Association
M.A.H.A.
277 Stinson
St. Paul, MN 55117

Harding Area Hockey Association
M.A.H.A.
964 Germain Ct.
St. Paul, MN 55106

Highland/Central Hockey Association
M.A.H.A.
1849 Juliet
St. Paul, MN 55104

West Side/West End Hockey Association
M.A.H.A.
207 E. Wyoming
St. Paul, MN 55107

Mendota Heights Hockey Association
M.A.H.A.
765 Lower Colonial Sr.
St. Paul, MN 55118

St. Croix Valley Hockey Association
M.A.H.A.
Box 295
Stillwater, MN 55082

West St. Paul Youth Athletic Association
M.A.H.A.
1066 Sperl
West St. Paul, MN 55118

White Bear Lake Hockey Association
M.A.H.A.
1915 LeMire Circle
White Bear Lake, MN 55110

Woodbury Area Hockey Association
M.A.H.A.
9286 Cornell Circle
Woodbury, MN 55125

Minnesota (Southern)

Blaine Youth Hockey Association
Phone: 612-434-6691
E-mail: jalexand@empros.com
17609 Jefferson St. NE
Ham Lake, MN 55304
Home Rink: Fogerty Arena
Rink Location: Blaine

Albert Lea Hockey Association
M.A.H.A.
P.O. Box 348
Albert Lea, MN 56007

Austin Youth Hockey Association
M.A.H.A.
304 21st St. NW
Austin, MN 55912

Cannon Falls Hockey Boosters
M.A.H.A.
6741 Eldorado Way
Cannon Falls, MN 55009

Centennial Hockey Association
M.A.H.A.
93 W. Golden Lake Rd.
Centennial, MN 55014

Chambridge-Asanti Hockey Association
M.A.H.A.
1508 309 Ave. NW
Chambridge, MN 55008

Fairbault Hockey Association
M.A.H.A.
511 SW 4th Ave.
Fairbault, MN 55021

Farmington Youth Hockey Association
M.A.H.A.
217 Hickory St. W
Farmington, MN 55024

Hastings Hockey Boosters
M.A.H.A.
1460 Truax Cr.
Hastings, MN 55033

Owatonna Youth Hockey Assocation
M.A.H.A.
c/o Vogel Arena
122 S. Garden
New Ulm, MN 56073

Northfield Hockey Association
M.A.H.A.
27 Jefferson Dr.
Northfield, MN 55057

Paynesville Youth Hockey Association
M.A.H.A.
28946 Koronis Ave.
Paynesville, MN 56362

Shakopee/Prior Lake Hockey Association
M.A.H.A.
15015 Aquila Ave. S
Prior Lake, MN 55372

Red Wing Amateur Hockey Association
M.A.H.A.
942 Burton St.
Red Wing, MN 55066

Redwood Falls Hockey Association
M.A.H.A.
Redwood Falls, MN 56283

Rochester Youth Hockey Association
M.A.H.A.
2507 27th Ave. NW
Rochester, MN 55901

Rosemount Area Hockey Association
M.A.H.A.
3930 137th St. W
Rosemount, MN 55068

Sleepy Eye Hockey Association
M.A.H.A.
RFD 1
Sleepy Eye, MN 56085

Worthington Hockey Association
M.A.H.A.
1380 Maplewood Drive
Worthington, MN 56187

Mankato Area Hockey Association
M.A.H.A.
110 Ivy Lane
Mankato, MN 56002

Michigan (Northern and Central)

United Scholastic Achievers, Inc.
Phone: 800-521-0600 ext. 3334
E-mail: aclem20577@aol.com
P.O. Box 321
Durand, MI 48429-0321
Home Rink: Iceland Arena
Rink Location: Flint
members.aol.com/aclem20577/
index.html

Mt. Clemens Wolves Travel
Phone: 313-885-0662
E-mail: james_miele@notes.mic.gmeds.com
1508 Hollywood
Grosse Pointe Woods, MI 48236
Home Rink: Mt. Clemens Ice Arena
Rink Location: Mt. Clemens

Jackson Area Hockey Association
Phone: 517-787-2406
E-mail: hecross@aol.com
P.O. Box 6044
Jackson, MI 49204
Home Rink: Optimist Ice Arena
Rink Location: 1300 W. North St.

Baraga Jr. Hockey
Phone: 906-353-6787
E-mail: apatovis@up.net
Rt. 1 Box 521
Baraga, MI 49908
Home Rink: Baraga
Rink Location: Baraga

Grosse Pointe Hockey Association
Southeastern Michigan
1536 S. Renaud
Grosse Pointe Woods, MI 48236
Home Rink: City Sports Center
Rink Location: Detroit

St. Clair Shores Hockey
Phone: 810-468-7643
E-mail: dc3meds@moa.net
38670 Hamon
Harrison Township, MI
Home Rink: S.C.S. Civic Arena
Rink Location: St. Clair Shores

Allen Park Hockey
M.A.H.A.
15800 White
Allen Park, MI 48101

Alpena Hockey
M.A.H.A.
P.O. Box 434
Alpena, MI 49707

Ann Arbor Amateur Hockey
M.A.H.A.
1334 Marlbough
Ann Arbor, MI 48104

Baraga Area Hockey
M.A.H.A.
P.O. Box 161
Baraga, MI 49908

Greater Battle Creek Ice Hockey
M.A.H.A.
P.O. Box 1682
Battle Creek, MI 49016

Big Rapids Area Junior Hockey
M.A.H.A.
Ferris State College
Big Rapids, MI 49307

Birmingham Hockey
M.A.H.A.
2300 East Lincoln
Birmingham, MI 48008

Flint IMA Hockey
M.A.H.A.
6045 Davison Rd.
Burton, MI 48509

I.M.A. Junior Sports Youth Hockey
M.A.H.A.
6045 Davison Rd.
Burton, MI 48509

Cadillac Area Youth Hockey
M.A.H.A.
201 Howard St.
Cadillac, MI 49601

Calumet Hockey
M.A.H.A.
Box 385
Calumet, MI 49913

Little Caesars Amateur Hockey
M.A.H.A.
7429 Kingsbridge
Canton, MI 48187

Cheboygan Hockey
M.A.H.A.
548 Bayview
Cheboygan, MI 49721

Team Michigan-Fraser
M.A.H.A.
28441 Anchor
Chesterfield, MI 48047

Dearborn Hockey
M.A.H.A.
P.O. Box 25
Dearborn, MI 48121

Dearborn Heights Hockey
M.A.H.A.
8597 Dixie Lane
Dearborn Heights, MI 48127

Detroit Hockey
M.A.H.A.
10500 Lyndon
Detroit, MI 48238

Greater Lansing Amateur Hockey
M.A.H.A.
P.O. Box 1238
East Lansing, MI 48823

Escanaba Area Junior Hockey
M.A.H.A.
P.O. Box 150
Escanaba, MI 49829

Upper Peninsula Hockey
M.A.H.A.
Box 151
Escanaba, MI 49829

Compuware Hockey Club
M.A.H.A.
31440 Northwestern Hwy.
Farmington Hills, MI 48018-5650

Farmington Hills Hockey Association
M.A.H.A.
29483 Shenandoah
Farmington Hills, MI 48331

Michigan National Hockey
M.A.H.A.
830 Westwood Dr.
Fenton, MI 48430

G.P.D. Hockey Club
M.A.H.A.
308 W. 8 Mile Rd.
Ferndale, MI 48220

Flint Eastern Michigan Hockey
M.A.H.A.
830 Westwood
Flint, MI 48430

Fraser Falcons
M.A.H.A.
34400 Utica
Fraser, MI 48026

Garden City Youth Athletic
M.A.H.A.
200 Log Cabin Road
Garden City, MI 48135

Otsego County Hockey
M.A.H.A.
P.O. Box 835
Gaylord, MI 49735

Gladwin Area Hockey
M.A.H.A.
4352 Riley Rd.
Gladwin, MI 48624

Grand Rapids Amateur Hockey
M.A.H.A.
P.O. Box 213
Grand Rapids, MI 49588-0213

Grosse Pointe Hockey
M.A.H.A.
1536 S. Renaud
Grosse Pointe Woods, MI 48236

Copper Country Junior Hockey
M.A.H.A.
1550 Birch St.
Hancock, MI 49930

Char-Em Youth Hockey
M.A.H.A.
4560 Heynia
Harbor Springs, MI 49740

Michigan Nationals Hockey Club
M.A.H.A.
P.O. Box 94
Inkster, MI 41841

Dickinson Amateur Hockey
M.A.H.A.
P.O. Box 313
Iron Mountain, MI 49801

Ironwood Polar Bears Hockey Club, Inc.
M.A.H.A.
P.O. Box 121 Greenbush St.
Ironwood, MI 49938

Jackson Area Hockey
M.A.H.A.
P.O. Box 6044
Jackson, MI 49204

Kalamazoo Optimist Hockey
M.A.H.A.
3600 Van Rick Dr.
Kalamazoo, MI 49007

Western Michigan Hockey
M.A.H.A.
6328 Queens Way
Kalamazoo, MI 49009

Kentwood Hockey & Skating
M.A.H.A.
P.O. Box 8247
Kentwood, MI 49508

L'Anse Hockey
M.A.H.A.
P.O. Box 215
L'Anse, MI 49946

Lincoln Park Hockey
M.A.H.A.
3525 Dix
Lincoln Park, MI 48146

Livonia Hockey
M.A.H.A.
33000 Civic Center Drive
Livonia, MI 48154

MIC MAC Hockey Club
M.A.H.A.
28009 Jamison
Livonia, MI 48154

Mackinaw City Skating Association
M.A.H.A.
P.O. Box 596
Mackinaw City, MI 49701

Manistique Hockey
M.A.H.A.
P.O. Box 332
Manistique, MI 49854

Marquette Junior Hockey Corp.
M.A.H.A.
P.O. Box 992
Marquette, MI 49855

Midland Amateur Hockey League
M.A.H.A.
P.O. Box 1304
Midland, MI 48641

Munising Hockey Association
M.A.H.A.
P.O. Box 813
Munising, MI 49862

Muskegon County Amateur Hockey
M.A.H.A.
P.O. Box 875
Muskegon, MI 49443

Iron Range Hockey
M.A.H.A.
P.O. Box 105
Negaunee, MI 49866

Tahquamenon Area Youth Hockey
M.A.H.A.
506 Newberry Ave.
Newberry, MI 49868

Ontonagon Amateur Hockey
M.A.H.A.
P.O. Box 3
Ontonagon, MI 49953

Mount Pleasant Amateur Hockey Association
M.A.H.A.
941 W. Wing
Pleasant, MI 48858

Michigan Capitals Womens Hockey
M.A.H.A.
P.O. Box 521 Wing St.
Plymouth, MI 48170

Plymouth-Canton Hockey
M.A.H.A.
900 Lilley Rd.
Plymouth, MI 48170

Port Huron Hockey
M.A.H.A.
P.O. Box 251
Port Huron, MI 48060

Redford Township Hockey
M.A.H.A.
12400 Beech Daly
Redford, MI 48239

River Rouge Hockey
M.A.H.A.
141 East Great Lakes
River Rouge, MI 48218

Michigan Travelers Hockey Club
M.A.H.A.
1457 Chestnut
Rochester, MI 48063

U.S.A. Spartans Hockey Club, Inc.
M.A.H.A.
385 Tanglewood
Rochester Hills, MI 48309

USA Hockey Club
M.A.H.A.
1675 John Rd.
Rochester Hills, MI 48307

R.F.B. Hockey
M.A.H.A.
23452 Astrid Lane
Rockwood, MI 48173

Royal Oak Hockey
M.A.H.A.
P.O. Box 782
Royal Oak, MI 48068

Greater Saginaw Amateur Association
M.A.H.A.
6129 Bay Rd.
Saginaw, MI 48604

Soo Michigan Hockey
M.A.H.A.
P.O. Box 241
Sault Ste. Marie, MI 49783

Livingston County Hockey
M.A.H.A.
11836 Four Lakes Dr.
South Lyon, MI 48178

South Lyon
M.A.H.A.
11836 Four Lakes Dr.
South Lyon, MI 48178

Southfield Hockey Club, Inc.
M.A.H.A.
P.O. Box 315
Southfield, MI 48037

Southgate Hockey
M.A.H.A.
14700 Reaume Dr.
Southgate, MI 48195

St. Clair Shores Hockey
M.A.H.A.
19924 Edmunton
St. Clair Shores, MI 48080

Macomb Hockey
M.A.H.A.
14415 Alpena
St. Hts., MI 48313

Iron Amateur Hockey
M.A.H.A.
P.O. Box 727
Stambaugh, MI 49964

Huron Hockey & Skating Association
M.A.H.A.
138 Anna
Tawas City, MI 48763

Grand Traverse Hockey
M.A.H.A.
P.O. Box 203
Traverse City, MI 49685

Trenton Hockey
M.A.H.A.
P.O. Box 42
Trenton, MI 48183

Berkley Hockey
M.A.H.A.
54 Evaline
Troy, MI 48098

Warren Hockey
M.A.H.A.
11886 Ridge
Utica, MI 48315

Gogebic Range Hockey
M.A.H.A.
P.O. Box 74
Wakefield, MI 49968

Adray Community
M.A.H.A.
27141 Shelbourne
Warren, MI 48093

Lakeland Hockey
M.A.H.A.
7330 Highland Rd.
Waterford, MI 48327

Wayne Youth Hockey
M.A.H.A.
4635 Howe Rd.
Wayne, MI 48184

North American Junior Hockey
M.A.H.A.
4051 Circle Dr.
West Bloomfield, MI 48033

Westland Hockey
M.A.H.A.
39301 Cambridge
Westland, MI 48185

Woodhaven Hockey
M.A.H.A.
21023 Tiffany
Woodhaven, MI 48183

Inter-City Girls Hockey
M.A.H.A.
19361 Lancaster Dr.
Woodhaven, MI 48183

Wyandotte-Riverview Hockey
M.A.H.A.
P.O. Box 664
Wyandottte, MI 48192

Elmwood Blues Hockey Teams
M.A.H.A.
7980 Todd Rd.
Yale, MI 48097

Michigan (Southern)

West Michigan Warriors-AAA-84's
Phone: 616-345-5369
E-mail: mike@spectrum-mm.com
6530 Twilight
Kalamazoo, MI 49004
Home Rink: Southside Arena
Rink Location: Grand Rapids

USA Hockey Club-Michigan
Phone: 810-851-7490
E-mail: 74262.2551@compuserve.com
888 Denison Ct.
Bloomfield Hills, MI 48302
Home Rink: Detroit Skate Club
Rink Location: Bloomfield Hills

West Side Coyotes Bantam "A" Hockey Club
Phone: 810-960-9636
2795 Woodbury
Walled Lake, MI 48390
Home Rink: University of Michigan at
Dearborn
Rink Location: University of Michigan,
Dearborn Campus

Birmingham Hockey Association
Phone: 810-433-3974
E-mail: rweekes@infoseek.com
18356 Bedford
Beverly Hills, MI 48009
Home Rink: Birmingham Ice Arena

Grosse Pointe Hockey Association
1536 S. Renaud
Grosse Pointe Woods, MI 48236

Eastern Michigan Hockey Association
Phone: 810-629-7637
830 Westwood Drive
Fenton, MI 48430
Home Rink: Iceland Arenas
Rink Location: Flint
members.aol.com/fpichler/
welcome.html

Royal Oak Hockey Association
Phone: 248-435-9309
E-mail: bobk@roha.org
P.O. Box 782
Royal Oak, MI, 48068-0782
Home Rink: John Lindell Memorial Arena
Rink Location: Royal Oak
www.roha.org

Missouri

Great Skate Roller Rink
Phone: 314-922-0512
E-mail: inlsk8@msn.com
1350 Blue Ridge Dr.
St. Peters, MO 63376
Home Rink: Great Skate
Rink Location: St. Peters

Webster Groves Hockey Association
Phone: 314-822-9928
E-mail: ktrum@seas.wustl.edu
1485 Dearborn Drive
St. Louis, MO 63122
Home Rink: Webster Groves
Rink Location: Webster Groves

Kirkwood Youth Hockey Association
Phone: 314-821-7507
868 North Kirkwood Road
Kirkwood, MO 63122-2656
Home Rink: Kirkwood
Rink Location: Kirkwood Park

Montana

Montana Amateur Hockey Association
Presidents
Bozeman Amateur Hockey Association
Phone: 406-586-6817
E-mail: reachrob@avicom.net
1117 S. Bozeman
Bozeman, MT 59715
Home Rink: Bozeman Ice Center
Rink Location: W. of Bozeman

Nebraska

O.M.A.H.A. Omaha Metropolitan Amateur
Hockey Association
Phone: 402-552-0230
E-mail: omahahoc@aol.com
6115 Maple Street
Omaha, NE 68104
Home Rink: Moylan; Tranquility IcePlex
Rink Location: Omaha

Gladiators Athletics
Phone: 402-339-3688
E-mail: mjmille1@wcc.com
5810 South 104 Ave.
Omaha NE 68127
Home Rink: Hitchcock
Rink Location: Omaha

Nevada

Las Vegas Mustangs
Phone: 702-795-7660
E-mail: desertpuck@aol.com
1500 East Tropicana Suite 109
Las Vegas, NV 89119
Home Rink: Santa Fe Hotel and Casino
Rink Location: Las Vegas

Southern Nevada Minor Hockey Association
Phone: 702-254-6046
E-mail: mikepen@accessnv.com
9716 Trailrider Dr.
Las Vegas, NV 89117
Home Rink: UNLV Thomas & Mack Arena
Rink Location: Las Vegas

New Hampshire

Hanover Hockey Association
Phone: 603-642-1342
E-mail: tsmbp@aol.com
P.O. Box 992
Hanover, NH 03755
Home Rink: James Campion Rink
Rink Location: Hanover, NH

Manchester Regional Youth Hockey
Association
Phone: 603-627-2651
E-mail: hkypuck@aol.com
237 Peak Street
Manchester, NH 03104
Home Rink: JFK / WSA
Rink Location: Manchester

Salem Saints Youth Hockey
Phone: 603-893-2694
E-mail: the.helinskis@worldnet.att.net
17 Mulberry Rd.
Salem, NH 03079
Home Rink: Skate 3
Rink Location: Tyngsboro, MA

Seacoast Spartans
Phone: 603-692-2263
E-mail: James@Nolin.mv.com
Somersworth, NH 03878
Home Rink: Rochester Arena
Rink Location: Rochester

Dover Stars Youth Hockey
Phone: 603-742-6699
E-mail: sallen@anselm.edu
46 Watson Rd.
Dover, NH 03820
Home Rink: Dover Arena
Rink Location: Dover

Keene Youth Hockey Club
Phone: 603-357-4217
E-mail: kroe@markem.com
27 Woodland Ave.
Keene, NH 03431
Home Rink: Cheshire Ice Arena
Rink Location: Swanzey

Rochester Youth Hockey
Phone: 603-335-1296
E-mail: dwd@dwd.mv.com
P.O. Box 583
Rochester, NH 03867
Home Rink: Rochester Arena
Rink Location: Rochester

Nashua Panthers Youth Hockey
Association
Phone: 603-672-7440
Fax: 603-465-9893
P.O. Box 911
Nashua, NH, 03061
Home Rink: Skate 3
Rink Location: Tyngsboro

New Jersey

Mighty Ducks Youth Hockey
Phone: 908-753-4248
E-mail: mdyh@aol.com
P.O. Box 696
Springfield, NJ 07081
Rink Location: South Brunswick

Philadelphia Little Flyers
Phone: 609-228-1082
E-mail: tschneid@ix.netcom.com
827 Hunters Lane
Deptford, NJ 08096
Home Rink: Twin Rinks
Rink Location: Pennsauken

Phila. Little Flyers Squirt AA
Phone: 609-589-7952
E-mail: jackcoach@jersey.net
32 Manchester Rd.
Sewell, NJ 08080
Home Rink: Twin Rinks of Pennsauken
Rink Location: Pennsauken

NJ Devils Youth Hockey
Phone: 201-334-9574
E-mail: dennis@mtlakes.csnet.net
Box 414 Rd #3 Boonton Ave.
Boonton, NJ 07005
Home Rink: South Mountain Arena
Rink Location: West Orange

New Jersey Devils Youth Hockey
Phone: 908-931-1111
E-mail: mjz@pipeline.com
29 Spring Hill Drive
West Orange, NJ 07052
Home Rink: South Mountain Arena
Rink Location: West Orange

Montclair Hockey Club
Phone: 201-744-1688
E-mail: hockeywave@aol.com
P. O. Box 43302
Upper Montclair, NJ 07043
Home Rink: Clarey Anderson
Rink Location: Montclair

Englewood Field Club
Phone: 201-569-8291
E-mail: smr3@columbia.edu
16 Ravine Road
Tenafly, NJ 07670
Home Rink: Englewood Field Club
Rink Location: Tenafly

Lawrence Flames Hockey Association
N.J. Y.H.L.
Phone: 609-599-9008
E-mail: nmonchak@aol.com.nick
12 Tartan Ct.
Lawrenceville, NJ 08648

American Eagles
A.Y.H.L.
4 Lusan Lane
Middletown, NJ 07734

Devils Youth
A.Y.H.L.
1010 Chatfield Drive
Pompton Plains, NJ 07444

Flyers Alumni
A.Y.H.L.
1 Meadowview Drive
Shamong, NJ 08088

Long Island Royals
A.Y.H.L.
270 Indian Head
Kings Park, NY 11754

Mercer Chiefs
A.Y.H.L.
6 Tennis Court
Hamilton Twp, NJ 08619

Morris County Colonials
A.Y.H.L.
8 Annabelle Lane
Florham, NJ 07932

New Jersey Rockets Squirt AA
Phone: 215-638-7864
E-mail: Bensalem@msn
2131 Joshua Dr.
Bensalem, PA 19020
Home Rink: BSA
Rink Location: Bridgewater

Jaguars Ice Hockey Club
Phone: 215-632-1283
E-mail: blueline@erols.com
P.O. Box 190
Medford, NJ 08050
Home Rink: Medford Ice Rink
Rink Location: Medford, New Jersey
www.erols.com/blueline

Lawrence "Flames" Hockey Assoc., Inc.
Phone: 609-599-9008
E-mail: NMonchak@aol.com
12 Tartan Ct.
Lawrenceville, NJ 08648
Home Rink: Iceland & Lawrenceville School
Rink Location: Central NJ

New York Islanders
A.Y.H.L.
2446 Seneca Ave.
Dix Hills, NY 11746

Philadelphia Jr. Flyers
A.Y.H.L.
292 Upper Gulph Road
Radnor, PA 19087

Philidelphia Little Flyers
A.Y.H.L.
26 Hillside Lane
New Hope, PA 18938

Ramapo Saints
A.Y.H.L.
4 Emerald Drive
Pomona, NY 10970

Suffolk Pal
A.Y.H.L.
10 Layton Lane
Centereach, NY 11720

Valley Forge
A.Y.H.L.
271 Beacon Drive
Phoenixville, PA 19460

Washington Lit Capitals
A.Y.H.L.
10220 Democracy Lane
Potomac, MD 20854

American Eagles
N.J. Y.H.L.
58 Warren Place
Middletown, NJ 07748

Bayonne Rangers Hockey Assoc.
N.J. Y.H.L.
110 Lord Ave.
Bayonne, NJ 07002

Brick Hockey Club
N.J. Y.H.L.
30 Edgewood Dr.
Brick, NJ 08724

Bridgewater Bears Hockey Club
N.J. Y.H.L.
588 Sudfbury Lane
Bridgewater, NJ 08807

Cranford Hockey Club
N.J. Y.H.L.
542 Willow Ave.
Garwood, NJ 07027

East Windsor P.A.L.
N.J. Y.H.L.
5 Edwards Drive
East Windsor, NJ 08520

Mercher Chiefs
N.J. Y.H.L.
4 Michele Ct.
East Windsor, NJ 08520

Morris County Colonials
N.J. Y.H.L.
228 Fairmount Ave.
Chatham, NJ 07928

New Jersey Gladiators Hockey Club
N.J. Y.H.L.
60 Strong Mountain Lane
Marlton, NJ 08053

New Jersey Mavericks
N.J. Y.H.L.
11 Treptow St.
Little Ferry, NJ 07643

New Jersey Rockets
N.J. Y.H.L.
157 Third Ave., Apt 3F
Westwood, NJ 07675

New Youth Sharks
N.J. Y.H.L.
117 Russek Dr.
Staten Island, NY 10312

Old Bridge Wings Hockey Association
N.J. Y.H.L.
44 Margaret St.
Old Bridge, NJ 08857

Princeton Youth Hockey Association
N.J. Y.H.L.
8 Birchwood Ct.
West Windsor, NJ 08648

Ramapo Youth Hockey Association
N.J. Y.H.L.
319 King St.
Chappaque, NY 10514

Shamong Hockey Leaders of America
Phone 609-268-1341
167 Jackson Rd.
Shamong, NJ 08088
Home Rink: Goshen Pond
Rink Location: Southern NJ

Staten Island Pirates
N.J. Y.H.L.
304 Kingdom Ave.
Staten Island, NJ 10312

Thunderbirds
N.J. Y.H.L.
2923 Belgrade St.
Philadelphia, PA 19134

Toms River Hockey Club
N.J. Y.H.L.
101 Twin Rivers Dr.
Toms River, NJ 08753

New York (Central)

Midstate Youth Hockey Association
Phone: 315-475-7673
E-mail: ccwallacej@aol.com
P.O. Box 648
Syracuse, NY 13201
Home Rink: NYS Fairgrounds Coliseum
Rink Location: Syracuse

West Point Youth Hockey
Phone: 914-938-8896
E-mail: yd0605@odia.usma.edu
USMA-DCFA Bldg. 500
West Point, NY 10996
Home Rink: Holleder Center/Tate Rink
Rink Location: USMA/West Point

Ogdensburg Minor Hockey Assoc.
Phone: 315-393-6094
E-mail: jhoward@ogdensburg.neric.org
P.O. Box 762
Ogdensburg, NY 13669
Home Rink: Ofa Golden Dome
Rink Location: Ogdensburg

Ithaca Youth Hockey Assoc.
Phone: 607-277-4474
E-mail: lhuw98a@prodigy.com
255 Burns Rd.
Ithaca, NY 14850
Home Rink: The Rink
Rink Location: Lansing

Oswego Minor Hockey Association, Inc.
Phone: 315-342-2636
E-mail: mathes@dreamscape.com
P.O.Box 5525
Oswego, NY 13126
Home Rink: Crisafulli The Fort
Rink Location: Oswego

Cortland Youth Hockey
Phone: 607-836-6103
E-mail: cahs1234@aol.com
3718 Route 41
Solon, NY 13040
Home Rink: Cortland State College
Rink Location: Cortland

West Seneca Wings
Bill McCormick
Phone: 716-743-3798
E-mail: bmcc@czn.com
197 Barnsdale Ave.
West Seneca, NY 14224
Home Rink: West Seneca Rec Cnt.
Rink Location: West Seneca

Massena Minor Hockey Assoc.
Phone: 315-769-6739
E-mail: ranmac@slic.com
25 Monroe Pkwy
Massena, NY 13662
Home Rink: Massena Arena
Rink Location: Massena

"Syracuse Stars" Midstate Youth Hockey
Association
Phone: 315-638-4558
E-mail: tcdowd@aol.com
8450 E. Mud Lake Rd.
Baldwinsville, NY 13027
Home Rink: NYS Fair Coliseum
Rink Location: Syracuse

Adirondack Blackflies
Phone: 518-863-4917
E-mail: martin@klink.net
322 North Reed St.
Northville, NY 12134
Home Rink: Buzz Fly Rink
Rink Location: Scotia

New York (Western)

Buffalo Hornets Minor Hockey
Phone: 716-685-1122
E-mail: SportsNiag@aol.com
3465 Broadway
Cheektowaga, NY 14227
Home Rink: Holiday Rinks
Rink Location: Cheektowaga

Chautauqua Co. Youth Hockey
Phone: 716-488-0499
21 Hess St.
Jamestown, NY 14701
Home Rink: Allen Park
Rink Location: Jamestown

Amherst Hockey Association
Phone: 716-636-4743
E-mail: kwill8030@aol.com
261 Shady Grove Dr.
East Amherst, NY 14051
Home Rink: Audubon
Rink Location: Amherst

Cheektowaga Hockey
Phone: 716-897-7218
c/o Cheektowaga Rec Center
2600 Harlem Rd. Cheektowaga, NY 14225
Home Rink: Cheektowaga Rec Center
Rink Location: Buffalo, NY suburbs

Twin Tier Tornadoes Junior C
E-mail: dsb10@cornell.edu
35 Belaire Dr.
Horseheads, New York 14845
Home Rink: Murray Center
Rink Location: Horseheads

Grand Niagara Cataract Hockey League
Phone: 716-791-4068
E-mail: genac1750@wzrd.com
2170 Florence Drive
Ransomville, NY 14131
Home Rinks: Niagara University
Rink Locations: Niagara University

Saints Hockey Club
Phone: 716-668-4243
E-mail: ekkq65a@prodigy.com
6 Northbrook Ct.
Lancaster, NY 14086
Home Rink: Various
Rink Location: Buffalo, NY suburbs

Lockport Tigers
Phone: 716-433-8770; 716-622-2563
E-mail: thurston@msmal.buffalo.edu
4 Rogers Avenue
Lockport, NY 14094
Home Rink: Hockey Outlet Ice Complex and
Niagara University Ice Arena
Rink Location: Wheatfield, Niagara Falls

Northern Chautauqua County Youth Hockey
Association
Phone: 716-792-4631
49 Old Mill Rd
Brocton, NY 14716
Home Rink: Fredonia State College Steele
Hall
Rink Location: Fredonia

Western New York Hockey League
Phone: 716-685-1122
E-mail: SportsNiag@aol.com
3465 Broadway
Cheektowaga, NY 14227
Home Rinks: Various rinks
www.webt.com/wnyah

New York (Eastern)

Clifton Park Youth Hockey Association
Phone: 518-877-5514
E-mail: kharper@albany.net
4 Noord Lane
Ballston Lake, NY 12019
Home Rink: Clifton Park Arena
Rink Location: Clifton Park
www.crisny.org/not-for-profit/coyha

Alexandria Bay Minor Hockey
Phone: 315-482-9077
E-mail: jrmiller@gisco.net
20739 St. Lawrence Park Rd.
Alexandria Bay, NY 13607
Home Rink: Alexandria Bay
Rink Location: Village of Alex Bay

New York City Cyclones
Phone: 212-563-4752
E-mail: wberke751@aol.com
145 4th Avenue
New York, NY 10003
Home Rink: Sky Rink at Chelsea Piers
Rink Location: New York

Schenectady Youth Hockey
Phone: 518-382-5104
460 State St.
Schenectady, NY 12306
Home Rink: Center City
Rink Location: Schenectady

Bear Mountain Hockey Club
Phone: 914-446-5107
E-mail: jgalu@aol.com
P.O Box 250
Highland Falls, NY 10928
Home Rink: Bear Mountain
Rink Location: Bear Mtn State Park

West Point Youth Hockey
Phone: 914-938-8896
E-mail: yd0605@odia.usma.edu
DCFA-USMA Youth Services
West Point, NY 10996
Home Rink: USMA-Tate Rink
Rink Location: West Point

Washingtonville Youth Hockey
Phone: 914-496-7223
E-mail: 2_reason@ny.frontiercomm.net
223 Sycamore Dr.
New Windsor, NY 12553
Home Rink: Ice Time Arena
Rink Location: Newburgh

Putnam Panthers
Phone: 914-878-4328
E-mail: mikeplustk@aol.com
7 Arbor Lane
Holmes, NY 12531
Home Rink: Trinity Pauling
Rink Location: Pauling

Clifton Park Youth Hockey Association
Phone: 518-877-5514
E-mail: kharper@albany.net
4 Noord Lane
Ballston Lake, NY 12019
Home Rink: Clifton Park Arena
Rink Location: Clifton Park

The Harvey Jr. Cavaliers
Phone: 914-232-3161
260 Jay Street
Katonah, NY 10536
Home Rink: Evarts Rink
Rink Location: Katonah

Nassau County Hockey
Phone: 516-571-7057
E-mail: parks1@co.nassau.ny.us
Cantiague Park, West John Street
Hicksville, NY 11801
Home Rink: Cantiague Park
Rink Location: Cantiague Park

Saratoga Youth Hockey, Inc.
Phone: 518-581-0704
E-mail: k.e-kane@worldnet.att.net
P.O. Box 247
Saratoga Springs, NY 12866
Home Rink: Weibel Ave, 2 rinks
Rink Location: Saratoga

Greater New York Stars
Phone: 718-435-2890
67 Parkville Avenue
Brooklyn, NY 11230
Home Rink: Abe Stark
Rink Location: Coney Island

Staten Island Sharks
Phone: 212-978-3813
E-mail: kjbreen@juno.com
237 Hamilton Ave.
Brooklyn, NY 11231
Home Rink: Clove Lake
Rink Location: Staten Island

Massena Minor Hockey
Phone: 315-769-6739
E-mail: ranmac@slic.com
25 Monroe Pkwy
Massena, NY 13662
Home Rink: Massena Arena
Rink Location: Massena

Farmingdale High School Hockey
Phone: 516-454-9683
E-mail: misdude@abest.com
41 Walnut Ave.
Farmingdale, NY 11735
Home Rink: Syosset Skating Acdamy
Rink Location: Syosset (NY, home of NY
Islanders)

Millbrook Youth Hockey
Phone: 914-223-7347
E-mail: glennn@vnet.ibm.com
RR2 Box 11
Verbank, NY 12585
Home Rink: Millbrook School
Rink Location: Millbrook

Suffern Youth Hockey
Phone: 914-368-3249
2 Tanchak Ct.
Suffern, NY 10901

Arrows Youth Hockey
Phone: 516-536-2716
E-mail: goalpost@msn.com
39 Gateway
Rockville Centre, NY 11570
Home Rink: Freeport Rec. Center
Rink Location: Freeport, Long Island

Eagles H.S. Hockey
Phone: 516-256-EAGLE
E-mail: eagle524@aol.com
P.O. Box 11
Valley Stream, NY 11582
Home Rink: Long Island Skating Academy
Rink Location: Syosset

Dix Hills Youth Hockey Association
Phone: 516-979-0343
E-mail: dhrebels@aol.com
5 Jamor Court
Nesconset, NY 11767
Home Rink: Dix Hills Park
Rink Location: Dix Hills

Dutchess Youth Hockey Association
Phone: 914 534-3463
E-mail: reubenr@earthlink.net
67 Reservoir Road
Cornwall, NY 12518
Home Rink: Civic Center
Rink Location: Poughkeepsie
home.earthlink.net/~reubenr/

Nassau County Hockey
Phone: 516-571-SCORE
E-mail: markshockey@msn.com
West John Street
Hicksville, NY 11580
Home Rink: Cantiague Park
Rink Location: Hicksville

Staten Island Sharks
Phone: 718-967-1925
E-mail: sharkssi@aol.com
117 Russek Drive
Staten Island, NY 10312
Home Rink: War Memorial Ice Arena
Rink Location: Staten Island

Adirondack Youth Hockey Association
Phone: 518-798-3946
E-mail: delly@capital.net
P.O. Box 940
Glens Falls, NY 12801
Home Rink: Glens Falls Recreation Center
Rink Location: Glens Falls

New Mexico

New Mexico I.C.E. Hockey Foundation
E-mail: nmice@flash.net
9530 Tramway Blvd. NE
Albuquerque, NM 87122
Home Rink: Our Post Ice Arena
Rink Location: Albquerque

New Mexico Amateur Hockey Association
Phone: 505-275-1493
E-mail: obrientp@aol.com
72 Abajo Drive
Edgewood, NM 87015
Home Rink: Blades Multiplex Arena
Rink Location: Rio Rancho Albuquerque
www.thuntek.net/nmaha/

Los Alamos Hockey Association
Phone: 505-662-7226
E-mail: haugen@lanl.gov
894 43rd St.
Los Alamos, NM 87544
Home Rink: Los Alamos County Ice Rink
Rink Location: Los Alamos

North Carolina

Greensboro Ice Sports
Phone: 910-333-1-ICE
E-mail: Kcowan@hpe.infi.net
P.O. Box 10122
Greensboro, NC 27404
Home Rink: Ice House of Greensboro
Rink Location: Greensboro

Cape Fear Youth Hockey Association
Phone: 910-487-1276
E-mail: bobkelly@foto.infi.net
7725 Scottsdale Drive
Fayetteville, NC 28314
Home Rink: Cleland Arena
Rink Location: Fort Bragg

Charlotte Amateur Hockey Association
Phone: 704-521-8885
E-mail: mikem@captor-time.com
P.O. Box 221472
Charlotte NC 28222
Home Rink: IceHouse of Charlotte
Rink Location: Pineville

TYHA Triangle Youth Hockey
Phone: 919- 933-8307
E-mail: larryg23@aol.com
One Dan Kidd Drive
Hillsborough, NC 27278
Home Rink: Sports Plex
Rink Location: Hillsborough

Raleigh Jr. Icecaps
E-mail: kpinkey@aol.com
Phone 919-363-4960
622 Wakehurst Drive
Apex, NC 27502
Home Rink: Cary Ice House
Rink Location: Cary

Raleigh Youth Hockey Association
P.O. Box 1314
Cary, NC 27512

Ohio

Brooklyn Youth Hockey Association
Phone: 216.351.8050
E-mail: sefchik@en.com
P.O. Box 44643
Brooklyn, OH 44144
Home Rink: Brooklyn Rec Center
Rink Location: Brooklyn
www.en.com/users/sefchik/byhahom.htm

Oakwood Ice Jacks
Phone: 937-296-1497
E-mail: king@dnaco.net
48 Ivanhoe Ave.
Oakwood Dayton, OH 45419
Home Rink: Sportstown Ice Center
Rink Location: Centerville

Youngstown Youth Hockey
Phone: 330-758-3928
E-mail:wahoono1@aol.com
8059 Forest Lake
Boardman, OH 44512
Home Rink: Ice Zone
Rink Location: Boardman

Cleveland Hts. Hockey League
Phone: 216-291-1048
E-mail: jon304@juno.com
1321 Yellowstone Road
Cleveland Hts, OH 44121
Home Rink: Heights Recreation Pavilion
Rink Location: Cleveland Hts

Garfield Heights "Bulldog" Youth Hockey
Phone: 216-779-6167
E-mail: mmw@ix.netcom.com
9508 Dorothy Avenue
Garfield Heights, OH 44125-1419
Home Rink: Dan Kostel Ice Rink
Rink Location: Garfield Heights

Dayton Bomber Youth Hockey
Phone: 513-429-0273
E-mail: OldieRadio@aol.com
3088 Ranchfield
Beavercreek, OH 45432
Home Rink: Kettering Rec Center
Rink Location: Kettering

Athens Hockey Association
Phone: 614-593-3152
E-mail: Rodgersj@ouvaxa.cats.ohiou.edu
15 Euclid Dr.
Athens, OH 45701
Home Rink: Bird Ice Arena
Rink Location: Athens Ohio U Campus

Cincinnati Amateur Hockey Association
E-mail: TheoWilk@msn.com
7718 Ashley View Dr.
Cincinnati, OH 45227
Home Rink: Icelands
Rink Location: Cincinnati

Dayton Bluehawk Travel Hockey
Phone: 513-836-6052
E-mail: phil.bellante@lexis-nexis.com
7013 Woodcroft Dr.
Englewood, OH 45322
Home Rink: Hobart Arena
Rink Location: Troy

Mentor Youth Hockey
Mentor, OH 44060
Home Rink: Mentor Civic Arena
Rink Location: Mentor

Dayton Bombers Youth Hockey League
Phone: 513-294-1258
E-mail: ad360@dayton.wright.edu
1473 Constance Ave
Kettering, OH 45409
Home Rink: Kettering Rec Complex
Rink Location: Kettering

Elyria Ice Hockey Booster Club, Inc.
Phone: 216-365-0301
P.O. Box 661
Elyria, OH 44036-0661
Home Rink: North Park Ice Rink
Rink Location: Elyria

Cleveland Suburban Hockey League
Phone: 216-842-7079
7400 Romilly Oval
Parma, OH 44129
Home Rink: 20 rinks/organizations
Rink Location: Cleveland and
surrounding area

Lorain County Hockey
Phone: 216-774-2515
P.O. Box 232
Oberlin, OH 44074-0232
Home Rink: Oberlin Ice Rink
Rink Location: Oberlin

Golden Triangle Youth Hockey
Phone: 937-859-5836
E-mail: kim.james@daytonoh.ncr.com
834 Park Ave.
Miamisburg, OH 45342
Home Rink: Hamilton Sports Arena
Rink Location: Hamilton

Kettering Fairmont Hockey Club
Phone: 937-833-4287
E-mail: gtipton@theonramp.net
206 June Place
Brookville, OH 45309
Home Rink: Brookville

Winterhurst Hockey Association
Cleveland Suburban Hockey League
Phone: 216-899-1313
E-mail: m.werner@popmail.csuohio.edu
P.O.Box 770468
Lakewood, OH 44107
wha.yhn.com

Parma Hts. Hockey Association
Phone: 216-846-1009
E-mail: mhicar@aol.com
20066 Trapper Trail
Strongsville, OH 44136-8764
Home Rink: Greenbriar Ice Rink
Rink Location: Parma Hts.

Troy Rec Jr. Hockey
Phone: 937-335-0427
E-mail: cozatt@erinet
4946 Rt. 41 East
Troy, OH 45373
Home Rink: Hobart Arena
Rink Location: Troy

Oklahoma

Tulsa Youth Hockey Association
E-mail: mrpaint@ix.netcom.com
6528 E. 101st St., Suite D-1, Box 445
Tulsa, OK 74133
Home Rink: Tulsa Ice Arena
Rink Location: Tulsa

Arctic Edge
Phone: 405-748-5454
14613 North Kelly Road
Oklahoma City, OK 73013
Home Rink: Arctic Edge
Rink Location: Oklahoma City

Oregon

Oregon State Hockey Association
Phone: 503-251-3830
E-mail: everetth@katu.com
10514 N.E. Halsey
Portland, OR 97220-3957
Home Rink: Various
Rink Location: Portland, Eugene
www.sk8pro.com/pdxhockey

Pennsylvania (Eastern)

Warwick Wildcats
Phone: 215-322-4320
E-mail: gxxg@msn.com
1521 Mearns Rd.
Warwick, PA 18974
Home Rink: Warwick Twin Rinks
Rink Location: Warwick

Valley Forge Minutemen-Revised
Phone: 610-363-9409
E-mail: jgehring@appliedc.com
302 Misty Autumn Drive
Exton, PA 19341
Home Rink: Center Ice
Rink Location: Oaks

Central Bucks East Blazers HS
Phone: 215-766-2255
E-mail: ihockey@bellatlantic.net
5259 Geddes Way
Pipersville, PA 18947-1142
Home Rink: Face Off Circle
Rink Location: Warminster

Bucks County Generals
Phone: 215-766-2255
E-mail: ihockey@bellatlantic.net
5259 Geddes Way
Pipersville, PA 18947-1142
Home Rink: Warwick Twin Rinks
Rink Location: Jamison

Lehigh Valley Comets
Phone: 610-434-6899
3323 7th Street
Whitehall, PA 18052
Home Rink: Lehigh Valley Ice Arena
Rink Location: Whitehall

Old York Road Raiders
Phone: 215-635-4817
E-mail: goldberg@vm.temple.edu
Church and Old York Roads
Elkins Park, PA 19027
Home Rink: Old York Road Skating Club
Rink Location: Elkins Park

Glaciers
Phone: 215-674-0150
E-mail: herik@ix.comcat.com
1185 York Road
Warminster, PA 18974
Home Rink: Face Off Circle
Rink Location: Warminster

Northeastern PA Youth Hockey Association
Phone: 717-474-0731
E-mail: winfield@epix.net
51 Farmhouse Road
Mountain Top, PA 18707
Home Rink: Ice-a-Rama
Rink Location: Wilkes-Barre

Philadelphia Jr. Flyers
Phone: 610-436-9670
E-mail: dombroski@enter.net
527 Hansen Road
Prussia, PA 19406-1831
Home Rink: Ice Line Triple Rinks
Rink Location: West Goshen

Philadelphia Little Flyers
Phone: 610-495-6671
E-mail: tschneid@ix.netcom.com
50 Railroad St.
Linfield, PA 19468
Home Rink: Twin Rinks
Rink Location: Pennsauken

Pottstown Penguins
Phone: 610-327-3476
E-mail: cassey#m#_rich@msgw.vf.lmco.com
1720 Farmington Ave.
Pottstown, PA 19464
Home Rink: The Hill School
Rink Location: Pottstown

Valley Forge Minutemen
Phone: 610-354-8970
431 West Valley Forge Rd
King of Prussia, PA 19341
Home Rink: Center Ice
Rink Location: King of Prussia

Hershey Jr. Bears
Phone: 717-534-3819
E-mail: billh@blueskycomputing.com
100 W. HersheyPark Drive
Hershey, PA 17033
Home Rink: HersheyPark Arena
Rink Location: Hershey
www.blueskycomputing.com/jrbears/
index.htm

Wolfpack Youth Ice Hockey
Phone: 610-370-WOLF
E-mail: leroy60@aol.com
P.O. Box 2502
West Lawn, PA 19609
Home Rink: Timberline Ice Arena
Rink Location: Reading

Jets~Sharks Youth Hockey Association
Deleware Valley Hockey League
Phone: 717-657-1793
E-mail: jets@paonline.com
P.O. Box 6121
Harrisburg, PA 17112-0121
Home Rink: Twin Ponds East and West
Rink Location: Harrisburg
jetshockey.yhn.com

Warwick Wildcats Youth Hockey
Association
Delaware Valley Hockey League
Phone: 215-322-4320
E-mail: gxxg@msn.com
1621 Mearns Road
Warwick, PA 18974
Rink Location: Warwick Twin Rinks
wildcats.yhn.com

Philadelphia Quakers
Phone: 610-429-4370 ext. 101
E-mail: jgraves@igi.net
1035 Andrew Drive
West Chester, PA 19380
Home Rink: Ice Line Triple Rinks
Rink Location: West Chester

Pennsylvania (Western)

Allegheny Hockey Association
765 New Texas Road
Pittsburgh, PA 15239
Home Rink: Golden Mile Ice Rink
Rink Location: Monroeville

Crawford County Youth Hockey
Phone: 814-724-4880
E-mail: ctfn123@aol.com
563 Sunset Drive
Meadville, PA 16335
Home Rink: MARC, Dearment Ice
Rink Location: Meadville

Erie Youth Hockey Association
Phone: 814-838-9407
E-mail: djhenning@aol.com
3442 West 41st St.
Erie, PA 16506
Home Rink: JMC
Rink Location: Erie

C.C.Y.H.A.
Phone: 814-425-7594
29745 Lake Creek Rd.
Cochranton, PA 16314
Home Rink: Meadville Area Rec Complex
Rink Location: Meadville

Eastern Hockey Association
Phone: 412-734-5931
E-mail: Nec9617@aol.com
325 Squire Circle
Pittsburgh, PA 15212-1976
Home Rink: Bladerunners Ice Complex
Rink Location: Harmarville

Mon Valley Youth Hockey Assoc
Phone: 412-722-1126
E-mail: rfw3+@pitt.edu
R.D. #1, Box 351
Ruffs Dale, PA 15679
Home Rink: Ice Garden
Rink Location: Rostraver

State College Youth Ice Hockey Assn.
Phone: 412-867-7825
E-mail: rjones@ciu10.com
2036 N. Oak Lane
State College, PA 16803
Home Rink: Penn State
Rink Location: Penn State Univ.

Pittsburgh Amateur Penguins
Phone: 412-941-8891
E-mail: cn1djd@gnc.com
144 Marion Drive
McMurray, PA 15317-2922
Home Rink: Blade Runners
Rink Location: Harmarville/Warrendale

Erie Youth Hockey
Phone: 814-899-0919
E-mail: gbrumba503@aol.com
Home Rink: JMC Ice Arena
Rink Location: Erie

South Hills Interscholastic Hockey League
Phone: 412-941-3181
E-mail: defazio+@andrew.cmu.edu
113 Sugar Camp Rd.
Venetia, PA 15367
Home Rink: 7 Rinks in the Pittsburgh area
Rink Location: Pittsburgh

Rhode Island

Northern R.I. Vikings
Phone: 401-949-4051
E-mail: nrihockey@aol.com
P.O. Box 427
Greenville, RI 02828
Home Rink: Smithfield Ice Rink
Rink Location: Smithfield

Woonsocket North Stars
Phone: 401-766-6089
P.O. Box 595
Woonsocket, RI 02895
Home Rink: Mt. St. Charles
Rink Location: Woonsocket

Edgewood R.I. Youth Hockey
Phone: 401-831-6048
E-mail: discopuck@aol.com
84 Lynde Street
Providence, RI 02908-1122
Home Rink: P.C. Schneider Arena
Rink Location: Providence

Newport Youth Hockey
Phone: 401-423-2607
E-mail: labyrinth@edgenet.net
P.O. Box 1331
Newport, RI 02840
Home Rink: St. Georges
Rink Location: Middletown
www3.edgenet.net/~sullivan

Rhode Island Panthers
Phone: 401-944-3935
E-mail: donald_wright@brown.edu
148 Fiat Street
Cranston, RI 02910
Home Rink: Cranston Veterans
Rink Location: Cranston
users.ids.net/~smo2/home.html

South Carolina

Greenville Youth Hockey Association
Phone: 864-292-5979
104 Gaithburg Sq.
Taylors, SC 29687
Home Rink: The Pavilion
Rink Location: Taylors
www.furman.edu/~pecoy/gyha.htm

Lowcountry Hockey Association
Phone: 803-769-5753
E-mail: kennethr@awod.com
2142 Hunter Creek Drive
Charleston, SC 29414
Home Rink: Carolina Ice Palace
Rink Location: North Charleston

South Dakota

Watertown Hockey Association
E-mail: bjblauw@basec.net
Watertown, SD 57201

Sioux Falls Youth Hockey Assn
Phone: 605-361-9836
4235 West Mesa Pass
Sioux Falls, SD 57106
Home Rink: Minnehaha Ice & Rec
Rink Location: Sioux Falls

Rapid City Youth Hockey Association
Phone: 605-348-6891
E-mail: grim0275@server1.natcol-rcy.edu
2903 Scott St. #55
Rapid City, SD 57701
Home Rink: Canyon Lake
Rink Location: Rapid City

Brookings Ice Skating Association
Phone: 605-692-5095
E-mail: bmuteh@brookings.net
1317 Orchard Drive
Brookings, SD 57006
Home Rink: Brookings Ice Arena
Rink Location: Brookings

Huron Hockey Association
Phone 605-352-7801
819 Kansas SE
Huron, SD 57350
Rink Location: Huron

Oahe Hockey Association
Phone: 605-224-0334
E-mail: opie7672@aol.com
316 East Broadway
Pierre, SD 57501
Home Rink: Schomer Building
Rink Location: Fort Pierre

Texas

SAIHA
Phone: 210-9814749
E-mail: iggy_man@msn.com
27118 Boerne Forrest
Boerne, TX 78006
Home Rink: Crystal Ice Palace
Rink Location: Boerne

AYHA
Phone: 512-327-7671
E-mail: Nomad37@aol.com
2704 Barton's Bluff Lane
Austin, TX 78746
Home Rink: Chaparral Ice Center
Rink Location: Austin

Dallas PeeWee Ice Hawks
Phone: 972-596-2339
E-mail: JBeckPlano@aol.com15100
15100 Midway Road
Addison, TX 75244
Home Rink: Iceoplex
Rink Location: Addison
members.aol.com/icehawks/index.html

Aerodrome In-House League
Phone: 713-847-5283 ext113
E-mail: robertjhooper@worldnet.att.net
8220 Willow Place North
Houston, TX 77070
Home Rink: Willowbrook Aerodrome
Rink Location: Houston
ourworld.compuserve.com/homepages/
rjhooper/aihlindx.htm.

Houston Jr. Aeros Hockey Assoc.
E-mail: kevin@hstn.expl.pgs.com
Houston, TX 77077
Home Rink: Sugarland Aerodrome
Rink Location: Sugarland

Houston Junior Aeros Hockey Association
Phone: 713-370-8925
E-mail: del3@ibm.net
12026 Knobcrest Dr.
Houston, TX 77070
Home Rink: Aerodrome or Sharpstown Ice
Rink
Rink Location: Sugarland or Houston

Dallas Junior Hockey Association
Phone: 214-234-8093
E-mail: renata@i-linknet
2408 Mesa Drive
Richardson, TX 75080
Home Rink: various
Rink Location: Dallas

Stampede Youth Hockey Association
Phone: 817-778-8380
E-mail: jerryrayb@aol.com
2609 Olympia Drive
Temple, TX 76502
Home Rink: Bell County Expo Center
Rink Location: Belton

Austinice Armadillos
Phone: 512-451-5102
E-mail: timothy_doherty@msn.com
7920 San Felipe #804
Austin, TX 78729
Home Rink: Austinice
Rink Location: Austin

Utah

Utah High School Hockey, Inc.
Phone: 801-393-4883
E-mail: coachbean@aol.com
4172 College Dr.
Ogden, UT 84403
Home Rink: The Ice Sheet
Rink Location: Ogden

Salt Lake Amateur Hockey Association
Phone: 801-566-5407
P.O. Box 26552
Salt Lake City, UT 84126
Home Rink: Bountiful Recreation Center
Rink Location: Bountiful

Virginia

Reston Raider Girls Travel Hockey Team
Phone: 703-573-3457
E-mail: chikwstic@aol.com
7803 Byrds Nest Pass
Annandale, VA 22003
Home Rink: Reston Ice Forum
Rink Location: Reston

Hampton Roads Jr. Admirals
Phone: 757-490-1341
E-mail: cdvg59a@prodigy.com
P. O. Box 62202
Virginia Beach, VA 23466
Home Rink: Iceland Skating Center
Rink Location: Virginia Beach

Northern Virginia Hockey Club
Phone: 703-414-6855
E-mail: kevin.mcfarland@mci.com
8703 Highgate Road
Alexandria, VA 22308
Home Rink: Mt. Vernon
Rink Location: Alexandria

American In-Line Skating
Phone: 703-277-2628
E-mail: keim@his.com
4255 Hunt Club Circle, Suite # 1412
Fairfax, VA 22033
Home Rink: Many
Rink Locations: Northern Virginia; Maryland;
Washington, DC

Vermont

Stowe Youth Hockey
Phone: 802-253-4512
E-mail: dcomm@together.net
P.O. Box 1197
Stowe, VT 05672
Home Rink: Jackson Arena
Rink Location: Stowe

Lyndon Area Youth Hockey
Phone: 802-626-5795
E-mail: taylor@kingcon.com
Lyndon Heights
Lyndonville, VT 05851
Home Rink: Fenton Chester Arena
Rink Location: Lyndonville

Brattleboro Hockey Association
Phone: 802-257-4148
E-mail: faceoff@sover.net
42 Carriage Hill Rd.
W. Brattleboro, VT 05301
Home Rink: Nelson Whithington
Rink Location: Brattleboro

Washington

Seattle Jr. Hockey, female program
Phone: 425-743-7849
Fax: 425-672-9134
E-mail: rwg@sprynet.com
17730 Spruce Way
Lynnwood, WA 98037-7431
Home Rink: Olympicview
Rink Location: Mountlake Terrace

Spokane American Youth Hockey
Phone: 509-327-7383
E-mail: dworden@nextdim.com
P.O. Box 9489
Spokane, WA 99209
Home Rink: Eagles Ice Arena
Rink Location: Spokane

Sno-King Amateur Hockey Association
(SKAHA)
Phone: 425-821-7133 ext. 3003, ext. 3001
Fax: 425-823-1367
E-mail: snoking@brigadoon.com
12526 N.E. 144th St.
Kirkland, WA 98034
E-mail: lrich417@aol.com 206-365-0035
Home Rink: Kingsgate Arena
Rink Location: Kirkland
www.snokinghockey.org

Seattle Junior Hockey Association (SJHA)
Phone: 206-743-7849
E-mail: rwg@sprynet.com
17730 Spruce Way
Lynnwood, WA 98037-7431
Phone: 206-672-7744
E-mail: dayleyh@wolfenet.com
22202 70th Ave. West
Mountlake Terrace, WA 98043
Home Rink: OlympicView Ice Arena
Rink Location: Mountlake Terrace

Tacoma Amateur Hockey Association
Phone: 206-926-3726
2701 40th St. E. Apt.B
Tacoma, WA 98443
Home Rink: Puget Sound Hockey Center
Rink Location: Tacoma

Tacoma Amateur Hockey Association
Phone: 253-529-9360
E-mail: salcedo@gte.net
329 S. 309th St.
Federal Way, WA 98003
Home Rink: Puget Sound Hockey Center
Rink Location: Tacoma

Wisconsin (Northwest)

Hayward Youth Hockey
Phone: 715-634-2815
E-mail: mfpc@win.bright.net
P.O. Box 455
Hayward, WI 54843
Home Rink: Hayward Sports Center
Rink Location: Hayward

Blackhawk Hockey Association
Phone: 715-698-2168
P.O. Box 259
Baldwin, WI 54002
Home Rink: Baldwin Ice Rink
Rink Location: Baldwin

Amery Youth Hockey Association
W.A.H.A.
P.O. Box 305
Amery, WI 54001

Ashland Youth Hockey Association
W.A.H.A.
P.O. Box 169
Ashland, WI 54806

Barron Youth Hockey
W.A.H.A.
320 S. Oak St.
Barron, WI 54812

Chippewa Youth Hockey Association
W.A.H.A.
P.O. Box 131
Chippewa Falls, WI 54729

Cumberland Youth Hockey Association
W.A.H.A.
1601 Western Ave Box 11
Cumberland, WI 54829

Grantsburg Youth Hockey Association
W.A.H.A.
11469 N. Shore Drive
Grantsburg, WI 54840

Hayward Youth Hockey Association
W.A.H.A.
P.O. Box 455
Hayward, WI 54843

Iron River Ice Facilities, Inc.
W.A.H.A.
P.O. Box 181
Iron River, WI 54847

Rice Lake Youth Hockey Association
W.A.H.A.
1204 Hammond Ave. Box 81
Rice Lake, WI 54868

Rusk County Youth Hockey Association
W.A.H.A.
911 Shady Lane
Ladysmith, WI 54848

Spooner Ice Association
W.A.H.A.
Box 375
Spooner, WI 54801

Superior Amatuer Youth Hockey Association
W.A.H.A.
1015 Oakes Ave.
Superior, WI 54880

Webster Youth Hockey Association
W.A.H.A.
P.O. Box 275
Siren, WI 54872

Wisconsin Selects
W.A.H.A.
Bob Anderson General Manager
P.O. Box 334
Superior, WI 54880

Wisconsin (Northeast)

W.A.H.A.
P.O. Box 462
Antigo, WI 54409

Wisconsin Junior Admirals
Phone: 715-842-5892
E-mail: jradmirals@aol.com.
1720 Roosevelt Street
Wausau, WI 54403
Home Rink: Sara Park
Rink Location: Tomahawk

Badger State Hockey League
W.A.H.A.
1680 Lighthouse Lodge Rd.
Rhinelander, WI 54521

Eagle River Recreation Association
W.A.H.A.
P.O. Box 1495
Eagle River, WI 54521

Lakeland Hawks Ice Association
W.A.H.A.
P.O. Box 290
Hazelhurst, WI 54531

Marathon County Youth Hockey Inc.
W.A.H.A.
P.O. Box 176
Wausau, WI 54403

Marathon County Senior Hockey Inc.
W.A.H.A.
1932 Emerson Street
Wausau, WI 54403

Marshfield Youth Hockey Association
W.A.H.A.
405 E. 17th Street
Marshfield, WI 54449

Medford Area Youth Hockey Association
W.A.H.A.
P.O. Box 302
Medford, WI 54451

Merrill Hockey, Inc.
W.A.H.A.
Phone: 715-536-6651
E-mail: glkautza@mail.wiscnet.net
P.O. Box 764
Merrill, WI 54452
Home Rink: Smith Mulit-Purpose
Rink Location: Merrill

Mosinee Hockey Club
W.A.H.A.
P.O. Box 214
Mosinee, WI 54455

North Lakeland Ice Inc.
W.A.H.A.
HC1 Box 446
Presque Isle, WI 54557

Park Falls Area Blue Line Club Inc.
W.A.H.A.
P.O. Box 133
Park Falls, WI 54552

Portage County Youth On Ice
W.A.H.A.
P.O. Box 966
Stevens Point, WI 54481

Price Ice Ltd.
W.A.H.A.
P.O. Box 212
Phillips, WI 54555

Rhinelander Ice Association
W.A.H.A.
P.O. Box 1188
Rhinelander, WI 54501

Shouth Wood County Youth Hockey
Association
W.A.H.A.
P.O. Box 111
Wisconsin Rapids, WI 54495

Shawano Hockey League
W.A.H.A.
313 S. Lincoln St.
Shawano, WI 54166

Tomahawk Youth Hockey
W.A.H.A.
P.O. Box 555
Tomahawk, WI 54487

Tomah Youth Hockey   •
Phone: 608-427-1315
E-mail: jiverson@wimsn.ang.af.mil
Tomah, WI 54660
Home Rink: Recreation Park
Rink Location: Tomah

Wisconsin (Central: Region 3, Green Bay Area)

Central Wisconsin AAA
Phone: 715-842-5892
E-mail: theeyres@dwave.net
1720 Roosevelt Street
Wausau, WI 54403
Home Rink: The MARC
Rink Location: Merrill

Everest Youth Hockey
Phone: 715-359-2102
E-mail: ppsportmom@aol.com
5406 DJ Lane
Weston, WI 54406
Home Rink: Greenheck Arena
Rink Location: Weston

Central Wisconsin Hockey Association
Phone: 715-623-5757
E-mail: bberg@newnorth.net
819 Martin Avenue
Antigo, WI 54409

Bay Area Youth Hockey Association
W.A.H.A.
P.O. Box 22072
Green Bay, WI 54305-2072

Brown County Youth Hockey Association
W.A.H.A.
875 Packer Drive
Green Bay, WI 54304

De Pere Youth Hockey Association
W.A.H.A.
P.O. Box 3052
Green Bay, WI 54115

Fox Valley Youth Hockey Association
W.A.H.A.
P.O. Box 2463
Appleton, WI 54913

Manitowoc County Youth Hockey
W.A.H.A.
P.O. Box 1943
Manitowoc, WI 54221-1943

Marinette-Menominee Youth Hockey Association
W.A.H.A.
P.O. Box 414
Marinette, WI 54143

Mauston Screemin' Eagles
608-847-4521
E-mail: jmcmurry@mwt.net
303 Grote Street
Mauston, WI 53948
Home Rink: Mauston
Rink Location: Mauston
www.mwt.net/~jmcmurry

Northeastern Wisconsin Hockey Association
W.A.H.A.
504 Hilltop Dr.
Green Bay, WI 54301

Oshkosh Skating Club Inc.
W.A.H.A.
1665 Chatham Dr.
Oshkosh, WI 54904

Tri-County Recreation Association Inc.
W.A.H.A.
700 E. Shady Lane
Neenah, WI 54946

Waupaca Area Youth Hockey Association
W.A.H.A.
157 Grand Season Drive
Waupaca, WI 54981

Wisconsin (Southeast)

Southwest Eagles Youth Hockey
Phone: 608-845-5270
613 Mahogany Way
Verona, WI 53593
Home Rink: Eagles Nest Ice Arena
Rink Location: Verona

Baraboo Youth "T-Bird" Hockey
W.A.H.A.
P.O. Box 433
Baraboo, WI 53913

Beloit Youth Hockey Association
W.A.H.A.
P.O. Box 1262
Beloit, WI 53512-1262

Dane County Hockey Officials
Association, Inc.
W.A.H.A.
3350 Clove Dr.
Madison, WI 53704

Dane County Youth Hockey Association
W.A.H.A.
1909 LaSierra Way
Madison, WI 53716

Dodgeville Area Youth Hockey
W.A.H.A.
713 W. Fountian St.
Dodgeville, WI 54533

Janesville Youth Hockey Club Inc.
W.A.H.A.
P.O. Box 724
Janesville, WI 53547-0724

Madison Capitals Youth Hockey Association
W.A.H.A.
525 N. Sherman
Madison, WI 53704

Madison Hawks Selects
W.A.H.A.
Box 2138
Madison, WI 53701

Madison Majors
W.A.H.A.
625 South Shore Drive
Madison, WI 53715

Madison Patriots Hockey Association
W.A.H.A.
P.O. Box 7822
Madison, WI 53716

Madison Westmorland Youth Hockey
Association
W.A.H.A.
2759 Tami Trail
Madison, WI 53711

McFarland Youth Hockey Association
W.A.H.A.
P.O. Box 264
McFarland, WI 53558

Monroe Hockey Association
W.A.H.A.
2703 9th St.
Monroe, WI 53566

Reedsburg Youth Hockey Association
W.A.H.A.
P.O. Box 304
Reedsburg, WI 53959

Sauk Prarie Youth Hockey
W.A.H.A.
P.O. Box 72
Prairie du Sac, WI 53578

Southwest Eagles Hockey Association
W.A.H.A.
P.O. Box 620287
Middleton, WI 53562

Stoughton Youth Hockey Association
W.A.H.A.
P.O. Box 301
Stoughton, WI 53589

Sun Prairie Youth Hockey Association
W.A.H.A.
1010 N. Bird St.
Sun Prairie, WI 53590

Waunakee Youth Hockey
W.A.H.A.
P.O. Box 156
Waunakee, WI 53597

West Madison Hockey Association-Flyers
W.A.H.A.
P.O. Box 56222
Madison, WI 53705

Wisconsin Dells Area Youth Hockey
W.A.H.A.
P.O. Box 358
Wisconsin Dells, WI 53965

Wisconsin Girls/Women's Hockey
Association
W.A.H.A.
546 Orchard Dr.
Madison, WI 53711

Wisconsin (Southern: Region 5)

Kenosha Blue Line Hockey Club, Inc.
Phone: 414-697-9829
E-mail: roger.crump@ln.ssw.abbott.com
11129 82nd St.
Kenosha, WI 53142
Home Rink: Kenosha County Ice Arena
Rink Location: Kenosha

McFarland Blues Youth Hockey
Phone: 608-838-3235
5412 Forest Lawn Circle
McFarland, WI 53558
Home Rink: McFarland Community Ice Arena
Rink Location: McFarland

Madison Jr. Monsters
Phone: 608-849-8700
E-mail: jrmonsters@geocities.com
P.O. Box 275
Waunakee, WI 53597-0275
www.geocities.com/Colosseum/5829

Washington Co. Youth Hockey
Phone: 414-335-1676
E-mail: lindy@hnet.net
1409 Chestnut St.
West Bend, WI 53095
Home Rink: Kettle Moraine
Rink Location: West Bend

Southwest Youth Hockey Assoc.
Phone: 608-845-5270
E-mail: kyledk@msn.com
103 Lincoln St.
Verona, WI 53593
Home Rink: Eagle's Nest Ice Arena
Rink Location: Verona

West Madison Flyers
Phone: 608-271-4055
E-mail: ladoga@execpc.com
1117 Valley Stream Drive
Madison, WI 53711-2438
Home Rink: Madison Ice Arena
www.execpc.com/~ladoga/flyers/

Pettit National Selects
Phone: 414-392-9632
33570 Hidden Valley Drive
Dousman, WI 53118
Home Rink: Pettit National Ice Center

Waukesha County Youth Hockey Assosiation
Phone: 414-548-8885
P.O. Box 4194
Waukesha, WI 53187
Home Rink: Two-Eble; Nagawaukee
Rink Location: Waukesha

ElmBrook Hockey Association
W.A.H.A.
P.O. Box 5007
Elm Grove, WI 53122

Fond Du Lac Blue Line Club
W.A.H.A.
P.O. Box 211
Fond Du Lac, WI 54936

Kenosha Blue Line Hockey Club
W.A.H.A.
7727 60th Avenue
Kenosha, WI 53142

Last Chance
W.A.H.A.
2370 Camelot Drive
Brookfield, WI 53005

Racine County Hockey Association
W.A.H.A.
5033 Deerwood Dr.
Racine, WI 53406

Sheboygan Blue Line Association
W.A.H.A.
1202 Wildwood Ave.
Sheboygan, WI 53081

Southeastern Hockey Association of
Wisconsin
W.A.H.A.
P.O. Box 21987
Milwaukee, WI 53132

Washington County Youth Hockey
Association
W.A.H.A.
P.O. Box 462
West Bend, WI 53095

Waukesha Youth Hockey Association
W.A.H.A.
P.O. Box 4194
Waukesha, WI 53187-4194

Waupun Youth Hockey Association
W.A.H.A.
P.O. Box 285
Waupan, WI 53963

Milwaukee Winter Club
W.A.H.A.
P.O. Box 17506
Milwaukee, WI 53217

Wisconsin Classic Hockey League
W.A.H.A.
33570 Hidden Valley Drive
Dousman, WI 53118

Dodgeville Area Youth hockey
Phone: 608-987-2782
E-mail: tomnanjo@mhtc.net
40 Jackson
Mineral Point, WI 53565
Home Rink: Dodgeville
Rink Location: Harris Park

Fond Du Lac Blueline Club
Phone: 414-921-2057
E-mail: blueline@fdldotnet.com
68 N. Butler Street
Fond Du Lac, WI 54935-3138
Home Rink: Blueline Family Ice Center
Rink Location: Fond Du Lac

Wisconsin (Western Associations)

AltoonaYouth Hockey Association
W.A.H.A.
P.O. Box 61
Altoona, WI 54720

Black River Youth Hockey Association
W.A.H.A.
P.O. Box 463
Black River Falls, WI 54615

Eu Claire Youth Hockey Association
W.A.H.A.
P.O. Box 1592
Eau Claire, WI 54702

Hudson Youth Hockey Association
W.A.H.A.
Phone: 715-386-3535
1820 Hanley Road
Hudson, WI 54016

Mauston Area Youth Hockey Association
W.A.H.A.
P.O. Box 443
Mauston, WI 53948

Menomonie Youth Hockey Association
W.A.H.A.
P.O. Box 492
Menomonie, WI 54751

New Richmond Youth Hockey Association
W.A.H.A.
P.O. Box 207
New Richmond, WI 54017

Onalaska Youth Hockey Association
W.A.H.A.
P.O. Box 503
Onalaska, WI 54650

Pierce County Youth Hockey Association
W.A.H.A.
W7858 490th Ave.
Ellsworth, WI 54011

River City Youth Hockey Association
W.A.H.A.
P.O. Box 2463
La Crosse, WI 54602

River Falls Youth Hockey Association
W.A.H.A.
P.O. Box 582
River Falls, WI 54022

Somerset Youth Hockey Association
W.A.H.A.
P.O. Box 98
Somerset, WI 54025

Sparta Youth Hockey Association
W.A.H.A.
P.O. Box 331
Sparta, WI 54656

Tomah Youth Hockey Association
W.A.H.A.
P.O. Box 126
Tomah, WI 54660

Viroqua Youth Hockey Association
W.A.H.A.
P.O. Box 55
Viroqua, WI 54665

West Salem Youth Hockey Association
W.A.H.A.
P.O. Box 15
West Salem, WI 54669

West Virginia

Charleston Amateur Hockey Association
Phone: 304-744-5996
E-mail: scottbuckley@newwave.net
105 Addison Drive
South Charleston, WV 25309
Home Rink: Tri-State Ice Arena
Rink Location: Huntington

Morgantown Hockey Association
Phone: 304-328-5636
E-mail: u5a88@wvnvm.wvnet.edu
Rt. 13 Box 167
Morgantown, WV 26505
Home Rink: Boparc Ice Rink
Rink Location: Morgantown

Wyoming

Casper Amateur Hockey Club
Phone: 307-234-0531
E-mail: cfarrel@trib.com
1210 Cornwall
Casper, WY 82609
Home Rink: Casper Ice Arena
Rink Location: Casper

Canada

Alberta

KC Knights Hockey Club
Phone: 403-463-1261
E-mail: ernie.waschuk@gov.ab.ca
3619 56th Street
Edmonton, AB T6L 2J6

Canadian Rocky Mountain Hockey
Academy
Paul Hughes-High Performance Program
Director
Phone: 800-KIK-PUCK
E-mail:kikpuck@banff.net
Box 3098
Canmore, AB T0L 0M0
Home Rink: Olympic Arena
Rink Location: Canmore

British Columbia

Sicamous & District Minor Hockey
E-mail: tawni@sicamous.com
Box 429
Sicamous, BC V0E 2V0
Home Rink: Sicamous

Westside Minor Hockey
Phone: 250-768-7248
E-mail: laredo@can-info.net
3207 Sunset Place
Westbank, BC V4T 1S3
Home Rink: Mt. Boucherie
Rink Location: Westside

Richmond Girls Ice Hockey
Phone: 604-271-7901
E-mail: chim@rgih.bc.ca
8720 Ashbrook Court
Richmond BC V6Y 2Z7
Home Rink: Richmond Ice Center
Rink Location: Richmond

Port Coquitlam Minor Hckey Association
Phone: 604-941-7314
E-mail: mgm@intergate.bc.ca
1262 Plymouth Crescent
Port Coquitlam, BC V3B 6G2
Home Rink: PoCo Recreation Centre

BC Amateur Hockey Association
Phone: 250-652-2978
E-mail: bcaha@vanisle.net
6671 Oldfirled Rd.
Saanichton Victoria, BC
www.bcaha.org/

Port Coquitlam International Bnatam Hockey
Tournament
Phone: 604-941-7314
E-mail: mgm@intergate.bc.ca
1261 Plymouth Crescent
Port Coquitlam, BC V3B 2G6
Home Rink: Port Coquitlam

Ridge Meadows Minor Hockey
Phone: 604-467-4632
E-mail: garth@intergate.bc.ca
24895 Ferguson Ave.
Maple Ridge, BC V2W 1H4
Home Rink: Cam Neely Arena
Rink Location: Maple Ridge

Fort St. James Minor Hockey
Phone: 250-690-7535
E-mail: bberland@onramp.hwy16.com
250 Ash St. West
Fort St. James, BC VOJ 1PO
Home Rink: Fort Forum

Victoria Racquet Club Minor Hockey
Association
Phone: 250-721-3599
E-mail: JDick9999@aol.com
4036 Hollydene Place
Victoria, BC V8N 3Z7
Home Rink: Gordan Head Complex
Rink Location: Victoria

Tri-Cities Female Ice Hockey Association
Phone: 604-941-2339
E-mail: coughlan@intergate.bc.ca
2544 Colonial Drive
Port Coquitlam, BC V3C 5X3
Home Rink: Coquitlam and Port Coquitlam
Rink Location: near Vancouver

Manitoba

St. James AA Hockey Club
Phone: 204-832-8563
E-mail: stjames@geocities.com
15 Sayer Ave.
Winnipeg MB R2Y 0C5
Home Rink: Allard
Rink Location: Winnipeg

Manitoba Mustangs
Phone: 204-663-2614
E-mail: dkroeker@ccco.net
32 Clydesdale Drive
Winnipeg Canada, MB R2E 0G6
Home Rink: Gateway Arena
Rink Location: Gateway/Bonner

Flin Flon Minor Hockey
Phone: 204-687-6906
E-mail: hfreebor@mb.sympatico.ca
180 Wright Ave
Flin Flon, MB R8A 0E3
Home Rink: Whitney Forum
Rink Location: Flin Flon

New Brunswick

New Brunswick Stars Elite Hockey
Program
Phone: 506-387-6080
P.O. Box 20038
Moncton, NB E1C 9M1
Home Rink: various
Rink Locations: throughout province

Ontario (Northern)

Beaverton Minor Hockey Association
Phone: 705-426-7630
E-mail: jfiume@lindsaycomp.on.ca
Box 691
Beaverton, ON L0K 1A0
Home Rink: Beaverton Community Center
Rink Location: Beaverton

StarFire International Hockey
Phone: 613-962-7224
E-mail: starfire@sympatico.ca
25 Hutton Dr.
Belleville, ON K8P 1E9
Home Rink: various
Rink Location: Trenton -Belleville

Sportszone International
Phone: 705-721-9622
24 Moore Place
Barrie, ON L4N 6N8
Home Rink: Eddie Busch
Rink Location: Collingwood

Hamilton Girls' Hockey Association
Phone: 905-575-0544
163 Darlington Dr.
Hamilton, ON L9C 2M4
Home Rink: Inch Park
Rink Location: Hamilton

Port Dover Minor Hockey
Phone: 519-428-7715
E-mail: deliot@nornet.on.ca
RR1 Port Dover
Port Dover, ON N0A 1N1
Home Rink: Port Dover
Rink Location: Port Dover

EMHA Chiefs M-Atom "AAA"
Phone: 519-262-2924
E-mail: bcoke@hay.net
201 Lakeview
Grand bend on Nom-1T0
Home Rink: Ice House
Rink Location: London

Peterborough Church Nationals
Phone: 705-743-4608
E-mail: mariner@oncomdis.on.ca
19 Ferndale Ave.
Peterborough, ON K9J-1M1
Home Rink: Kinsmen Civic Center
Rink Location: Peterborough

Russell Minor Hockey Association
Phone: 613-445-5511
E-mail: renrich@direct-internet.net
P.O. Box 281
Russell, ON K4R 1C8
Home Rink: Russell
Rink Location: 30 minutes from Ottawa,
Canada

Brampton Vipers Hockey Club
Phone: 905-840-6689
E-mail: mnaraine@pathcom.com
4 Wishart Place
Brampton, ON L6Z 3H5
Home Rink: The Ice Gardens
Rink Location: York University

Beaverton Minor Hockey Association
Phone: 705-426-5796
E-mail: jfiume@lindsaycomp.on.ca
RR#2
Beaverton, ON L0K 1A0
Home Rink: Beaverton
Rink Location: Beaverton

Jr. Eskis Hockey Club Inc.
Phone: 705-232-4603
E-mail: scottie@ntl.sympatico.ca
P.O. Box 1131
Iroquois Falls, ON P0K 1G0
Home Rink: Jus Jordan Arena
Rink Location: Iroquois Falls

Ontario (Southern)

Chinguacousy Minor Hockey Association
Phone: 905-458-9734
E-mail: spunker@total.net
20 Victoria Cres.
Brampton, ON L6T 763
Home Rink: Victoria Park Arena
Rink Location: Brampton

Dundas Minor Hockey Assoc.
Phone: 905-628-2702
E-mail: ghill@gowebway.com
31 Napier St. N.
Dundas, ON L9H 2Z6

Rosedale Minor Hockey
Phone: 905-574-9391
103 Pinewarbler Drive
Hamilton, ON L9A 4Z5
Home Rink: Rosedale Arena
Rink Location: Hamilton

Georgetown Minor Hockey
Phone: 905-873-2689
E-mail: gerry@castle
26 College St.
Georgetown, ON l7G 2N7
Home Rink: Georgetown
www.castle.on.ca

Quinte Regional Minor Hockey Association
Phone: 613-968-9186
E-mail: freeland@connect.reach.net
245 Bridge Street East
Belleville, ON K8N 1P2
Home Rink: Wally Dever Arena
Rink Location: Belleville

Mississauga North Stars
Phone: 905-270-9741
E-mail: clancy@globalserve.on.ca
312-135 Hillcrest Ave.
Mississauga, ON L5B 4B1
Home Rink: Tomken Arena
Rink Location: Mississauga

Windsor Minor Hockey Association
Phone: 519-254-1739
E-mail: mobile@mnsi.net
P.O. Box 713 Station A
Windsor, ON N9A 6N4
Home Rink: Windsor-Adie Knox
Rink Location: Windsor

Brockville Minor Hockey Association
Phone: 613-342-1900
E-mail: saunded@mail.lgboe.edu.on.ca
1322 Lily Bay Drive North
Elizabethtown, ON K6V 7C5
Home Rink: Brockville Youth Arena
Rink Location: Brockville

Rideau-St. Lawrence Minor Hockey
Association
Phone: 613-925-2904
E-mail: shalpenny@mulberry.com
Box 285
Prescott, ON K0E 1T0
Home Rink: Leo Boivin Community Centre
Rink Location: Prescott
www.mulberry.com/~shalpenny/
kings.htm

Waterford & District Minor Hockey
Phone: 519-443-5458
E-mail: jball@nornet.on.ca
166 Church Street West
Waterford, ON N0E 1YO
Home Rink: Tricenturena
Rink Location: Waterford

Metcalfe & District Hockey Association
Phone: 613-821-4733
E-mail: mailit@direct-internet.net
P.O. Box 436
Greely, ON K4P 1N6
Home Rink: The Larry Robinson Arena
Rink Location: Metcalfe
www.direct-internet.net/mdha

Peterborough Community Church Hockey
League Nationals
Phone: 705-743-4608
E-mail: mariner@pipcom.com
19 Ferndale Ave.
Peterborough, ON K9J-1M1
Home Rink: Kinsmen, Evinrude Center,
Northcrest Arenas
Rink Location: Peterborough

Lawfield Minor Hockey
Phone: 905-387-3542
E-mail: jwoodw7269@aol.com
150 Folkstone Ave.
Hamilton, ON L8V 4R6

London Devilettes Girls Hockey
Association
Phone: 519-659-2024
E-mail: devilett@execulink.com
108 Speight Cres.
London, ON N5V 3W8
Home Rink: Argyle Arena
Rink Location: East London
www.devilettes.on.ca

BLOMHA
Phone: 905-333-9717
E-mail: hockey@blomha.on.ca
3333-75 New Street
Burlington, ON L7N 1N1
Home Rink: Burlington

Prospects
Phone: 519-579-9284
E-mail: prospect@golden.net
198 Blackwell Drive
Kitchener, ON N2N 2S2
Home Rink: University of Guelph
Rink Location: Guelph

Quinte Regional Minor Hockey
Phone: 613-966-2981
E-mail: stephunt@connect.reach.net
6457 Huntingwood Dr. East
Belleville, ON K8N 4Z5
Home Rink: Quinte Sports Center
Rink Location: Belleville

Quebec

Cote-St-Luc Houseleague
E-mail: dkramer@total.net
5852 Shalom
Montreal, Quebec H4W 2Z1
Home Rink: Samuel Moskovitch
Rink Location: Shalom an Cavendish

Hockey Mineur Beauport Inc.
Phone: 418-661-8448
Fax: 418-661-5509
2 Rue Du Fargy
Beauport, Quebec G1E 6P4

Association du Hockey Mineur de Sainte-Foy
Fax: 418-654-4012
E-mail: gasselin@quebectel.com
930 Avenue Roland-Beaudin
Sainte-Foy, Quebec, G1V AH8
Home Rink: Centre Sportif de Sainte-Foy
Rink Location: Sainte-Foy
www.globetrotter.qc.ca/
ahm_gouverneurs

Hockey Mineur de Magog, Inc.
Phone: 819-868-2125
E-mail: ahmm96@multi-medias.ca
C.P 416
Magog, Quebec, J1X 3X7
Home Rink: Arena de Magog
Rink Location: Magog
www.multi-medias.ca/ahmm96

Vics de Granby
Phone: 514-777-1216
E-mail: renles@granby.mtl.net
180 9e Rang Ouest
Granby, Quebec, J2G 8C9
Home Rink: Léonard Grondin
Rink Location: Granby

Saskatchewan

Saskatchewan Wheatland AAA
Phone: 306-286-3624
E-mail: vanessa@sk.sympatico.ca
Box 208
Leroy, SK SOK 2PO
Home Rink: Regina & Saskatoon
Rink Location: Saskatchewan

Western Canada Invitational
Phone: 306-347-8305
E-mail: Fredmcbeth@eagle.wbm.ca
79 Groome Ave.
Regina, SK S4S 6S3
Home Rink: Balfour
Rink Location: Regina

Regina Flyers Midget AA
Phone: 306-525-6461
E-mail: jfodey@bfsmedia.com
1400 Horace Street
Regina, SK
Home Rink: Mahone Arena
Rink Location: Regina

S.A.S.K. CAN
Phone: 306-858-2266
E-mail: barkerdc@sk.simpatico.ca
Box 338
Lucky Lake, SK SOL 1ZO
Rink Location: Saskatoon

Outside North America

Français Volants de Paris
Phone: 33 1 47 06 23 08
E-mail: heidet1@opsi.worldnet.fr
82 Rue de Verdun
Champigny, France 94500

Bulldogs Brno
Riegrova 7
Brno, Czech 61200

Pumas Youth Hockey Mexico
Phone: 52-5-812-1486
E-mail: sportica@mail.internet.com.mx
Noche De Paz 38 Cuajimalpa
Mexico City d.f. 05100
Home Rink: Sportica
Rink Location: Mexico City

SK Iron
E-mail:
nils.hakan.svensson@uppsala.mail.telia.com
Ramsjovagen 176
740 30 Bjorklinge, Sweden

Hockey Boulogne Billancourt 92
Phone: 33 1 46 21 20 00
E-mail: easi2k@easynet.fr
30 Rue des Peupliers
Boulogne Billancourt, France 92100
Home Rink: Boulogne Billancourt
Rink Location: Boulogne Billancourt

Adult Hockey

We don't have a ready-made list of adult hockey organizations, but there are several organizations out there. The best way to find out about adult recreational hockey is to contact Hockey North America (800-4-HOCKEY) or visit their Web site at www.hna.com. Hockey North America has more than 20 leagues in the U.S. and Canada — and you don't need to be a hockey expert because HNA has plenty of programs for beginners.

NHL: Directory of Addresses

This directory gives you contact information for the NHL offices, the NHL Players' Association, and the NHL teams. If you want the Web address for any NHL team, check the listing given in Chapter 12.

NHL offices

National Hockey League, L.P.
1251 Ave. of the Americas
47th floor
New York, NY 100120
Phone: 212-789-2000
Fax: 212-789-2020

75 International Boulevard, Suite 300
Rexdale, ON M9W 6L9
Phone: 416-798-0809
Fax: 416-798-0819

NHL Players Association (NHLPA)

777 Bay Street, Suite 2400
Toronto, ON M5G2C8
Phone: 416-408-4040
Fax: 416-408-3685

NHL Teams

Anaheim Mighty Ducks
Arrowhead Pond of Anaheim
2695 East Katella Avenue @ Douglas Road
Anaheim, CA 92803
Phone: 714-704-2500
Tickets: 714-704-2400
Seating capacity: 16,223

Boston Bruins
FleetCenter
One FleetCenter Suite 200
Boston, MA 02114
Phone: 617-523-3030
Tickets: 617-227-3200 or 800-828-7080
Seating capacity: 17,565

Buffalo Sabres
Marine Midland Arena
One Seymour H. Knox III Plaza
Buffalo, NY 14203
Phone: 716-855-4100
Tickets: 716-852-5000
Seating capacity: 18,595

Calgary Flames
Canadian Airlines Saddledome
P. O. Box 1540 Station M
Calgary, AB T2P 3B9
Phone: 403-261-0475
Tickets: 403-270-6700
Seating capacity: 20,000

Carolina Hurricanes
5000 Aerial Center Parkway
Morrisville, NC 27560
Phone: 919-467-7825
Tickets: 888-645-8491
Seating capacity: 21,000

Chicago Blackhawks
United Center
1901 West Madison Street
Chicago, IL 60612
Phone: 312-943-7000
Tickets: 312-559-1212
Seating capacity: 20,500

Colorado Avalanche
McNichols Sports Arena
1635 Clay Street
Denver, CO 80204
Phone: 303-893-3865
Tickets: 303-830-8497
Seating capacity: 16,061

Dallas Stars
Reunion Arena
777 Sports Street
Dallas, TX 75207
Phone: 214-939-2770
Tickets: 214-467-8277
Seating capacity: 16,924

Detroit Red Wings
Joe Louis Arena
600 Civic Center Drive
Detroit, MI 48226
Tickets: 810-645-6666
Seating capacity: 19,275

Edmonton Oilers
Edmonton Coliseum
7424 118th Avenue
Edmonton, AB T5B 4M9
Phone: 403-471-2191
Tickets: 403-451-8000
Seating capacity: 16,437

Florida Panthers
Miami Arena
100 Northeast Third Ave.
Miami, FL 33301
Phone: 305-530-4400
Tickets: 305-530-4400 Ext. 4444
Seating capacity: 14,700

Los Angeles Kings
The Great Western Forum
3900 West Manchester Boulevard
Inglewood, CA 90308
Phone: 310-673-1300
Tickets: 310-673-6003
Seating capacity: 17,317

Montreal Canadiens
Molson Centre
1260 Gauchetiere Street West
Montreal, Quebec H3B 5E8
Phone: 514-932-2582
Tickets: 514-932-2582
Seating capacity: 21,273

New Jersey Devils
Continental Airlines Arena
P.O. Box 504
East Rutherford, NJ 07073
Phone: 201-935-6050
Tickets: 201-507-8900
Seating capacity: 19,040

New York Islanders
Nassau Veterans' Memorial Coliseum
1255 Hempstead Turnpike
Uniondale, NY 11553
Phone: 516-794-9300
Tickets: 516-888-9000
Seating capacity: 16,297

New York Rangers
Madison Square Garden
2 Pennsylvania Plaza
New York, NY 10121
Phone: 212-465-6040
Tickets: 212-308-NYRS
Seating capacity: 18,200

Ottawa Senators
Corel Centre
1000 Palladium Drive
Kanata, ON K2V 1A4
Phone: 613-599-0100
Tickets: 613-599-0300
Seating capacity: 18,500

Philadelphia Flyers
CoreStates Center
1 CoreStates Complex
Philadelphia, PA 19148
Tickets: 215-336-2000
Seating capacity: 17,380

Phoenix Coyotes
America West Arena
201 East Jefferson Street
Phoenix, AZ 85004
Phone: 602-379-2000
Fax: 602-379-7800
Seating capacity: 19,023

Pittsburgh Penguins
Civic Arena
300 Auditorium Place
Pittsburgh, PA 15219
Phone: 412-642-PENS
Tickets: 412-642-PENS
Seating capacity: 17,181

St. Louis Blues
Kiel Center
1401 Clark Avenue
St. Louis, MO 63102
Phone: 314-622-5435
Tickets: 314-968-1800
Seating capacity: 18,500

San Jose Sharks
San Jose Arena
525 West Santa Clara
San Jose, CA 95113
Phone: 408-287-9200
Tickets: 408-999-5765
Seating capacity: 17,449

Tampa Bay Lightning
Ice Palace
401 Channelside Drive
Tampa Bay, FL 33602
Phone: 813-229-8800
Tickets: 813-229-8800
Seating capacity: 28,000

Toronto Maple Leafs
Maple Leaf Gardens
60 Carlton Street
Toronto, ON M5B 1L1
Phone: 416-977-1641
Tickets: 416-870-5000
Seating capacity: 15,642

Vancouver Canucks
General Motors Place
800 Griffiths Way
Vancouver, BC V6B 6G1
Phone: 604-899-7400
Tickets: 604-280-4400
Seating capacity: 18,422

Washington Capitals
US Air Arena
1 Harry S Truman Drive
Landover, MD 20785
Phone: 301-386-7000
Tickets: 410-481-SEAT or 202-432-SEAT
Seating capacity: 18,130

Appendix C
Hockey Signals

This appendix is a collection of the most common signals that the hockey officials make during a game. In fact, these signals are also used in roller (in-line) hockey, too. If you need more details, check out Appendix A, which is a glossary of some common hockey terms. In addition, Part I of this book has more descriptions — and maybe a diagram or two to help you.

Boarding

Boarding is called when you check another player into the boards with more than just your average force. The degree of violence and the manner in which the player is thrown into the boards (tripped, elbowed, body checked, and so on) help determine the penalty.

Gesture: Striking the closed fist once into the open palm of the other hand.

Butt ending

Jab a player with the shaft (butt-end) of your stick . . . and you get called for butt ending!

Gesture: Moving the forearm, fist closed, under the forearm of the other hand that is held palm down.

Charging

A charge is called when you take more than two steps or strides to run or jump into another player.

Gesture: Rotating clenched fists around one another in front of the chest.

Checking from behind

When you try to get between your opponent and the puck by using your body and/or your stick, you are checking. When you check your opponent from behind, however, you draw the attention of the officials!

Gesture: Placing the arm behind the back, elbow bent, forearm parallel to the surface.

Cross checking

If you pick your stick off the ice and hold it in two hands to check your opponent (using the shaft of the stick), you get whistled for cross checking.

Gesture: Extending both clenched fists forward and back from the chest.

Delayed calling of penalty

If an infraction calls for a minor, major, misconduct, game misconduct, or match penalty on a player of the team *not* in possession of the puck, the referee blows his whistle and imposes the penalty after completion of the play by the team with the puck. (The play is considered completed when the team in possession of the puck loses possession!)

Gesture: Extending the non-whistle hand straight above the head and pointing to the penalized player.

Delayed (slow) whistle

You are onside when either of your skates are on your own side of the blue line (or on the line) at the moment the puck completely crosses the outer edge of that line — no matter where your stick is. However, while an offside call is delayed, if players of the offending team clear the zone, the official drops his arm and the play is no longer offside.

Gesture: Extending the non-whistle hand straight above the head.

Delaying the game

If you shoot, bat, or throw the puck outside the playing area, you are delaying the game. You are also guilty of this infraction if you deliberately move the goal (by displacing a goalpost) to keep the opposition from scoring.

Gesture: Placing the non-whistle hand (palm open) across the chest and then fully extending it in front of the body.

Elbowing

If you use your elbow in any way to contact or foul another player, you are guilty of elbowing.

Gesture: Tapping the elbow with the opposite hand.

Fighting

Fisticuffs are not tolerated!

Gesture: Punching motion to the side with the arm extending from the shoulder.

Goal scored

This is the signal you'll love to see — as long as your team is the one to score the goal!

Gesture: Pointing at the goal (in which the puck entered) with the non-whistle hand while blowing the whistle.

Hand pass

This isn't baseball. You can't close your hand on the puck or pick it up from the ice — unless, of course, you're the ref.

Gesture: Placing the non-whistle hand (open hand) and arm alongside the body and swinging forward and up in an underhand motion.

High sticking

You get called for high sticking if you injure an opposing player by carrying any part of your stick above your waist.

Gesture: Holding a clenched fist, with the hands one above the other, at the side of the head.

Holding

Impeding the progress of an opponent by holding is frowned upon!

Gesture: Clasping the wrist of the whistle hand well in front of the chest.

Holding the face mask

If you can't get away with holding your opponent's face mask in the NFL, do you think you can do it in the NHL?

Gesture: Holding the closed fist in front of the face, palm in, and pulling down in one straight motion.

Hooking

Imagine that the blade of the hockey stick is a hook. If you use this hook to impede another player (pulling or tugging on the hook), you commit hooking.

Gesture: Tugging with both arms, as if pulling something toward the stomach.

Icing

So you think you can just send that puck from behind your red line down the length of the ice whenever you want? No, you can't. See Chapter 3 for all the details on icing. In roller or in-line hockey, this infraction is known as "clearing."

Gesture: Extending the arm (without whistle) over the head.

Interference

If you impede the progress of another player who does not have the puck, you are interfering. That means you can't check an opponent who does not have the puck. You are also called for interference if you deliberately knock the stick out of your opponent's hands or prevent your opponent from picking up a dropped stick or other piece of equipment.

Gesture: Crossing and keeping the arms in front of the chest with fists closed.

Kneeing

Don't use your knees against your opponent!

Gesture: Tapping once the right knee with the right hand, keeping both skates on the surface.

Match penalty

A match penalty involves the suspension of a player for the remainder of the game. This usually occurs when you try to injure an opponent (such as kicking). After five minutes playing time, the suspended player can be replaced by another.

Gesture: Patting flat of hand on top of the head.

Misconduct

Misconducts include basic, game, and gross misconduct levels (see Chapter 3 for details).

Gesture: Placing both hands on hips.

Offside

If you precede the puck into the attacking zone (over the blueline), you get called for offside. (Offside is explained and illustrated in Chapter 3.)

Gesture: Extending the free arm over the head.

Penalty shot

Certain infractions force a referee to award a penalty shot (such as when you take your opponent down from behind if he is on a breakaway). This is a free skate and shot on goal, with only the goalie being allowed to stop the shot.

Gesture: Crossing arms (fists clenched) above head.

Slashing

When you hit another player with your stick, you are guilty of slashing. It doesn't matter if you are holding the stick with one or two hands or even if you miss the player you are aiming for — it's still slashing.

Gesture: Chopping once the hand across the straightened forearm of the other hand.

Spearing

Spearing is sort of the opposite of butt ending. If you poke another player with the blade tip of your stick — or if you only make the attempt — you are guilty of spearing.

Gesture: Making a single jabbing motion with both hands together, thrust forward from in front of the chest then dropping the hands to the side.

Time-out

In the NHL, each team can have one thirty-second time-out during a game. This time-out must be taken during a normal stoppage of play.

Gesture: Making a T with both hands.

Tripping

No matter how you trip your opponent — with your stick, knee, foot, arm, or hand — it still adds up to tripping.

Gesture: Striking the side of the leg and following through once, keeping the head up and both skates on the surface.

Wash-out

A referee uses this signal to indicate that no penalty occurred or no goal was scored — and play can continue. A linesman makes this gesture to show that no icing, offside, or high-sticking took place.

Gesture: Swinging both arms laterally across the body at shoulder level with palms down.

Appendix D
Hockey: The Lists

From Hall of Famers to Stanley Cup winners, from career milestones to single-season achievements, this appendix has something for any hockey enthusiast.

The Hockey Hall of Fame

The Hockey Hall of Fame was formed in 1943. In 1961, the Hockey Hall of Fame opened its doors to the public in a building located on the grounds of the Canadian National Exhibition in Toronto. The Hockey Hall of Fame moved to its new site at BCE Place and welcomed the hockey world on June 18, 1993. Visit its Web site at www.hhof.com.

There were 307 Honored Members in the Hockey Hall of Fame as of 1997: 209 have been inducted as players, 85 as builders, and 13 as Referees/Linesmen. Other inductees include media personnel who have made a significant contribution to hockey. This is a list of the players in the Hall of Fame, broken down by forwards/defensemen and goalies.

Forwards and defensemen

A forward (F) is usually classified as a center (C), a right wing (RW), or a left wing (LW). A defenseman (D) is, well, a defenseman. Until the 1930s, there was also the position of rover (RO) — a player who roamed the entire rink.

Pos. = position	A = assists
GP = games played	Pts. = points
G = goals scored	PIM = penalties in minutes

Player	Election Year	Pos.	GP	G	A	Pts.	PIM
Sid Abel	1969	C	613	189	283	472	376
Jack Adams	1959	C	243	134	50	184	307
Syl Apps	1961	C	423	201	231	432	56
George Armstrong	1975	RW	1187	296	417	713	721
Ace Bailey	1975	RW	313	111	82	193	472
Dan Bain	1945	C	Unavailable				
Hobey Baker	1945	RO	Unavailable				
Bill Barber	1990	LW	903	420	463	883	623
Marty Barry	1965	C	509	195	192	387	231
Andy Bathgate	1978	RW	1069	349	624	973	624
Bobby Bauer	1996	RW	327	123	137	260	36
Jean Beliveau	1972	C	1125	507	712	1219	1029
Doug Bentley	1964	LW	566	219	324	543	217
Max Bentley	1966	C	646	245	299	544	175
Toe Blake	1966	LW	578	235	292	527	272
Leo Boivin	1986	D	1150	72	250	322	1192
Dickie Boon	1952	D	42	10	XX	10	XX
Mike Bossy	1991	LW	752	573	553	1126	210
Butch Bouchard	1966	D	785	49	144	193	863
Frank Boucher	1958	C	557	161	262	423	119
George Boucher	1960	F/D	457	122	62	184	739
Russell Bowie	1945	C	80	234	XX	234	XX
Punch Broadbent	1962	RW	302	122	45	167	553
John Bucyk	1981	LW	1540	556	813	1369	497
Billy Burch	1974	C	390	137	53	190	251
Harry Cameron	1962	D	312	174	27	201	154
King Clancy	1958	D	592	137	143	280	904
Dit Clapper	1947	RW	833	228	246	474	462
Bobby Clarke	1987	C	1144	358	852	1210	1453
Sprague Cleghorn	1958	D	377	163	39	202	489

Player	Election Year	Pos.	GP	G	A	Pts.	PIM
Neil Colville	1967	C/D	464	99	166	265	213
Charlie Conacher	1961	RW	460	225	173	398	523
Lionel Conacher	1994	D	500	80	105	185	882
Bill Cook	1952	RW	586	322	196	518	483
Fred Cook	1995	LW	473	158	144	302	449
Art Coulter	1974	D	465	30	82	112	543
Yvan Cournoyer	1982	RW	968	428	435	863	255
Bill Cowley	1968	C	549	195	353	548	143
Rusty Crawford	1962	LW	245	110	3	113	51
Jack Darragh	1962	RW	250	194	21	215	88
Scotty Davidson	1950	RW	40	42	XX	42	XX
Hap Day	1961	LW	581	86	116	202	602
Alex Delvecchio	1977	C	1549	456	825	1281	383
Cy Denneny	1959	LW	368	281	69	350	210
Marcel Dionne	1992	C	1348	731	1040	1771	600
Gord Drillon	1975	LW	311	155	139	294	56
Graham Drinkwater	1950	L/D	37	40	XX	40	XX
Woody Dumart	1992	LW	771	211	218	429	99
Tommy Dunderdale	1974	C	290	225	XX	225	XX
Red Dutton	1958	D	449	29	67	96	871
Babe Dye	1970	RW	270	202	41	243	190
Phil Esposito	1984	C	1282	717	873	1590	910
Arthur Farrell	1965	F	26	29	XX	29	XX
Fern Flaman	1990	D	910	34	174	208	1370
Frank Foyston	1958	C	357	242	7	249	32
Frank Fredrickson	1958	C	327	170	34	204	206
Bill Gadsby	1970	D	1248	130	437	567	1539
Bob Gainey	1992	LW	1160	239	262	501	585
Herb Gardiner	1958	D	233	44	9	53	52
Jimmy Gardner	1962	LW	112	63	XX	63	XX
Boom Boom Geoffrion	1972	RW	883	393	429	822	689

(continued)

(continued)

Player	Election Year	Pos.	GP	G	A	Pts.	PIM
Eddie Gerard	1945	F/D	201	93	30	123	106
Rod Gilbert	1982	RW	1065	406	615	1021	508
Billy Gilmour	1962	RW	32	26	XX	26	XX
Moose Goheen	1952	D	Unavailable				
Ebbie Goodfellow	1963	C	554	134	190	324	511
Mike Grant	1950	D	55	10	XX	10	XX
Shorty Green	1962	RW	103	33	8	41	151
Si Griffis	1950	RO/D	117	39	XX	39	XX
Joe Hall	1961	F/D	198	105	1	106	145
Doug Harvey	1973	D	1113	88	452	540	1216
George Hay	1958	LW	373	179	60	239	84
Bryan Hextall	1969	RW	447	187	175	362	227
Tom Hooper	1962	F	11	12	XX	12	XX
Red Horner	1965	D	490	42	110	152	1264
Tim Horton	1977	D	1446	115	403	518	1611
Gordie Howe	1972	RW	1767	801	1049	1850	1685
Syd Howe	1965	F/D	691	237	291	528	214
Harry Howell	1979	D	1411	94	324	418	1298
Bobby Hull	1983	LW	1063	610	560	1170	640
Harry Hyland	1962	RW	157	199	XX	199	9
Dick Irvin	1958	C	249	152	23	174	76
Busher Jackson	1971	LW	636	241	234	475	437
Ching Johnson	1958	D	435	38	48	86	808
Moose Johnson	1952	LW/D	270	123	XX	123	XX
Tom Johnson	1970	D	978	51	213	264	960
Aurel Joliat	1947	LW	654	270	190	460	752
Duke Keats	1958	C	256	183	19	202	112
Red Kelly	1969	C	1316	281	542	823	327
Ted Kennedy	1966	C	696	231	329	560	432
Dave Keon	1986	C	1296	396	590	986	117
Elmer Lach	1966	C	664	215	408	623	478

Player	Election Year	Pos.	GP	G	A	Pts.	PIM
Guy Lafleur	1988	LW	1126	560	793	1353	399
Newsy Lalonde	1950	C/RO	315	428	27	455	122
Jacques Laperriere	1987	D	691	40	242	282	674
Guy Lapointe	1993	D	884	171	451	622	893
Edgar Laprade	1993	C	501	108	172	280	42
Jack Laviolette	1962	D/LW	178	58	0	58	0
Jacques Lemaire	1984	C	853	366	469	835	217
Herbie Lewis	1989	LW	484	148	161	309	248
Ted Lindsay	1966	LW	1068	379	472	851	1808
Mickey MacKay	1952	C/RO	388	246	19	265	79
Frank Mahovlich	1981	LW	1181	533	570	1103	1056
Joe Malone	1950	C/LW	125	146	18	164	35
Sylvio Mantha	1960	D	543	63	72	135	667
Jack Marshall	1965	C/D	132	99	XX	99	XX
Fred Maxwell	1962	RO	Unavailable				
Lanny McDonald	1992	RW	1111	500	506	1006	899
Frank McGee	1945	C/RO	23	71	XX	71	XX
Billy McGimsie	1962	F	Unavailable				
George McNamara	1958	D	121	39	XX	39	XX
Stan Mikita	1983	C	1394	541	926	1467	1270
Dickie Moore	1974	RW	719	261	347	608	652
Howie Morenz	1945	C	550	270	197	467	531
Bill Mosienko	1965	RW	711	258	282	540	121
Frank Nighbor	1947	LW/C	348	136	60	196	266
Reg Noble	1962	LW/C/D	534	180	79	259	770
Buddy O'Connor	1988	C	509	140	257	397	34
Harry Oliver	1967	F	603	216	85	301	147
Bert Olmstead	1985	LW	848	181	421	602	884
Bobby Orr	1979	D	657	270	645	915	953
Brad Park	1988	D	1113	213	683	896	1429
Lester Patrick	1947	D/RO/G	207	130	XX	130	XX

(continued)

(continued)

Player	Election Year	Pos.	GP	G	A	Pts.	PIM
Lynn Patrick	1980	LW	455	145	190	335	270
Gilbert Perreault	1990	C	1191	512	814	1326	500
Tommy Phillips	1945	LW	33	57	XX	57	XX
Pierre Pilote	1975	D	890	80	418	498	1251
Didier Pitre	1962	D/RO/RW	282	238	17	255	59
Denis Potvin	1991	D	1060	310	742	1052	1354
Babe Pratt	1966	D	517	83	209	292	453
Joe Primeau	1963	C	310	66	177	243	105
Marcel Pronovost	1978	D	1206	88	257	345	851
Bob Pulford	1991	LW	1079	281	362	643	792
Harvey Pulford	1945	D	96	6	XX	6	XX
Bill Quackenbush	1976	D	774	62	222	284	95
Frank Rankin	1961	RO	Unavailable				
Jean Ratelle	1985	C	1281	491	776	1267	276
Ken Reardon	1966	D	341	26	96	122	604
Henri Richard	1979	C	1256	358	688	1046	928
Maurice Richard	1961	RW	978	544	421	965	1285
George Richardson	1950	Unavailable					
Gordon Roberts	1971	LW	166	203	XX	XX	XX
Larry Robinson	1995	D	1384	208	750	958	793
Art Ross	1945	D	167	85	0	85	0
Blair Russell	1965	RW/C	67	110	XX	110	XX
Ernie Russell	1965	RO/C	98	180	XX	180	XX
Jack Ruttan	1962	Unavailable					
Borje Salming	1996	D	1148	150	637	787	1344
Serge Savard	1986	D	1040	106	333	439	592
Fred Scanlan	1965	F	31	16	XX	16	XX
Milt Schmidt	1961	C	778	229	346	575	466
Sweeney Schriner	1962	LW	484	201	204	405	148
Earl Seibert	1963	D	650	89	187	276	768

Player	Election Year	Pos.	GP	G	A	Pts.	PIM
Oliver Seibert	1961	D	Unavailable				
Eddie Shore	1947	D	550	105	179	284	1037
Steve Shutt	1993	LW	930	424	393	817	410
Babe Siebert	1964	LW/D	593	140	156	296	972
Joe Simpson	1962	D	340	76	19	95	176
Darryl Sittler	1989	C	1096	484	637	1121	948
Alf Smith	1962	RW	65	90	XX	90	XX
Clint Smith	1991	C	483	161	236	397	24
Hooley Smith	1972	RW	715	200	215	415	1013
Tommy Smith	1973	LW/C	XX	240	XX	240	XX
Allan Stanley	1981	D	1244	100	333	433	792
Barney Stanley	1962	RW/D	216	144	XX	144	XX
Black Jack Stewart	1964	D	565	31	84	115	765
Nels Stewart	1962	C	651	324	191	515	943
Bruce Stuart	1961	F	45	63	XX	63	XX
Hod Stuart	1945	D	33	16	XX	16	XX
Cyclone Taylor	1947	D/RO/C	186	194	XX	194	XX
Harry Trihey	1950	C	30	46	XX	46	XX
Norm Ullman	1982	C	1410	490	739	1229	712
Jack Walker	1960	LW/RO	361	135	8	143	18
Marty Walsh	1962	C	59	135	XX	135	XX
Harry E. Watson	1962	C	Unavailable				
Harry P. Watson	1994	LW	Unavailable				
Cooney Weiland	1971	C	509	173	160	333	147
Harry Westwick	1962	RO	87	87	XX	87	XX
Fredrick Whitcroft	1962	RO	9	5	XX	5	XX
Gord Wilson	1962	D	Unavailable				

Goaltenders

GP = games played   SO = shutouts   Min. = minutes
Avg. = average   GA = goals against

Player	Election Year	GP	Min.	GA	SO	Avg.
Clint Benedict	1965	362	22321	863	57	2.32
Johnny Bower	1976	552	32077	1347	37	2.52
Frank Brimsek	1966	514	31210	1404	40	2.70
Turk Broda	1967	629	38167	1609	62	2.53
Gerry Cheevers	1985	418	24394	1175	26	2.89
Alex Connell	1958	417	26030	830	81	1.91
Ken Dryden	1983	397	23352	870	46	2.24
Bill Durnan	1964	383	22945	901	34	2.36
Tony Esposito	1988	886	52585	2563	76	2.92
Chuck Gardiner	1945	316	19687	664	42	2.05
Ed Giacomin	1987	610	35693	1675	54	2.82
George Hainsworth	1961	465	29415	937	94	1.91
Glenn Hall	1975	906	53464	2239	84	2.51
Riley Hern	1962	60	XX	281	1	4.68
Hap Holmes	1972	410	6510	1191	41	2.90
Hughie Lehman	1958	403	3047	1451	23	3.60
Percy LeSueur	1961	156	XX	718	4	4.60
Harry Lumley	1980	804	48097	2210	71	2.76
Paddy Moran	1958	201	XX	1094	2	5.44
Bernie Parent	1984	608	35136	1493	55	2.55
Jacques Plante	1978	837	49533	1965	82	2.38
Chuck Rayner	1973	425	25491	1295	25	3.05
Terry Sawchuk	1971	971	57114	2401	103	2.52
Billy Smith	1993	680	38431	2031	22	3.17
Tiny Thompson	1959	553	34174	1183	81	2.08
Vladislav Tretiak	1989	Unavailable				
Georges Vezina	1945	328	11564	1145	15	3.49
Gump Worsley	1980	862	50232	2432	43	2.90
Roy Worters	1969	484	30175	1143	66	2.27

Stanley Cup Winners

The Stanley Cup is awarded annually to the team winning the National Hockey League's best-of-seven final playoff round. (The number of times that a team has won the Stanley Cup is given in parentheses next to the winning team's name.)

Season	Champion	Finalist	Games	Head Coach
1997	Detroit Red Wings (8)	Philadelphia Flyers	4	Scotty Bowman
1996	Colorado Avalanche (1)	Florida Panthers	4	Marc Crawford
1995	New Jersey Devils (1)	Detroit Red Wings	4	Jacques Lemaire
1994	New York Rangers (4)	Vancouver Canucks	7	Mike Keenan
1993	Montreal Canadiens (23)	Los Angeles Kings	5	Jacques Demers
1992	Pittsburgh Penguins (2)	Chicago Blackhawks	5	Scotty Bowman
1991	Pittsburgh Penguins (1)	Minnesota North Stars	6	Bob Johnson
1990	Edmonton Oilers (5)	Boston Bruins	5	John Muckler
1989	Calgary Flames (1)	Montreal Canadiens	6	Terry Crisp
1988	Edmonton Oilers (4)	Boston Bruins	4	Glen Sather
1987	Edmonton Oilers (3)	Philadelphia Flyers	7	Glen Sather
1986	Montreal Canadiens (22)	Calgary Flames	5	Jean Perron
1985	Edmonton Oilers (2)	Philadelphia Flyers	5	Glen Sather
1984	Edmonton Oilers (1)	New York Islanders	5	Glen Sather
1983	New York Islanders (4)	Edmonton Oilers	4	Al Arbour
1982	New York Islanders (3)	Vancouver Canucks	4	Al Arbour
1981	New York Islanders (2)	Minnesota North Stars	5	Al Arbour
1980	New York Islanders (1)	Philadelphia Flyers	6	Al Arbour
1979	Montreal Canadiens (21)	New York Rangers	5	Scotty Bowman
1978	Montreal Canadiens (20)	Boston Bruins	6	Scotty Bowman
1977	Montreal Canadiens (19)	Boston Bruins	4	Scotty Bowman
1976	Montreal Canadiens (18)	Philadelphia Flyers	4	Scotty Bowman
1975	Philadelphia Flyers (2)	Buffalo Sabres	6	Fred Shero
1974	Philadelphia Flyers (1)	Boston Bruins	6	Fred Shero
1973	Montreal Canadiens (17)	Chicago Blackhawks	6	Scotty Bowman
1972	Boston Bruins (5)	New York Rangers	6	Tom Johnson

(continued)

(continued)

Season	Champion	Finalist	Games	Head Coach
1971	Montreal Canadiens (16)	Chicago Blackhawks	7	Al MacNeil
1970	Boston Bruins (4)	St. Louis Blues	4	Harry Sinden
1969	Montreal Canadiens (15)	St. Louis Blues	4	Claude Ruel
1968	Montreal Canadiens (14)	St. Louis Blues	4	Toe Blake
1967	Toronto Maple Leafs (11)	Montreal Canadiens	6	Punch Imlach
1966	Montreal Canadiens (13)	Detroit Red Wings	6	Toe Blake
1965	Montreal Canadiens (12)	Chicago Blackhawks	7	Toe Blake
1964	Toronto Maple Leafs (10)	Detroit Red Wings	7	Punch Imlach
1963	Toronto Maple Leafs (9)	Detroit Red Wings	5	Punch Imlach
1962	Toronto Maple Leafs (8)	Chicago Blackhawks	6	Punch Imlach
1961	Chicago Blackhawks (3)	Detroit Red Wings	6	Rudy Pilous
1960	Montreal Canadiens (11)	Toronto Maple Leafs	4	Toe Blake
1959	Montreal Canadiens (10)	Toronto Maple Leafs	5	Toe Blake
1958	Montreal Canadiens (9)	Boston Bruins	6	Toe Blake
1957	Montreal Canadiens (8)	Boston Bruins	5	Toe Blake
1956	Montreal Canadiens (7)	Detroit Red Wings	5	Toe Blake
1955	Detroit Red Wings (7)	Montreal Canadiens	7	Jimmy Skinner
1954	Detroit Red Wings (6)	Montreal Canadiens	7	Tommy Ivan
1953	Montreal Canadiens (6)	Boston Bruins	5	Dick Irvin
1952	Detroit Red Wings (5)	Montreal Canadiens	4	Tommy Ivan
1951	Toronto Maple Leafs (7)	Montreal Canadiens	5	Joe Primeau
1950	Detroit Red Wings (4)	New York Rangers	7	Tommy Ivan
1949	Toronto Maple Leafs (6)	Detroit Red Wings	4	Hap Day
1948	Toronto Maple Leafs (5)	Detroit Red Wings	4	Hap Day
1947	Toronto Maple Leafs (4)	Montreal Canadiens	6	Hap Day
1946	Montreal Canadiens (5)	Boston Bruins	5	Dick Irvin
1945	Toronto Maple Leafs (3)	Detroit Red Wings	7	Hap Day
1944	Montreal Canadiens (4)	Chicago Blackhawks	4	Dick Irvin
1943	Detroit Red Wings (3)	Boston Bruins	4	Jack Adams
1942	Toronto Maple Leafs (2)	Detroit Red Wings	7	Hap Day
1941	Boston Bruins (3)	Detroit Red Wings	4	Cooney Weiland

Season	Champion	Finalist	Games	Head Coach
1940	New York Rangers (3)	Toronto Maple Leafs	6	Frank Boucher
1939	Boston Bruins (2)	Toronto Maple Leafs	5	Art Ross
1938	Chicago Blackhawks (2)	Toronto Maple Leafs	4	Bill Stewart
1937	Detroit Red Wings (2)	New York Rangers	5	Jack Adams
1936	Detroit Red Wings (1)	Toronto Maple Leafs	4	Jack Adams
1935	Montreal Maroons (2)	Toronto Maple Leafs	3	Tommy Gorman
1934	Chicago Blackhawks (1)	Detroit Red Wings	4	Tommy Gorman
1933	New York Rangers (2)	Toronto Maple Leafs	4	Lester Patrick
1932	Toronto Maple Leafs (1)	New York Rangers	3	Dick Irvin
1931	Montreal Canadiens (3)	Chicago Blackhawks	5	Cecil Hart
1930	Montreal Canadiens (2)	Boston Bruins	2	Cecil Hart
1929	Boston Bruins (1)	New York Rangers	2	Cy Denneny
1928	New York Rangers (1)	Montreal Maroons	5	Lester Patrick
1927	Ottawa Senators (4)	Boston Bruins	2	Dave Gill
1926	Montreal Maroons (1)	Victoria Cougars	4	Eddie Gerard
1925	Victoria Cougars (1)	Montreal Canadiens	4	Lester Patrick
1924	Montreal Canadiens (1)	Vancouver Maroons Calgary Tigers	2 2	Leo Dandurand
1923	Ottawa Senators (3)	Vancouver Maroons Edmonton Eskimos	4 2	Pete Green
1922	Toronto St. Pats (1)	Vancouver Millionaires	5	Eddie Powers
1921	Ottawa Senators (2)	Vancouver Millionaires	5	Pete Green
1920	Ottawa Senators (1)	Seattle Metropolitans	5	Pete Green
1919	No decision*	No decision*	5	
1918	Toronto Arenas (1)	Vancouver Millionaires	5	Dick Carroll

* In 1919, the Montreal Canadiens went to Seattle to play Seattle, Pacific Coast Hockey League champions. After five games (two wins apiece and one tie), the local Department of Health called off the series because of the influenza epidemic and the death of Joe Hall from influenza.

NHL "Mosts"

No sport is without its "most this or that" list, and hockey is no exception. Here are some if the most interesting NHL achievements! (You'll find some of these feats repeated in the next section on NHL career milestones — but with more information on who else ranks in the same category.)

Most Seasons Played: 26, Gordie Howe

Most Games Played: 1767, Gordie Howe

Most Consecutive Games Played: 964, Doug Jarvis

Most 40-Goal (or more) Seasons: 12, Wayne Gretzky

Most 50-Goal (or more) Seasons: 9, Wayne Gretzky, Mike Bossy

Most 60-Goal (or more) Seasons: 5, Wayne Gretzky, Mike Bossy

Most 100-Point (or more) Seasons: 15, Wayne Gretzky

Most Three-Goal (or more) Games in a Career: 49, Wayne Gretzky

Most Career Games for a Goalie: 971, Terry Sawchuk

Most Games in One Season for a Goalie: 79, Grant Fuhr

Most 30-Win (or more) Seasons for a Goalie: 8, Tony Esposito

Most 40-Win (or more) Seasons for a Goalie: 3, Jacques Plante

Most Consecutive Complete Games for a Goalie: 502, Glenn Hall

Most Victories in One Season for a Goalie: 47, Bernie Parent

Most Career Shutouts for a Goalie: 103, Terry Sawchuk

Most Shutouts in One Season for a Goalie: 22, George Hainsworth

Longest Winning Streak for a Goalie: 17, Gilles Gilbert

Longest Unbeaten Streak for a Goalie: 32 (24-0-8), Gerry Cheevers

Longest Consecutive Shutout Streak for a Goalie: 461:29, Alex Connell

Most Career Points: 2705, Wayne Gretzky

Most Career Goals: 862, Wayne Gretzky

Most Career Assists: 1843, Wayne Gretzky

Most Career Points Scored by a Defenseman: 1444, Paul Coffey

Most Career Goals Scored by a Defenseman: 381, Paul Coffey

Most Career Assists Scored by a Defenseman: 1063, Paul Coffey

Most Points Scored in One Season: 215, Wayne Gretzky

Most Goals Scored in One Season: 92, Wayne Gretzky

Most Assists Scored in One Season: 163, Wayne Gretzky

Most Three-Goal (or more) Games in One Season: 10, Wayne Gretzky

Most Points Scored by a Defenseman in One Season: 139, Bobby Orr

Most Goals Scored by a Defenseman in One Season: 48, Paul Coffey

Most Assists Scored by a Defenseman in One Season: 102, Bobby Orr

Most Points Scored by a Rookie in One Season: 132, Teemu Selanne

Most Goals Scored by a Rookie in One Season: 76, Teemu Selanne

Most Assists Scored by a Rookie in One Season: 70, Peter Stastny, Joe Juneau

Most Points Scored by a Rookie Defenseman in One Season: 76, Larry Murphy

Most Goals Scored by a Rookie Defenseman in One Season: 23, Brian Leetch

Most Assists Scored by a Rookie Defenseman in One Season: 60, Larry Murphy

Most Points Scored by a Goalie in One Season: 14 (0 goals, 14 assists), Grant Fuhr

Most Points Scored in One Game: 10 (6 goals, 4 assists), Darryl Sittler

Most Goals Scored in One Game: 7, Joe Malone

Most Assists Scored in One Game: 7, Billy Taylor, Wayne Gretzky

Most Points Scored by a Defenseman in One Game: 8, Tom Bladon, Paul Coffey

Most Goals Scored by a Defenseman in One Game: 5, Ian Turnbull

Most Assists Scored by a Defenseman in One Game: 6, Babe Pratt, Pat Stapleton, Bobby Orr, Ron Stackhouse, Paul Coffey, Gary Suter,

Most Shorthanded Goals Scored in One Season: 13, Mario Lemieux

Longest Consecutive Point-Scoring Streak: 51 games, Wayne Gretzky

Longest Consecutive Point-Scoring Streak for a Defenseman: 28 games, Paul Coffey

Longest Consecutive Goal-Scoring Streak: 16 games, Punch Broadbent

Longest Consecutive Assist-Scoring Streak: 23 games, Wayne Gretzky

NHL Career Milestones

This section is a sampling of some great career milestones in the NHL — and some of these "milestones" are still growing because these lists also contain current players and coaches (players or coaches who were active during the 1996–97 season are in **bold**). A good place to go for hockey statistics is the World Wide Web. For an archive of statistics, try the LCS Guide to Hockey at www.lcshockey.com. Current season statistics are readily available at the National Hockey League site, so also give www.nhl.com a visit. And for a listing of all active players' statistics (career and current season), no place is better than the National Hockey League Players Association at www.nhlpa.com.

Forwards and defensemen

Seasons

Gordie Howe (RW)	26
Alex Delvecchio (C)	24
Tim Horton (D)	24
John Bucyk (LW)	23
Stan Mikita (C)	22
Doug Mohns (D)	22
Dean Prentice (LW)	22

Games played

Gordie Howe (RW)	1,767
Alex Delvecchio (C)	1,549
John Bucyk (LW)	1,540
Tim Horton (D)	1,446
Harry Howell (D)	1,411
Norm Ullman (C)	1,410
Stan Mikita (C)	1,394
Doug Mohns (D)	1,390
Larry Robinson (D)	1,384
Dean Prentice (LW)	1,378
Mike Gartner (RW)	1,372
Ron Stewart (RW)	1,353
Marcel Dionne (C)	1,348
Wayne Gretzky (C)	1,335
Red Kelly (C)	1,316
Larry Murphy (D)	1,315
Dave Keon (C)	1,296
Ray Bourque (D)	1,290
Phil Esposito (C)	1,282

Jean Ratelle (C)	1,281
Bryan Trottier (C)	1,279
Mark Messier (C)	1,272

Goals

Wayne Gretzky (C)	862
Gordie Howe (RW)	801
Marcel Dionne (C)	731
Phil Esposito (C)	717
Mike Gartner (RW)	696
Bobby Hull (LW)	610
Jari Kurri (RW)	596
Dino Ciccarelli (RW)	586
Mark Messier (C)	575
Mike Bossy (RW)	573
Mario Lemieux (C)	563
Guy Lafleur (RW)	560
John Bucyk (LW)	556
Michel Goulet (LW)	548
Maurice Richard (RW)	544
Stan Mikita (C)	541
Steve Yzerman (C)	539
Frank Mahovlich (LW)	533
Bryan Trottier (C)	524
Dale Hawerchuk (C)	518

Assists

Wayne Gretzky (C)	1,843
Paul Coffey (D)	1,063
Gordie Howe (RW)	1,049
Marcel Dionne (C)	1,040
Ray Bourque (D)	1,001
Mark Messier (C)	977
Ron Francis (C)	944
Stan Mikita (C)	926
Bryan Trottier (C)	901
Dale Hawerchuk (C)	891
Mario Lemieux (C)	881
Phil Esposito (C)	873
Denis Savard (C)	865
Bobby Clarke (C)	852
Alex Delvecchio (C)	825
Gilbert Perreault (C)	814
John Bucyk (LW)	813
Steve Yzerman (C)	801
Larry Murphy (D)	797
Guy Lafleur (RW)	793

Points

Wayne Gretzky (C)	2,705
Gordie Howe (RW)	1,850
Marcel Dionne (C)	1,771
Phil Esposito (C)	1,590
Mark Messier (C)	1,552
Mario Lemieux (C)	1,494
Stan Mikita (C)	1,467
Paul Coffey (D)	1,444
Bryan Trottier (C)	1,425
Dale Hawerchuk (C)	1,409
Jari Kurri (RW)	1,376
John Bucyk (LW)	1,369
Ray Bourque (D)	1,363
Guy Lafleur (RW)	1,353
Ron Francis (C)	1,347
Steve Yzerman (C)	1,340
Denis Savard (C)	1,338
Gilbert Perreault (C)	1,326
Mike Gartner (RW)	1,308
Alex Delvecchio (C)	1,281

Penalty minutes

Dave Williams (LW)	3,966
Dale Hunter (C)	3,343
Tim Hunter (RW)	3,146
Marty McSorley (D)	3,078
Chris Nilan (RW)	3,043
Bob Probert (LW)	2,653
Willie Plett (RW)	2,572
Rich Tocchet (RW)	2,469
Basil McRae (LW)	2,457
Jay Wells (D)	2,359

Goaltenders

Seasons

Terry Sawchuk	21
Gump Worsley	21
Glenn Hall	18
Gilles Meloche	18
Jacques Plante	18
Billy Smith	18
Don Beaupre	17
Andy Moog	17

Tony Esposito	16
Eddie Johnston	16
Harry Lumley	16
Rogie Vachon	16
Grant Fuhr	16
Johnny Bower	15
Reggie Lemelin	15
Cesare Maniago	15

Games played

Terry Sawchuk	971
Glenn Hall	906
Tony Esposito	886
Gump Worsley	862
Jacques Plante	837
Harry Lumley	804
Rogie Vachon	795
Gilles Meloche	788
Grant Fuhr	748
Billy Smith	680
Don Beaupre	667
Mike Liut	663
Dan Bouchard	655
Turk Broda	629
Andy Moog	671
John Vanbiesbrouck	657
Kelly Hrudey	649
Ed Giacomin	610
Bernie Parent	608
Greg Millen	604

Minutes

Terry Sawchuk	57,205
Glenn Hall	53,484
Tony Esposito	52,585
Gump Worsley	50,232
Jacques Plante	49,553
Harry Lumley	48,107
Rogie Vachon	46,298
Gilles Meloche	45,401
Grant Fuhr	42,273
Billy Smith	38,431
Turk Broda	38,173
Mike Liut	38,155
Dan Bouchard	37,919
Don Beaupre	37,396
Ed Giacomin	35,693

Goals against average

Alex Connell	1.91
George Hainsworth	1.91
Chuck Gardiner	2.02
Lorne Chabot	2.04
Tiny Thompson	2.08
Dave Kerr	2.17
Ken Dryden	2.24
Roy Worters	2.27
Clint Benedict	2.32
Norm Smith	2.32
Bill Durnan	2.36
Gerry McNeil	2.36

Games won

Terry Sawchuk	435
Jacques Plante	434
Tony Esposito	423
Glenn Hall	407
Rogie Vachon	355
Andy Moog	354
Grant Fuhr	353
Patrick Roy	349
Gump Worsley	335
Harry Lumley	332

Shutouts

Terry Sawchuk	103
George Hainsworth	94
Glenn Hall	84
Jacques Plante	82
Tiny Thompson	81
Alex Connell	81
Tony Esposito	76
Lorne Chabot	73
Harry Lumley	71
Roy Worters	66

Coaches

Games coached

Scotty Bowman	1,736
Al Arbour	1,606
Dick Irvin	1,437
Billy Reay	1,102

Jack Adams	982
Sid Abel	963
Bryan Murray	916
Toe Blake	914
Punch Imlach	879
Bob Berry	860

Games won

Scotty Bowman	1,013
Al Arbour	781
Dick Irvin	690
Billy Reay	542
Toe Blake	500
Bryan Murray	467
Glen Sather	464

Most Stanley Cup wins by coach

Toe Blake	8
Scotty Bowman	7
Hap Day	5
Al Arbour	4
Dick Irvin	4
Punch Imlach	4
Glen Sather	4
Jack Adams	3
Pete Green	3
Tommy Ivan	3

NHL Single-Season Milestones

This is a selection of single-season achievements that can give you some idea of how the game has changed from year to year. Players who were active during the 1996–97 season are in **bold**.

Forwards and defensemen

Goals

1981–82	**Wayne Gretzky**	92
1983–84	**Wayne Gretzky**	87
1990–91	**Brett Hull**	86
1988–89	**Mario Lemieux**	85
1971–72	Phil Esposito	76

1992–93	**Alexander Mogilny**	76
1992–93	**Teemu Selanne**	76
1984–85	**Wayne Gretzky**	73
1989–90	**Brett Hull**	72
1982–83	**Wayne Gretzky**	71
1984–85	**Jari Kurri**	71
1991–92	**Brett Hull**	70
1987–88	**Mario Lemieux**	70
1988–89	Bernie Nicholls	70
1978–79	Mike Bossy	69
1992–93	**Mario Lemieux**	69
1995–96	**Mario Lemieux**	69
1980–81	Mike Bossy	68
1973–74	Phil Esposito	68
1985–86	**Jari Kurri**	68
1972–73	Phil Esposito	66
1982–83	Lanny McDonald	66
1988–89	**Steve Yzerman**	65
1981–82	Mike Bossy	64
1992–93	Luc Robitaille	63
1986–87	**Wayne Gretzky**	62
1989–90	**Steve Yzerman**	62
1995–96	**Jaromir Jagr**	62
1985–86	Mike Bossy	61
1974–75	Phil Esposito	61
1975–76	Reggie Leach	61
1982–83	Mike Bossy	60
1992–93	**Pavel Bure**	60
1993–94	**Pavel Bure**	60
1977–78	Guy Lafleur	60
1981–82	Dennis Maruk	60
1976–77	Steve Shutt	60

50-goal seasons

	Seasons	Consecutive
Mike Bossy	9	9
Wayne Gretzky	9	8
Guy Lafleur	6	6
Marcel Dionne	6	5
Phil Esposito	5	5
Brett Hull	5	5
Steve Yzerman	5	4
Mario Lemieux	6	3
Bobby Hull	5	2
Michel Goulet	4	4
Tim Kerr	4	4
Jari Kurri	4	4

Points

1985–86	**Wayne Gretzky**	215
1981–82	**Wayne Gretzky**	212
1984–85	**Wayne Gretzky**	208
1983–84	**Wayne Gretzky**	205
1988–89	**Mario Lemieux**	199
1982–83	**Wayne Gretzky**	196
1986–87	**Wayne Gretzky**	183
1988–89	**Wayne Gretzky**	168
1987–88	**Mario Lemieux**	168
1980–81	**Wayne Gretzky**	164
1990–91	**Wayne Gretzky**	163
1992–93	**Mario Lemieux**	160
1995–96	**Mario Lemieux**	161
1988–89	**Steve Yzerman**	155
1970–71	Phil Esposito	152
1988–89	Bernie Nicholls	150
1987–88	**Wayne Gretzky**	149
1995–96	**Jaromir Jagr**	149
1992–93	**Pat Lafontaine**	148
1981–82	Mike Bossy	147
1973–74	Phil Esposito	145
1989–90	**Wayne Gretzky**	142

Penalty minutes

1974–75	Dave Schultz	472
1981–82	Paul Baxter	409
1991–92	Mike Peluso	408
1977–78	Dave Schultz	405
1992–93	Marty McSorley	399
1987–88	Bob Probert	398
1985–86	Joey Kocur	377
1988–89	Tim Hunter	375
1975–76	Steve Durbano	370

Goaltenders

Shutouts

1928–29	George Hainsworth	22
1925–26	Alex Connell	15
1927–28	Alex Connell	15
1969–70	Tony Esposito	15
1927–28	Hal Winkler	15
1926–27	George Hainsworth	14
1926–27	Clint Benedict	13

1926–27	Alex Connell	13
1927–28	George Hainsworth	13
1953–54	Harry Lumley	13
1928–29	John Roach	13
1928–29	Roy Worters	13

Index

• A •

abdominal strength exercises. *See also* training
  circuit 1, 93
  circuit 2, 93–94
  circuit 3, 94–95
  performance of, 92
adult hockey, 189–190, 322
aerobic fitness
  beginning, 79
  benefits of, 69
  defined, 69
  frequency of, 79
agitators
  Clarke, Bobby, 140
  goalies as, 141
  honorable mention, 141
  Lemieux, Claude, 140
  Samuelsson, Ulf, 140
  Smith, Billy, 141
  Tikkanen, Esa, 139
  Williams, Dave "Tiger," 141
Alabama hockey organizations, 272
Alaska hockey organizations, 272
Alberta hockey organizations, 317
All-Star Game Program, 169
All-Star team, 164
altercations, 37, 259
American Hockey League, 60
American Hockey Magazine, 169
Amonte, Tony, 152
Anaheim Mighty Ducks
  information, 322
  watching on television, 150
  Web site, 164
Arizona hockey organizations, 273
Arkansas hockey organizations, 273
Arrowhead Pond in Anaheim, 159
Art Ross Trophy, 30

assists. *See also* passes
  defined, 30, 259
  records, 30
attacking zone. *See* offensive zone

• B •

back checking, 40, 181, 259, 326
backhand pass, 176
basic misconduct, 36, 329
Baun, Bobby
  as best hitter, 227
  photograph, 228
Beck, Barry
  as best hitter, 227
  photograph, 228
The Beckett Hockey Monthly, 170
Beliveau, Jean, 214–215
Bettman, Gary, 50
black ice, 192
blades
  curve of, 184
  skate, 18
  stick, 19, 184
  tape for, 119
blocker, 23, 259
blue lines. *See also* hockey rink
  defined, 11, 259
  illustrated, 12
boarding, 259, 325
boards, 102, 116, 259
body check, 134, 260
Boivin, Leo, 229
books, 170
Bossy, Mike, 128
Boston Bruins
  information, 322
  Web site, 164
Bourque, Ray, 126
Bower, Johnny, 249–250

Bowman, Scotty
  background, 101
  as coach of Montreal Canadians
      1976-1979, 224–225
  defined, 97
  left-wing lock, 106, 148, 265
  locker room talks, 112
  practices, 101–107
box formation, 128, 129, 260
breakaways
  defending, 178
  defined, 34, 260
breakout, 103, 260
British Columbia hockey organizations,
    317–318
Broadbent, Punch, 347
Brown, Dave, 136
Buffalo Sabres
  information, 322
  watching on television, 151
  Web site, 164
butt ending, 260, 325

● *C* ●

Calgary Flames
  information, 322
  Web site, 164
California hockey organizations, 273–275
Callander, Jock, 250
Campbell, Colin, 97–100, 108, 110, 112
camps, 191
Canadian Hockey Association, 190, 271
Canadian youth hockey organizations,
    317–321
career milestones. *See also* milestones
  assists (forwards and defensemen),
      349
  games coached, 352–353
  games played (forwards and
      defensemen), 348–349
  games played (goalies), 351
  games won (coaches), 353
  games won (goalies), 252
  goals (forwards and defensemen), 349
  goals against average (goalies), 352

minutes (goalies), 351
  penalty minutes (forwards and
      defensemen), 350
  points (forwards and defensemen), 350
  seasons (forward and defensemen),
      348
  seasons (goalies), 350–351
  shutouts (goalies), 352
  Stanley Cup wins (coaches), 353
Carolina Hurricanes
  information, 322
  Web site, 165
catcher, 23, 260
CBC, 168
center ice, 11
centers. *See also* forwards; positions
  common traits of, 14
  defined, 14, 260
  during power play, 117
  face-offs and, 177
  first-line, 14
  moving puck and, 184
  power plays and, 178
  second-line, 14
  third-line, 14
Central Hockey League, 60, 61, 62
changing on the fly, 104, 109
  coaches and, 112
  defined, 32, 104, 260
  odd-man rush and, 104
  practicing, 104–105
  stages, 109
charging. *See also* penalties
  defined, 38, 260, 325
  illustrated, 39
  signal, 325
Charlestown Chiefs, 226
checking
  back, 40, 181, 259, 326
  body, 134, 260
  cross, 36, 261, 326
  defined, 326
  in-line/street hockey and, 199
  pond hockey and, 193
  role, 110
  stick, 181, 269

sweep, 269
in women's hockey, 64
Cheevers, Gerry, 345
Cherry, Don, 243–244
Chicago Blackhawks
information, 323
Web site, 165
Clarke, Bobby, 140
coaching (NHL)
assistants, 100
before season, 98
career milestones, 352–353
changing on the fly, 111
cuts and, 99
defensive game, 108
difficulty of, 97
during games, 108–111
during play-offs, 112–113
during season, 99–101
exhibitions, 99
locker room talks, 111–112
match-ups, 110–111
player fitness and, 100
practices, 100, 101
speed and pressure game, 108
systems, 108
training camp, 98
video tape and, 99–100
watching, 152
Coffey, Paul
in all-time power-play unit, 127
longest consecutive point-scoring
streak for a defenseman, 347
most career assists scored by a
defenseman, 345
most career goals scored by a
defenseman, 345
most career points scored by a
defenseman, 345
most goals scored by a defenseman in
one season, 346
college hockey
graduates, 63–64
NHL versus, 63
revival, 62
structure of, 62–63

teams, 63
women's, 64
Colonial Hockey League, 60, 62
Colorado Avalanche
information, 323
Web site, 165
Colorado hockey organizations, 275
Conference Finals, 55
Conference Quarterfinals, 55
conferences (NHL), 51–53
Conn Smythe Trophy, 179
Connecticut hockey organizations, 276
Connell, Alex, 345
cordura, 198
crease, 11, 12, 261
cross checking, 36, 261, 326
cycling. *See also* practices
defined, 107
practicing, 107
cycling training, 68

● *D* ●

Dallas Stars
information, 323
Web site, 165
*A Day in the Life of the National Hockey
League,* 170
deep hollow, 18
defense
looking at the puck and, 185
playing, 185–186
two-on-one, 186
defensemen. *See also* positions
50-point seasons milestone, 354
assists career milestone, 349
defined, 16, 261
on five-on-three power play, 126
games played career milestone,
348–349
goals (career milestone), 349
goals (single-season milestone),
353–354
Hall of Fame, 333–339
Norris Trophy, 186

(continued)

defensemen *(continued)*
  penalty minutes (career milestone),
    350
  penalty minutes (single-season mile-
    stone), 355
  points (career milestone), 350
  points (single-season milestone), 355
  power plays and, 116, 117
  seasons milestone, 348
  timing, 186
  types of, 16
defensive zone, 11, 118, 261
dekers, 178, 261
Delaware hockey organizations, 277
delayed off-side, 262, 326
delaying the game penalty, 327
Detroit Red Wings
  best team 1950-1955, 224
  information, 323
  watching on television, 148
  Web site, 165
diamond formation, 128, 129, 262
draw. *See* face-offs

• *E* •

East Coast Hockey League, 60
Edmonton Oilers
  as best team 1984-1990, 226
  information, 323
  watching on television, 151
  Web site, 165
elbow pads, 26, 198
elbowing, 134–135, 137, 262, 327
equipment
  blocker, 23, 259
  catcher, 23, 260
  for children, 27
  choosing, 25–27
  cost of, 26
  fitting, 255
  goalie, 22–23
  helmets, 21, 24, 25
  history of, 23–24
  in-line/street hockey, 198–199
  protective, 21–23
  purchasing, 26–28

  skates, 17–19, 25
  sticks, 19–20, 26
  where to buy, 27–28
ESPN
  hockey coverage, 167
  Sportszone Web site, 166
Esposito, Phil
  in all-time power-play unit, 128
  as best hockey personality, 244
  most 30-win seasons for a goalie, 344
exercise
  hockey as, 206
  routines need for, 73
Ezinicki, Bill, 229

• *F* •

face-off circles
  defined, 11
  illustrated, 12
  for power play, 115
face-offs
  defined, 11, 262
  five-on-three power play, 124
  Mark Messier on, 177–178
  power play beginning, 115
  set plays off, 178
fans, 204–205
feather pass, 175
Fedorov, Sergei, 217
Ferguson, John
  as best hockey personality, 244
  as top fighter, 136
Fetisov, Viacheslav, 217–218
Fielder, Guyle, 250
fighting. *See also* penalties
  defined, 40
  hockey and, 41
  illustrated, 41
  NHL best list, 136–137
  punishment for, 135
  signal, 327
firm pass, 175
Fischler's Illustrated History of Hockey, 9
fisticuffs. *See* fighting
Fitness for High Performance Hockey, 69,
  73, 80

five-hole, 178, 262

five-on-three power play. *See also* power plays

close to the net, 126–127

control, 124

defined, 123

face-off, 124

illustrated, 124

not scoring during, 127

one-timers and, 124, 266

setup, 123–124

flat pass, 176, 263

Florida hockey organizations, 277–278

Florida Panthers

information, 323

Web site, 165

forechecking

defined, 104, 263

left-wing lock, 106

practicing, 104

Forsberg, Peter, 218

forwards. *See also* centers; positions; wings

50-goal seasons milestone, 354–355

assists career milestone, 349

defined, 13, 263

in five-on-three, 123

games played milestone, 348–349

goals (career milestone), 349

goals (single-season milestone), 353–354

Hall of Fame, 333–339

on off sides, 127

penalty minutes (career milestone), 350

penalty minutes (single-season milestone), 355

points (career milestone), 350

points (single-season milestone), 355

power, scoring as, 180–181

seasons milestone, 348

tandems, 129

Fotiu, Nick, 245

Fox Broadcasting, 146, 167

FoxTrax puck, 146

Fuhr, Grant

most games in one season for a goalie, 344

most points scored by a goalie in one season, 346

• **G** •

Gainey, Bob, 131

Gamble, Dick, 250

game misconduct, 36, 329

games

best all-time, 235–241

Bruins versus Canadiens - April 8, 1971, 237

Canada versus Sweden - September 7, 1996, 240

Canadian and Swedish Olympic teams - February 27, 1994, 238

Canadians versus Central Red Army team - December 31, 1975, 237

coaching, 108–111

delaying penalty, 327

Maple Leafs versus Canadiens - May 2, 1967, 236

Montreal Maroons versus Red Wings - March 24, 1936, 235

Penguins versus Capitals - April 24, 1996, 239

pickup, 192–193

Rangers versus Devils - May 25, 1994, 239

sudden death, 31

U.S. Olympic team versus Soviet Union - February 22, 1980, 238

USA versus Canada - September 12, 1996, 241

The Game, 170

Gartner, Mike, 184–185, 186

gear. *See* equipment

Geoffrion, Bernard "Boom Boom," 246

Georgia hockey organizations, 278

Gerry Crosby's, 27–28

Gilbert, Gilles, 345

Glover, Fred, 251

gloves, 26, 199

goal
  crease, 11, 12, 261
  defined, 11
  dimensions, 11
  holes, 179
  illustrated, 12
  line, 29
  moving, 327
  post, 11
goal judges, 42, 264
goalies. *See also* positions
  as agitators, 141
  blocker, 23, 259
  defined, 13, 264
  games played career milestone, 351
  games won career milestone, 352
  goals against average career milestone, 352
  Hall of Fame, 340
  instincts, 16
  minutes career milestone, 351
  number carried on teams, 13
  protection for, 22–23
  protection history, 24
  puck handling, 184
  pulling, 267
  qualities of, 15
  seasons milestone, 350–351
  shutouts (career milestone), 352
  shutouts (single-season milestone), 355–356
  sticks, 20
  substitutions, 32
  training for, 71
  verbal nature of, 134
goals (score)
  defined, 29, 263
  records, 30
  scoring, 29–30
  signal, 327
GP (games played), 53, 264
Great One, 127, 175, 264
Gretzky, Wayne
  in all-time power-play unit, 127
  as best player, 209–210
  in best power-play unit, 125
  hockey history, 209

longest consecutive assist-scoring streak, 347
longest consecutive point-scoring streak, 347
most 40-goal seasons, 344
most 50-goal seasons, 344
most 60-goal seasons, 344
most 100-point seasons, 344
most assists scored in one season, 30, 345
most career assists, 30, 345
most career goals, 30, 345
most career points, 345
most goals scored in one season, 30, 345
most points scored in one season, 345
most three-goal games, 344
most three-goal games in one season, 346
on passing, 175–176
photograph, 150, 210
Gretzky's office, 176
gross misconduct, 36, 329
Gruhl, Scott, 251

• H •

Hainsworth, George, 345
half board power play. *See also* power plays
  defined, 122
  illustrated, 122
  version 2, 123
Hall, Glenn
  as best player, 215
  most consecutive complete games for a goalie, 345
hand pass signal, 327
Hanson Brothers, 137
Harvey, Doug
  in all-time power-play unit, 128
  as best player, 213–214
  hockey history, 213
  photograph, 214
Hasek, Dominik
  as best goalie, 151
  as best player, 218–219

hockey history, 218
photograph, 151, 219
hat trick, 264
helmets. *See also* equipment; protection
choosing, 25
importance of, 21
in-line skating, 197
introduction of, 24
wearing, 254
Hextall, Ron, 184
high triangle, 121
high-sticking. *See also* penalties
defined, 39, 264, 328
illustrated, 40
signal, 328
hitters, best, 227–233
hitting
importance of, 133
methods, 134–135
hockey
adult, 189–190, 322
best personalities in, 243–248
camps, 191
college, 62–64
exercise as, 206
fans, 204–205
fighting and, 41
goal of, 12
growth of, 207
history of, 9–11
in-line, 197–199
international, 65–66, 207
listening to, 153
North American origins, 10
pond, 191–194
print, 169–170
professional origins, 10–11
schools, 191
speed, 203
street, 197–199, 269
tips, 253–255
watching in person, 155–161
watching on television, 145–153
Web sites, 163–166
women's, 64

The Hockey Digest, 170
Hockey For Dummies
how to use, 3
icons, 5–6
organization, 3–5
purpose of, 1–2
why you need, 2–3
Hockey Hall of Fame
defined, 171
forwards/defensemen, 333–339
founding of, 333
goalies, 340
location of, 333
Hockey Illustrated, 169
Hockey Night in Canada, 168, 243
The Hockey News, 27, 169, 191
hockey organizations
adult, 322
Canadian Hockey Association, 190, 271
NHL, 322–323
USA Hockey, 206, 271
youth, 272–321
hockey rink, 11–12
attacking zone, 11, 259
blue lines, 11, 259
center ice, 11
defensive zone, 11, 261
dimensions of, 11
face-off circles, 11
goals, 11
ice, 155, 157
illustrated, 12
neutral zone, 11, 12, 265
red line, 11, 268
watching, 156
hockey signals
boarding, 325
butt ending, 325
charging, 325
checking from behind, 326
cross checking, 326
delayed (slow) whistle, 326
delayed calling of penalty, 326
delaying the game, 327
elbowing, 327

(continued)

hockey signals *(continued)*
  fighting, 327
  goal scored, 327
  hand pass, 327
  high sticking, 328
  holding, 328
  holding the face mask, 328
  hooking, 328
  icing, 328
  interference, 329
  kneeing, 329
  match penalty, 329
  misconduct, 329
  offside, 329
  penalty shot, 330
  slashing, 330
  spearing, 330
  time-out, 330
  tripping, 331
  wash-out, 331
hockey teams. *See also* positions;
    specific teams
  best all-time, 223–226
  college, 63
  goalies on, 13
  members of, 13
  minor league, 60–61
  NHL, list of, 50–51
  NHL ownership, 49
  penalties for, 13
  rosters, 31–32
  substitutions, 32
  Web sites, 164–165
holding. *See also* penalties
  defined, 264, 328
  face mask, 328
  signal, 328
holes. *See also* goal
  defined, 179
  five, 178, 262
  illustrated, 179
hooking. *See also* penalties
  defined, 38, 264, 328
  illustrated, 38

signal, 328
Horton, Tim, 230
Howe, Gordie
  in all-time power-play unit, 127
  as best intimidator, 137
  as best player, 212
  hockey history, 212
  most games played, 344
  most seasons played, 344
  photograph, 212
Hull, Bobby, 246
Hull, Brett
  in best power-play unit, 126
  on getting free in front of the net,
    183–184

• *I* •

ice
  black, 192
  pond hockey, 192
  rink, 155, 157
  safety, 192
  thin, avoiding, 254
icing. *See also* infractions
  defined, 33, 265, 328
  illustrated, 33
  signal, 328
  time and, 130
icons, this book, 5–6
Idaho hockey organizations, 278
Illinois hockey organizations
  Central, 280
  Northern, 278–280
  Southern, 280
Indiana hockey organizations, 280–281
infractions
  defined, 32
  icing, 33, 265
  offside, 33–35, 329
in-line hockey
  defined, 197, 265
  equipment, 198–199
  gloves, 199

growth of, 197
leagues, 197
playing of, 197–198
pucks, 198
rules, 199
sticks, 198
values, 198
in-line skating
beginning of, 195
equipment, 197
skates, 196
interference, 39, 265
international hockey
best players in, 217–222
countries participating in, 206
growth of, 66
IIHF, 65
Web site, 65
youth organizations, 321
International Hockey League, 10, 60
International Ice Hockey Federation
(IIHF)
defined, 65
information, 190–191
phone number, 190
Web site, 191
international television, 168
intimidation
all-time best at, 137–139
importance of, 133
speed and, 135
tactics, 134–135
verbal, 134
Iowa hockey organizations, 281

● J ●

Jagr, Jaromir
as best player, 220
in best power-play unit, 126
hockey history, 220
photograph, 221
Jarvis, Doug
as best penalty killer, 131
most consecutive games played, 344
jawing, 133–134
juniors, 61

● K ●

Kansas hockey organizations, 282
Kariya, Paul
in best power-play unit, 125
photograph, 150
Keenan, Mike, 112
Kentucky hockey organizations, 282
Kharlamov, Valeri, 219
kids
leagues for, 189–190
power plays and, 121
youth hockey organizations, 272–321
killing penalties
all-time best at, 131
approaches to, 128
box formation, 128, 129, 260
defined, 128, 266
diamond formation, 128, 129, 262
methods for, 130
tandems, 129
team, 130
units, 128, 266
kit, 9
kneeing, 265, 329
Kocur, Joey, 136
Kurri, Jari, 220
Kurtenbach, Orland, 137

● L ●

leagues
adult, 189–190
college, 62–64
competitive, 190
in-line/street hockey, 197
international, 190–191
joining, 190
junior, 61
midget, 61
minor, 59–62
NHL, 47–58
recreational, 190
types of, 207

(continued)

leagues *(continued)*
  what to look for in, 190
  women's, 64
  youth, 189–190
Leetch, Brian
  in best power-play unit, 125
  most goals scored by rookie
    defenseman in one season, 346
  photograph, 187
  on playing defense, 185–187
left-wing lock, 106–107, 148, 265
Lemaire, Jacques, 149
Lemieux, Claude, 140
Lemieux, Mario
  in all-time power-play unit, 127
  as best player, 210
  in best power-play unit, 126
  hockey history, 210
  most shorthanded goals scored in one
    season, 347
Lethbridge Arena, 161
Let's Play Hockey, 170
Lindros, Eric
  as best intimidator, 139
  photograph, 182
  on shooting off the pass, 182
Lindsay, Ted, 129, 138
line change
  defined, 104
  illustrated, 105
  perfecting, 109
  practicing, 104–105
  puck during, 109
  stages of, 109
lines
  centers and, 14
  checking role, 110
  components of, 13
  defined, 13
  first, 110
  fourth, 110
  number carried on teams, 13
  second, 110
  third, 110
  wings and, 15

linesmen, 42, 265
locker room talks, 111–112
Los Angeles Kings
  information, 323
  Web site, 165
lower body training
  alternating lunges with barbells, 91
  alternating lunges with dumbbells, 90
  calf extensions, 92
  circuit 1, 88–90
  double leg hamstring curls, 89
  hip abduction, 89–90
  leg extension, 92
  sliding double leg press, 88
  squats, 91
  thigh variations, 90–91
  variations, 90–92

• *M* •

MacInnis, Al
  in best power-play unit, 126
  on shooting from the point, 179–180
Madison Square Garden, 159
magazines, 169–170
Maine hockey organizations, 282
major penalties, 36
Malone, Joe, 30, 346
Manitoba hockey organizations, 318
Maple Leaf Gardens, 160
Marchment, Bryan, 230
Marshall, Willie, 251
Maryland hockey organizations, 282–283
Massachusetts hockey organizations,
  283–286
match penalty, 329
match-ups. *See also* coaching
  home advantage in, 110–111
  post-game, 110
  pre-game, 110
McSorley, Marty, 136
McVie, Tom, 246–247
Messier, Mark
  as best intimidator, 138
  as best player, 213
  on face-offs, 177–178

hockey history, 213
photograph, 177
Michayluk, Dave, 251
Michigan hockey organizations
Northern and Central, 291–295
Southern, 295–296
midget leagues, 61
milestones
career, 348–353
single-season, 353–356
Minnesota hockey organizations
Central, 287–289
Northern, 286–287
Southern, 290
minor leagues
best players in, 249–252
franchises, 60
hockey play in, 59
NFL affiliation of, 61
NHL versus, 62
popularity of, 62
teams, finding, 60–61
minor penalties, 35
misconduct penalties
basic, 36
defined, 329
game, 36
gross, 36
signal, 329
Missouri hockey organizations, 296
Molson Centre, 160
Montana hockey organizations, 296
Montreal Canadians
best team 1956-1960, 224
best team 1965-1969, 224
best team 1976-1979, 224–225
Habs, 224, 264
information, 323
Web site, 165
Montreal Forum, 135
Murphy, Larry, 346

• *N* •

National Hockey Association (NHA), 10,
48
National Hockey League. *See* NHL
Nebraska hockey organizations, 296
Neely, Cam, 128
net. *See also* goal
defined, 11
five-on-three power play and, 126–127
getting free in front of, 183–184
netminders. *See* goalies
neutral zone
defined, 11, 265
illustrated, 12
trap, 149
New Brunswick hockey organizations,
318
New Hampshire hockey organizations,
296–297
New Jersey Devils
information, 323
watching on television, 149
Web site, 165
New Jersey hockey organizations,
297–299
New Mexico hockey organizations, 303
New York hockey organizations
Central, 300–301
Eastern, 301–303
Western, 300–301
New York Islanders
as best team 1980-1984, 225
information, 323
Web site, 165
New York Rangers
information, 323
watching on television, 149–150
Web site, 165
newspapers, 170
NHL. *See also* Stanley Cup
beginning of, 10
best all-time teams, 223–226
best fighters, 136–137

(continued)

NHL *(continued)*
  best players, 209–216
  career milestones, 348–353
  changes in, 49
  coaching, 97–113
  college hockey versus, 63
  commissioner, 50
  conferences, 51–53
  directory of addresses, 322–324
  divisions, 51–53
  employees, 49
  exhibitions, 99
  expansion, 51, 52–53
  history of, 47–48
  minor league affiliations, 61
  minor leagues versus, 62
  "mosts" list, 344–347
  offices, 322
  off-season conditioning regimen, 71–72
  personnel, 50
  player salaries, 49
  players, 57–58
  Players Association (NHLPA), 322
  play-off format, 55
  single-season milestones, 353–356
  standings, 53–54
  team ownership, 49
  teams, 50–51
  today, 49
  training camps, 98–99
  Web site, 164–165
Nike, 199
Norris Trophy, 186
North Carolina hockey organizations,
    303–304

• O •

odd-man rush. *See also* line change
  defined, 104
  illustrated, 105
off side pass. *See* two-line pass
offensive zone, 11, 119, 259
Official Guide and Record Book, 169
officials
  goal judges, 42
  linesmen, 42, 265
  off-ice, 42–43, 265
  referee, 42, 268
  video goal judge, 43
*The Official National Hockey League 75th
    Anniversary Commemorative Book,*
    170
offside. *See also* infractions
  defined, 33, 266, 329
  delayed, 262, 326
  illustrated, 34, 35
  infraction, 329
  two-line pass, 34, 35
Ohio hockey organizations, 304–305
Oklahoma hockey organizations, 305
one-timers, 14, 124, 266
Ontario Hockey League, 61
Ontario hockey organizations
  Northern, 318–319
  Southern, 319–320
O'Ree, Willie, 252
Oregon hockey organizations, 305
organization, this book, 3–5
Orr, Bobby
  in all-time power-play unit, 127
  as best player, 211
  hockey history, 211
  most assists scored by a defenseman
      in one season, 346
  most points scored by a defenseman in
      one season, 346
  photograph, 211
Ottawa Senators
  best team 1919-1927, 223
  information, 323
  Web site, 165
Owchar, Dennis, 231
Ozolinsh, Sandis, 125

• P •

Pacific Coast Hockey Association
    (PCHA), 47–48
Pacific Coast League (PCL), 10, 11
pads. *See also* protection

elbow, 26, 198
shoulder, 21, 24, 25
pants, 22, 26, 198
Parent, Bernie, 345
Park, Brad, 128
passes
backhand, 176
crisp, 120
feather, 175
firm, 175
first (power play), 15–17
flat, 176, 263
forehand, 176
hand, 327
importance of, 119
second (power play), 118
shooting off, 182
short, 119
third (power play), 119
two-line, 34, 35
umbrella, 120, 270
Wayne Gretzky on, 175–176
passion, 204
penalties
back checking, 40, 181, 259, 326
boarding, 259, 325
butt ending, 325
charging, 28, 38–39, 260, 325
cross checking, 36, 261, 326
defined, 35, 266
delayed calling of, 326
delayed off-side, 262, 326
delaying the game, 261, 327
elbowing, 134–135, 137, 262, 327
fighting, 40–41, 327
high sticking, 39–40, 264, 328
holding, 264, 328
hooking, 38, 264, 328
interference, 39, 265, 329
killing, 128–131, 266
killing units, 128, 266
kneeing, 265, 329
majors, 36
match, 329
minors, 35
misconducts, 36, 329
power play, 13

receiving, 37
roughing, 37–38, 268
slashing, 39, 134, 268, 330
spearing, 269, 330
tripping, 270, 331
types of, 35–36
penalty shots, 36, 267, 330
Pennsylvania hockey organizations
Eastern, 305–307
Western, 307
periods, 31
Philadelphia Flyers
information, 323
watching on television, 148
Web site, 165
Phoenix Coyotes
information, 323
Web site, 165
pickup games, 192–193
pipe. *See* goal, post
Pittsburgh Penguins
information, 324
Web site, 165
Plager, Bob
as best hitter, 231
photograph, 232
Plante, Jacques, 344
players. *See also* NHL; *specific players*
accommodating, 205
background of, 57
best in international hockey, 217–222
best in minor leagues, 249–252
best in NHL, 209–216
fatigue of, 100
fitness of, 100
opposing, watching, 157–158
past, background of, 58
practices, 100, 101
salaries, 49
size of, 58
speed of, 58
strength of, 58
talking to each other, 133–134
team, 254
training, 67–95
training camp shape of, 99
voting on All-Star team, 164

play-offs. *See also* Stanley Cup Championship
  coaching during, 112–113
  format, 55
  mental preparation for, 113
  mistakes, avoiding, 113
  number of teams eligible for, 55
  short-term view in, 112
point
  defined, 115, 267
  shooting from, 179
  slap shots from, 115
pond hockey
  checking in, 193
  enjoyment of, 191–192, 193
  etiquette, 193
  good ice for, 192
  ice safety, 192
  illustration, 194
  pickup games, 192–193
  rules, 193
  slap shots in, 193
positions
  centers, 14
  defensemen, 16
  forwards, 13, 180–181, 263
  goalies, 13, 15–16
  illustrated, 13
  list of, 13
  wings, 14–15, 270
Potvin, Denis
  as best hitter, 232
  photograph, 233
power forward, 180–181
Power Play Magazine, 169
power plays
  all-time best unit, 127–128
  beginning of, 115
  best units in hockey, 125–126
  center in, 117
  centerman and, 178
  control and, 119–122
  defensemen in, 116, 117
  defined, 13, 115, 267
  first pass, 115–117
  five-on-three, 123–127

half board, 122–123
high triangle, 121
importance of, 115
kids and, 121
pass importance, 119
Pittsburgh Penguin, 118
quarterback, 116, 117
second pass, 118
studies in, 118
third pass, 119
two-on-one, 121
umbrella, 119–120, 270
wingers in, 116
power skating, 184–185
practices
  breakout, 103, 260
  cycling, 107
  fatigue and, 101
  forechecking, 104
  line change, 104–105, 107
  overall view of, 107
  player age and, 101
  Scotty Bowman, 101–107
  shooting drills, 102–103
  skill, 105
  team health and, 100
  time for, 107
  warm ups, 101–102
print media
  books, 170
  magazines, 169–170
  newspapers, 170
Probert, Bob, 136
protection. *See also* equipment
  elbow pads, 26
  gloves, 23, 26
  goalie, 22–23
  helmets, 21
  history of, 23–24
  in-line/street hockey, 198–199
  padded pants, 22, 26
  shin guards, 26
  shoulder pads, 21, 25
PTS (points), 53, 267
pucks
  catching, 119
  clearing, 261

dimensions, 23
directing, 262
during line changes, 107
during warm ups, 102
following on television, 145–146
FoxTrax, 146
freezing, 263
funneling, 106
handling as goalie, 184
handling with head up, 254
in-line/street hockey, 198
materials, 23
overhandling, 184
"ping," 153
provision of, 23
smothering, 269
trapping, 108, 109, 270
treating, 119

• *Q* •

Quebec hockey organizations, 320–321
Quebec Major Junior Hockey League, 61

• *R* •

radio broadcasts, 169
Randall, Ken, 48
RDS, 168
rebounds, 181
red line. *See also* hockey rink
  defined, 11, 268
  illustrated, 12
referees, 30, 37, 42, 268
Rhode Island hockey organizations, 308
Richard, Maurice, 213
rink. *See* hockey rink
Roberts, Gary, 180–181
roller hockey. *See* in-line hockey
roughing, 37–38, 268
rules
  infractions, 32–35
  in-line/street hockey, 199
  officials and, 42
  penalties, 35–41

periods, 31
rosters, 31–32
scoring, 29–30
running training, 68

• *S* •

St. Louis Blues
  information, 324
  Web site, 165
Salming, Borje, 220
Samuelsson, Ulf
  as agitator, 140
  as best hitter, 232
  photograph, 233
San Jose Arena, 161
San Jose Sharks
  information, 324
  Web site, 165
Saskatchewan hockey organizations, 321
Sather, Glen, 149, 150
save, 124, 268
Sawchuk, Terry
  as best player, 216
  most career games for a goalie, 344
  most career shutouts for a goalie, 345
schools, 191
scoring
  body position and, 181
  as power forward, 180–181
  records, 30
  rules, 29–30
  shoot-out, 31, 268
Selanne, Teemu, 246
Shanahan, Brendan, 125
shin guards, 26, 198
shooting drills. *See also* practices
  drill 1, 102
  drill 2, 103
  illustrated, 102, 103
  off the pass, 182
  time for, 103
shoot-outs, 31, 268
Shore, Eddie
  as best intimidator, 138
  as best player, 214
  hockey history, 214

shorthanded. *See* killing penalties;
　　power play
shots
　on goal, 330
　left-handed, 14
　one-timing, 14
　penalty, 36, 267, 330
　right-handed, 14
　slap, 19, 193, 268
　snap, 19
shoulder pads
　choosing, 25
　positions and, 24
　types of, 21
signals. *See* hockey signals
single-season milestones. *See also*
　　milestones
　50-goal seasons, 354–355
　goals, 353–354
　penalty minutes, 355
　shutouts, 355–356
Sittler, Darryl, 30, 346
skates. *See also* equipment
　blades, 18
　choosing, 25
　design of, 17–18
　illustrated, 19
　materials used in, 17–18
skating
　in-line, 195–197
　learning, 253
　power, 184–185
　training, 68–69
　warm ups, 101
slap shot
　defined, 19, 268
　from point, 115
　pond hockey and, 193
slashing. *See also* penalties
　calling of, 39
　defined, 39, 268, 330
　signal, 330
slot, 183, 269
Smith, Billy, 141
sniper, 21, 269
South Carolina hockey organizations,
　308

South Dakota hockey organizations, 308
spearing, 269, 330
speed, 203
speed and pressure game, 108
Sports Illustrated for Kids, 169
Sportsline Web site, 165–166
SRC, 168
Stairmaster training, 69
standings (NHL) 1996-1997, 53–54
　determination of, 53
　points, 53
Stanley Cup
　defined, 55, 269
　disappearance of, 56
　history of, 55–56
　security, 57
Stanley Cup Centennial book, 170
Stanley Cup Championship. *See also*
　　play-offs
　beginning of, 10
　broadcast, 49
　winners, 341–343
Stastny, Peter
　as best player, 221
　most assists scored by a rookie in one
　　season, 346
　photograph, 222
sticks
　blades, 19, 184
　choosing, 26
　flex degrees, 19, 263
　goalie blades, 184
　heel, 20, 264
　illustrated, 20
　in-line/street hockey, 198
　knocking out, 39, 329
　materials, 19
　regulations for, 20
　shot types and, 19
　tape on, 176
　using properly, 255
Storey, Red, 247
street hockey
　curriculum, 199
　defined, 197, 269
　equipment, 198–199
　gloves, 199

leagues, 197
playing of, 197–198
pucks, 198
rules, 199
sticks, 198
trying, 255
stretching. *See also* training
  arms, 78
  calf, 79
  circuit, 73–79
  groin, 74, 76
  hamstrings, 76
  knees, 78
  quads, 78
  shoulders, 78
  warm up, 101
  when to do, 73
substitutions
  changing on the fly, 32
  general, 32
  goalie, 32
sudden death, 31
Summer Hockey School Guide, 191
sweaters, 22, 269

● *T* ●

Tampa Bay Lightening
  information, 324
  Web site, 165
tandems, 129
taxi squad, 31
television. *See also* watching hockey
    (television)
  CBC, 168
  ESPN, 167
  Fox, 167
  international, 168
  RDS, 168
  regional cable, 168
  SRC, 168
  TSN, 168
Texas hockey organizations, 309
Thornson, Len, 252
three-on-one, 104
three-on-two, 104

Tikkanen, Esa, 139
time-outs, 330
tips, hockey, 253–255
Toronto Maple Leafs
  best team 1947-1951, 223
  best team 1962-1967, 224
  information, 324
  Web site, 165
training
  abdominal strength, 92–95
  aerobic fitness, 69, 79
  cycling, 68
  exercise routine need and, 73
  fitness, tracking, 70
  for goalies, 71
  into hockey shape, 72–73
  leg strength, 73
  NHL off-season conditioning regimen,
    71–72
  running, 68
  skating, 68–69
  Stairmaster, 69
  stretching, 73–79
  weight training, 69–70, 79–95
training camps. *See also* NHL
  opening of, 98
  in the past, 98
  players' reporting to, 99
traps. *See also* coaching
  defined, 107, 270
  Florida, 107, 108
  neutral zone, 149
  New Jersey, 107, 108
Tretiak, Vladislav, 221
tripping, 270, 331
Trottier, Bryan, 30
TSN, 168
Turnbull, Ian, 347
two-line pass
  defined, 34, 270
  illustrated, 35
two-on-one
  creating, 121
  defending, 186
  defined, 104
  power plays, 121

• U •

umbrella. *See also* power plays
  defined, 119–120, 270
  illustrated, 120
  passes, 120
United States Olympic hockey team
      (1980), 226
upper body training. *See also* weight
      training
  alternating seated bicep curls with
      dumbbells, 84
  bench flys with dumbbells, 83
  bench press, 80
  bicep curls, 82, 86
  chest variation, 85
  circuit 1, 80–82
  circuit 2, 82–84
  dumbbell row, 84
  forearms variation, 85
  inclined bench press, 85
  lat pull-downs, 81
  palm-down/palm-up arm extensions, 87
  pec-deck flys, 88
  seated tricep extension with barbell, 83
  shoulder abduction, 87
  shoulder extension, 82
  shoulders variation, 87–88
  standing upright row, 84
  tricep extensions, 81, 86
  upper arms variation, 86
  variations, 85–88
  wrist curls, 85
USA Hockey, 190, 205, 271
USA Hockey InLine, 197, 198
USA Hockey In-Line Magazine, 169
Utah hockey organizations, 309

• V •

Vancouver Canucks
  information, 324
  Web site, 165
Vermont hockey organizations, 310
Vernon, Mike, 178, 180
video goal judge, 43

video tape, 99–100
Virginia hockey organizations, 309–310

• W •

warm ups, 101–102
Washington Capitals
  information, 324
  Web site, 165
Washington hockey organizations,
      310–311
wash-out, 331
watching hockey (in person)
  at Arrowhead Pond in Anaheim, 159
  attention and, 155
  culinary delights and, 158
  enjoyment of, 205
  fan temperament and, 158
  hockey tip, 254
  at Madison Square Garden, 159
  at Maple Leaf Gardens, 160
  at Molson Centre, 160
  opposing players, 157–158
  at San Jose Arena, 161
  seat position for, 156
  whole rink, 156
  women, 206
watching hockey (television). *See also*
  Anaheim Mighty Ducks, 150
  Buffalo Sabres, 151
  Detroit Red Wings, 148
  Edmonton Oilers, 151
  following the puck and, 145–146
  listening and, 153
  New Jersey Devils, 149
  New York Rangers, 149–150
  old-time, 147
  Philadelphia Flyers, 148
  play formation, 147
  video replays, 147
  what's missed by, 152–153
water skiing. *See* hooking
Web sites
  Canadian Hockey Association, 271
  ESPN, 166
  The Hockey Hall of Fame, 171

IIHF, 191
NHL, 163–164
Sportsline, 165–166
team, 164–165
USA Hockey, 206, 271
USA Hockey InLine, 197, 198
Youth Hockey Network, 272
weight training. *See also* training
abdominal, 92–95
alternating lunges with barbells, 91
alternating lunges with dumbbells, 90
alternating seated bicep curls with
dumbbells, 84
bench flys with dumbbells, 83
bench press, 80
benefits of, 69
bicep curls, 82, 86
calf extensions, 92
double leg hamstring curls, 89
dumbbell row, 84
frequency, 80
hip abduction, 89–90
inclined bench press, 85
lat pull-downs, 81
leg extension, 92
lower body: circuit 1, 88–90
lower body variations, 90–92
palm-down/palm-up arm extensions, 87
pec-deck flys, 88
seated tricep extension with barbell, 83
shoulder abduction, 87
shoulder extension, 82
sliding double leg press, 88
squats, 91
standing upright row, 84
trainers, 70
tricep extensions, 81, 86
upper body: circuit 1, 80–82
upper body: circuit 2, 82–84
upper body variations, 85–88
weight amount in, 79
wrist curls, 85
Wenger, Dr. Howie, 69, 72–73, 79
West Coast Hockey League, 60

West Virginia hockey organizations, 317
Western Hockey League, 60, 61
Williams, Dave "Tiger"
as best agitator, 141
as best hockey personality, 247
wings. *See also* positions
defined, 14, 270
during power play, 116
left, 14
lines and, 15
right, 14
scoring, 15
types of, 15
Wisconsin hockey organizations
Central, 312–313
Northeast, 311–312
Northwest, 311
Southeast, 313–314
Southern, 314–316
Western, 316
women
hockey Web links, 205
playing hockey, 64, 205
watching hockey, 205
Worsley, Lorne "Gump," 248
Wyoming hockey organizations, 317

youth hockey organizations
Alabama, 272
Alaska, 272
Alberta, 317
Arizona, 273
Arkansas, 273
British Columbia, 317–318
California, 273–275
Colorado, 275
Connecticut, 276
Delaware, 277
Florida, 277–278
Georgia, 278
Idaho, 278

(continued)

youth hockey organizations *(continued)*
Illinois (Central), 280
Illinois (Northern), 278–280
Illinois (Southern), 280
Indiana, 280–281
International, 321
Iowa, 281
Kansas, 282
Kentucky, 282
Maine, 282
Manitoba, 318
Maryland, 282–283
Massachusetts, 283–286
Michigan (Northern and Central),
    291–295
Michigan (Southern), 295–296
Minnesota (Central), 287–289
Minnesota (Northern), 286–287
Minnesota (Southern), 290
Missouri, 296
Montana, 296
Nebraska, 296
New Brunswick, 318
New Hampshire, 296–297
New Jersey, 297–299
New Mexico, 303
New York (Central), 300
New York (Eastern), 301–303
New York (Western), 300–301
North Carolina, 303–304
Ohio, 304–305
Oklahoma, 305
Ontario (Northern), 318–319
Ontario (Southern), 319–320
Oregon, 305
Pennsylvania (Eastern), 305–307
Pennsylvania (Western), 307
Quebec, 320–321
Rhode Island, 308
Saskatchewan, 321
South Carolina, 308
South Dakota, 308
Texas, 309

Utah, 309
Vermont, 310
Virginia, 309–310
Washington, 310–311
West Virginia, 317
Wisconsin (Central), 312–313
Wisconsin (Northeast), 311–312
Wisconsin (Northwest), 311
Wisconsin (Southeast), 313–314
Wisconsin (Southern), 314–316
Wisconsin (Western), 316
Wyoming, 317

• Z •

Zamboni, 155, 157, 270

ORDER THE BOOK
FITNESS FOR HIGH PERFORMANCE HOCKEY
BY DR. HOWIE WENGER
NEW YORK RANGERS FITNESS CONSULTANT

SPECIAL Order by Feb 28/98 **15% OFF** fax orders on this form only

ORDER FORM

Contact Name: _____ Team: _____

Address: _____

Province/State: _____ Country: _____ Postal/Zip Code: _____

Phone: ( ) _____ Fax: ( ) _____

ORDER INFORMATION:

If ordering	Price per
1–29 copies	$29.95 CNDN$
30+ copies	$25.15 CNDN$

(Approx US$
21.95
18.95)

Please send _____ copies @ _____ = _____

Packaging & Handling ($1.50 + $1.00 per book) _____

SUBTOTAL = _____

Less 15% if fax orded by Dec 31/97 _____

Plus Shipping _____

please indicate your shipping option

GROUND ☐   AIR ☐   RUSH ☐

We will add taxes if applicable = _____

TOTAL = _____

Credit Card Type _____ No. _____ Exp. _____

Name on card _____

PREVIEW AND ORDER ON-LINE AT: HTTP://WWW.TRAFFORD.COM/ROBOTS/97-0001.HTML

OR, MAIL/FAX FORM
WITH PAYMENT TO:

TRAFFORD Publishing

Suite 2, 3050 Nanaimo St.
Victoria, B.C. V8T 4Z1, CANADA

Phone	250-383-6864
Toll-free	1-888-232-4444 (Canada & US)
Fax	250-383-6804
E-mail	sales@trafford.com
Web site	www.trafford.com

A DIVISION OF TRAFFORD HOLDINGS LTD.

FREE ISSUE! FREE HAT!

Hey hockey enthusiast, here is your chance to read all about your favorite NHL® Teams. NHL POWERPLAY® is the official magazine of the players and teams of the NHL® and NHLPA®. NHL POWERPLAY® Magazine is packed with amazing facts, stats, and sports tips. That's why we want to send you a complimentary issue – absolutely FREE – to explore. We know the future of the NHL® begins with Power Players like you!

If you decide to subscribe, an official NHL POWERPLAY® Magazine Hat is yours absolutely FREE!

FREE ISSUE
FREE HAT